American Regional Dialects

American Regional Dialects

A Word Geography

Craig M. Carver

Ann Arbor   The University of Michigan Press

First paperback edition 1989
Copyright © by The University of Michigan 1987
All rights reserved
Published in the United States of America by
The University of Michigan Press
Manufactured in the United States of America

1990   1989   1988   1987   4   3   2   1

Library of Congress Cataloging-in-Publication Data

Carver, Craig M., 1947–
  American regional dialects.

  Bibliography: p.
  Includes index.
  1. English language—Dialects—United States.
2. Americanisms.   I.   Title.
PE2841.C37 1987   427'.973   86-16007
ISBN 0-472-10076-9 (alk. paper)
ISBN 0-472-08103-9 (pbk.: alk. paper)

Acknowledgments

Grateful acknowledgment is made to the following authors and publishers for the right to reprint adaptations of maps and figures from copyrighted material:

American Geographical Society for figure 27 from "Building in Wood in the Eastern United States" by Fred Kniffen and Henry Glassie, in volume 56, *The Geographical Review,* 1966; and figure 4 from "Classical Town Names in the United States: The Historical Geography of an American Ideal" by Wilbur Zelinsky, in volume 57, *The Geographical Review,* 1967.

Association of American Geographers for material from the *Annals of the Association of American Geographers:* map from "Physiographic Divisions of the United States" by Nevin M. Fenneman, in volume 18, 1928; figure 26 from "An Approach to the Religious Geography of the United States: Patterns of Church Membership in 1952" by Wilbur Zelinsky, in volume 51, 1961; figure 14 from "The Urban Street Pattern as a Culture Indicator: Pennsylvania 1682–1815" by Richard Pillsbury, in volume 60, 1970; figure 3 from "The Imprint of Upper South on Mid-Nineteenth Century Texas" by Terry Jordan, in volume 57, 1967; map on page 657 of "The Hispanic-American Borderland" by R. L. Nostrand, in volume 60, 1970; figure 2 from "American Wests: Preface to a Geographical Interpretation," by D. W. Meinig, in volume 62, 1972.

Robert F. Dakin for figures 172 and 173 from volume 3 of "The Dialect Vocabulary of the Ohio River Valley: A Survey of the Distribution of Selected Vocabulary Forms in an Area of Complex Settlement History." Ph.D. dissertation, University of Michigan, 1966.

Alva L. Davis for maps on pages 115 and 121 of "A World Atlas of the Great Lakes Region." Ph.D. dissertation, University of Michigan, 1949.

Gale Research Company for a map from *The Linguistic Atlas of the Upper Midwest in Three Volumes* by Harold B. Allen. (Copyright 1973, 1975, 1976 by the University of Minnesota; reprinted by permission of Gale Research Company), All rights reserved, University of Minnesota.

Joseph W. Glass for a map on page 257 of "The Pennsylvania Culture Region: A Geographical Interpretation of Barns and Farmsteads." Ph.D. dissertation, Pennsylvania State University, 1971.

Houghton Mifflin Company for maps facing pages 140, 150, 154, 168, and 236 of *The Expansion of New England: The Spread of New England Settlement and Institutions to the Mississippi River 1620–1865* by Lois Kimball Mathews, 1909.

Prentice-Hall for a map from Wilbur Zelinsky, *The Cultural Geography of the United States,* © 1973, p. 118. Adapted by permission of Prentice-Hall, Englewood Cliffs, New Jersey.

Roger W. Shuy for maps 3, 9, and 37 from "The Northern-Midland Dialect Boundary in Illinois" by Roger W. Shuy, in volume 38, *Publication of the American Dialect Society,* 1962.

University of California Press for maps on pages 49, 51, 53, 55, 64, 79, 81, and 101 from *A Word Geography of California and Nevada* by Elizabeth S. Bright. Berkeley: University of California Press, 1971.

University of Pennsylvania Press for figures 7, 8, and 9 from *Pattern in the Material Folk Culture of the Eastern United States* by Henry Glassie. Philadelphia: University of Pennsylvania Press, 1968.

University of Texas Press for a map adapted from *Imperial Texas: An Interpretative Essay in Cultural Geography* by D. W. Meinig. Copyright © 1969. By permission of the author and the University of Texas Press.

University of Washington Press for map 4 from *Cultural Regions of the United States* by Raymond D. Gastil. Seattle: University of Washington Press, 1975.

H. G. H. Wilhelm for figures 16, 21, and 27 from *The Origin and Distribution of Settlement Groups: Ohio 1850* by H. G. H. Wilhelm. Athens, Ohio: Department of Geography, Ohio University, 1982.

Preface

This book attempts to define the geography and character of American English dialects using lexical and morphological data collected for the various linguistic atlases and for the *Dictionary of American Regional English (DARE)*. It is in the tradition of Hans Kurath's *A Word Geography of the Eastern United States,* but with important differences. The emphasis here is on the analysis and discovery of the dialect regions of the United States and on their historical and cultural origins. Individual isoglosses are treated only insofar as they shed direct light on the dimensions of a region. Accordingly, only a few maps show the distributions of specific words.[1] Most of the linguistic maps are instead composites or generalizations of numerous individual distributions.

Much time, however, is spent on the characteristic words of a particular dialect, especially as their histories and meanings throw light on the cultural underpinnings of a region. The old idea that language reflects the culture from which it arises is one of the operating principles of this book. This is not the place, however, to treat every dialect word exhaustively. That is more properly the function of a dictionary, and the reader is referred to the authoritative *Dictionary of American Regional English* (Frederic G. Cassidy, editor in chief).

Although speech variation for certain areas of the country has been effectively mapped, notably a portion of the Atlantic seaboard, the Upper Midwest, and the North Central states, no study has been done for the country as a whole. Despite the surveys completed by the various sectional linguistic atlases, prior to the completion of the *DARE* fieldwork in 1970, there were no truly comparable data covering all fifty states. Moreover, except for a few published works (see Allen 1973–76; Kurath 1939–43, 1949), the data of the atlases are virtually inaccessible at this time. Most of the materials are in a very raw state either as original field work sheets stored at nearly a dozen different places or, very recently, as expensive microform.[2]

The present work makes extensive use of the available atlas materials, but it is especially indebted to the *DARE* fieldwork, which is both comprehensive and accessible, a data base having been created for the editing of the dictionary. This data took five years to collect (1965–70), using nearly a hundred trained field-workers and a hefty questionnaire containing over 1,800 questions, and is additionally a rich source of cultural and sociological information. A lagniappe in using the *DARE* data is that, since it was completed nearly forty years after the early linguistic atlas fieldwork, notably in New England, it offers an opportunity to look at how the dialects and their regions have changed during that period of upheaval (ca. 1930–70).

This book is also heavily indebted to the great dictionaries of the English language, which allow the investigator a wealth of easily obtained information about the origins and uses of words. Foremost among these are the *Oxford English Dictionary* and its four volume *Supplement, A Dictionary of American English, Dictionary of Americanisms,* the *English Dialect Dictionary,* the *Scottish National Dictionary,* and *Webster's Third New International Dictionary.* Other important, more specialized dictionaries consulted were the *American Dialect Dictionary, Dictionary of Jamaican English, Dictionary of Bahamian English, Dictionary of Newfoundland English,* and *Dictionary of Canadianisms.*

A constant companion reference work in the writing of this book was *This Remarkable Continent: An Atlas of United States and Canadian Society and Cultures* (Rooney et al. 1982). It is the cooperative effort of many cultural geographers and is invaluable to the student of American dialects who seeks to place language variation in a larger context.

The introductory chapter presents a brief history of linguistic geography, defines terms and concepts used throughout the book, and lays out the method of analysis. The following six chapters derive the dialect regions of the country, each chapter devoted to a major region and its subregions. Settlement history and cultural geography are explored in their relation to the dialect areas, and the characterizing lexicons are described in detail to give a feel for each region's speech. The concluding chapter gives an overview of America's dialect regions and shows how it is a new definition partially at odds with the traditional three-part division of American linguistic geography.

I would like to thank Timothy Frazer, William Kretzschmar, James Hartman, and Frederic Cassidy for reading brief portions of this work and giving me valuable comments. I would also like to thank the (unidentified) readers of the original manuscript for their part in the early development of this book and Richard W. Bailey for his insightful criticism at several stages in that development. I am indebted to Frederic Cassidy for permission to use the *DARE* materials and to the numerous people—fieldworkers, pre-editors, computer programmers—who made it all possible.

NOTES

1. Many of the words discussed here are mapped in *DARE,* which should be consulted for the specific range of a given expression.
2. The field records of *LAGS (Linguistic Atlas of the Gulf States),* LANCS (Linguistic Atlas of the North Central States), and *LAMSAS (Linguistic Atlas of the Middle and South Atlantic States)* are now available on microform. Although invaluable in their own right, the extreme "rawness" of their data does not resolve the accessibility problem. A very recent giant step toward a solution, however, has been made with the efforts of William Kretzschmar and Lee Pederson to computerize some of these data. Kretzschmar, who took over the editorship of *LAMSAS* and LANCS in 1984, is now in the process of creating a computer data base of those materials. For the computerizing of the *LAGS* materials see Pederson et al. 1986.

Contents

Maps

CHAPTER 1

Introduction

English Dialectology and the Linguistic Atlas

A dialect is a variety of language distinguished from other varieties by a set of gram-matical, phonetic, and lexical features. When these features are distributed geograph-ically over a restricted and relatively uniform area, it is a *regional dialect*. When they are shared by speakers of a social grouping, it is a *social dialect*. Regional dialectology, the older approach, was born out of nineteenth-century philology, a creation of the comparative method, one of the important methodologies in the history of linguistics.

This approach assumed that language is a material phenomenon, a field of tangible objects—sounds, words, phrases, and whole texts—that can be observed and even collected, an assumption behind the fieldwork method developed late in the nine-teenth century. Words from different languages could be compared, not unlike the way a zoologist compares different species or varieties: *father* (English), *fadar* (Gothic), *fater* (Old High German), *pater* (Latin), *pitar* (Sanskrit). Like scientists, linguists could discover the "laws" of language change by discerning the systematic differences in the related or cognate forms. One of the first of these "scientists" was Jakob Grimm (of Grimms' fairy-tale fame), who in 1822 formulated his famous law of consonant change. It was also this approach that gave us the first accurate and detailed etymologies.

With Darwinian eyes, they saw language as an evolving, organic phenomenon, a diversifying continuum in time. It was no accident that they readily adopted the meta-phor of an Indo-European family "tree" of languages. When it was discovered, how-ever, that languages did not always or even usually change suddenly, splitting the parent form into new language branches, and that the parent language itself had varieties that played an important role in change, the tree metaphor became an inadequate model.

As Johannes Schmidt argued in 1872, language change was better conceived as a process of spatial diffusion; waves were a better, or at least needed additional, model. Linguistic innovations spread over a speech area in particular geographical patterns. The need to study these individual patterns created linguistic geography; maps became tools for unraveling the history of the language.[1]

In order to take advantage of this new tool, the German scholar Georg Wenker set out in the 1870s to gather specimens of dialect around Düsseldorf. Eventually he extended his survey to cover the whole German empire, sending by mail a prepared list of forty sentences to some forty-four thousand schoolteachers who then translated them into their local speech. Although overwhelmed by this massive amount of noncomputerized data, Wenker nevertheless plotted some of his findings on a base map of Germany and published in 1881 six maps that previewed the full atlas (1926).

Because Wenker relied on the extremely variable abilities of schoolmasters to "translate" High German sentences into dialectal ones using their own phonetic spellings, his method was not very reliable. Thirty or so years later in France, Jules Gilliéron used a more refined, direct method that is the basis of modern fieldwork. To get data that was less influenced by the transcribing abilities of the speakers themselves, he separated the function of the investigator or *field-worker* from the speaker whose speech was being investigated, the *informant*. He sent a trained field-worker to some six hundred communities throughout France to capture the speech of the peasantry. This was done using the fine mesh of a questionnaire containing some two thousand items.

The product was nearly two thousand full-scale maps published between 1902 and 1910 in five heavy, handsomely bound tomes. "Carte no. 1200," for example, is a black and white outline map of France, its provinces marked by dotted lines, and the assigned number of each informant printed in its appropriate location. Next to each number is the field-worker's transcription of the way the informant pronounced *savoir* (= to know). The map shows that in central France the pronunciation is nearly standard, "sava," but toward the mountainous Spanish border, the informants pronounce it either as "sabe" or "sapye." Since the publication of the *Atlas linguistique de la France,* numerous European and American atlases have appeared (see Trudgill 1975, 231 for a list of most of these).

In America, linguistic geography faced formidable problems. The sheer size of the country with a large but dispersed population made fieldwork extremely difficult. The initial thrust of American dialectology was primarily toward producing a dialect dictionary. Toward this end the American Dialect Society was founded in Cambridge, Massachusetts, in 1889; among its founders were George Kittredge, Edward Sheldon, and James Russell Lowell. By 1917 over twenty-six thousand words and phrases had been collected and printed in the society's publication, *Dialect Notes;* but an American dialect dictionary was nowhere on the horizon.

In 1924, Sir William Craigie, who was one of the editors on the great *Oxford English Dictionary (OED),* began work on the *Dictionary of American English (DAE).* This was to be the American counterpart of the *OED,* a dictionary primarily of standard written American English based on historical principles.

In 1929 American dialectology's energies turned away from the idea of a dictionary and toward the concept of an atlas. In that year the American Council of Learned Societies (of which the American Dialect Society is a member) published a circular outlining a proposed American "Linguistic Atlas" and designating Hans Kurath as director. For a decade or so, Kurath's progress reports dominated the issues of *Dialect Notes.* New England was chosen as the first area to be explored, because it was compact in size and had three hundred years of well-documented history.

Kurath's field-workers elicited words or phrases using "work sheets" consisting of over seven hundred questions arranged according to topics. There was, however, no standard form for the questions themselves; it was left to the field-worker to formulate the question.[2] By 1935 the fieldwork was completed and the editing of the results was well underway, a necessary and big step prior to mapping. After experimenting with elaborate custom-made typesetting, in 1939 the first hand-drafted, lithoprinted maps of the first volume of the *Linguistic Atlas of New England (LANE)* appeared. Volume two followed in 1941, volume three in 1943.

The field survey of the Atlantic states continued and in 1949 Kurath summarized some of the findings in *A Word Geography of the Eastern United States* (abbreviated here as *WG*). It was at about this time that the dream of a Linguistic Atlas of the United States and Canada was abandoned as a single project. The size of the task was far beyond the available financial resources. Instead, different scholars took it upon themselves to do research in particular sections of the country. Because each used the same general methodology, their results are comparable, though their individual approaches have important differences.

Hans Kurath and Raven I. McDavid, Jr., continued with the *Linguistic Atlas of the Middle and South Atlantic States (LAMSAS)*. Primarily for reasons of time and money, they decided to abandon cartography altogether and only to list the informant locations and responses, enabling other scholars to do the mapping for themselves. In 1980 the first two fascicles of *LAMSAS* were published.

During the late 1930s Albert H. Marckwardt started the fieldwork for the Linguistic Atlas of the North Central States (LANCS), which covers Wisconsin, Michigan, southwestern Ontario, Illinois, Indiana, Ohio, and Kentucky. In chapters 3 and 4 of the present work, three interpretations of the LANCS field records are compared in detail with generalizations made from the *DARE* records: Alva L. Davis's (1948) "A Word Atlas of the Great Lakes Regions," Roger Shuy's (1962) "The Northern-Midland Dialect Boundary in Illinois," and Robert Dakin's (1966) "The Dialect Vocabulary of the Ohio River Valley." All three studies identify major boundaries in this section of the country.

Other than *LANE,* the only other sectional atlas to be published in book form is the *Linguistic Atlas of the Upper Midwest (LAUM)* under the direction of Harold B. Allen (1973–75). The raw field records or "protocols" of the *Linguistic Atlas of the Gulf States (LAGS)* were made available on microfilm in 1981, but there has been little interpretation of this detailed and excellent data base (see Pederson 1969, 1974, 1976, 1981; Pederson et al. 1986).

Having used a version of the work sheets customized to elicit the vocabulary of the Southwest, E. Bagby Atwood published *The Regional Vocabulary of Texas* (1962), a detailed description of the speech in Texas and adjacent areas. His fieldwork is used to help describe the limits and subregions of the Delta South (chap. 5) and the Southwest (chap. 7).

Three hundred interviews in California and Nevada were completed in 1959 for the Linguistic Atlas of the Pacific Coast (LAPC) by David W. Reed and Allen A. Metcalf. Carroll E. Reed separately investigated the Pacific Northwest, but completed fieldwork only for Washington and scattered other areas. Only the California and Nevada records have had close scrutiny (Bright 1971; Metcalf 1973). The subdialects of

California based on Bright's study are explored in chapter 7. Fieldwork has also been completed for Oklahoma, Missouri, and Colorado, but only preliminary work has been done in the other western states.[3]

Although the present study draws heavily on the available atlas materials, it is primarily indebted to the fieldwork completed for the *Dictionary of American Regional English (DARE)* from 1965 to 1970. Because that fieldwork covers the entire United States, it offers a unique opportunity for viewing the dialect regions nationwide. However, despite the respectable number of communities investigated (1,002), its major drawback is its relatively sparse geographical coverage. Nevertheless we can derive a reliable general picture of the regional dialects of the United States.

The *DARE* questionnaire was modeled on the *LANE* work sheets and on the questionnaires used for the English and Scottish atlases (see Cassidy 1953). Unlike the work sheets, the *DARE* questionnaire followed the English atlas in using set questions, avoiding variation in the way the field-workers elicited the responses. Its 1,847 questions (two and one-half times the number in the various atlas work sheets) are arranged topically into forty-one categories and are framed so as to avoid using words that the informant might possibly give as a response. This was done by using three basic forms of questions.

One of the most common forms is the *context completion question,* which is especially useful for evoking verbs. For example, questions OO37a–b ask for the past and participle forms of *shrink*: "Talking about clothes shrinking: 'The first time my wool socks were washed they _____.' " " 'I can't get them on because they've _____ (too much).' "

The *defining question* was formulated in two ways. It gave a definition for which the informant provided his or her vernacular usage (qu. AA21: "What joking expressions do you have about a wife who gives the orders and a husband who takes them from her?"; qu. GG42: "A reckless person, who takes foolish chances."). Or it asked for alternate terms for a standard term (qu. V9: "What nicknames do people have around here for a 'policeman'?"; qu. GG40: "Words or expressions meaning 'violently angry.' ").

The *open question* was used infrequently because it was very nonspecific, for example, question I44: "What kinds of berries grow wild around here?" The intent of this type was to catch as many terms as possible without having to formulate a tedious series of individual questions for (in this case) all the kinds of berries.

The questionnaire has a rural emphasis, but it is considerably less lopsided than the atlas work sheet questions. There are the usual questions about calls to animals; others ask about the trappings of farming, about harnesses, plows, and work animals. But a good portion of the questionnaire also asks about more urban concerns, like names for vehicles and modes of transportation, terms for certain sections of a town or city, and expressions for legal and criminal activities.

Most, however, cut across urban/rural lines: questions about weather, topography, houses, furnishings, foods, and games. In addition to these are the innovative questions that go beyond previous fieldwork. These are the questions for abstractions like honesty and dishonesty, buying and selling, emotions, manner of action or being, and relationships among people. In short, the questionnaire targets the language of a broad spectrum of human activities and behavior.

The eighty-two *DARE* field-workers in five years of interviewing netted some two-and-one-half million individual responses. The informants were primarily older, somewhat rural and middle class, many with at least a high school education, as indicated by the statistical profile of the informant sample.

Another method of gathering data developed in America by Alva Davis (1948) and used later by Wood, Atwood, Allen, Foscue, and others, is the use of *checklists*. This approach, usually conducted by mail, employs written questions, each having a brief list of possible responses. The informant circles the words in the list he is familiar with and writes any other words he knows or has heard but that are not on the list.

Statistical Profile of the DARE Informant Sample

	Number of Informants	Percentage
Community Types		
1. Metropolitan area with population over a million	165	6.0
2. Large city, population hundreds of thousands	138	5.0
3. Small city, tens of thousands	550	20.0
4. Town or village, population in the thousands	1,046	38.0
5. Rural areas with population in the hundreds	853	31.0
Age		
Old: 60 years and up	1,824	66.3
Middle-aged: 40 to 59	663	24.1
Young: under 40	265	9.6
Education		
At least 2 years of college	865	31.3
High school	1,128	41.0
Grade school	649	23.6
5 years or less grade school	77	2.8
Unknown	33	1.3
Race		
White	2,549	92.7
Black	188	6.8
Other	15	0.5
Sex		
Male	1,354	49.2
Female	1,398	50.8

Typically two or three times as many responses are elicited by the checklist question as are by the same oral question. On the level of the individual isogloss, the checklist usually gives considerably different results. But, as Davis showed, dialect boundaries derived from the checklist are very similar to those derived from questionnaire data (see also Frazer 1971).

Because many of the possible dialect responses are already provided in the checklist, the informant does not have to pull them out of his own vocabulary. He need only recognize the word or phrase, even though he himself may never actually use it. In general, this method documents the *latent* regional vocabulary of its informants. In contrast, the oral questionnaire leaves it completely up to the informant to provide the responses. Typically his responses will be those words "on the tip of his tongue," words that tend to be from his *active* vocabulary.

The way the question is phrased, however, can affect whether the response is active or latent. For example, to *DARE* question NN7 ("Exclamations of surprise: 'They're getting married next week. Well, _____.' "), 109 informants, most of them from the South, responded *I declare*. But this expression is "known" throughout the country, as the 400 informants who gave the same response, but to a different question (NN32), testify. Unlike NN7, question NN32 cues the informant with the *I* in the exclamatory phrase *I declare* ("Exclamations like 'I swear' or 'I vow': 'I _____!' "). The cue is enough to evoke this particular response. Thus, *I declare* is actively regional, but latently nonregional.

This is not an uncommon situation: often a word or phrase is "known" every-where, but is actually commonly used only in a certain region. A regional lexicon, therefore, has two general types of lexical features: those that are unique to the region, and those that might be widely known, but are used significantly more often in the region.

A lexicon, however, is only one measure of a dialect region. The boundaries generalized from phonological and grammatical features may not necessarily coincide with generalized word boundaries, because there are forces of change operating on words that do not affect pronunciation and grammar. Many, perhaps most regionalisms, are attached to a culture's evolving practices in cooking, home remedies, recreation, and so on. Moreover, cultural attitudes are to a degree reflected in the language. The lexicon of a dialect, then, is bound to be closer to the nature and geographical spread of a culture, and by extension its economy, than are the pronunciation and grammar. For example, the decreasing currency of regionalisms for "cottage cheese" (*sour-milk cheese, pot cheese, smearcase, clabber cheese,* etc.) can be accounted for by the decrease in the number of homes that make their own cheese and the concomitant proliferation of supermarkets.

The relationship between word and phonetic geography has never been fully explored. Kurath and McDavid (1961) discovered in the linguistic atlas materials for the Atlantic states that the two geographies coincide fairly well, though the isoglosses and boundaries often appeared to have unequal weight. That is, a sharp lexical boundary often did not have a correspondingly sharp phonetic boundary. In any case, this impor-tant question is left for future studies to answer.

Regional Dialect

Region

Because regional dialectology describes language variation in terms of geographical areas, and because language is a cultural artifact, linguistic geography is as much a branch of *cultural geography* as it is of linguistics, and it is a synthesis in its own right. One of America's foremost cultural geographers, Wilbur Zelinsky, defines a region as "any portion of the earth's surface, large or small, that stands apart from others in terms of a given characteristic or set of characteristics" (Rooney et al. 1982, 3). For the cultural geographer these characteristics are a diverse lot and include types of food, housing, religion, town street patterns, farming methods, and of course, language, to name only a few. Linguists usually talk in terms of *features* instead of characteristics, and these are broken down into phonetic, syntactic, and lexical or morphemic elements, these last being the domain of the present study.

Zelinsky's region is a *uniform* or *formal region*. Regions of this type are relatively homogeneous within a certain range of features. As a method of description the assumption of the formal region is that

> whatever is stated about one part of [the region] is true of any other part; it is the largest area over which a generalisation remains valid. . . . With multi-feature regions very rarely is each feature completely uniform throughout." (Minshull 1967, 38).

In terms of lexical geography, a region is defined by its use of a particular set of words and expressions, its *lexicon;* but the degrees of usage will vary within the region itself.

The other major type of region is a *nodal* or *functional region* that is more dynamic and is based, not on a set of frozen features, but on the interaction between a center or node and a surrounding hinterland. The geography of migration and settlement can be described as a functional region. Broadly speaking, settlement in the United States spread westward from cultural nodes or foci on the coast, the influence of the nodes diminishing with distance. There are five original coastal centers from which most American dialects developed: Boston, Philadelphia, tidewater Virginia, Charleston, and New Orleans. These cultural *hearths* may continue to have functional relationships with their settlement areas, as is the case of Boston on Eastern New England and perhaps of New Orleans on the Delta South; or the relationship may be chiefly historical only surviving as a set of features, which is more or less the case with the other hearths.[4]

Settlement

Because the United States and its language are so new, the influence of settlement patterns plays a more immediate role in explaining its dialect regions. This is now virtually an axiom in American regional dialectology. In his seminal essay on "The

Morphology of Landscape" (1925), the eminent geographer, Carl O. Sauer, formulated the relationship between settlement patterns and cultural regions. Groups of immigrant or American-born settlers carried their culture with them westward, which through time shaped the evolution of the landscape. Thus, to understand the character of a region, to explain its features and boundaries, we must begin by examining the contrasting cultures of the human carriers and the geography of their movements. Of course the newly settled area is never a complete cross section of the older society, but develops a character of its own, especially to the degree that it is a blend or hybrid of various regional cultures and sometimes imported or non-American cultures.

Another geographer of American culture, D. W. Meinig (1972, esp. 162–63), developed a four-stage model of settlement in terms of four general categories: population, circulation (traffic and communication patterns), political areas, and culture. Although his model grows out of his work with the cultural history of the West, it can usefully be applied on a national level.[5]

In the first phase, migrants move to an area whose special environmental qualities they find attractive, transplanting the culture of the source region or hearth. The settlement, located within a huge, chiefly unorganized territory, is relatively isolated, with seasonal traffic and little outflow of goods. As we will see, these first effective settlements often leave traces in the linguistic geography, usually as boundaries marking off dialect subregions. This happens when the early settled area has time to develop a new, characteristic speech pattern that contrasts with adjacent areas settled later. It is most apparent in the Upper North and Lower South where streams of settlement created regional ponds or areas that remained relatively stable and uniform for a time, but that eventually overflowed with a new and large wave of immigration. Despite the overflow or spread of settlement beyond the borders of the early cultural pond, those borders remain more or less intact.

In the second phase, the frontier of free, readily available land is completed and the identity of the culture begins to emerge. The new amalgam of people forms a cohesive society adjusted to its environment and begins to develop a regional system of transportation and communication, first with improved roads and riverboats, and then with railroads and telegraph connections. In this stage, the political area is brought more closely in line with the emerging functional region.

The third phase is the result of the impact of national culture and commerce. An interregional transportation and communications network develops as an integral part of a nationwide system. Railroads become well established and paved highways and motor vehicles eventually follow. This period ends, especially in the West, with the appearance of the first airlines. With the strong influence of national culture, only those subcultures with tenacious social features, such as religion, language, and ethnic background, survive. The present work attempts to describe the regional language of America in this third phase as it has developed out of the first two phases.

Although Meinig does not say as much, his model may predict the demise of sharply distinctive dialects, or at least their shapes and extensions. The fourth phase is characterized by the "metropolitanization" of the landscape. The high mobility of a large urban and suburban population, the expansion of freeways, nonstop air service to national and international centers, and communications systems (including television and satellite transmission), all have a hand in the "dissolution of historic regional cultures" (Meinig 1972, 163).

Such a dissolution of dialects, however, remains to be seen. There is evidence that this may not be true for regional dialects. Where there is earlier linguistic atlas data to compare with the *DARE* fieldwork, as in New England, the Ohio River Valley, and elsewhere, linguistic regions reveal themselves to be very hardy, persisting despite the radical change or obsolescence of the features that earlier defined them.

Another, more likely possibility exists for the future of regional dialects. It also happens in the fourth phase of this model that new innovative centers emerge with a new awareness of the values of local culture and environment. These may be the future nodes for linguistic innovation, from which new regional dialects will develop.

The study of spatial diffusion is another way of approaching the definition of a region and has several applications to linguistic geography, both in relation to settlement and to the theory of language variation and change. The two most relevant types of spatial diffusion are *relocation* and *expansion diffusion* (see Gould 1969). *Relocation diffusion* occurs when a group of people move from an initial area or hearth so that they are diffused through time and over space to a new set of locations. As already discussed, the region defined by this process is essentially a functional one until settlement is complete, when often it gradually becomes a formal or uniform region.[6]

In terms of cultural features, this is a straightforward and often observable process. For example, different methods of wood construction carried into the frontier by two main groups of settlers have been recorded in the field and charted on maps (see map 1.1). These field records reveal the underlying settlement and, by extension, cultural patterns. The building methods used in the New England hearth spread almost due west into New York, the northern portions of Ohio, Indiana, and Illinois, and northward into Michigan and Wisconsin—the same pattern we will see in the dimensions of the Upper North dialect region. The second group built cabins and other structures primarily in the manner of the Scotch-Irish, dispersing from Pennsylvania down the Appalachians and into the inland South. In a similar way, whole groups of words or lexicons diffused with settlement from the hearth regions.

But not all the words unique to the lexicon of a dialect region originate in the hearth. New words, such as terms for four-lane highways or for broken-down cars, spread throughout a region long after settlement patterns have given it its primary shape. This type of diffusion is called *expansion diffusion* and is the process involved in the spread of new linguistic forms from an innovating center. More generally, it is the communication of ideas from knowers to nonknowers, so that the number of knowers is always increasing. Theories about language variation and change must take into account expansion diffusion. For example, implicational theory, as well as its underlying wave model, are attempts to explain the diffusion of new forms and linguistic variants in a language (see C.-J. Bailey 1973a, 1973b; Weinreich et al. 1968).

One of the important shaping forces in the diffusion of settlement is physical geography. As the pioneers moved west they encountered a series of differing physiographic provinces, each with distinct soils, topography, and climate. The interplay between the migrating peoples and physiography created regional economies suited to the natural conditions and imported habits of the settlers. Regions were born. The shape

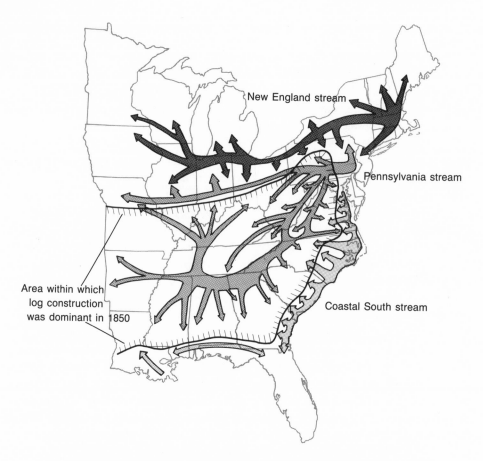

1.1. The Diffusion of Different Methods of Wood Construction. The historical forces that created areas where certain styles of architecture and building methods predominate are the same forces that helped shape four major dialect regions. The Upper South was defined early by log construction brought to the frontier by Pennsylvanians. Frame construction dominant in New England and the southern tidewater hearths was likewise carried with settlers into the Upper North and Lower South respectively. Later Pennsylvania settlement along the National Road came after the heyday of log construction and helped establish the Lower North, which is characterized by very mixed features. (Source: Kniffen and Glassie 1966.)

of the land, its rivers, mountains, piedmont and tidewater, plateaus and plains, formed natural areas and boundaries that affected settlement, which in turn influenced the cultural and linguistic patterns on the land.

Methodology: Mapping Dialect Regions and Boundaries

Primarily two cartographic methods of deriving dialect boundaries have been used in American linguistic geography, the *bundle method* and the *grid method*. Both tend to distort the picture more than is necessary.

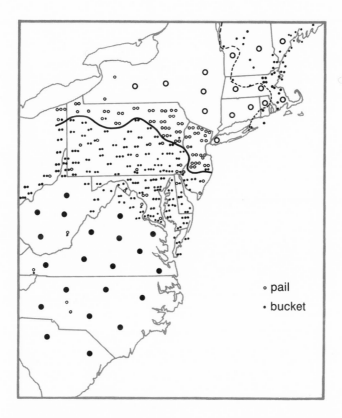

1.2. The Isoglosses for Bucket/Pail. Based on the fieldwork completed in the 1930s and 1940s for the linguistic atlas project, this map illustrates a common, though not necessary, phenomenon in linguistic geography: the complementary distribution of terms. *Pail* is used in the North and is the complement of the Midland *bucket*. Note in eastern New England that even though both terms are used, an isogloss can still be drawn. (Source: *WG,* fig. 66.)

In the first method, the linguist locates each informant who gave a particular interview response on a map. When all the responses are charted, and if they tend to cluster in a specific area of the country, a line or *isogloss* can be drawn around the outer limits of the geographical spread. In map 1.2, from Hans Kurath's *A Word Geography of the Eastern United States* (1949, fig. 66), the northern limits of the spread of *bucket* is traced with such a line.

When several different isoglosses "bundle" together, that is, when they roughly coincide as in map 1.3, a dialect boundary emerges. Major dialect boundaries have a larger number of line isoglosses than do minor boundaries. Map 1.4, one of the best known in American linguistic geography (from *WG,* fig. 3), shows the major and minor dialect regions in the East as derived by the compound line or bundle method.

The grid method was introduced to American linguistic geography by Alva Davis in his 1948 dissertation. He based this method on Wenzel's system of grids that are formed by drawing lines half-way between the communities where interviews were

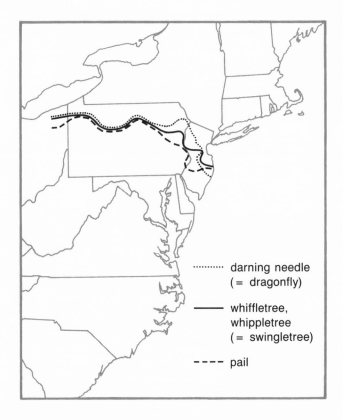

1.3. Bundling of Three Northern Isoglosses. Hans Kurath used this and other bundles of isoglosses to derive the generalized Northern boundary of map 1.4. (Source: *WG,* fig. 5a.)

conducted. If the communities are approximately equidistant from each other, as in Roger Shuy's intensive study of northern Illinois, then a honeycomb gridwork is created (map 1.5*A*).

Instead of a free-form line, the distribution of a feature is plotted along the sides of the grids. In map 1.5*B* two features are mapped; the resulting isoglosses divide those communities that have the features from those that do not. To discover boundaries, many feature distributions (often twelve or more) are plotted on a single grid map, and a count is made of the number of times each section of the grid is a part of an isogloss. The sections that participate in the largest number of isoglosses form themselves into a dialect boundary (map 1.5*C*). This method has the advantage of deriving boundaries from distributions that do not apparently coincide.

Both of these methods rely heavily on linear boundaries and do not represent the graded spread of dialect features. Notice in map 1.2, for example, that the occurrences of *pail* and *bucket* intermingle. It is virtually impossible to represent this situation accurately with a line. Lines imply a sharpness that belies the continuity and blurred

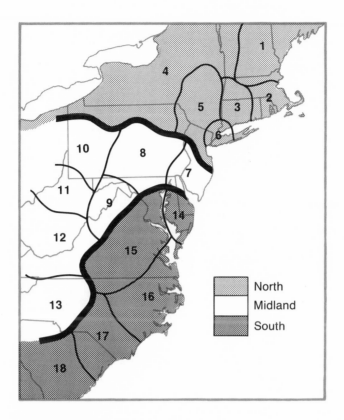

1.4. Dialect Regions of the Eastern United States by Kurath. In this well-
known map, Hans Kurath defined three major dialect regions (North, Midland,
and South), which had considerable influence on subsequent analysis, classification, and naming of the speech regions west and south of the Appalachians. He
further divided these three primary regions into eighteen subregions. In the
North these are: (1) Northeastern New England, (2) Southeastern New England,
(3) Southwestern New England, (4) Upstate New York and western Vermont,
(5) the Hudson Valley, and (6) Metropolitan New York. In the Midland these
are: (7) the Delaware Valley (Philadelphia area), (8) the Susquehanna Valley,
(9) the Upper Potomac and Shenandoah valleys, (10) the Upper Ohio Valley
(Pittsburgh area), (11) northern West Virginia, (12) southern West Virginia, and
(13) western North and South Carolina. In the South these are: (14) Delamarvia,
(15) the Virginia Piedmont, (16) northeastern North Carolina, (17) the Cape
Fear and Peedee valleys, and (18) South Carolina. (Source: *WG*, fig. 3.)

edges of language variation. A line isogloss is a convenient fiction existing in an
abstract moment in time. Like the lines we use to divide society into social classes, an
isogloss is at best an approximation.

    A line dialect boundary accurately describes the distribution of linguistic features
under only one circumstance as shown schematically in this first speaker-word matrix.[7]
Here speakers I–IV use a lexicon or set of words *a–g,* while speakers V–IX do not use
the lexicon at all. In this situation, it is accurate to draw a line boundary and assign the

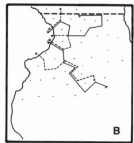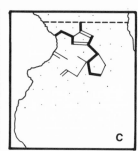

1.5. The Grid-Count Method. Describing the dialect geography of northern Illinois, *A* shows the base or grid formed by drawing lines midway between the communities investigated (represented here by dots). *B:* the solid line separates those communities whose speakers pronounce *humor* with the on-glide /j/ from those communities that do not have this pronunciation. The dashed line is the isogloss for the pronunciation of /č/ in *rinses*. *C* shows the tabulation of multiple isoglosses. The dark lines represent those sections of the grid where 12 to 17 isoglosses coincide. The dual lines represent 10 to 11 shared isoglosses and the single line 9 isoglosses. (Source: Shuy 1962, 6, 23, 68.)

speakers to either dialect X or Y. But this situation almost never happens. The typical situation is more closely represented by the second matrix.

Here it is more difficult to say just where the boundary is between dialect X and Y. Clearly speakers I–V should be grouped together. But what of the rest? As we move spatially toward the right the number of words used by each speaker decreases. This quantitative change is impossible to represent with a single line without being arbitrary and misleading.[8]

To show this gradient another method must be used. Applying simple cartographic principles, we can translate the matrix into a schematic map (map 1.6). The

					Speakers				
Words	I	II	III	IV	V	VI	VII	VIII	IX
a	+	+	+	+	−	−	−	−	−
b	+	+	+	+	−	−	−	−	−
c	+	+	+	+	−	−	−	−	−
d	+	+	+	+	−	−	−	−	−
e	+	+	+	+	−	−	−	−	−
f	+	+	+	+	−	−	−	−	−
g	+	+	+	+	−	−	−	−	−

region X   region Y

spatial area

Speakers

Words	I	II	III	IV	V	VI	VII	VIII	IX
a	+	+	+	+	+	+	+	+	−
b	+	+	+	+	+	+	+	+	−
c	+	+	+	+	+	+	+	−	−
d	+	+	+	+	+	+	−	−	−
e	+	+	+	+	+	+	−	−	−
f	+	+	+	+	+	+	−	−	−
g	+	+	+	+	+	+	−	−	−
h	+	+	+	+	+	−	−	−	−
i	+	+	+	+	+	−	−	−	−
				spatial area					

degree to which a community participates in a particular dialect can be gauged by counting the number of words (shown in parentheses) that each representative speaker (I–IX) uses. The numbers fall naturally into regional groups bounded by the sudden drop-off in the word count. Dialect X has a *core* area located by representative speakers I–IV where the greatest number of features are, or as Whittlesey puts it, "where the characteristics of the region find their most intense expression and their clearest manifestation" (1954, 41). A secondary area or *domain* can be discerned that includes the locations of speakers V and VI, and a tertiary area or *sphere* extends to speakers VII and VIII.[9] This representation has the advantages of showing areas (two dimensions) as well as boundaries (lines), and of revealing the internal organization of regions.

Map 1.6 is a rudimentary *participation map,* a term and methodology introduced by H. Rex Wilson in his 1958 dissertation. Clyde Hankey uses the method in his word

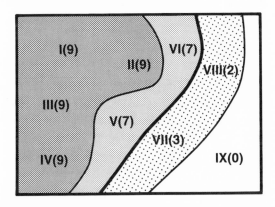

1.6. Schematic Participation Map. This is the cartographic representation of hypothetical speakers I through IX who used 0 to 9 of the words of a lexicon.

geography of Colorado (1960) and Robert Dakin employs it (1966, 3:89) in his study of the Ohio River Valley region. But in these works, it is given only a small place. Hankey contends that a participation boundary

> is not equivalent to the isogloss bundle but [is] rather a less definite boundary. While large bundles of isoglosses represent distinct dialect boundaries, the participation boundary represents at best a tentative dialect boundary—one that may have been, or may become, more definite. (1960, 38)

Isogloss bundles, however, are rarely any more definite; it is difficult to find more than a handful at a time that coincide very closely. Instead they have the annoying habit of intertwining over broad areas, creating boundaries often a hundred miles wide (see, for example, Marckwardt's 1957 North Central "boundaries").

But despite the apparent differences among the three methods, there is remarkable agreement among the boundaries they display. As we will see, especially in chapters 2 and 3, the participation method comes up with essentially the same results as Davis's grid in the North Central states, and Kurath's bundles in New England.

The participation method, especially as it is used here to interpret the "layers" of a dialect region, has several advantages over the others. First, because it gives an areal picture, and not just a linear one, the internal organization of the dialect region—the variation in the extent to which subareas participate in the dialect as measured by a given set of features—is made apparent. Second, many of the irrelevant differences and complications are smoothed out; the background noise is muted.

This latter effect is enhanced by the surprisingly large number of regionalisms that *DARE*'s lengthy questionnaire reaped. What the *DARE* data lack in geographical coverage is made up in lexical depth. This means that many more areal isoglosses can be used in the mapping than have usually been used in past studies—for example, five or six times as many isoglosses as Kurath typically used in his *Word Geography*. The larger the number, the greater the averaging and leveling effect on the anomalies that are created by the wide mesh of the informant sample, by the unevenness of the informants' social levels, and by other distorting factors inherent in fieldwork.

Dialect Layers

The topographic model, particularly the geologic metaphor of strata and rock layering, is useful in analyzing and mapping regional dialects. A typical dialect region has several strata of features. A single *layer* of features is the composite of a unique set of areal isoglosses, the geographical spread of its lexicon. To composite these isoglosses means to add, as in map 1.6, the number of terms that are used in each community investigated. For example, the Delta South layer is defined in map 5.5 as a composite of 15 *DARE* areal isoglosses, the numbers on the map signifying both location and quantity of lexicon words recorded there. The number of isogloss terms occurring in a given community roughly represents the relative degree to which the speakers of the community know the lexicon unique to this dialect pattern or region.

Not all layers have the same importance or "weight." The South II layer (map 4.5), for example, has more weight than the Midland layer (map 6.5) because its lexicon is larger—84 words, as opposed to 40. A layer, then, has both qualitative (it is made up of a particular lexical material) and quantitative aspects (it is thicker or thinner, to use the geologic metaphor, depending on the size of the lexicon).

There is of course no reliable way of precisely measuring how many defining words there are in a dialect's lexicon. But because most of the layers derived in this book are based on the *DARE* fieldwork, the number of areal isoglosses that could readily be collected in the *DARE* map files is taken to be a rough estimate of a layer's relative weight. As a quick review of the files shows, most of the responses to the questionnaire do not cluster in any kind of regional pattern, but are scattered in a random fashion throughout the country. The initial step in culling the regional from the nonregional expressions was to check every response given by eight or more informants to every question. Because the data base is so massive it would be virtually impossible to do this if it were not for *DARE*'s computer-generated, schematic map. This step produced between fifteen thousand and twenty thousand maps that were deemed to have possible regional significance.

However, because one of the purposes of this book is to discover and map the dialect regions of the country, only unequivocally regional distributions were used to derive the layers. Thus, the second step was to cull from the thousands of initially sifted distributions, all the *DARE* responses that were clearly regional. In effect a random sampling was taken. Although the weighting of layers based on the number of culled responses is not a precise measurement of a layer's relative weight, it is a generally reliable one.

Like all formal regions, the uniformity of a dialect layer is not complete. As Whittlesey puts it: "There is always a certain range of characteristics permitted by the criteria, and there are irrelevant differences which are disregarded" (1954, 36; see also Minshull 1967, 38). But we must be careful to distinguish between "irrelevant differences" and differences that reveal something about the internal shape of dialect regions.

In map 1.6 the heterogeneity is an aspect of the internal order. Dialect layer X has a sloping regional pattern, which in a larger context might appear as a hill, the core being the hilltop. In short, a layer has internal details. Subregions emerge; a landscape is formed. Clusters of relatively low numbers appear as valleys and depressions; sudden drop-offs in the numbers define plateaus and mesalike areas.[10] The core of the Northeast (see map 2.9), for example, runs like a mountain range through western New England, into New York and northeastern Pennsylvania.

In many cases, the core will correspond with the hearth of the layer, as western New England does for the Northeast region (see map 2.9).[11] Unless drastic social or other changes have occurred, the source area will usually conserve more of the original lexicon than its settlement areas, which have additional competing cultural forces and other regionally specific influences on the language, such as the regional economy and commerce. In general we can expect the area of highest isogloss density to be the core and historical source of a given region.

Sometimes the internal order of a region will include other topographical features, such as the ridge of high numbers in the South I layer (see map 4.3) along the Chattahoochee River in Georgia forming part of the Atlantic South dialect boundary; or the depression of sparse isoglosses in Alabama and Tennessee in two layers of the South (see maps 4.3 and 4.5); or the broad valley in Montana and the Dakotas in the extension of the North into the West (see map 7.4). These linguistic patterns on the land were shaped by the streams of migration and the elements of history.

This method, then, describes the dialect of a specific area in terms of the relative degree to which it participates in the lexicons of the layers that overlap its area. This is measured by the number of lexicon expressions recorded in each community. The Hudson Valley in New York, for example, is defined more by its weak participation in two Northern layers (see maps 3.3 and 3.7), than it is by Hudson Valley terms, expressions used only or most commonly there. Its speakers use fewer Northern expressions than speakers in surrounding areas.

The reasons for this are rooted in the Dutch settlement of the Hudson Valley, which provided many dialect terms for the American English that came to dominate the region. In time these terms died out or were replaced by standard expressions or other regionalisms. By the 1960s only one or two words distinctive to the region survived. But the settlement pattern had set a trend, one that persists in the speech of the region. The layer maps, however, will not tell us what Northernisms are least common in the valley.

A dialect layer, like the formal region it is, presumes to have only *relative* uniformity of features: the lexicon is relatively evenly distributed throughout. The isogloss sums that best define the New England layer (see map 2.4), for example, range primarily between 15 and 22. But there are always anomalies in the structure of a layer, and these are usually the effect of social variables. Because of the nature of the linguistic atlas and *DARE* fieldwork, the social range of the informants is chiefly nonurban, older, generally middle to lower-middle class, and without close ethnic ties.

Often when there are irrelevant differences, it is due to informants who are outside this social range. For example, in the New England layer, much of eastern New England is covered by a secondary level of numbers generally ranging between 15 and 18 or 19. But the informants in Auburn and Framingham, Massachusetts, each used only four words from the lexicon. As one might suspect, neither fits the general informant social range; both have strong Jewish and ethnic backgrounds, their parents having emigrated from Eastern Europe.

Other instances include the St. Meinrad, Indiana, informant whose strong German background—the town itself being a German settlement—shows up as an anomaly in the South I layer (represented by 19 isoglosses in southern Indiana in map 4.3). Age and education play a role in the responses of the young, college-educated informants in University City, Missouri (outside St. Louis; represented by 3 isoglosses in map 4.3), and in Lewiston in central Pennsylvania (see map 3.3). Cities also appear as having anomalously low numbers in many layers (see, for example, Boston in map 2.4), revealing the extent of the rural bias of the fieldwork.

Other less systematic variables also affect the homogeneity of a layer, such as the occasional prompting that field-workers resorted to when the informant got stuck in answering a question. This tends to disappear, however, in the averaging effect of compositing many areal isoglosses.

Dialect Region

A dialect layer, however, is not a dialect region. A layer has regionality and represents a definable or restricted area characterized by the lexicon; but a layer is only a single aspect in the analysis of a dialect region. To get a more complete picture of the speech of an area, all of the layers overlapping that area must be taken into account. In addition, the relative weights of the layers and the intensity or strength of each in the region must be evaluated. The dialect region of the South, for example, is not fully defined until the relationships among the various layers composing it are examined—the two major layers, the South I and II (see maps 4.3 and 4.5), and the more minor layers, the South-and-West (see map 4.8), the Midland (see map 6.5), and the several layers of the Upper and Lower South.

In the present work, the layers and their lexicons are first analyzed in detail and then combined to derive a fuller picture of the dialect region. This latter step is done in two different ways, areally and linearly. In the linear interpretation, the boundaries of relevant layers are combined on a single map. When they bundle together a major or super boundary is formed constituting an important defining feature of the dialect region (see, for example, maps 2.6, 3.14, 3.15).

In the areal interpretation the overlapping cores and domains of the layers are shown as gradient shadings depending on the strength of the combinations (see, for example, map 5.9). For example, an area covered by overlapping cores has greater strength or intensity represented by a darker shade than an area covered by a core and a domain, which in turn has a greater intensity of features than an area covered only by domains.

The combinations and permutations of layers and their internal organization can get extremely complicated, as is the case in the midlands (see map 6.20). But not making a distinction between dialect layers and regions has resulted in a certain amount of confusion in dialect geography. It has, for example, misled researchers into positing the existence of a Midland *dialect* on the basis of a single set or layer of features (a topic dealt with in detail in chap. 6).

A map of language variation is merely a static representation of a phenomenon whose most salient characteristic is its fluidity. When we speak, our utterance is a virtually unbroken stream of sounds—quite different from the discrete words and letters of writing and printing. It is also a continuum through time, ever changing despite the desperate attempts of prescriptive grammarians to fix it. Language variation is a continuum along the social dimension. And of course, despite its enormous variety, it is an almost seamless fabric covering the land. A person traveling southward from Superior, Wisconsin, to Mobile, Alabama, would be aware of the differing speech patterns but would not be able to say at what points along the route the changes occurred.

What follows, then, is not the definitive description of regional dialects in America, because such a description is impossible. It is merely one attempt to seize the linguistic river as it flowed through early-twentieth-century America and to describe it from a spatial or geographical point of view.

NOTES

1. See Bloomfield 1933, chaps. 18–19; Samuels 1972, chap. 6; Weinreich et al. 1968, 151–55.
2. For a more detailed description of the work sheet methodology, see Atwood 1963, 13–16; Davis, McDavid, and McDavid 1969; and Kurath 1939.
3. For a more detailed history of the atlases see McDavid 1958, 494–99; McDavid 1983; and especially McDavid 1984; Atwood 1963; Allen 1977.
4. The wave model used to describe language variation and change, first conceived in 1872 by Johannes Schmidt (Bloomfield 1933, 317) and revived a hundred years later by C.-J. Bailey (1973a, 1973b), makes use of the nodal or functional region.
5. John Fraser Hart (1974) explores another dynamic version of the settlement of the eastern United States, which he argues passes through three "frontier" stages: "the frontier of occupance (two persons per square mile), the frontier of settlement (six persons per square mile), and the frontier of agriculture (eighteen persons per square mile)."
6. In Meinig's scheme, phase one begets a nodal region, two and three approximate formal regions, and the fourth phase sees the creation of new nodal regions.
7. William Labov (1973, 344) developed this matrix to show semantic ranges.
8. Note that a diagonal line is not possible because it cannot be represented spatially, that is, on a map.
9. D. W. Meinig (1965) coined *core, domain,* and *sphere* to describe the Mormon cultural region.
10. Computers have enabled dialectologists to create a three-dimensional representation of just such a landscape (see, for example, Southard 1983). Computer cartography offers exciting new ways of mapping regional dialects, especially when color is added.
11. There is, however, no necessary connection between the core and the hearth as Whittlesey (1954, 41) points out in a more theoretical vein:

> In nodal regions, the core is the most representative portion of the entire area and the part most closely tied to the focus [= the hearth of a settlement region]. . . . It should be noted that the core and the focus are not synonymous, even though the focus ordinarily lies within the core. The focus is one of the salient features of the nodal region's structure; the core is the epitome of the region's character, whether uniform or nodal.

CHAPTER 2

New England and the Northeast

The New Englander's penchant for dropping postvocalic *r*'s ("don't pa'k it in the ya'd"), for inserting *r*'s where they "don't belong" ("it's an idear, anyway"), and for pronouncing *aunt* and *glass* like a proper Englishman using the vowel [ɑ] are shibboleths often recognized by non-Yankee speakers. It is remarkable that this distinctive dialect with its strong "accent" is the origin of the quite different Northern dialect. Somewhere in time and space this strongly conservative parent dialect, which hangs onto old, even relic expressions and which is generally less colloquial than any other American regional dialect, gave rise to the lexically innovative North, whose speech is heavy with new coinages and with regional colloquial and slang usage.

Settlement

The history of New England settlement has been told in admirable detail in the *Handbook of the Linguistic Geography of New England* (Kurath 1939; henceforth referred to as simply *Handbook*), so it is only necessary to sketch the important patterns that have helped shape the dialect areas.

The first colonists established two dominant centers from which sprang New England's subregional characteristics. These earliest cradles of settlement were the Massachusetts Bay area and the Lower Connecticut River Valley. The Massachusetts Bay Colony was founded over a period of about twenty years beginning with the landing of the 102 Mayflower pilgrims at Plymouth and ending with the last of the 4,000 or so families of the "Great Migration." By 1640, this first hearth was well established along the Massachusetts coast, which was dotted with more than a dozen towns and villages. The basic cultural features were in place and would persist unaltered by the arrival of newcomers.

The second settlement hearth, however, was only about midway in its development. In 1635 several groups of families came overland on the Connecticut Path from the Boston area to settle Windsor, Wethersfield, and Hartford on the lower Connecticut River (see map 2.1). Although they came from the Bay Colony (especially from Cambridge, Dorchester, and Watertown), they had only recently arrived from England. Living on the small, alotted parcels of poor Massachusetts land had been a hardship. So like later immigrants arriving in the Massachusetts Colony, they soon moved west to new lands.

It is not surprising that they chose the Lower Connecticut River Valley. To the

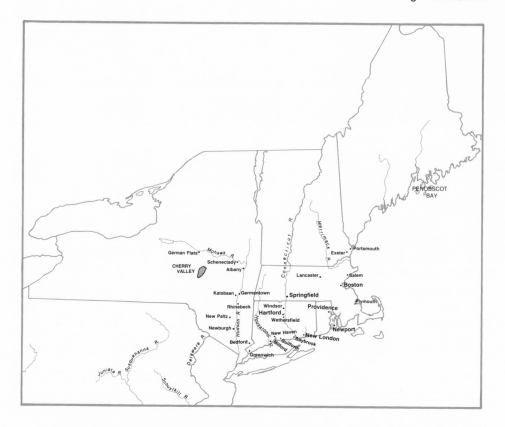

2.1. Important Colonial Towns in New England and New York

seventeenth-century colonists, waterways were an integrative force, a means of trade
and communication. The coastal lowlands and *intervales* along the rivers were also
generally the most fertile. Consequently the New England towns established to about
1675 were all accessible by water. The greatest New England river, the Connecticut
River, with its broad fertile valley meandering among the low mountains, was the
inevitable site of the second hearth.

The Connecticut settlement continued to grow with colonists arriving directly
from England, particularly from southeastern England. Saybrook was established at the
mouth of the Connecticut in 1636 primarily as a military outpost, but its influence on
later surrounding settlement was considerable. English Puritan merchants settled New
Haven in 1638 at what seemed to be an ideal commercial site with a large harbor and
navigable rivers. A year later a group from England settled Milford and Guilford on
either side of New Haven. The last town to be founded by this initial wave of colonists
was New London, established at the mouth of the Thames River by a mixture of
settlers, most of whom were from Massachusetts.

The Connecticut Colony had no true nucleus. As a hearth it was relatively
decentralized, spread out along the river and coast; whereas, in Massachusetts the
Boston Bay area was the distinct center, like a hub (*neb* to some Essex County old-
timers) from which spokes of migration radiated.

The general cohesiveness of the arriving groups reinforced the internal unity of the two colonies. Numbers of families, usually members of the same congregation led by an elected minister, sailed en masse to America to settle as neighbors in the same areas. The first settlers came primarily from eastern and southern rural England bringing with them the farming, fishing, and shipping expressions that have characterized the New England lexicon down to the present.

In general, the two hearths in this first period of colonization (1620–40) were settled directly from England. The second period lasting to about 1675 saw the settlement of surrounding areas, not so much by Englishmen, who were now preoccupied with the Puritan revolution and its political turmoil, but by citizens of the two core colonies.

During the second period the first front of settlement pushed inland from the Massachusetts coast. By 1675 civilization extended along the entire coast from Cape Cod to the Penobscot Bay in Maine. Inland it tended to follow first the larger rivers and "creeks" or saltwater inlets and then the well-known Indian trails. In that same year the inland frontier line extended from Dover and Exeter in New Hampshire; to Groton, Lancaster, and Worcester in Massachusetts; to Woonsocket and Providence in Rhode Island (map 2.2).

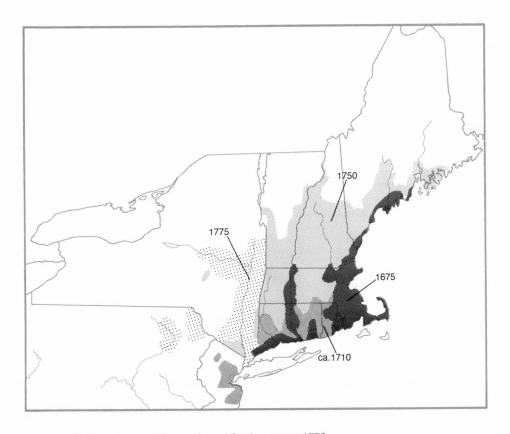

2.2. New England Expansion of Settlement to 1775

In the meantime the Connecticut settlement filled the coastline and proceeded up the Connecticut River to Springfield, Massachusetts, where it met settlers coming overland from the Massachusetts Colony. Here along the Massachusetts section of the Connecticut River Valley the two migrations mingled and spread northward as far as Northfield. By the end of the second period of colonization marked by the war with the Indians known as King Philip's War (1674–76), there were about one hundred twenty thousand New England citizens.

Religious motivation was behind the settlement of Rhode Island, New England's refuge for dissenters and malcontents in the way New England itself was England's refuge. It essentially is a very early offshoot of the Massachusetts Bay Colony, with few settlers arriving directly from England. By 1638, thirteen families from Salem and Boston were settled at Providence. In that year Anne Hutchinson and her followers founded Portsmouth. A part of her group afterward broke off and withdrew to Newport. These early towns subsequently drew their population mainly from Rehoboth, a 1644 Massachusetts Bay Colony outpost, and from the old colony made up of Plymouth and its surrounding settlements.

The Rhode Island Colony was not a fountainhead from which other areas of New England were settled, except perhaps for southwestern Vermont, but was like a gradually filling pool on two sides of which two major settlement streams flowed. To the west was the Connecticut hearth expanding northward, and to the north was the Massachusetts hearth spreading west and northward.

The Regions of New England According to *LANE*

As the *Linguistic Atlas of New England* (Kurath 1939–43) showed, these streams and pools of settlement shaped the geography of New England speech. From the atlas fieldwork, Kurath (*Handbook,* 8–25) delimited two major dialect "regions"—Eastern and Western New England—and seven "subregions," depending on how you cut it (map 2.3). These latter are the Boston area, the Lower Connecticut River Valley, the Narragansett Bay area (Rhode Island), Worcester County–Upper Connecticut River Valley, and three, more minor areas: the Plymouth area, which includes Cape Cod; the Merrimack Valley–New Hampshire Bay area; and Coastal Maine. The New London area, Kurath suggests, may also be a faint subregion.

As outlined by Kurath, *LANE*'s seven subregions also correspond closely with the smaller whorls and eddies of settlement, probably in part because Kurath relies heavily in a somewhat circular fashion on the settlement patterns themselves to help define these dialect areas. Only two have substantial representative isoglosses: Eastern New England and the Narragansett Bay area. The other subdialects could only faintly be heard in the 1930s with just two or three relics left to testify.

The Plymouth and New London areas, and the Worcester County–Upper Connecticut River Valley almost totally lack any linguistic evidence conclusive in itself. Assuming that these areas ever actually existed as subdialect regions, they were by the 1930s moribund. Without a knowledge of the history of New England, it would be very difficult to pick out many of these areas. This may have been why Kurath gave a quite

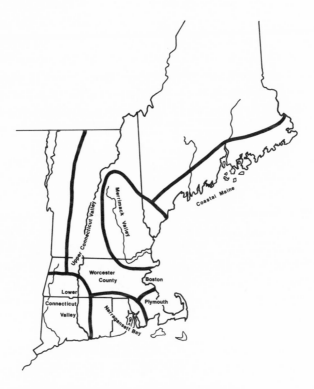

2.3. The Regions of New England According to *LANE*

different picture of New England in *A Word Geography of the Eastern United States* (1949), published ten years after the *Handbook,* reducing the subdivisions to three: Northeastern, Southeastern, and Southwestern New England (see map 1.4).

Because the *DARE* data were collected some thirty-five years after *LANE,* we have the rare opportunity of observing how the distributions of many eastern words have changed and whether these changes have affected the dialect boundaries. After the cataclysmic political, economic, and social upheavals of the mid-twentieth century, we can expect comparable linguistic changes. Specifically, the mass exodus of people from the country to the cities during this period and the dramatic shift to a commercially and technologically based economy and life-style accelerated the decline of the old, rural folk terms and precipitated the spatial and semantic drift of other regionalisms.

Some words we would expect to be rare and dying out. The rather stately old *grandsire* or *grandsir* for grandfather is preserved in *DARE* by only one aged North Leverett informant (northcentral Massachusetts), while *spindle* for corn tassel was known by only two informants—one in Cape Cod, the other in Augusta, Maine. *Orts,* an English dialect term for scraps or garbage was at one time well known in Essex County (northeastern Massachusetts); in the 1960s it still survived in the vocabulary of a Bar Harbor, Maine, informant and a New Bedford, Massachusetts, native, who knew it in the collocation *orts bag* (= garbage sack).

Similarly *blare* (= the cry of a calf) and *bannock* (= a thin corn cake) seem to be well on their way out of usage. These all survived into the late 1960s as relics. It is not surprising that such forms as *webbins* (= lines for driving a horse), *blart* (= the low of a cow), *creeper* (= a cast-iron skillet) and *minnim* (= minnow) are probably obsolete today, since they had no great currency in the New England of the 1930s.

But the strong *LANE* isoglosses that Kurath used to derive some of the sub-regions and particularly the primary boundary of Eastern New England have also changed drastically.

Eastern New England

The boundary separating Eastern from Western New England is of the first order in the hierarchy of New England regions. Kurath is very specific about where this boundary lies (*Handbook,* 8): beginning at the mouth of the Connecticut River, it runs due north to the southern border of Franklyn County in westcentral Massachusetts, where it veers west for about fifty miles to the Berkshire Hills, then turns north again, running along the crest of the Green Mountains to the Vermont-Canadian border (map 2.3).

As he notes elsewhere (Kurath 1972, 41), the sparsely settled areas through which this line runs impeded communication between Eastern and Western New England, thereby emphasizing and stabilizing the boundary. Moreover, Eastern and Western New England each developed a transportation system, notably railroads, which radiated from the old centers outward to the peripheral settlements. These separate systems helped individually consolidate the two regions economically, socially, and culturally.

Kurath uses numerous individual word distributions to support the definition of this primary dialect boundary. But many of these words that were alive and well in the *LANE* era are virtually nonexistent today. No *DARE* informants, for example, gave *LANE*'s Eastern New England term *sour-milk cheese* (*WG,* figs. 8, 10, 126) as a response to the direct question designed to elicit synonyms for "cottage cheese." Only three informants knew the old New Englandism *intervale* (= bottomland along a river; *WG,* fig. 91) and two of them pronounced it ['ɪn,tɚ,vəl] instead of ['ɪn,tɚ'vel].

Another formerly strong Eastern New England isogloss, *the necessary* or *necessary house* for "outhouse" (*WG,* fig. 55), seems to be obsolescent and not just because the object it refers to has gone the way of the horse and buggy. Two *DARE* informants, one in Connecticut and one in Pennsylvania, used this euphemism for outdoor toilet, but two others, one in Massachusetts and one in Pennsylvania, used it in reference to an indoor toilet. Similarly, only two Massachusetts informants knew *go 'long* (*WG,* fig. 107) as a call for driving horses.

Another group of Eastern New England words in *LANE* has changed but not as radically. Today none of these have great currency and would not be very useful in mapping New England's boundaries. A sizable portion of *DARE* informants using these terms were located outside of New England, often in the settlement areas in New York, New Jersey, and Ohio, but not always.

Bonnyclabber or *bonnyclapper* (= thick sour milk; *WG,* figs. 2, 10, 124), a strong Eastern New England isogloss in *LANE,* is nearly as common by *DARE* measurements in New Jersey as in New England proper. Similarly in *DARE, sap orchard* (= sugar maple orchard; *WG,* fig. 144) is an Upstate New York word. *Drag* or *stone drag* (= a wheelless vehicle used to remove fieldstones, *WG,* figs. 9, 78) were well-defined clusters in *LANE.* According to *DARE,* the former is widespread and not regional (149 informants) and the latter expression, though most common in New England, is also found in New Jersey, New York, and Ohio. Like *drag, coal hod* (= a container for coal; *WG,* fig. 82) is spread throughout most of the United States.

Four important *LANE* terms, to *team* (= to haul; *WG,* fig. 76), *raised bread* (= homemade wheat bread; *WG,* fig. 115), *toro* and *top cow* (= a bull; *WG,* fig. 94), are from *DARE*'s view more common outside New England than inside, though none of these expressions is known by many informants.

A good number of Eastern New England words have actually expanded in usage since *LANE,* breaking out of their former dialect boundaries and spreading primarily throughout the Northeast. This is true of *carting* (= hauling; *WG,* fig. 76). *Eaves spout* (= rain gutters) extends throughout the Upper North; *whitebread* (= wheat bread; *WG,* 67), *comforter* (= bed quilt), and *sire* (= a bull; *WG,* fig. 94) are as common in the North-and-West as in New England.

Only a very few *LANE* words have held their ground in Eastern New England. *Double runner* (= bobsled; *WG,* fig. 80) is still essentially eastern and *tumble* (= hay cock; *WG,* fig. 59) is northern New England. *Tonic* (= carbonated soft drink) seems to have gained in currency but stayed primarily in Massachusetts and southeastern New Hampshire. Except for these few, virtually none of *LANE*'s Eastern New England terms would today qualify as regionally defining.

The picture for the other *LANE* subregions is essentially the same; none have more than a handful of representative isoglosses and most of these have completely faded from use.

The Merrimack Valley and New Hampshire Bay area, which was settled primarily by pioneers from Essex County, Massachusetts, has in *LANE* only about four unique terms: *mudworm* (= earthworm; *WG,* fig. 140), *blare* (= the bawl of a calf), *how be you?,* and *white-arsed hornet* (*Handbook,* chart 22 on p. 37). In the five *DARE* communities in this area, none of these expressions were recorded.

The Worcester County–Upper Connecticut River Valley area corresponds to the confluence of the settlement streams from the Lower Connecticut and Boston Bay hearths. But in *LANE* only about three isoglosses are presented as evidence of the region's existence (*Handbook,* chart 24 on p. 38). *High beams* and *great beams* (= barn loft) seem to have disappeared altogether, and of the nine *DARE* informants who use *toro* as a euphemism for a bull, all except one, an Upstate New Yorker, were in the southwestern United States.

Belly-bunt (= belly-flop), however, is still current in New England and largely confined to this subregion, though two informants in the Hudson Valley and one each in northeastern Ohio and northern Wisconsin (all New England settlement areas) also knew it. Even though Kurath discusses *fishworm* (= earthworm; *Handbook,* 18) as a lexical example of the settlement expansion from the Massachusetts coast westward and up the

Connecticut Valley, it does not qualify as a defining isogloss of this subregion since even in the 1930s it was not unique to New England (see *WG*, fig. 139). According to *DARE,* it is known throughout the Northeast and most of the rest of the northern United States.

The Boston area is presumably the most seminal speech region of New England, since all of Eastern New England, as Kurath noted, tends to be "oriented in cultural matters toward Boston and hence receptive to Boston speech" (*Handbook,* 12). However, there are to date no studies showing the relationship of Boston speech to that of the rest of New England. Though Kurath gives little evidence to show that the Boston area is a separate speech subregion, as with most large influential urban areas it has its own complex and distinctive mix of regional and social dialects (see Carlson 1973; Parslow 1967).

The Lower Connecticut Valley, a portion of the Connecticut hearth, has only about five characterizing isoglosses from *LANE* (*Handbook,* 20–21), all of which seem to be fading out of use. Even though there was a direct *DARE* question for "corn tassel," no informants gave *topgallant* as a response. Similarly the question for "seesaw" elicited no *tinter* or *teenter* responses. Only one Connecticut speaker (Bridgeport) used *round clam,* the old southwestern New England name for the quahog. Two eastern Connecticut informants (Jewett City and Lebanon) and one southwestern Massachusetts informant knew *angledog* as a synonym for earthworm. The fifth isogloss, *ivy* (= mountain laurel), did not have a direct *DARE* question to elicit it.

The Narragansett Bay area is the best documented *LANE* subregion, having about twelve isoglosses (*Handbook,* 13–15). All have significantly changed their geography in one way or another. *Cade* (= a pet lamb), *apple slump* (= a deep-dish apple dessert), and *shacket* (= a yellow-jacket hornet) seem to be well on their way out of use, if not completely gone. *Eace worm* (= earthworm) was in the 1930s an important isogloss, but only one *DARE* informant in Rhode Island used it (recorded by the field-worker as "east worm").

A peculiarly distributed group of *DARE* informants knew the Narragansett terms *closet* or *kitchen closet* for pantry. Two informants were in New Hampshire and one in Rhode Island, while the remaining five were scattered in the South. Though faint here, we will see more of this regional pattern where the same words are used in both New England and the Lower South.

Two Narragansett terms cited by Kurath were not representative isoglosses at all though they are regionalisms. *Johnnycake* (= a corn griddle cake) is known throughout the Upper North, and *clothes press* (= a clothes closet) is more common outside of New England though confined to the Northeast. A few others that Kurath cites have become widespread in the United States and have lost their regional status (assuming they ever had any). *Crib* or *corn crib* (= a structure for storing corn) and *fry pan* (= skillet) are essentially known everywhere, as is *loft* (= hay mow) though it seems to be more common in the South and Lower North.

Only two *LANE* isoglosses seem to have remained Narragansett regionalisms: *dandle* or *dandle board* (= seesaw) and *quahog* (= an edible American clam) as distinct from the northeastern New England (especially Massachusetts) *cohog.*

In the Plymouth area *coop!* (= a call to chickens; *WG,* fig. 106) is unknown to *DARE* informants, and only three Massachusetts informants used the formerly common *tilting board* or *tilt* (= seesaw; *WG,* fig. 79). *Tempest* (= rain storm) and *mummichog* (= saltwater minnow or killifish), however, have remained alive and have held their ground in this area.

New England regional English, then, underwent considerable change during the middle third of this century. By the late 1960s, most of the *LANE* isoglosses had lost their regionally defining status. Some had spread to other parts of the country, but a large number had become obsolescent or were outright relics.

The New England Layer

What effect has this impressive lexical "drift" had on New England's dialect boundaries? Have they drifted also?

Map 2.4 is a composite of 45 *DARE* areal isoglosses, only 20 of which can be found at all in the *LANE* maps. Of those 20, Kurath discusses only 4 in *WG: belly-bump(er), piazza, rock maple,* and *rowen.* In short, map 2.4 is based largely on "new"

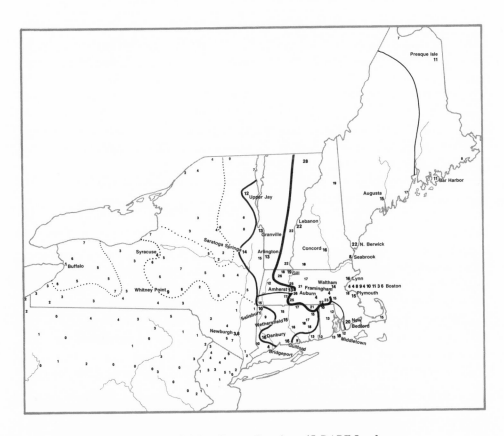

2.4. The New England Dialect Layer Based on 45 *DARE* Isoglosses

isoglosses, replacing most of the old ones in *LANE,* which are no longer useful for discovering dialect boundaries.

Of the twenty-five other isoglosses, most are completely unknown to American word geography. They are either very recent coinages like *grinder* (= a hero or sub-marine sandwich) and *rotary* (= a traffic circle), or they are terms that only a lengthy, detailed questionnaire would catch. *LANE* simply didn't go after words for the soft rolls of dust under furniture (*kittens* or *kitties*) or names for a hair bun (a *pug*) or the kind of day when clouds come and go continually (an *open-and-shut* day).

The dominant landmark on this map is the Upper Connecticut River Valley. Here the "highest" or densest isoglosses occur where the two hearth streams mingled. The rapid drop in density to the west of the valley in central Vermont indicates that this is a major boundary. West of the boundary is a flat region (12 to 15 isoglosses) extending into eastern New York where again the count drops off marking the western boundary of the general New England dialect layer. This boundary is continuous wending southeastward through Connecticut.

East of the Upper Connecticut Valley is a dense isogloss plateau extending from the Penobscot Bay in Maine, down across the Merrimack Valley and central Mas-sachusetts to the Plymouth area. This is essentially the domain of the Massachusetts Bay hearth. With a comparable isogloss density, the domain of the Connecticut hearth is also evident covering most of the state. Rhode Island also appears as a separate area. The areas of relative density bounded by sudden drop-offs or slopes form a pattern that roughly corresponds with the *LANE* subregions (map 2.3) but with some important differences.

Map 2.5 is a generalized version of the *DARE* composite (map 2.4) and allows easier comparison with the *LANE* areas (map 2.3). All of the major boundaries remain intact in the *DARE* map, notably the boundary dividing Eastern from Western New England, though the east-west division is vague in the southern section.

Western New England in map 2.5 is shown as a clearly defined subregion that is separated into northern and southern areas. The southwestern section is in general agreement with the *LANE* version (map 2.3). The northwestern section, however, is another story. Though Kurath also separates Southwestern New England out as a faint subregion in *WG,* he generally treats Western New England and particularly North-western New England as the eastern edge of the Inland North and not as a subregion in its own right, in part because it apparently lacks a unique vocabulary in contrast to the large Eastern New England lexicon. As he notes, its regional vocabulary was dispersed westward to the Great Lakes leaving only a couple of localized survivals like *angledog* (= earthworm) and *callathump* (= shivaree) (*WG,* 26).

Northwestern New England in map 2.5, however, is a clearly defined area covering northwestern Massachusetts, western Vermont, and northeastern New York. Despite the strong western boundary present in this layer, other evidence, which we will be looking at shortly, suggests that this subregion—particularly Northwestern New England—is primarily a transitional speech area between the major Eastern New England dialect and the Inland North.

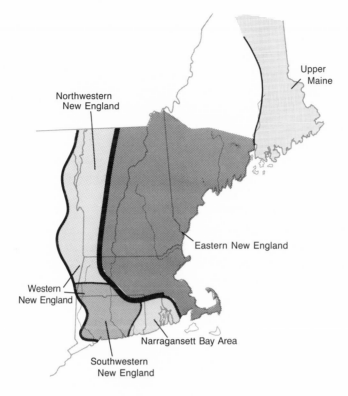

Upper
Maine

Northwestern
New England

Eastern New England

Western
New England

Narragansett Bay Area

Southwestern
New England

2.5. The Regions of New England Generalized from Map 2.4

The Narragansett Bay area is also clearly defined in map 2.5, though it appears somewhat shrunken from its *LANE* version, in part due to the transitional nature of its western section.

The Merrimack Valley and Plymouth areas, however, are not distinguished at all in the map and may have slipped through *DARE*'s wide-meshed fieldwork. On the other hand, because these two subregions were never very clearly documented in *LANE* in the first place, but seemed to be established primarily on the basis of settlement patterns, the absence of *DARE* evidence may indicate the absence of the subregion. In any case, the lack of evidence in map 2.4 for these purported subdialects is probably not due to any kind of linguistic change occuring since the 1930s.

Maine (in map 2.5) appears as two separate regions: lower and upper Maine. The boundary between the two naturally falls at the Penobscot Bay, which was the northernmost point of settlement along the New England coast throughout the entire colonial period. Lower Maine is essentially an extension of Eastern New England, while upper Maine, with its very different settlement history that includes ties with New Brunswick, appears as a subdialect region in its own right. This is borne out in the maps for the Northeast (map 2.8) and the Upper North (map 3.7).

Clearly the Connecticut River Valley is the dominant feature in the dialect geography of New England and has remained so since the first settlements. Of the 45 isoglosses of map 2.4, over half remain almost entirely east of this valley (see app. A for a list of these). The river valley, however, loses its sharpness as a dividing line between the two New Englands (eastern and western) in southern New England, specifically in Connecticut. In northern New England this boundary is clearly present (map 2.5) as far south as the Connecticut-Massachusetts border where it turns eastward, separating Rhode Island from Massachusetts. Then as if splitting into two, more minor boundaries, it continues southward on either side of Rhode Island. From the *LANE* evidence we would expect the western side of Rhode Island to be the continuation of the primary boundary. This is indirectly corroborated in the maps for the Upper North (map 3.7) and the North (map 3.3) layers (see maps 3.3, 3.7, and 3.9).

The three Northern layers (see maps 3.3, 3.7, and 3.9) define New England as a whole, and particularly Eastern New England, by the relative absence of isoglosses. This is best seen in the Inland North map, which shows a very sparse isogloss count in New England (maps 3.9 and 3.10). But in all three layers we can see a boundary of various magnitudes separating Eastern from Western New England. At the same time Western New England, particularly the Southwestern section, is separated from the Inland North. Map 2.6 shows how the Northern layers help define New England.

The Eastern New England bundle of boundaries in map 2.6 is coherent along the Upper Connecticut Valley but diverges considerably in Massachusetts. The Upper North line runs further east than the others, as might be expected, since New England is parent to the Upper North and would therefore be most likely to share the greatest number of words of any of the Northern layers. The more westerly meanderings of the North line in central Massachusetts and eastern Connecticut suggest that this (approximately the dotted area) is a transitional speech region between the colonial hearths of the Lower Connecticut River Valley on the one hand and of Rhode Island and eastern Massachusetts on the other. In any case, the primary boundary in southern New England runs west of the Rhode Island subarea.

The relatively coherent bundle through Connecticut and Massachusetts forms a strong boundary separating Western New England from the Hudson Valley. The line dividing Northwestern New England from New York evident in the New England layer (map 2.4) and to a lesser extent in the Upstate New York isoglosses (map 2.7) is so weak in the Northern layers that it is not possible to draw a definite line. This suggests that Southwestern New England, where the western isogloss bundles are coherent, is clearly a subdialect area of New England, whereas Northwestern New England is only a minor subregion, perhaps primarily transitional in character between the Inland North and New England.

Despite the enormous change in the geography of individual New England words that established the *LANE* areas of map 2.3, the major and several minor New England dialect boundaries remain relatively unchanged. If anything the *DARE* data affirm and, in the case of Western New England and Maine, clarify the boundaries. It is proof that dialect expressions inevitably spread or die out, but that dialect boundaries remain relatively stable and alive. The more pronounced the boundary, that is, the higher and

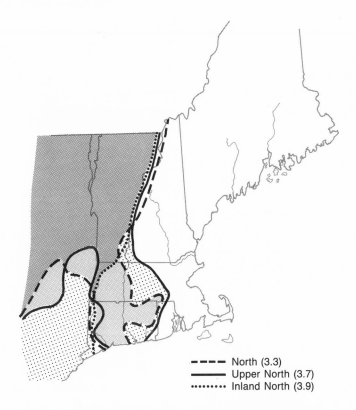

2.6. Isogloss Bundles of Three Northern Layers in New England. Shading
shows relative density of Northern terms, the darkest area in Vermont and northeast New York representing the heaviest concentration of terms from all three
layers, eastern New England using the least percentage of the Northern lexicons.
Note that the Hudson Valley is roughly outlined by the relative lack of North
and Upper North terms, and differs from the similarly shaded area in central
Massachusetts and south-central Connecticut, by the presence of the Inland
North lexicon, whereas the Upper North lexicon characterizes the latter area.

steeper the slope—as in the case of the western edge of the Upper Connecticut River
Valley—the more likely is the boundary to remain intact.

Lexicon

New England from the first was closely tied to the sea. Ship building and fishing have
long been a feature of coastal New England life, peppering its speech with nautical and
sea weather terms. Many of the first immigrants came from the western counties of
England where the major occupations had to do with fishing and shipping. They spoke
of *nor'easters* and *nor'westers,* of winds *lulling down* or sometimes *breezing up* into a
tempest. All of these old expressions can still be heard in New England, particularly
along the coasts.

Two nautical terms that penetrated much further inland originally referred to parts of a ship. A *bulkhead* in the early seventeenth century, as now, was a partition separating the cabins or compartments of a ship. But once the term came ashore, it was enlisted as a name for the sloping doors that give access to a cellar. This must have been a common term early on. Thoreau used it with complete familiarity in *Walden* (1854). The term had penetrated well into Western New England by the nineteenth century, but abruptly stopped its drift at the western boundary. Today it is virtually an exclusive New England expression.

Hatchway, on the other hand, has spread throughout Upstate New York, even into northeastern Ohio (a New England settlement area) and competes with its cousin synonym *bulkhead* in Western New England. *Hatchway* originally referred to the square opening in a ship's deck through which cargo was lowered. The earliest known record of the term occurs ironically in a 1626 treatise written by one of New England's first heroes, Captain John Smith. But the term faded from the coast, perhaps being pushed out by *bulkhead.* Today it is not much used in Eastern New England.

It was the common experience of the colonists to encounter in the New World phenomena for which they had no satisfactory names. The changeable New England sky, for example, in contrast to the relatively constant weather of England, created a need for a new expression. In eighteenth-century nautical parlance, *open* meant weather free of fog or mist. An *open day,* then, would be a clear sunny day. And as New England folk logic would have it, an *open-and-shut day* would be a changeable day when clouds continually come and go.

Another unfamiliar phenomenon to the settlers was a mountain pass. *Notch* was the word they picked for this, a typical transference of a common English word. Today it is used throughout New England, often in place-names, just as it was when the Massachusetts colonist Samuel Sewall used it in his 1718 diary.

Snakes of course were not a New World surprise, but the term *adder,* which the colonists brought with them, has remained primarily a New England and New York usage. It has also survived in the Lower South. *Mummichogs* (= saltwater minnows or killifish) and *quahogs* (= thick-shelled edible American clams), however, were new to them and, as was often done for many New World discoveries, they adopted Indian names, in this case, the Narragansett terms *moamitteaug* (= literally: they go in great numbers) and *poquauhock* (= dark or closed shell). *Pogy* and *scup* (= menhaden) were also Indian borrowings. These last terms have stayed in the coastal areas and especially in southeastern New England.

Most of the recorded New England lexicon, however, is rural in nature and pertains to the farming and domestic life of an older and simpler time. Most of these terms are new coinages or new adaptations of old words. *Creepers,* for example, were metal cleats fastened to boot soles enabling a man to work surefootedly in the icy winters. During winter, sleighs were more than just a convenience and played an important role in the settlement of New England and eventually New York, since they afforded smooth passage over rough or unbroken ground. There are many terms for many different kinds of sleighs, but at least two are unique to New England. A *double runner* is a bobsled and is also known in New England as a *double ripper* or *traverse sled.* Sleighs were used on the farm to haul loads, or as a Yankee is apt to say, to *cart* or *team* loads, such as firewood. One of the most common New England names for such a sleigh is *pung,* which is probably an abbreviation of an early folk version of "toboggan," *tom pung* (1801).

In preparing for a sleigh ride the New Englander might strap the harness to the horse with a *belly-girt* and straighten the *webbins* or reins. Instead of commanding the horse to "get up!", he would be likely to say *go 'long!* or *go on!* And if he were going downtown, it would not be unusual to hear him say he was going *downstreet.*

If the horse were balky or bad tempered, our Yankee might say it was being *ugly,* a term he would also use with reference to an ornery cow. An ugly *top cow,* however, is not an unmanageable cow, but a bull. This is one of the numerous euphemisms that U.S. folk speakers almost universally feel compelled to use, especially in mixed company where *bull* (at least the word) is taboo. *Toro* and *sire* were also once New England euphemisms. But today the former is more likely to be heard in the Southwest and the latter throughout much of the North and West.

"Manure" is also euphemized in Yankee speech to *dressing,* usually in combinations like *top, meadow, cow,* or *horse dressing.* Oddly enough, where an Ozarker might cringe in company to hear the word *titman,* the New England farmer uses the term unabashedly when talking about the runt of a sow's litter. *Tit* here means small and originally the whole expression referred to a stunted or very short man. Thoreau used it when he called modern man "A race of tit-men [who] soar but little higher in our intellectual flights than the columns of the daily paper" (*Walden,* 1854). This is still a solidly New England and Upstate New York expression in common rural use.

Given the importance of the production of maple sugar and syrup in New England, it is surprising that there are not more expressions relating to it in the lexicon. *Sap orchard* for a sugar maple grove was apparently once a fairly common usage in New England (see *WG,* fig. 144), but in the *DARE* responses only one Mainer and two western New Yorkers used it. *Rock maple,* however, is a common New England term for the sugar maple itself.

In the rocky New England soil farmers removed stones from their fields with a horse-drawn, wheelless vehicle called a *stone drag* or more often simply *drag.* The latter may have been unique to the New England lexicon, but by the mid-twentieth century, *drag* was used in much of the rural United States. *Stone drag,* however, stays close to New England where it is used alongside the more common Upper North term *stoneboat.*

The hilly landscape also fostered the *side-hill plow,* which has a cutting apparatus that can be reversed. The earliest known citation for the term is from an 1830 North Carolina newspaper, so it is likely that though this two-way plow is or was in widespread use, this term for it died out except in New England and New York. A similar situation probably obtains for a *wheel harrow,* a term used almost exclusively in New England for the common farm implement that breaks up lumps of dirt in a newly plowed field. In clearing his field of brush, the New England farmer might use a *bush scythe* that he has sharpened with a *rifle* or emery-covered whetter.

Among the weeds he would want to remove would be couch grass or quack grass, which he would know as *witch grass,* a New Englandism since the American revolutionary period. *Swale grass,* however, which grows naturally in damp places, the New England farmer might be inclined to let grow as hay. Such a damp area, specifically a marshy depression in level land, has been known in New England as a *swale* since at least 1667 when it was recorded in the public records of Dedham, Massachusetts. It may have come originally from English dialect with the colonists from the eastern counties of England where the term is still in use.

After cutting his hay, the farmer would then *tedder* it. This name comes from a farm machine invented in mid-nineteenth-century America. It stirred and spread the hay to promote its drying. The verb *to ted,* however, goes back to fifteenth-century England and means to spread or scatter (new mown grass) for drying. In the convolutions of language change, *ted* the verb gave rise to *tedder* the noun that then became *tedder* the verb with the same meaning as the original *ted* verb.

Once the hay has been teddered, it may be stacked for curing into haycocks or as some New England farmers call them, *tumbles.* Finally, he would *mow it away,* that is, store it in the barn or hay mow. If a second crop or aftermath were allowed to grow in the hayfield, he would refer to it as *rowen,* a fourteenth-century term still very much alive in twentieth-century New England.

As with many major cultural regions, New England has its share of recipes and related food terminology. Some of these terms are dialectal because the dishes themselves are regional. This is the case with *brown bread,* or in full, *Boston brown bread,* which is a kind of dessert bread usually made with cornmeal and rye flour, sweetened with molasses, and steamed.

But most of the food regionalisms refer to dishes that are eaten virtually everywhere. The well-known submarine sandwich, for example, in New England is often called a *grinder;* and the hot dog or frankfurter is frequently shortened to *frankfurt,* as is hamburger shortened to *hamburg.* These all-American sandwiches are washed down, especially in Massachusetts, with a *tonic* or carbonated soft drink. Nearly everyone has at one time or another eaten a poached egg, but only New Englanders call it a *dropped egg.*

The Indians of the region left their imprint not only on the lexicon but on the cuisine when they introduced the New England pilgrims to maize or Indian corn. *Indian pudding,* known throughout New England and parts of New York, is cornmeal mush with milk and molasses, which is sometimes eaten as a dessert. This rather unassuming dish, which is probably served with minor variations on many tables throughout the United States, is also called *hasty pudding.* It is likely that the Indians themselves introduced the dish, for when Samuel Sewall visited an Indian chief in his wigwam in 1714, he was served "roste Alewife and very good Hasty Pudding."

Bannock is a thin corn cake, the kind one can find almost anywhere in the South. To Scottish and northern English colonists, "bannock" was a flat loaf of unleavened bread made with oats or barley. It was a simple matter for them to transfer this Old World name to the New World corn bread. The term itself, however, seems to be dying out.

Bread made from wheat flour and yeast in contrast to unleavened cornbread is known in the South as *light bread* and in New England as *raised bread.* However, with the decline of home baking in the face of the ubiquitous white stuff sold by super-markets—what old folks know as "store-bought bread"—*raised bread* has lost most of its currency.

In New England and New York a thick cream soup made with corn is known as *corn chowder,* which would never be made with *cow corn,* called elsewhere "field corn," since that variety of maize is usually reserved for animal feed. The *DARE* informants, however, said that very young cow corn is fine for human consumption.

The small white beans used in most parts of the United States are called in New England and New York *pea beans,* which because they are dried, can be stored in a pantry or *buttry.* This variant of the older British *butlery* is a New Englandism that has spread in sparse fashion to most of the major New England settlements in Ohio, Michigan, Minnesota, and elsewhere. It is still most often used in New England, however. Vegetables that have been stored too long in the buttry are said to be *gone by,* that is, they have become tough and inedible. *Gone by* is also a New England euphemism for "died," which might be heard in conjunction with a funeral wake, also known here as the *calling hours.*

In New England, especially among older speakers, a funnel is often called a *tunnel,* whereas a *funnel* can refer to the old-fashioned stovepipe. In using a tunnel, if the liquid which one is pouring comes out a little at a time, it would be said to be coming out by *dribs and drabs,* a phrase most often heard in inland New England among all age groups.

A *tenement* in this region is an apartment building. Tenement houses were first erected in the early nineteenth century in New York City where this term has taken on connotations of poverty and squalor. These connotations seem to be absent from the New England usage. Although tenements rarely have verandas, many New England homes do and these are often called *piazzas.* English colonists brought this term to the eastern colonies when it still meant a colonnade or covered walkway. In time its meaning shifted to refer to a usually covered porch, but for some reason this shift took place only in New England and the Atlantic South where *piazza* is in common regional use today.

Among the children's games, winter sports are especially popular and have fostered at least two regionalisms. The method of coasting on a sled face down has been particularly productive of regional expressions. The New England version is called a *belly-bump* or *belly-bunt,* terms used along with the Northern *belly-flop.* The ice-skating game called "crack-the-whip" is also known in New England and New York as *snap-the-whip.* In New England marble games, a superior playing marble, especially the taw or shooter, is an *allie.* This term is an abbreviated form of "alabaster," the material that quality marbles were made of.

There are numerous other, more miscellaneous New Englandisms. A *fusspot* is the inland New England term for a finicky or fussy person. The Upper North-and-West *fussbudget* is also used in New England.

If one takes a shortcut or direct route from one point to another, in this region it is called *going* or *cutting cross-lots.*

A festering or suppurating wound is said to be *matterating.*

A woman with her hair done up in a bun on the top of her head is wearing a *pug*.

Giving an unexpected hint or warning is called *putting a flea in one's ear,* elsewhere known as "putting a bee in one's bonnet."

A-yuh is one of the favorite New England folk forms of "yes." An equally gruntlike expression is *vum,* which is actually an old form of "I vow" (= I swear) going back to Revolutionary times. "We must fight for liberty / And vum we'll 'fend it, if we die," proclaimed a bit of doggerel published in a 1785 edition of the *Massachusetts Spy,* a well-known newspaper at the time. Today it is usually an exclamation: "I'll be vummed," or "I vum!", or just "Vum!" are most likely to be heard.

Two contemporary regionalisms were created with the highway system. In New England a traffic circle is called a *rotary.* Primarily in Western New England and adjacent areas of New York, a divided highway with extensive plantings or natural foliage is called a *parkway.*

The New England lexicon, then, is rooted in the colonial period giving it a slight archaic flavor spiced here and there with older nautical terms and early Indian borrowings. It tends to be conservative, having few recently coined expressions and very few terms that might be considered slang in nature.

New York

The faint extension of the New England dialect into New York as a thin layer of isoglosses (map 2.4) is the linguistic counterpart of the extension of New England settlement into New York. New Englanders first pushed into New York when it was still known as New Netherland. Around 1640 they established Southold and Southhampton on Long Island. A hundred years later a flood tide of New Englanders had settled the area east of the Hudson River. Dutchess and Ulster counties had doubled their population between 1750 and 1770. Expansion northward had been impeded by the war with France, but with the Treaty of 1763 and the expulsion of the French from North America, northern New York soon saw the arrival of Yankees from Vermont and western Massachusetts.

Meanwhile in 1740 a bold party of Scotch-Irish from Londonderry, New Hampshire, were the first pioneers in the western frontier beyond the Hudson Valley. About fifty miles west of Albany they established the community of Cherry Valley (see map 2.1). This was to become the springboard for later settlement in central New York.

Beginning around 1760 the settlement of New York primarily by New Englanders expanded in two general directions. One branch pushed northward up the Hudson Valley beyond Albany where towns with New England names like Cambridge, Greenwich, and Salem were established. The other branch extended westward into the upper Susquehanna basin as a continuation of the beginning at Cherry Valley. At the same time newcomers filled both sides of the Mohawk River. The movement westward culminated in the 1790s with "Genesee fever," which drove migration from New England through Albany to the Genesee Valley in far western New York. One Albany observer in the winter of 1795 counted over five hundred sleds loaded with household belongings passing westward in a single day.

The New York colony by the time of the Revolution had three broad cultural regions: the highly cosmopolitan New York City area; the Yankee region, which in the east included most of Long Island and the land bordering New England, and in the west the Susquehanna, Genesee, and Delaware settlements; and the Dutch area of the Hudson Valley, along with its German and Huguenot settlements. Each of these broad colonial cultural regions left its imprint in various ways on the linguistic regions of New York.

The Hudson Valley

In 1664 at the end of Dutch rule, New Amsterdam (New York City) had no more than fifteen hundred residents. All of New Netherland (southeastern New York) had only about eight thousand compared to the twenty-five thousand inhabitants of the New England colony. Even with such small numbers and such a short occupation, the Dutch culture and language persisted tenaciously. By mid-eighteenth century, Albany, for example, was still completely Dutch in character. The Dutch language was still predominant in the Hudson Valley and still quite common in New York City.

In 1709 another large non-English-speaking group began settling the valley: the Palatine Germans. Arriving as whole families, they were the largest single (non-English) European group to migrate to New York during the colonial period. Their settlement along the Hudson and later the Mohawk and Schoharie rivers strengthened the non-English character of the region and helped divert the flood of New England settlers to the north and west. This was their greatest impact on the regional geography. Today very little of the Dutch or German speech has survived except in place-names.

Unlike Western New England, the Hudson Valley at the time of the atlas survey (ca.1935) had a substantial unique lexicon and was clearly a dialect subregion in its own right. Kurath discovered at least a dozen isoglosses that defined the area, but almost all of these have either disappeared or changed to such a degree that they have lost their unique defining ability.

As might be expected, over half of the atlas isoglosses for this area are anglicized remnants of the Dutch vocabulary. Some of these, especially the food terms, had already become obsolescent by the 1930s, such as *olicook* (= doughnut; *WG*, fig. 120) from Dutch *oliekoek* (= oil cake) and *rolliche* (= roulade; *WG*, 24) from *rolletje* (= little roll). These terms were unknown to *DARE* informants. *Thick milk* (= clabber) was another obsolescent term in the Hudson Valley, though in both the atlas (see *WG*, figs. 23, 124) and *DARE* fieldwork it survives independently in Pennsylvania, deriving not from Dutch but from Pennsylvania German *dickemilch*.

Suppawn (= cornmeal mush) was borrowed by the Dutch from the Indians. In *WG* (figs. 2, 13), it it used as a representative isogloss for the Hudson Valley, but by 1965 it was virtually obsolete. No *DARE* informants gave the term in response to the specific question designed to elicit names for this rudimentary dish. The reason for *suppawn*'s precipitous fall from usage after being current for some three hundred years is puzzling, though, as with other food terms, the impact of commercialization doubtless played a large role.

It may also have been commercialization that affected *cruller* but in just the opposite way. *Cruller,* another term for doughnut or sweet cake (from Dutch *krulle* = curly cake), gained considerable currency in the nineteenth century. The atlas collected instances of it from northern Virginia to southern Maine, but east of a line through eastern Maryland, eastern Pennsylvania, and southeastern New York (*WG,* figs. 14, 120). By the late 1960s, *cruller* had spread throughout the Northeast and inland through Ohio, to Illinois and Wisconsin, with scattered usage further west, especially in California; however, it had not penetrated the South any further than northern Virginia and eastern West Virginia.

Other former Hudson Valley terms that have spread outside of the region are: *hay barrack* (= a structure with a sliding roof for covering haystacks; from Dutch *hooiberg*), *stoop* (= a small porch; from Dutch *stoep*), *saw-buck* (= saw horse; from Dutch *zaagbok*) and *teeter-totter* (= seesaw). *Barrack* or *hay barrack,* which has by far the least currency of these, was known by only eight *DARE* informants, only one of whom was in the Hudson Valley. At the time of the atlas fieldwork, *stoop* (*WG,* fig. 7) and *saw-buck* (*WG,* fig. 81) were in use throughout the Northeast except in Eastern New England. They are even more widely spread in *DARE.*

Teeter-totter, however, is one of Kurath's "representative" isoglosses (*WG,* fig. 13) for the Hudson Valley. The *DARE* map shows a quite different picture with 386 informants using this term throughout the North-and-West except in Eastern New England and central and southern Pennsylvania. But is this a case of linguistic spreading? Alva Davis in his dissertation on the Great Lakes region, completed a year before Kurath published *A Word Geography,* found that *teeter-totter* was common everywhere in Illinois, Indiana, Ohio, and Michigan. This is, then, simply a matter of the limitations of the earlier atlas fieldwork that Kurath uses, which left off at the Appalachian Mountains. In any case, like the other terms, *teeter-totter* does not qualify as a representative isogloss for the Hudson Valley.

About four isoglosses remain that in *DARE* retain to one degree or another some of their defining or representative value. *Kip* (= a call to chickens; *WG,* fig. 106) is still a Hudson word, though with only four informants it is probably dying out. Likewise only seven informants knew *sap bush* (*WG,* fig. 145) for a sugar maple grove and only three of these were in the region proper. With so few informants these shrunken isoglosses can only hint at the presence of the region.

Pot cheese, on the other hand, with forty-four informants giving it as a synonym for cottage cheese (from Dutch *potkaas* = cheese prepared or stored in pots), provides much stronger evidence of the old Dutch cultural region. Of these forty-four, twenty-six are scattered primarily along the valley or in New York City; seven are in northern New Jersey, and two in southwestern Connecticut (map 2.7). Given the widespread commercial preparation of this food and the according predominance of the term "cottage cheese," which has virtually displaced the numerous other old dialect terms for it, it is surprising that *pot cheese* has survived for so long. Of the forty-four informants, however, three-quarters were old speakers and only two were under thirty-five years of age.

Skimmilton also approaches being a representative isogloss. This term for a shivaree or the good-natured hazing of newlyweds (not from Dutch, but from English dialect) was known by seventeen informants so tightly clustered in this region that it is possible to mark off its distribution with a line (the broken line in map 2.7). None of the informants used the variant *skimmerton,* though one used *skimmington* and another said *skimbling.* Despite this good informant representation, all but one were old speakers— almost certain evidence that the term is disappearing fast.

As with the subdialects of New England, the atlas isoglosses defining the Hudson Valley have undergone enormous change. Some have expanded far beyond the borders of the valley; others have died out or are mere relics. In either case, their function as evidence of a viable dialect is essentially nullified. It would be virtually impossible to define a region based on the isoglosses discussed here. And even those two old standbys, *pot cheese* and *skimmilton,* are apparently vanishing from use. Perhaps more importantly there seem to be no new or recently discovered isoglosses to replace the old regionally defining terms.

But what the Hudson Valley lacks in positive lexical evidence, it makes up in indirect evidence. Nearly every map of the North reveals the outlines of this region either in total (see maps 2.6, 3.3, 3.7, 3.9) or in part, as when the western boundary of New England (map 2.4) coincides with the eastern boundary of the Hudson Valley area. That the region still exists seems assured, but the nature of its speech is not readily apparent from the *DARE* data. A more detailed study is needed. In any case, if it persists as a separate linguistic area, it will not be on the basis of its Dutch vocabulary as it has been in the past.

Upstate New York

We saw in map 2.4 the thin, though nonuniform layer of New England terms spread over New York state as a result of early Yankee settlement. The greatest number of these eighteen isoglosses (see app. A) are shared with western and central New England (except western Connecticut); and the least number with Eastern New England, especially the coastal areas from Narragansett Bay to northern Maine.

Map 2.7 shows the distributions of nine words that are almost exclusive to New York. But even here the affinity of New York with Western New England is apparent. *Throughway* (= expressway), for example, is well attested in Western New England, and *lobbered milk* (= clabber) is common in Southwestern New England. *Brush broom* (= whisk broom) and *horning* (= shivaree) are also well documented in *LANE.*

Despite its undeniably close historical and cultural relationship with New England, Upstate New York—all of the state except the greater New York metropolitan area—is a viable, if minor, dialect area in its own right. But as map 2.7 suggests, it is hardly a uniform region, having as complicated a geography as New England. Gastil (1975, map 29 on p. 139), for example, maps off six cultural districts within the state (cf. map 3.1). In map 2.7, the Hudson and Mohawk valleys appear as a separate area of thin isoglosses surrounded by denser areas. The sparse isoglosses near the St. Lawrence River in northern New York are perhaps a faint indication of another subarea. But to generalize further about New York's subregions based on map 2.7 is risky since there are so few isoglosses that the picture in its details is bound to be misleading.

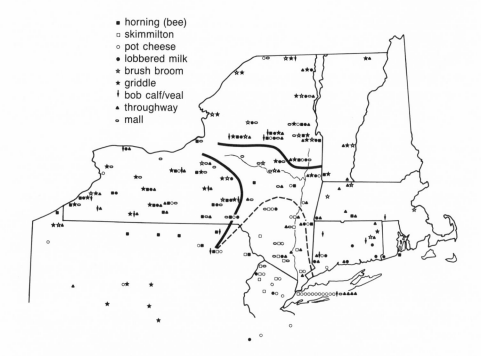

- ■ horning (bee)
- □ skimmilton
- ○ pot cheese
- ● lobbered milk
- ☆ brush broom
- ★ griddle
- † bob calf/veal
- ▲ throughway
- ○ mall

2.7. Selected Upstate New York Isoglosses from the *DARE* Fieldwork.
Note that the distributions of *skimmilton* (the dashed line) and, to a lesser
extent, *pot cheese* outline the Hudson Valley. Together with the Mohawk
Valley, the southeast corner of the state is marked off by the near absence of
bob calf, griddle, and *brushbroom.*

Lobbered or *loppered milk* (= clabber) in America was a Western New England
expression that was diffused throughout much of New York. It derives from Middle
English *lopren,* which later became dialectal in England. It was this dialectal *lobber* or
lopper that Scottish and northern English immigrants carried to the Connecticut Colony.
LANE (map 298; *WG,* fig. 124) shows particular concentrations of *lobbered milk* in
Connecticut and *loppered milk* in Rhode Island and Northwestern New England, which
received a certain amount of Rhode Island settlement. It also shows, as might be
expected, a mixed usage of the two forms in New York. Map 2.7 tells a similar story,
though the proportions are not quite the same. Significantly there are no informants in
Vermont.

Horning or *horning bee,* the Upstate counterpart to the Hudson *skimmilton,* may
be a Rhode Island invention that arrived in New York via Northwestern New England.
WG (fig. 154) shows the term neatly isolated in Rhode Island, with scattered instances
in Northwestern New England, central New York, and northern Pennsylvania. The
DARE map is in basic agreement, but also shows two informants in Michigan.

A whisk broom is often called a *brush broom* in Upstate New York. *LANE* (map
155) also shows its use in Western New England. This Americanism may be a late
coinage that originated in New York and, reversing the historical trend, spread into New

England. The *Dictionary of Americanisms* (*DA*) gives what may be circumstantial evidence for this in its earliest citation taken from a 1910 *Dialect Notes* glossary of central west New York.

Bob calf or *bob veal* is an example of one common feature of American folk speech: redundancy (q.v. *American Dialect Dictionary*). These expressions for a calf used for veal have their roots in English dialect, which uses *bob* to refer simply to a young calf.

In addition to the standard sense of a flat cooking pan, a *griddle* in this region also means the round lid of a wood-burning stove. Because the old-fashioned wood-burners that were stoked through lidded, round holes on the top are essentially things of the past, the terms for its once well-known parts are also essentially obsolescent. Most of the informants using *griddle* were over sixty years old in 1965. The same is true of the previous four Upstate New York terms. They were all used to one degree or another primarily by old informants.

But two other solid isoglosses suggest that this subdialect region is not passing away with the older customs and ways of life. *Throughway* (= freeway or expressway) and *mall* (= median strip in a highway) are two obviously modern terms. The 1939, second edition of the *Merriam-Webster Dictionary* gives only one sense of *throughway*, "a through street." But the third edition (1961) gives the additional sense, "expressway," though it doesn't recognize the regional status. The *DARE* isogloss is almost paradigmatic for the layer: the informants are neatly spread throughout New York (four in New York City) and Western New England. Here is a term that had no part in settlement spread, yet its geography mimics that spread as if it had. It is clear evidence of the coherence and internal communication of a living dialect region.

Mall offers a qualification on this theme. No *DARE* informants in New England used this term to mean a highway median strip. Of the thirty-four informants, all are Upstate except three: one each in New York City, northern New Jersey, and anomalously, southern Indiana. It may be that the *DARE* fieldwork caught this term at the moment prior to its spread into Western New England. Or it may be that this is an example of the transitional nature of the Western New England region, which has a tendency to share only parts of the lexicons east and west of it. Or perhaps the unusual containment of this term within a single state has some other word-specific reason, perhaps political in nature, such as the use of the term in maps or other state publications. At any rate, these last two isoglosses suggest that Upstate New York is a separate and viable dialect region.

The Northeast Layer

The Northeast is essentially an extension of New England settlement first into New York, where, through its contact with the old western frontier, a unique brand of Yankee speech quite different from Eastern New England's evolved. Settlement then spread into northern Pennsylvania, Ohio, and points west, ultimately creating the Upper North. At the same time, the southeastern Pennsylvania hearth centered on Philadelphia spread westward, picking up the influence of the secondary hearth in the western section centered on Pittsburgh, and continuing westward mingling on its northern margin with the sweep of settlement from New York and New England.

One of the first effects of this early movement out of the Northeast was to establish a dialect layer older in its evolution than that formed by the great surge westward beyond Ohio, but younger than the stabilized colonial hearths of New England and eastern Pennsylvania. The Northeast is in many ways a transitional yet relatively distinct area between the New England and eastern Pennsylvania axis and the full extension of the Northern region.

This is at least evident in the speech of the Northeast—roughly New England, New York, and most of New Jersey and Pennsylvania—which has a considerable number of characteristic regionalisms. Map 2.8 plots these. Although all 37 isoglosses are clearly concentrated in the Northeast, many are scattered to one degree or another throughout the North, particularly the Upper North. A few, notably *mud wasp, macadam, cruller, whiffletree,* and *route,* could almost as easily have been mapped with the Upper North isoglosses (map 3.7), except that a predominant number of the informants in each case were located in the Northeast in a tightly clustered pattern. In the case of *soda* and *brook,* the scattering outside of the Northeast includes parts of the South as well as the North.

The Northeast layer is a good example of the correspondence that often exists between the core of a dialect layer and the historical source or hearth of the region. Accordingly, the densest isoglosses occur in Western New England, particularly in Southwestern New England, the area of the Connecticut hearth. Map 2.9 generalizes the isoglosses of map 2.8 into areas of relative density. The importance of the rest of New England, particularly the southern portion, as well as northern New Jersey and the lower Hudson and upper Susquehanna valleys to the region as a whole, is apparent from the area of secondarily high numbers, 15 to 19 isoglosses.

The extension of the Northeast layer westward is faintly present in Ohio, Michigan, and Wisconsin as low but significant isogloss numbers spread somewhat erratically. The layer also thinly covers the Virginia tidewater region, diluting its "Southerness"—a situation we will see amplified in the maps of the South—and adding to the uniqueness of this Southern subarea.

Just how discrete a dialect region the Northeast is is not clear. There are, for example, no significant isogloss bundles or boundaries that distinctly segregate the region. Moreover, the numbers tend to be mixed, making it not only difficult to draw boundaries, but making the isogloss ranges of map 2.9 a continual compromise. Nevertheless, the spatial concentration of a body of words clearly indicates a speech region, even if its borders are blurred. This is the region of the early Northern dialect, a variety of American English closer to its Western New England and New York origins than to the rest of the North, closer geographically, historically and, because of a shared lexicon, linguistically.

That the Northeast is especially close to its New England roots is also apparent in the regional origins of many of the terms in the lexicon, insofar as their geographical histories can be traced or deduced. Among the most likely of these are *brook, button-*

2.8. The Northeast Dialect Layer Based on 37 *DARE* Isoglosses

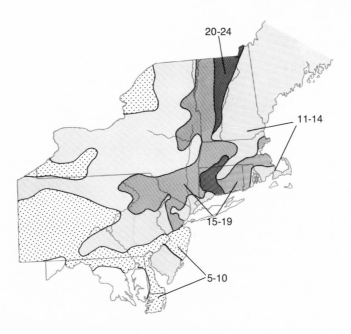

2.9. Relative Isogloss Densities of the Northeast Layer. The core of this
layer is roughly the area of two darkest shadings (15 to 24 isoglosses) and the
domain is the remaining shaded portion.

wood and *buttonball, clapboard, double house, stone wall, thank-you-ma'am, hamburg,*
and probably *mud wasp* and *corn broom.*

New England, however, is not the only source of the Northeast lexicon. The
Hudson Valley's *cruller,* Metropolitan New York's *guinea* and *Jersey mosquito,* and the
New Jersey area's *hop-toad* indicate at least three minor source areas. In addition, a few
slang and colloquial expressions, such as *can, get a wiggle on,* and *cowboy,* suggest a
more recent non-Yankee source.

The lexicon is particularly rich in nature terms. *Brook* (= a small stream), which
appears in numerous colonial New England records beginning as early as 1622, has long
been known to be regional. Professor Schele de Vere, a nineteenth-century scholar of
American language, observed in 1872 that "*kill* of New York is a *brook* in New
England, a *run* in Virginia, and, alas! a *crick,* or creek, almost everywhere else" (p.
460). His observation would be quite different today. *Brook* is still strong in New
England, but it has spread throughout the Northeast, and is well known in most of the
rest of the United States, though probably as a book word. It easily replaced the Hudson
Valley *kill* (from Dutch), which is rarely used today except in place-names (Catskill
Mountains, Schuylkill River, etc.).

A Northeast weather expression that may have originated with the New England
penchant for taking nautical expressions ashore is *mackerel sky,* which is a sky covered
with numerous small cumulus clouds forming a pattern reminiscent of the markings on a
mackerel.

When the colonists arrived in North America, they encountered a very large spreading tree they had never seen before and for which they of course had no name. Though it later became best known as the *sycamore,* an older name for this tree is *buttonwood,* first used in seventeenth-century Eastern New England from where it spread throughout the Northeast. A century and a half later the variant *buttonball* appeared in Western New England apparently with reference to the tree's small ball-like fruit. This new name soon took hold and, for as yet unknown reasons, usurped the earlier expression, *buttonwood* (see *WG,* 76–77), but only in Western New England and in the greater Hudson Valley area, creating an unusual regional contrast. The contrast is especially clear in the atlas fieldwork, which shows *buttonball* in Connecticut, western Massachusetts, most of New York, and East Jersey, sandwiched between the *button-wood* area of Eastern New England, Vermont, eastern Pennsylvania, and most of West Jersey (*WG,* fig. 146). The *DARE* fieldwork shows essentially the same contrasting distributions except that the two terms in Pennsylvania intermingle more.

Hen hawk is a Northeast term usually referring to the red-tailed hawk, but is also applied to other buteonine hawks that raid chicken yards. This decidedly rural name is rare in Pennsylvania and New Jersey and is known in widely scattered locales in the Atlantic states all the way to Florida.

The small tree frogs that set up a cacophony of peeping, especially in the springtime, are known in the Northeast as *spring peepers* or more commonly simply *peepers.* Another purely folk invention is the Northeast name for the toad: *hop-toad* or *hoppy toad* or occasionally even *hopper toad.* In an 1827 edition of the *Massachusetts Spy,* a Yankee writer observed with Brahman condescension both the regionality and folk redundancy of the expression: "An inhabitant of the Middle States talks of 'hop-toads,'—as if all toads were not hoppers." By "Middle States" the writer presumably means New Jersey, Delaware, and probably Maryland. This and the tight cluster of *DARE* informants in West Jersey suggest that this area was a minor source for the Northeast lexicon. That the informants were disproportionately old and had little formal education also indicates the folk level of usage.

The widespread North-and-West *nightcrawler* (= a large earthworm) has in the Northeast the variant *nightwalker.* Like *LANE, DARE* found this in scattered use in Massachusetts and Connecticut, but additionally in New York, northern New Jersey, and northern Pennsylvania. Unlike any of the other Northeasternisms, *nightwalker* was not found outside of the region. *Mud wasp* (= a wasp that builds a nest from mud), on the other hand, is spread throughout the North and much of the West, but with obvious concentration in the Northeast where it originated, specifically in all probability in Eastern New England.

Another Northeast insect is the *Jersey mosquito,* an especially large and voracious mosquito, most commonly referred to with citified trepidation of the natural world by speakers in the Metropolitan New York area including all of northern New Jersey, where the term probably originated in the mid-nineteenth century. It is particularly common among urban informants, but its total absence among *DARE*'s Boston and Philadelphia speakers helps certify its New York–New Jersey pedigree. It is also well known in central Pennsylvania and southern New England, but is virtually unheard of outside of the Northeast. Many Northeasterners use the heightened variants *Jersey bomber, Jersey bird,* or *Jersey robin.*

The Northeast also has its share of expressions used on the farm. As the New England farmer plowed his rocky land, especially in the early days, he had to contend with numerous *cobblestones* or *cobbles,* two old words known everywhere but most often used in the Northeast. These small boulders or rocks which are often smooth and rounded and at the very least the size of a fist were used to make sturdy *stone walls,* built without mortar and serving as fences between neighboring farms. (It is a stone wall that Robert Frost's protagonist repairs in "Mending Wall.") This resourceful use of fieldstones was brought to America from England with the very first colonists, for there is mention of stone walls as early as 1651 in the Portsmouth, Rhode Island, colonial records.

Dry wall or *dry fence,* though having much less currency, is a Northeast synonym of *stone wall,* apparently in allusion to its mortarless (dry) construction. It has spread from the Northeast into the Appalachians in southern Pennsylvania, West Virginia, Maryland, and Virginia, but is not much used in the rest of Pennsylvania or New Jersey.

The Upper North *whippletree* (= the pivoting bar to which the traces of a harness are fastened) has the Northeast variant *whiffletree,* which is also used in scattered parts of the North. More *DARE* informants responded *whiffletree* than the older form, *whippletree,* which accords with Kurath's observation that there is a trend toward the former (*WG,* 58). The trend, however, is primarily confined to the Northeast.

In addition to a whiffletree, among the devices involved in the harnessing of draft animals to a wagon is the wagon tongue or *pole* as it is known in the Northeast as well as in much of the Upper North. The wagon itself is often kept when not in use in a *wagon shed,* one of the numerous kinds of buildings found on many Northeastern farms, especially in central and western Pennsylvania.

The rural roads on which farmers drive their wagons and modern machinery are called in the Northeast *routes* when they are assigned numbers or letters. In the rest of the United States, when referring to these lesser traveled, often country roads, speakers are apt to use only the road number, sometimes preceded by "highway" or "U.S." or "U.S. highway." The Northeast *route* such-and-such is also common throughout Ohio and Illinois, but not in Indiana or the other adjacent states. This situation where most of the informants within a given state use the term and where state borders play an obvious role in the distribution pattern, may be the result of the adoption of the term by state or county departments of transportation or other government agencies. Whatever the mechanism behind the spatial placement of *route,* its geography is ultimately shaped by the same forces of human geography that shaped the northern dialect regions.

When referring to a road generically, a Northeasterner might use *macadam,* especially if the road is surfaced with asphalt. Originally this term referred to a road made of layers of crushed rock, a composition invented by John L. McAdam, an early-nineteenth-century British engineer. This term has spread from the Northeast in sparse fashion into most of Ohio and the Upper North as well as southward into western Virginia and even into parts of central North Carolina.

Many times a macadam will have a short dip whose sudden appearance often takes driver and passengers by surprise. Such a depression in the road has been known in the Northeast as a *thank-you-ma'am* since the early 1800s. The origin of this expression may be as simple and folksy as the suggestion made by one of the characters in Henry Wadsworth Longfellow's prose tale *Kavanagh* (1849): "The driver called them thank-you-ma'ams because they made everybody bow."

Expressions relating to the home and food always form a large part of regional lexicons and the Northeast is no exception. The very unregional "hamburger" is often shortened to *hamburg*, especially in New England and Upstate New York. At home a hamburg is often eaten with *panfried potatoes* or *pan fries,* more commonly called (except in New England) *home fried potatoes* or *home fries.* The beverage of choice with such an all-American meal is a *soda,* one of the most common names in the Northeast for a carbonated soft drink. This is the abbreviated form of *soda water,* which originally contained sodium bicarbonate. Though *soda* is by far most common in the Northeast, the *DARE* map shows scattered usage throughout the United States with a mysteriously strong concentration of informants in southwestern Illinois and eastern Missouri.

Although *scallions* (= small green onions usually eaten raw) is probably known by cooks everywhere, it is heard primarily in the speech of Northeastern ones. Also in the Northeast one can hear *grass,* a jocular term for asparagus that is almost as common in the Pacific Coast states.

A deep-fried sweet cake or doughnut is often called a *cruller* in this region as well as other parts of the North westward to the Mississippi River and in California.

Back in the days when brooms were usually homemade, in New England they were made from the panicles of broomcorn, a variety of common sorghum, and appropriately enough called *corn brooms,* a name that was still easily recollected in the 1960s by some seventy chiefly Northeastern informants, most of whom, however, were well over sixty years of age.

A house that is constructed with rooms on each side of a main entrance hall was in Boston as early as 1707 called a *double house.* From its New England origin both this type of house and its name spread throughout the Northeast and westward to central Indiana. In time, with the rise of large-scale apartment living, these old double houses were converted into two family dwellings and the name shifted its meaning to refer to what is more commonly called today, a *duplex.* This later sense, however, did not develop in New England to the degree it did in the rest of the Northeast, so the *DARE* map shows the greatest concentration of informants in Ohio, Pennsylvania, Delaware, southern New Jersey, and parts of Maryland and New York, and the least concentration in southeastern New York, northern New Jersey, and New England.

The Northeast has a handful of expressions that can be considered slang or very colloquial. One of the most recent is *can* (= buttocks), which entered United States speech sometime this century and may be related to *can* meaning a toilet. It seems to be primarily an urban usage. *Guinea* (= an Italian or person of Italian descent) has an even greater urban profile and probably originated in Metropolitan New York with the early-twentieth-century influx of southern European immigrants, especially Italians. It is primarily used by young speakers and males. But despite its recent origin, this derogatory expression has its roots in the eighteenth-century-term *guinea,* used to refer to a Negro slave newly brought from Africa, specifically from the Guinea coast. This earlier usage also had considerable, if not exclusive, currency in New England.

Another recent colloquialism probably from the late 1930s is *cowboy* referring to a reckless driver. It does not, however, have any greater currency in the towns and cities than it does in the rural areas; nor does *rummy* (= a drunkard), which entered Northeast speech in the nineteenth century. With only twenty-eight informants it seems to have dwindling currency though over half of the informants were middle-aged or younger.

Among the more miscellaneous terms of the lexicon are *dowsing rod* or *dowser.* This instrument, also called a *dowsing stick,* is usually a forked stick used to divine underground water. The diviner himself is called a *dowser. Dowse* first appeared in English dialect in the seventeenth century from unknown origins.

More recent is the term to *jack,* which means to hunt deer illegally at night with a light or a *jacklight,* a lantern held high on a pole whose brightness stuns the deer long enough for the hunter to take an easy shot. *Jacking* or *jacklighting* is known in the North Central states as *shining* and in the West as *spotlighting.*

Finally, in much of the Northeast an affectionate nickname for one's grandmother is *nanna* and to hurry is to *get a wiggle on.*

The Northeastern United States, then, is a general speech region characterized by the features of the Northeast layer. But because the New England and New York layers overlap large sections of the Northeast, the region as a whole is only very loosely unified. Three broad subregions emerge when all three layers (maps 2.4, 2.7, and 2.8) are conflated: Eastern New England, Western New England, and New York (fig. 1).

Of these three subregions, Eastern New England is the most conservative and self-contained, being strongly separated from the region westward (Western New England and the Inland North) by a bundle of boundaries from at least four different layers: the New England, Upper North, North, and Inland North layers. Eastern New England is itself broken into several subregions including the Narragansett Bay area and upper Maine.

Western New England, is much less distinct than its sister region to the east, especially its northern portion. It divides into northern and southern subareas: Northwestern and Southwestern New England. Northwestern New England is a weakly defined subregion unto itself and is largely transitional between Eastern New England and Upstate New York, though it has greater affinity with the latter. The speech of Southwestern New England or the Lower Connecticut River Valley area, is the dialect of the second New England hearth and is somewhat more distinctive than Northwestern New England speech.

New York is almost as diverse a speech region as New England and divides into three major subregions: Metropolitan New York, the Hudson Valley, and Upstate New

Layers
New England (map 2.4)
New York (map 2.7)
Northeast (maps 2.8 and 2.9)

Regions

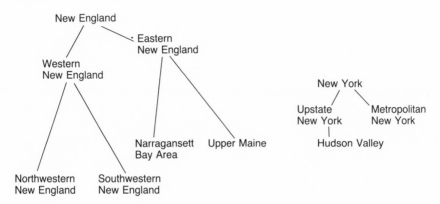

Fig. 1. Summary of the layers and regions of New England and the Northeast

York, this last being a broadly defined area that includes most of the state except the metropolitan area. Upstate New York and Northwestern New England are in many respects both the historical and linguistic parents of the rest of the Upper North.

The number of subregions in the Northeast testifies to a remarkable cultural diversity: the Dutch and German influence in the Hudson Valley; the seafaring background of Eastern New England; the rural farming life of Upstate New York and Western New England. Moreover, despite the enormous changes in the distribution and currency of the regional vocabulary during the middle third of the twentieth century, these subregions and their particular dimensions have remained intact, testimony to the durability of dialect regions in general.

CHAPTER 3

The North

As European civilization spread over the New World landscape, physical barriers and natural conduits contoured the emerging cultural regions. Early in the westward expansion the Ohio River, for example, and later the Great Lakes, gave the northeastern colonists relatively easy access to the northern interior. In time the Ohio became a natural boundary roughly dividing the eastern United States into two major sections, the North and the South, which have dominated American geography since the frontier farmers crossed the Appalachians. It is no accident that the Ohio River formed much of the line separating the Union and Confederate states. And it is no accident that the Northern cultural region is usually defined broadly as the territory north of this great river (map 3.1). But because rivers are rarely barriers or conduits to long-term settlement, the Ohio only approximates the actual cultural boundary, which was pushed north of the river as much as one hundred miles into southern Indiana and Illinois by migration from the Upper South.

The North itself originates in two cultural and linguistic hearths: New England and southeastern Pennsylvania. Like adjacent streams, these two cultures flowed westward, at times and places intermingling, but generally keeping within their own banks. The two streams, for example, remained relatively separate in their architecture styles (see Peirce 1975) and early methods of wood construction (see map 1.1). As we will see, their relative separateness formed the two major Northern dialect regions: the Upper North, defined in this chapter by three important layers; and the Lower North, described in chapter 6 as a very complex region of overlapping layers where the North meets the South.

In other ways these two streams were not so distinct. The diffusion of ideas (map 3.2), for example, suggests why the typical situation in linguistic geography is blurred boundaries and mingling of features. Because the spread of culture in the United States from one region to another rarely remains completely discrete, the immigrant streams from New England and Pennsylvania and the cultures they carried often blended and mixed, sharing certain features that came to characterize the North as a whole. For this and other reasons, such as the prevailing industrial and commercial base of the Northern economy, the North is unified as a linguistic region by at least one dialect layer, the North layer.

The North Layer

One of the commonest distributions of the *DARE* isoglosses covers roughly the area north of the Ohio river and much of the territory west of the Mississippi. The 82

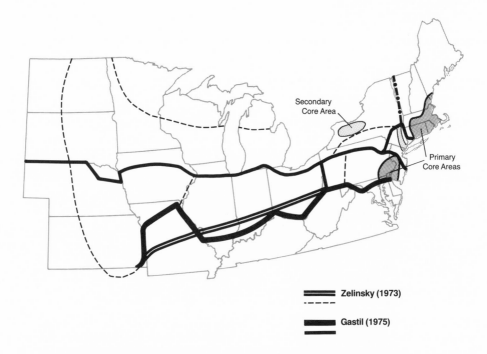

3.1. The Cultural Geography of the North. (Source: Zelinsky 1973 and Gastil 1975.)

isoglosses of this pattern are conflated in map 3.3. This layer could have been further reduced to two sublayers distinguished from each other by whether they extend into the Far West or not. Of the 82 isoglosses of the North layer, 35 are concentrated primarily east of Minnesota, north of the Ohio River, and throughout the Northeast including all of Pennsylvania and New Jersey. This distribution is referred to here as Eastern North, and roughly corresponds to the cultural region east of Minnesota and Iowa and north of the primary boundaries shown in map 3.1.

The remaining 47 isoglosses of the North layer have a similar distribution east of Minnesota, but additionally fan out into the West. When discussing the lexicon this distribution is referred to as North-and-West. (App. A lists separately the Eastern North and North-and-West isogloss subsets.) This western fan of isoglosses is a pattern we will see again in the Upper North (see map 3.7) and Inland North (see map 3.9) layers and plays an important role in the definition of the linguistic geography of the West (see map 7.3).

Generally speaking, especially east of the Mississippi River, the isogloss count of the North layer (map 3.3) slopes southward from a high density plateau in the Upper North to a low but significant density as far south as Tennessee and the central Appalachians. An irregular series of high numbers interrupts the slope in the southern portions of Ohio and Indiana. In the Northeast this slope disappears and becomes a jumble of ridges and valleys.

Extreme southwestern Connecticut, the Metropolitan New York area, and east-

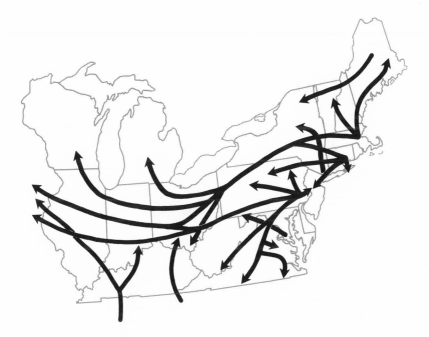

3.2. The Movement of Ideas in the North. Settlement patterns and the flow
of information through commerce and other forms of communication are among
the shaping influences on the cultural and linguistic regions of the North.
(Source: Glassie 1968.)

ern and central New Jersey all appear as a continuous area of strikingly low numbers, as
low as those in central Appalachia. This may be due to the urban influence, since most
of this region is dominated by an urban corridor extending from Bridgeport in southwestern Connecticut, to New York City to Trenton, New Jersey, to Philadelphia.

In addition, there are several dialect boundaries that cut across New Jersey.
History and language separate East Jersey from West Jersey, as atlas and other studies
have shown. The Philadelphia-Trenton axis is a hearth area for Lower North speech,
whereas Metropolitan New York, which dominates East Jersey, is a Northern subdialect
in its own right.

Some of the complexity of Pennsylvania as a linguistic and cultural region (see
maps 6.8 through 6.12) is apparent in the web of boundaries that divide it into at least
three major areas: northern Pennsylvania, which is in the Upper North; southeastern
Pennsylvania, which is complicated by the mix of Pennsylvania German culture and
the urban influence of Philadelphia and environs; and western and central eastern
Pennsylvania.

A major boundary separates Pennsylvania from most of Maryland and West
Virginia. As we will see in chapter 6, this is the major southern boundary of the Lower
North region, just as it is here for the linguistic and cultural North region (map 3.1). But
as it enters Ohio (map 3.3), it veers northward away from the Lower North boundary.

Map 3.4 is generalized from map 3.3 and gives an overview of the North dialect

3.3. The North Layer Based on 82 _DARE_ Isoglosses. The heaviest line (primary) encloses the area of generally highest numbers and marks a relatively steep drop-off in the magnitude of the numbers. The other two lines (secondary and tertiary) bound diminishing but discrete areas of the layer. The larger numeral near a community name represents the location of that community.

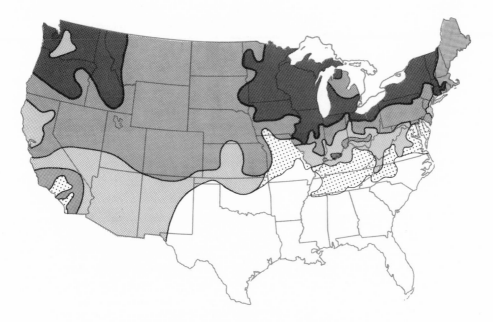

3.4. Overview of the Relative Densities of the North Layer. The darkest shading covers the area where generally the largest number of the layer's terms occur, while the lowest number occur within the dotted area.

layer. The heart of the region, the darkest shaded area, is roughly that of the Upper North layer (see map 3.8) with the addition of most of the Northwest. Both the Ohio River along the Kentucky border and the Mississippi along the western Illinois border form natural, though relatively minor, dialect boundaries, additional evidence of the influence of these great rivers on American geography.

Finally, though the West generally seems to continue the north-south division of the East, the more densely populated Pacific states, particularly southern California, show considerable mixing of small isogloss areas. This indicates the probability of a heterogeneous speech region.

Lexicon

Much of the North layer's lexicon is coined in America and has very few archaisms or survivals of an earlier English. It also has strikingly few loanwords—virtually none borrowed from the Indian languages, and only a handful of recent ones from the European.

One of these is German *fest* for "a festival or holiday," which entered American English sometime in the latter half of the nineteenth century. It is almost always used as the second element in numerous expressions and denotes a lively gathering of one sort or another. It is most often used in *gabfest,* which is known throughout the United States, for a gossip session or informal meeting where conversation is the main activity. *Talkfest* is a synonymous North-and-West expression that is surprisingly rare in Pennsylvania, home of a major German-American community.

Except for *gabfest,* other combinations with this highly productive loanword tend to be Eastern North. Usually they are self-explanatory. A *beerfest* or *drinkfest* is a party or social gathering where a lot of drinking is done. A *slugfest* is a brawl, and a *funfest* is a small local carnival, usually sponsored by a school or church. But a great many of the forms have to do with a gathering of prattling people; hence, *blarneyfest, henfest, yackfest, jaw-, chin-* or *tongue-fest, bullfest,* and *blabberfest,* to mention just a few.

Another very common German loan is *gesundheit,* which is used as a wish of good health to a person who has just sneezed. This Northern version of the Southern counterpart, *scat,* probably did not appear in American English with any currency until the twentieth century, so it seems doubtful that it is a borrowing from the long-time infusion of German immigrants. This is borne out by its appearance in other world varieties of English at about the same time (1914; see *OEDS*).

Babushka was adopted from the Russian for "grandmother," though probably not directly from Russian immigrants to the United States. Many Eastern North speakers have transferred it to refer to a head scarf that is usually folded in a triangle and tied under the chin, presumably the way Russian and east European grandmothers and old women are in the habit of doing. This too is a very recent borrowing first recorded in England in 1938. It tends to be an urban usage heard from well-educated speakers.

Beginning late in the nineteenth century and extending well into the twentieth, the North-and-West received massive immigration primarily from Europe. The South by contrast received very few immigrants. A map showing the foreign-born population density, say, for 1900 (see Lord and Lord 1955, 115), shows the Ohio River as a sharp line separating these two regions, the entire South except for Florida and southern Louisiana being conspicuously empty.

But the impact of immigrant speech on American English is relatively negligible compared to the influence of colonial non-English speech. This is why the non-English-speaking Europeans who distinguished the demography of the North, left little linguistic trace on its lexicon, while the various non-English languages of the colonial period (Spanish, French, and Indian) provided the South and its subregions with a significant number of loanwords.

The North layer lexicon, however, acknowledges the presence of several of these immigrant groups with appellations that are usually derogatory. Germans, for example, are sometimes known as *Dutchmen,* a misnomer based on the German word for "German," *Deutsch* (hence also "Pennsylvania Dutch"). More derogatory in the lexicon are the nicknames for Poles and Irishmen.

Polack is a recent revival of the seventeenth-century British word adopted from Polish, *Polak,* "a Polishman." It first appears in America in the *Congressional Record* for 1900, where it is used by a Congressman without a trace of derision. Today, however, it usually cannot be used without derogatory force. *Mick,* probably from the proper name Michael, is an early-nineteenth-century Americanism that seems to have had derogatory connotations from the beginning. Its earliest written example is from a California newspaper that presages the word's twentieth-century usage throughout the West as well as the Eastern North.

In addition to these ethnic epithets, the North as a whole has a substantial number of slang and strictly colloquial expressions. Most of these stay primarily east of the Rockies. Strenuous physical work makes one *sweat like a butcher,* an expression that might be used on a strictly figurative level with reference to a *grind* or someone who studies all the time. *Grind* probably originated as student slang sometime in the late nineteenth century. Not surprisingly, a disproportionate number of *DARE* informants who used this term were college educated. More uncomplimentary is the term for an old man: a *duffer.* Oddly enough this response was given primarily by old speakers.

Vivid metaphors are often the source of many regional colloquialisms. A cigar, for example, is called a *rope,* or more facetiously with reference to the famous Cuban varieties, *el ropo* or *el ropo stinkadoro.* Cigarettes are sometimes grimly called *coffin nails,* a well-worn twentieth-century coinage that has wide currency throughout the North-and-West.

In contrast to these more or less perjorative terms is a small group of euphemistic expressions. "To vomit" is euphemized as *to toss one's cookies,* which has many verb variants including *to shoot, spill, drop,* or *park one's cookies.* "Menstruation" has traditionally had numerous euphemisms, but one of the more puzzling and apparently illogical is *falling off the roof.* This expression is also used in scattered parts of the South, but is best known in the North.

"Hell" is occasionally euphemized as *perdition* and the universal exclamation "son of a bitch" is altered to *son of a sea cook. Bitch,* however, is by no means always avoided, especially by young and urban speakers, who sometimes use it to mean "complain or gripe." This usage is undoubtedly known everywhere, but its commonest occurrence is in the North-and-West. Men are also more apt to use it than women, which suggests that it still has taboo import.

Like most of the regional lexicons, the North layer as a whole is rich in popular fauna and flora names. The dogtooth violet, for example, is called *adder's tongue* primarily east of the Mississippi River. It probably originated in New England around 1800 and spread westward with the settlement. In a somewhat broader region, the wild snapdragon is known as *butter-and-eggs* and Queen Anne's lace is often called *wild carrot.* These last two, particularly "wild carrot," are also used in scattered fashion throughout the West and areas of the Upper South, especially the Appalachians. The prickly seeds of certain weeds are often called *burrs* or *sticktights,* the latter having a somewhat anomalous distribution. It is rare in New England but well known in southern Illinois, Kentucky, and scattered parts of the South.

In the North the various American blackbirds of the Icteridae family are lumped together under the name *grackle,* a usage that probably originated in New England though the word itself reaches back into Latin antiquity. The *hairy woodpecker,* a common North American variety, seems to be primarily recognized as distinctive in the Eastern North, though the earliest dictionary citations place the term in North Carolina. This name is not clearly linguistically regional since the range of the bird itself is the eastern United States north of the Lower South states.

In any case we might see these birds eating earthworms and caterpillars, or in the lexicon of the region, *nightcrawlers* and *woolly bears.* The former expression is well known throughout the North-and-West despite its very recent genesis sometime during the early part of this century. *Woolly bear,* on the other hand, is chiefly used in the Eastern North, and was probably carried to the United States by dialect speakers from England.

Among the aquatic animals, the snapping turtle is often called the *snapper turtle* or just the *snapper.* A bullfrog, and less often the smaller varieties of croaking frogs, are sometimes called *croakers.* Because the landlubber toad is frequently called a *toad-frog* in the South, the simple *toad* is by default a regionalism of the North-and-West.

The sap or resin of coniferous trees is frequently called *pitch* in the North-and-West in contrast to the preference in the South for *rosin* or *rosum.* As for trees themselves, at least three kinds have American-born names used primarily in the North. Since the founding of the early New England colonies, the linden tree has been called the *basswood tree.* The colonists and their northern heirs also call the mayapple a *mandrake,* a Middle English word for the narcotic herb whose root was thought to resemble the body of a man. Why this name should be transferred to the mayapple is a mystery. The sugar maple is known in the North, except for Eastern New England, as the *hard maple.* This term, which probably originated in Western New England in the eighteenth century, is well known today north of the Ohio River.

In addition to the hard maple, the North-and-West farmer often cultivates three other plants which he refers to with regional American names. Rhubarb has been called *pie plant* in the North since the early 1800s, doubtless with reference to the tart-tasting pies made from it. The well-known winter squash, *hubbard squash,* is also a favorite crop in this region. A favorite meadow grass grown for hay is *timothy grass,* which is first mentioned in print by Ben Franklin in 1747, but was named after Timothy Hanson, who promoted the grass's popularity by taking it to the Carolinas from New York in the early eighteenth century. All three of these plant names have considerable currency as far south as Tennessee and parts of the southern Appalachians.

As always in this rurally slanted account of American dialects, farming has contributed a substantial number of terms to the lexicon, but to a considerably lesser degree than in the South. The relatively strong urban character of the Eastern North has often cast the farmer as an unsophisticated rube, so much so that *farmer* is used with derogatory force for any awkward, ridiculous person. This is, however, a relatively late development coming into currency around 1900. By the late 1960s it was used primarily by young or middle-aged and, not surprisingly, well-educated speakers. Most of the *DARE* informants, however, were in small towns where speakers are most likely to be insecure about their supposed midpoint status between the sophisticated urbanite and the countrified cultivator.

Country-folk prudishness in contact with the farm bull has produced a number of preferred regional euphemisms, particularly when in mixed company. The unlikely expression, *gentleman cow,* is a New England euphemism that has spread throughout the rural North. *Sire* is also used but has additionally spread into the West.

The North-and-West farmer has a relatively small regional vocabulary that refers exclusively to the tools and activities of his trade. When fields were plowed using draft animals, he was likely to use a *gang plow* or a *sulky plow,* which he hitched to his horses with traces or *tugs*. If his horses or cows were doing poorly and were slat ribbed, he would be likely to refer to them at one time or another as *crowbait*. A writer in 1851 noted that he had "hired a mule . . . called a 'Crowbait' in Yankeeland" (cited in [1968] *Amsp* 43:93). Like many Northern terms this one probably originated in New England and spread westward.

If our Northern farmer were hauling a small or partial wagon load of, say, *sweet corn*, the North-and-West version of the South's *roasting ears*, he would likely say that he was hauling a *jag* of corn, a term also used by his English dialect counterpart. After *tedding* the hay in the field with a *tedder* or *hay tedder*, a machine that stirs and spreads the hay for curing, he would transport it to the barn on a *hay rack* or hay wagon and store it in the *mow*. To thresh grain in earlier days, he might have done it by hand using a *flail*. Though this method has largely died out, nevertheless a remarkable number of informants knew the term. Finally, a Northern farmer would sharpen his tools with a *wetstone*, the unaspirated version of "whetstone" perhaps altered by folk etymology since whetstones are wetted with water or oil when used.

Northern domestic expressions—especially terms used in the kitchen—are considerably more plentiful than the farming regionalisms. *Piccalilli*, a chopped, pungently spiced vegetable relish, is primarily a Northern condiment. Likewise *dandelion greens*, which are usually eaten raw on salads, is primarily a Northern dish. Root vegetables are often stored in a *root cellar* where it is dark and cool, forestalling their becoming tough and *woody*.

The outer covering of peas is widely known as the *pod*, but because *pod* is much more common in the North-and-West it has regional status. The green stem on strawberries, a tiny and usually unnoticed item which has given the American language a surprising number of regionalisms, is most commonly known in the North-and-West as the *hull*.

On the farm where milk is often drunk fresh from the cow, it sometimes has traces of the unwanted flavor of the weeds and grasses that the cow has grazed on, especially if she has gotten into a patch of bitterweed. In the North-and-West this milk would be called *tainted*, though the typical consumer rarely has occasion for this particular usage, given the strict standards placed on commercial milk.

It is the frugal custom throughout America to use leftover cold mush, especially cornmeal mush, by slicing and sauteeing it, and serving it with butter and maple syrup. In the North-and-West this is called simply *fried mush* or, especially in New England, *fried pudding*. *Griddle cake* is a Northern term for pancake especially when made of wheat or buckwheat flour. This term probably arrived in New England sometime in the late eighteenth century though it is not recorded in America until 1850. In the linguistic atlas materials gathered in the 1930s, it was still confined primarily to New England and was "new" in New York City, eastern New Jersey, and parts of Pennsylvania (*WG*, 20). By the time of the *DARE* survey, however, the expression had established itself in much of the North.

A more recent breakfast food is the sweet roll or in the North, *Danish pastry*, also called *Danish roll* or simply *Danish*. Doughnuts are also commonly eaten for breakfast and have numerous regional names. In the North-and-West they are sometimes jokingly called *sinkers,* an Americanism that may have originated on the frontier West where it was first applied to biscuits and dumplings.

For lunch a Northerner might have a *submarine sandwich,* or *submarine* or *sub* for short. This name for the famous *poor boy,* a large sandwich made with a long bun or portion of French bread and a variety of meats and cheeses, is of very recent vintage, perhaps as late as the 1940s and was probably introduced commercially. It is known throughout the North-and-West and in widely scattered parts of the rest of the country.

Homemade bread was once a commonplace food, but as it began to be dispossessed by commercial bakeries and supermarkets, new terms were needed to distinguish homemade from purchased bread. In the North-and-West, any goods that are not handmade at home, such as clothes or bread, are said to be *boughten.* More universal in this region than *boughten bread,* however, is *baker's bread* or *baker bread.* This expression seems to have originated in England just as the industrial revolution was picking up steam. Jane Austen first used it in writing in a letter of 1813.

Bread made of wheat flour in this same region is called *whitebread* in reference to the bleached flour that is usually used. Its Southern counterpart is *light bread.* When bread dough is covered and set aside in a warm place to let the yeast work, the Northern home baker might say "it *raised* quickly" or "it *had* not yet *raised* enough," using *raised* as the verb form for both the preterite and past participle.

Bread was sometimes used externally for medicinal purposes as in a *bread and milk poultice.* The soggy warmed bread was placed in a cloth and applied to an inflamed area providing a soothing, if not quite healing, effect.

Sweetbread is not bread at all but beef pancreas or thymus eaten by a few hearty Northerners. A loaf meat made of the head (brain, tongue, etc.) and sometimes heart and feet of a pig is well known throughout the North-and-West as *headcheese* and in the South as *souse* or *souse meat.* As the *Dictionary of Americanisms* points out, the Dutch *hoofdkaas* is used in the same sense and seems a likely source of *headcheese* given the influence of the Dutch in the Northeast.

Of the Northern dwellings, a *flat* is an apartment on one floor of a building, usually the entire floor and usually having a private entrance. Among its furnishings we might find tucked into a corner a *knickknack shelf* cluttered with figurines and other odds-and-ends. A truly *persnickety* or overly meticulous housekeeper would never allow *dust kittens* or *dust kitties* to collect under the furniture, which is what happens when one habitually *gives* the place *a once over* or a superficial cleaning.

In the North, babies don't usually crawl, they *creep,* a usage that probably originated in New England.

In older Northern homes one might be asked to *douse* the light or occasionally to *douse the glim* (or *glimmer* or *gleam*), an expression originally used with reference to lanterns and flame-type lights but later transferred to the electric light. *Comforter* is used in these same homes as well as in the West for a bedcover usually filled with down or these days with a comparable synthetic fiber. This term seems to have expanded its usage considerably since the 1930s when the linguistic atlas surveys found it primarily in New England with only scattered instances in the Upper North. The data from

LANCS presented by Alva Davis (1948, 74) also shows usage confined to the most northern portion of the North Central states; but by the 1960s the term was well known throughout the North-and-West and even in scattered parts south. This may be the result of the commercial use of the term.

Children's activities have contributed a small vocabulary to the lexicon including *belly-flop* or *belly-flopper,* which is common throughout the North-and-West for the act of *coasting* on a sled face down. With reference to a more or less unsuccessful dive in which the abdomen and chest strike flat against the water, *belly-flop* has even wider currency in this region.

A children's outdoor game called *statues* is played in this region in various ways but always with the element that on a given signal players freeze in whatever position they find themselves, as if becoming statues. Glass playing marbles, especially clear ones, are called in this same wide area *glassies,* another instance of the ubiquitous *-ie* ending found in marble terminology.

To divide marbles or other items into shares is to *divvy* them up. This slang alteration of "to divide" is a relatively recent American coinage first surfacing into print in 1872. In the game of hide-and-seek, the person who is "it" calls out *allee-allee (all) in free* when he or she has caught the first of the hiders (who then becomes "it"). In the West they sometimes use the more elaborate variant *allee-allee oxen (all in) free,* whereas *all (in) free* is the universal formula.

Much of the rest of the lexicon mapped here is a miscellany of Americanisms, born and bred in the North. Two are almost exclusively Northern expressions: *chestnut* (= an old joke or cliché) and *bobsled.* The rest are common in the West as well. Of these, *rapids* (= a place in a stream where the water descends rapidly and turbulently) is the oldest, entering Northeast speech in the eighteenth century and spreading westward.

Two of the most widely known expressions extending into Tennessee and the central Appalachians are *crazy bone* (= the elbow or funny bone) and *potluck.* The latter was used in the sixteenth century and alluded to one's luck as to what may be in the dinner pot, especially when having a meal on the spur of the moment without any special preparation. But the North-and-West regional usage has extended this to mean a social gathering to which persons bring a dish to share. Though *potluck dinner* is a regionalism, the social event is virtually a universal feature of American culture.

If two people don't get along with one another, they don't *jibe* and may even get a little *riled* or upset. *Rile* derives from "roil" which means to make water or any liquid turbid or muddy by stirring up sediment. It was a simple and natural matter of extending this to refer to vexed or stirred up emotions. By means of a common vowel change characteristic of Southern and New England folk speech, "roil" became *rile* in New England around 1800 and from there it spread throughout the North-and-West.

A much more recent expression (1902) with nearly the opposite meaning is *all in.* To be *all in* is to be tired and enervated.

Finally, one of the few old terms to survive as a regionalism in the North-and-West is the fourteenth-century word for a whitlow or inflammation usually on the finger or toe and involving the bone: *felon.* The Southern counterpart is the fuller form *bone felon* or *bone fellum.*

The Upper North

The Upper North can be viewed as the core of the North. It is a distinctive and clearly defined area having the greatest number of unmixed North features—in this study, lexical features. The history of this region is primarily the story of the expansion of New England westward. Just as Upstate New York portrayed in maps 2.4 and 2.7 is like an area of overflow from New England, so the entire Upper North speech region is primarily an extension of New England and its early settlements in New York. This is implicit in the cultural geography of the North (map 3.1), in the movement of ideas westward from the New England and Pennsylvania hearths (map 3.2), and in the regional spread of wood construction methods (map 1.1).

Whole communities from New England were transplanted to the North Central states. Among them was Granville, Massachusetts, which pulled up stakes and moved to what is now Granville, Ohio. Granby, Connecticut, became Worthington, Ohio. Orland, Indiana, is a transplant from Windham County, Vermont. Vermontville, Michigan, is from East Poultney, Vermont; Delavan, Illinois, from Rhode Island, and so on. Map 3.5 portrays isochronically the Yankee expansion to the Mississippi River and provides a point of comparison for the linguistic geography of the region.

Northeastern New Jersey was one of the first New England settlement areas, beginning in the 1660s. A typical emigration took place in 1666 when thirty New Haven, Connecticut, families relocated in what is now Newark. Northern New Jersey's fertile soil, liberal land policies, friendly Indians and close proximity to New York's markets, attracted many subsequent pioneers from Massachusetts, New Hampshire, and Rhode Island, who brought with them the same unique culture and language that are also features of later Upper North settlements.

Northern Pennsylvania by contrast was settled in the early and mid-nineteenth century. As New Englanders and their New York cousins gradually pushed southward some fifty miles into the wooded hills of northern Pennsylvania, southeastern Pennsylvanians had already moved northward up the Susquehanna Valley. The broad sparsely populated belt that came to separate the two groups in the dense forest section of northern Pennsylvania also separates Upper North speech from Lower North. Map 3.6 shows the lines of migration in New Jersey and Pennsylvania and the resultant Upper North dialect boundary as derived by Kurath in *WG* from atlas materials (cf. map 1.4).

In late-eighteenth-century New England, overcrowding, high land prices, steep taxes, and extreme religious and social conservatism drove settlers west beyond New York to the Ohio frontier. Movement west was also encouraged by the numerous "improved" roads that were constructed after the Revolution and that were especially easy to travel on just before the spring thaw when sleds heaped with household goods could glide easily over the rugged terrain.

Travel by river was also a favored mode, making the Ohio River a virtual highway into the wilderness. A flatboat, appropriately called a *family boat* because it could carry an entire family and their belongings, was large enough to allow life to go on with little disruption. It was not an unusual sight to see a mother washing clothes, cooking, or churning butter, while the children romped or did chores and the father

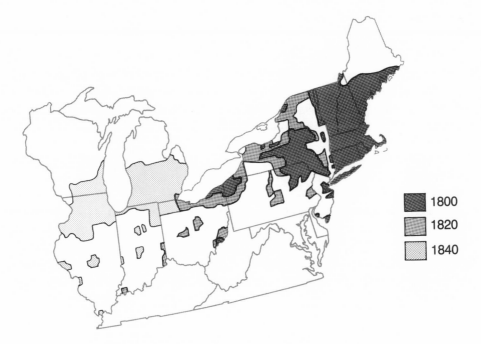

3.5. New England Settlement Areas. (Source: Mathews 1909.)

3.6. Northern Settlement Routes

chopped wood, made repairs, or steered at the helm. At the end of the trip, the family boat was dismantled and its wood used in building a cabin.

The first New England settlement in Ohio was founded in the spring of 1788 by a group of Massachusetts and Connecticut pioneers. Arriving by river in southeastern Ohio, they immediately began to build near its banks a typical New England village, which they named Marietta. For many years Marietta was a speech island in a region dominated by South and Lower North speakers, but today has lost most of its Yankee character (see Clark 1972).

The major New England region in Ohio is the so-called Western Reserve in the northeastern corner of the state (map 3.6). In 1795 the Connecticut Land Company sent Moses Cleaveland as agent to survey the large wilderness tract and to lay out towns such as the one planned at the mouth of the Cuyahoga River, which took the agent's name. Settlers, almost all from New England, began flooding into the area by way of the Great Genesee Road and an extension carved out from Erie to Cleveland. By 1800 the attraction of cheap land at a dollar per acre had drawn some thirteen hundred people to the Western Reserve, where they settled along Lake Erie or inland in the Mahoning and Cuyahoga valleys.

In general, the rest of Ohio was settled by a crescent of population gradually spreading north and westward from the Ohio River, which was the most important early route of ingress to the interior. Most of this spread originated in the adjacent areas of Kentucky and in the Mid-Atlantic states—Pennsylvania, Maryland, Virginia, and New Jersey. This complex mix of Pennsylvania and Upper South culture and speech contrasts sharply with the originally homogeneous New England area of northeastern Ohio and accentuates the steepness of the Upper North boundary in Ohio.

In Indiana the push of settlement from the east and south, particularly from the western counties of Virginia and North Carolina via Kentucky, nearly covered the entire state essentially excluding Indiana from the Upper North region. For decades Indiana's bad public image as a swampy wasteland and the high prices that greedy speculators demanded for its acreage diverted the stream of New England settlers northward to the counties along the Michigan border or farther west to northern Illinois.

The continuing improvement in transportation also shaped the course of migration. Probably the most important development was the opening of the Erie Canal in 1825. It deflected the new surge of migration in the 1830s from New York and New England away from the Ohio River Valley to the Great Lakes, reinforcing the Northern element in the Western Reserve and populating Michigan. The all-water route between East and West was now easy and inexpensive. The entire trip from the Hudson Valley on horse-drawn barge to Buffalo and then by steamer to Detroit cost only about ten dollars. After 1833 thousands of settlers arrived by regular steamer service in Detroit's bustling lake port. From there they fanned north and west into the fertile Michigan countryside or moved down the Chicago Road to northern Illinois (map 3.6).

Not only did the Erie Canal facilitate movement out of the Northeast, but because the bounty of western grain and wool could now be cheaply delivered to the East, it helped undermine the New England farms, whose rocky land could not produce competitive crops. The New England farmer was forced to move either into the cities and their growing industries, or as was usually the case, into the western wilderness where land was cheap and fertile. By 1850 New England farmers had settled most of lower Michigan in a line that reached from Saginaw Bay to Oceana County on Lake Michigan (see map 3.5).

As in Indiana and southern Ohio, southern hillmen settled the bottom la..ds of southern Illinois. Others, notably Kentuckians, moved further north along the Mississippi and Illinois Rivers. In 1822, Colonel James Johnson arrived in northwestern Illinois with Kentucky miners and 150 slaves to begin mining lead in the mineral rich region. Soon a mining rush was on and by 1830 some ten thousand frontiersmen had established the boom town, Galena, and were shipping seventy-five hundred tons of lead yearly to New Orleans. This region attracted a very mixed population and consequently created a linguistic island separate from the surrounding North dialect.

With the construction of the National Road (map 3.6), the central portions of Illinois, Indiana, and Ohio received an influx of settlers from the East, particularly from western Pennsylvania. As in Ohio this emphasized the difference between the lower section of Illinois and its northeastern region, which was predominantly settled by New Englanders and New Yorkers coming by way of the Great Lakes.

In 1845, for example, steamboats landed over twenty-thousand passengers at Chicago. Such numbers increased the population of Chicago sevenfold in the decade of the 1840s. Most arrivals, however, did not stay in the rapidly growing city but settled in northern Illinois, first on the choice lands of the Rock and Illinois River valleys, then in the forested uplands between. The prairies were avoided altogether. The vision of the treeless prairie extending beyond the horizon, a sea of man-height grass waving in the wind, was awesome and formidable to the pioneers, who had always sought densely wooded areas where their frontier techniques were of use. Inevitably as the land filled up, new farming methods were developed to cope with the thick sodded prairie. Roads were built to give access to crop markets and to forests for wood needed to construct buildings and fences. By 1850 Illinois was completely settled.

In the meantime the prosperity of northern Illinois spilled over into Wisconsin. By 1840 over thirty-thousand pioneers had cleared out farms along the Rock and Wisconsin rivers or along the federal road that ran adjacent to Lake Michigan from Chicago to Ft. Howard (map 3.6). In the next decade the flood of New Englanders increased the population of Wisconsin tenfold. In addition, immigrants from western Europe, particularly Germany, but also from Norway and Ireland, had settled in this area, eventually giving the state its unique brand of Northern culture.

Just in terms of settlement, then, the Upper North is generally the region of New England expansion shown in map 3.5 and is consequently a region where New England features of all kinds form the basic substratum of the culture and language. South of this region is the Lower North, one of the most complex dialect areas in the country. At least two major boundaries and several minor ones crisscross its length.

The Upper North Layer

The boundaries of the Upper North come into sharper focus in map 3.7, which is based on 62 isoglosses. Like the North layer, a subset of Upper North isoglosses extends into the West. The Upper North layer, however, has considerably less influence in the West

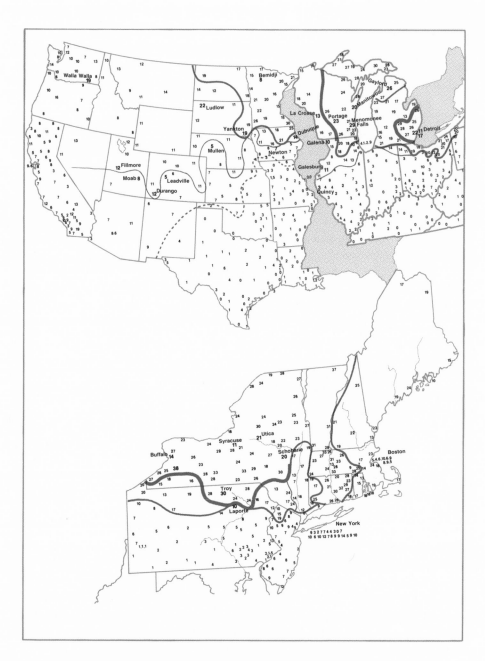

3.7. The Upper North Dialect Layer Based on 62 *DARE* Isoglosses. Alaska has 7 (Anchorage) and 9 (Juneau-Sitka) and Hawaii has 3, 10, and 4 (Honolulu). Primary, secondary, tertiary, and quaternary boundaries.

than does the North layer, only 27 percent (or 17) of its 62 isoglosses composing the Upper North-and-West sublayer compared to the 57 percent share that the North-and-West sublayer has of the North layer. Accordingly, Eastern Upper North isoglosses, which generally cover the area of two darkest shades in map 3.8, dominate the Upper North layer (see app. A).

The Upper North layer by no means covers a homogeneous speech region, but is broken up by isogloss ridges or steep slopes usually running east and west, but also occasionally north and south. Boundary definition is sharpest east of the Mississippi River becoming increasingly indefinite westward. As the heart of the North, this layer reinforces many of the internal patterns evident in the North layer. Especially noticeable is the close correspondence between the primary boundary of the North layer (map 3.3) and the secondary Upper North boundary (map 3.7) running from northern New Jersey, through northern Pennsylvania and Ohio, then along the Michigan-Indiana border.

Both the North and Upper North layers have their densest isoglosses in Western New England and Upstate New York, the hearth or seminal region of the Upper North. In map 3.7, Eastern New England including the Narragansett Bay area, but not central Massachusetts, is separated off as a region of relatively low isogloss numbers ranging from about 13 to 25, but averaging around 17 (excluding Boston and one or two anomalies).

The Hudson Valley is clearly outlined as an area of low numbers bounded by steep slopes to the east and west, a gradually increasing slope to the north and decreasing slopes to the south. This delineation is in remarkable agreement with Kurath's definition of Hudson Valley (map 1.4). The early-settled Mohawk River Valley is also separated off from higher numbers to the north and south, but blends almost imperceptibly into the coextensive Hudson Valley region.

The steepest slope in the Northeast, that is, the line of greatest disparity between isogloss numbers, runs from the Hudson Valley southwestward through the upper Susquehanna Valley in Pennsylvania, then veers northwestward back into New York to Lake Erie. Except in north-central Pennsylvania, this major boundary runs considerably north of Kurath's version. However, a smaller but distinct secondary boundary through Pennsylvania closely corresponds with Kurath's description, though it stops short in northwestern New Jersey. According to this map northern New Jersey is not within the primary region of the Upper North layer. It may be that the dominating influence of Metropolitan New York is masking the Upper North features. The relatively low isogloss numbers in the urban areas, notably Boston, New York City, Buffalo, Detroit, and Chicago reinforce this notion.

The secondary boundary through Pennsylvania continues westward into northern Ohio and along the Michigan-Indiana border. Although this secondary isogloss ridge is not as high, that is, the numbers are not as large as those in the core areas of New York and Western New England, it is as steep and thus as pronounced since the numbers immediately to the south drop off as precipitously as they do for the primary boundary in southern New York and north-central Pennsylvania. Interrupted by Lake Michigan, this ridge picks up again in northeastern Illinois skirting the Chicago area, then like Shuy's boundary (map 1.5C) heads due north. ·

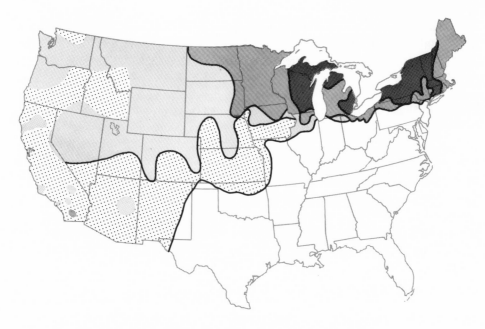

3.8. Overview of the Relative Densities of the Upper North Layer

A tertiary boundary runs southwestward through northern Illinois to the Mississippi River corresponding to the primary line in the North layer map. As it crosses the river it abruptly shifts northward continuing on the other side of the river near Dubuque, Iowa. This fault-line effect is the result of settlement history and can be seen in other layers (see Carver 1986). The tertiary boundary continues to meander westward, like the North layer secondary line, bifurcating the West into north and south sections. The Upper North quaternary line, corresponding to the North layer's tertiary, wends its way across the northeastern corner of Missouri into Iowa, then southward near the Kansas-Missouri border, across northern Oklahoma, and down across central New Mexico.

Map 3.8 gives a more generalized aerial view of the Upper North layer, its influence and limits. It shows that Michigan has two areas of high density, the Upper Peninsula and northern Michigan, and southeastern Michigan. Although these two sections share the Upper North lexicon, it is likely that their very different histories have given them different varieties of speech.

Wisconsin has an atypical boundary running north and south, west of which relatively low isoglosses extend into eastern Minnesota (map 3.7). This is in part the record left by settlers from the Mississippi Valley and Lower North who migrated up the Mississippi and St. Croix rivers into Minnesota and Wisconsin, mixing with Northeasterners, and establishing towns and farms along or inland from the river. The boundary through Wisconsin is probably the extension of Shuy's northern Illinois boundary (map 1.5*C*).

In the Upper Midwest there is a mixture of large and small numbers (map 3.7). This is the same situation that Allen describes in terms of minor dialect lines (see map

3.13) that indicate either "a complete blocking of some Northern terms" or the expansion of Midland forms and the recession of Northern forms (Allen 1971, 93). In the Upper North layer, for example, Ludlow, South Dakota, would be a continuation point in the secondary boundary line from Yankton except that surrounding distant communities interrupt that continuity.

This patchwork of isogloss numbers becomes more pronounced the further west one proceeds until in southern California line boundaries become almost totally meaningless. This suggests, as we will see more conclusively in chapter 7, that the West is still in an early state of dialect development. The recentness of its settlement, which is in some respects still in progress, has not yet allowed the language boundaries of this vast region to settle into fixed patterns. Even so, an inchoate boundary seems to be taking shape as a tertiary line in map 3.7 meandering like the goosenecks of a river through Nebraska, Colorado, Utah, and Nevada.

Lexicon

This layer essentially outlines the major Upper North dialect region, whose unique vocabulary as represented by a sample of about one hundred Upper North terms including those of map 3.7 is distinctive on several counts, especially in relation to the lexicons of New England and the South. Upper North terms tend to be relatively recent innovations or coinages, most coming into use in the nineteenth century, and many others not appearing until the twentieth. This means that there are relatively few relics or archaisms, few terms which have survived in the region while dying out in New England and in other areas of the United States.

Like the North layer, there are very few loanwords unique to this lexicon, fewer than in the Lower Southern lexicons, though there is another contingent of derogatory regionalisms for certain immigrant groups, such as *canuck* (= Canadian), *sheeny* (= Jew), *mick* (= Irishman), and *bohunk* (= Eastern European, especially a Bohemian). And like its sibling layer, the North, slang and purely colloquial terms make up a significant percentage of its lexicon. To be *strapped,* for example, is American slang meaning to be without money, to be "broke," and has been in Upper North currency since the mid-nineteenth century. *Ass-end-to* is Upper North for "backwards or reversed."

Most of the slang relates to types of people or their characteristics and is decidedly derogatory. A *squealer,* for example, is an informer and was at one time criminal argot. It is an extended meaning of the earlier Americanism referring to "a complainer." The *DARE* informants, however, were responding to a question specifically about children who are "squealers" or "tattle-tales."

A weak timid person is sometimes called a *milquetoast,* which derives from H. T. Webster's character, Caspar Milquetoast, who appeared in the syndicated comic strip, "The Timid Soul" (1924). A person nearly the opposite of a milquetoast is someone with a lot of *crust,* someone who is aggressively and abrasively bold or forward. A *fussbudget* is a finicky and fussy person in the Upper North-and-West, while a drunk is often called a *souse* though not usually in the West.

Among the more offensive slang expressions are *canuck* for a Canadian and *sheeny* for a Jew. Both are nineteenth-century American inventions that are not much used in the West. *Nigger heaven,* also originating in the last century, is the upper balcony of a theater. It is known throughout the region including the West and is a response primarily given by old *DARE* informants. Not surprisingly, no black informants used it.

Finally, among Upper North slang expressions are *yap* for mouth and *schnozz* for the appendage above the yap. The latter is a shortened form of *schnozzle,* also an Upper North term, which is probably a mid-twentieth century alteration of Yiddish *schnoitsl* (= "snout") perhaps blended with *nozzle.*

The lexicon also has an unusually high number of colloquial phrases, though this may reflect the method of collection rather than a characteristic of Upper North speech. All but one of these phrases is primarily confined to the older area of the Upper North, the section east of the Mississippi River. *All the tea in China* is known throughout the Upper North-and-West in negative collocations such as "I wouldn't do that for all the tea in China." This recently coined phrase is particularly common among both urban and young speakers and like many of the Upper North phrases is rarely found in print.

Several other phrases are equally vivid metaphors. In the eastern section, if two people are *at swords' points* they are at odds with each other, in which case one may get an advantage over the other, or in the lexicon, *get the best of* the other person. If in trying to *get the better of* someone, a person does it in a complicated or roundabout way, he would be said to be *going around Robin Hood's barn* to get the desired results. This barn of circumlocution is also known in Maine as *Robinson's barn,* which may have made more sense in the practical folk mind than the Nottingham setting.

Equally nonsequitur is the comparative phrase for a particularly aggressive and mean person: *meaner than dirt.* Although not recorded in any dictionary before *DARE,* this expression probably has been around for awhile since most of the informants who knew it were old. A disporportionate number were also female, which suggests its euphemistic nature.

Another nonsequitur phrase employs *dog's age* to mean "a long time." This first appeared in writing in a colorful bit of New England dialect in 1836: "That blamed line gale has kept me in bilboes such a dog's age" (*DAE*). Time has worn this expression down into a featureless cliché; almost all of the forty-nine informants who used it were old and none were young.

If something is *on the fritz,* often a machine of some kind, it is defective or out of order. This recent phrase (1903) may have come to America from Britain as a show business term. In any case, it tends to be an urban usage especially common among educated and young informants. Something, say a car, might be on the fritz because the mechanic repaired it *by guess and by gosh;* that is, he repaired it without knowing what he was doing, working instead "with a hope and a prayer" or "by hit or miss." Finally, among the Upper North phrases is the locution *for all of me* meaning "for all I care."

The lexicon is particularly rich in folk terms for plants and animals. Some of these are centuries-old British expressions, like *angleworm* (= earthworm) and *pollywog* (= tadpole), which are also common today throughout the western states. *Bloodsucker* for "leech" dates back to the fourteenth century. Because this term survives so vigorously in the Upper North, it has essentially made the standard term "leech" a regional usage confined to the rest of the country.

Like most of the expressions in the lexicon, most of the flora and fauna names are Americanisms. The bullish appearance of several kinds of freshwater catfish led the New England colonists sometime in the seventeenth century to name them *bull catfish, bullhead cats,* or just *bullheads.* The harmless snake known most commonly as the "king snake" is called in the Upper North a *milk snake* from the erroneous belief that it drinks cow's milk. Its propensity for milk houses, however, is due to its taste for mice and rats and not for milk.

One of the very few linguistic legacies that the Indians may have left in this lexicon is *no-see-um,* a tiny stinging fly or midge. Thoreau mentions its Indian origins in *Maine Woods* (1848). Like much of the regional vocabulary, the term probably originated in New England and was disseminated from there throughout the Upper North.

The common dragonfly has probably elicited more names from the linguistic folk imagination than any other critter. In New England and the Upper North it is called the *devil's darning needle* or more commonly, *darning needle.* It got this name from the folk myth that the dragonfly can sew together the fingers or toes of a vulnerable, sleeping person.

"Poplars" are also known as *popples* in the Upper North especially in its northeastern section, and the hawthorn tree is also called a *thorn apple tree* with reference to its prickly fruit. The spiked and prickly seeds of various weeds and grasses are often called *pitchforks* or *stickers,* both terms probably coined fairly recently in America.

The Upper North lexicon has relatively fewer ruralisms, specifically farming terms, than any other major U.S. dialect region. This is not too surprising given the industrial and urban character of the North in contrast to the South. Nevertheless, the rural bias of the *DARE* questionnaire netted a number of terms that can be heard today on Upper North farms.

The frugality and ingenuity of the Northern farmer is illustrated in the *stump fence,* which was a simple fence made of the bothersome tree stumps that dotted the newly cleared landscape. This term may be regional because the fence itself may have been constructed nowhere else. At any rate, since most of the informants were old and none were young, both the term and the fence are probably well on their way to obsolescence.

On the Upper Northern farm one would feed or *swill* the hogs, remove stones from a field with a *stoneboat,* and stack hay for curing in the field into *cocks* or *haycocks.* One would refer to the valuable sugar maple grove as a *sugar bush* and probably without knowing it would be using a Dutch word carried west by New York pioneers (*busch, bosch*). The outer covering of certain of the farm's produce, such as beans or walnuts, would be referred to as the *shuck* and to remove this covering would be called *shucking* it. Guinea fowl are raised throughout the rural United States, but Upper North farmers tend to call them, unremarkably, *guinea hens,* whereas the rest of the country, especially the South and Lower North, tends to refer to them as simply *guineas.*

Calls to animals have from the beginning of linguistic geography in America been recognized as one of the best-defined sets of regionalisms since they are almost purely oral forms, rarely found in print. *So-boss,* for example, is the Upper North-and-West call to cows and calves. *Boss* and *bossy* referring to a cow are themselves a part of this lexicon, so that other combinations such as *co-boss* and *come-boss* are also heard primarily in this region. *Boss* was an English dialect form brought to America, probably to New England. In the mid-nineteenth century, it had gotten as far as the plains where it was also used as one of the names for a buffalo. *Ko-day,* or occasionally *ko-dack,* was originally a New England call to sheep that has established itself in the Upper North lexicon.

Onomatopoeic words for animal sounds are also frequently regional. The Upper North version of the bawl of a cow or calf is a *blat,* which is also the sound that an Upper North sheep makes. *Whinner* is the sound of a horse.

Finally among the ruralisms are terms dealing with horse-drawn wagons and carriages. A light wagon usually having two seats and drawn by two horses is sometimes known as a *Democrat wagon* or just a *Democrat.* The pivoting crossbar to which the traces are fastened is called a *whippletree,* or very occasionally, a *whiffletree.* The whippletrees are in turn fastened to both ends of the *evener,* which divides the work of the two horses. On a buggy the two outer shafts between which the horse is harnessed are known as the *thills* or (except in New England) the *fills.*

Also in this rural jargon, a wagon's wheel axle is sometimes called an *exle,* or more often, an *ex* or *ax.* These two latter terms are remarkable survivals of a very old word that in English goes back before 700 A.D.: *æx,* which has the same meaning, the axle of a wheel or the axis of rotation. It is cognate with the Old High German and Old Teutonic form *ahsa* and is related to Latin *axis* and Sanskrit *aksha.* But as the *Oxford English Dictionary* (*OED*) points out, the word is not found by itself in English after the Old English period, and even in combinations such as *ax-nail* and *ax-pin* is now obsolete except in British dialect. And yet it is alive and well in a dialect of American English.

All of these wagon terms are from a bygone era. Even so, they still had considerable currency when the *DARE* fieldwork was being completed. Their imminent demise, however, is foreshadowed by the old age of most of the informants and by semantic confusion. For example, the standard name for the horse on the left side of a team is "near horse," or in the Upper North, *nigh horse.* But of the eighty-five *DARE* informants who said *nigh horse,* twenty-six were responding instead to the question for the horse on the right side. The term itself was still remembered in the region, but the thing it refers to—the position of a horse in a team—was beginning to be unfamiliar, doubtless from disuse.

Like the farming vocabulary, the number of domestic and culinary terms in the lexicon is relatively low for a major dialect area. *Beet greens* as a dish is one of the few Upper North foods. *Johnnycake* is a kind of corn bread, which was at one time so well known in New England that Yankees were called *johnnycakes* and New England was the *land of johnnycake.*

Also, as the expression itself indicates, the *New England boiled dinner,* consisting of meat, usually corned beef, boiled together with vegetables, originated in New England. But today in the Upper North, it is usually called simply *boiled dinner*. When older residents take their tea or coffee without anything added to it, they sometimes say they take it *clear*.

Two old-fashioned kitchen items are the *stove-handle* for lifting the round lids on a wood-burning stove, and a *spider*, which is a heavy iron skillet that originally had long legs for cooking over coals. Both terms and items seem to be fading from use. A more recent and very current item one might find in a kitchen, often stored on door knobs, is a rubber band, or in the lexicon, an *elastic band* or simply an *elastic*.

The three- or four-inch baseboards that run along the wall where it joins with the floor are frequently called in the Upper North-and-West *mopboards*, a nineteenth-century Americanism still very much alive. *Eaves trough* is also a current term for the metal channel that runs along the edge of a roof for carrying off rainwater. This term has several variants including *eave(s) troth* or *troft* and *eave(s) spout*.

A May Day folk custom has given us the *May basket*, a small basket filled with flowers or candy and left on a friend's doorstep on May first. The night of May first is accordingly called *May basket night*. Among the dances of the region is the *polka;* and *cribbage* is a favorite card game.

Duck on a (or *the*) *rock* or *duck on drake* is a children's game played in the Upper North-and-West and also known among English boys as *duck* or *duckstone*. In this game each player places a stone on a rock and they all try to knock the others' stones off. In another game, the universal "hide-and-seek," the place where "it" waits is called in the Upper North the *goal* or *gool*.

There are a number of miscellaneous terms, many of which are not generally known to be dialectal. A crossroads in the Upper North is often called *four-corners*. Buildings situated on diagonal corners opposite each other are said to be *kitty-corner* from each other. An area surfaced with smooth black pavement or "black top" is sometimes called *tarvia*, a trade name which has become a generic in the region.

The Upper North has two unusual terms meaning "crooked or askew": *skew-gee* and *galley-west*. The former, which has the variants *screw-gee* and *skew-haw*, was coined toward the end of the nineteenth century and also means "confused or mixed up." *Galley-west* is a folk etymology of English dialect "colly-west" or "Colly Weston," usually used in the idiom "It's all along o' Colly Weston," meaning that something has gone wrong or is awry. John Cheever, a Massachusetts author, used it in a recent novel: "He stopped so abruptly that several men banged into him, scattering the dream galley-west" (*Falconer* 1977, 108).

If two people just don't get along well, they don't *hitch*. In other words, they can't *go* each other.

In the Upper North-and-West a splinter of wood, specifically when it is accidentally run under the skin, is a *sliver*, which might make a squeamish milquetoast feel sick *to* his stomach.

To throw something, especially something weighty, is to *heave* it. To lust and chase after members of the opposite sex is to be *on the make*. More exclusively Upper North are *mammoth* for "large or enormous" ("a mammoth bullhead cat"), *gooms* for "gums," and *down cellar* for "in" or "into" the cellar. Finally in this survey is the odd locution used for an informal "goodbye" or "see-you-later": *see-you-in-church.*

The Inland North Layer

The third major Northern layer is shown in map 3.9, a composite of 51 isoglosses that fall into four geographical subcategories. Just as the North layer (see map 3.3) is defined by two sets of isoglosses (the Eastern North and the North-and-West), so the Inland North layer is a combination of the inland sections of the four major Northern patterns we've seen so far: Eastern Upper North, Upper North-and-West, Eastern North, and North-and-West (see app. A).[1]

The distinctive pattern of the Inland North, however, is that New England is excluded, as indicated by the very low isogloss numbers in Eastern New England. These are only slightly higher in Western New England, gradually increasing into New York. The gradualness of the slope inland makes it difficult to interpret the area with lines, though a minor boundary can be seen following the upper Connecticut River and near the western borders of Massachusetts and Connecticut.

A clearly defined line runs through central Pennsylvania, considerably south of the Upper North layer, and continues into the North Central states staying somewhat south of the roughly parallel Upper North boundary. In the southern half of Ohio, Indiana, and Illinois, high and low isoglosses intermingle, indicative of a complex, heterogeneous region. The same thing occurs in the North layer (maps 3.3 and 3.4).

The primary boundary in central-west Illinois loses much of its definition on the other side of the Mississippi River. There in Iowa near Keokuk, an old frontier town, it continues as a diminished secondary boundary along the Iowa-Missouri border into Nebraska, abruptly running northward. Again the Mississippi along the Illinois border deflects additional Northern features northward. The primary boundary that left off in central-west Illinois begins on the west side of the river one-hundred fifty miles north near Dubuque. From there it dips through central Iowa.

Unlike the other maps of the North that include the West, the Inland North layer reverses the general trend in which boundaries are sharper in the East: lines of isogloss difference are clearer the farther West one goes. The primary Inland North boundary is especially strong through Iowa, southern South Dakota, Montana, central Idaho, and Oregon. Like the other North layers, however, the West as a whole is set off in map 3.9 by the now familiar line through Missouri, Oklahoma, and New Mexico.

Lexicon

Because New England is the primary historical source of the Upper North culture, it is a little surprising to find a group of words with general Upper North distribution that excludes New England. Clearly settlement pattern doesn't tell the whole story of the origin of a dialect region or layer. Some features doubtless were carried west and then died out for one reason or another in New England. This seems to be the case with *wheatcake* (= pancake), which was used by at least one Bedford, New Hampshire,

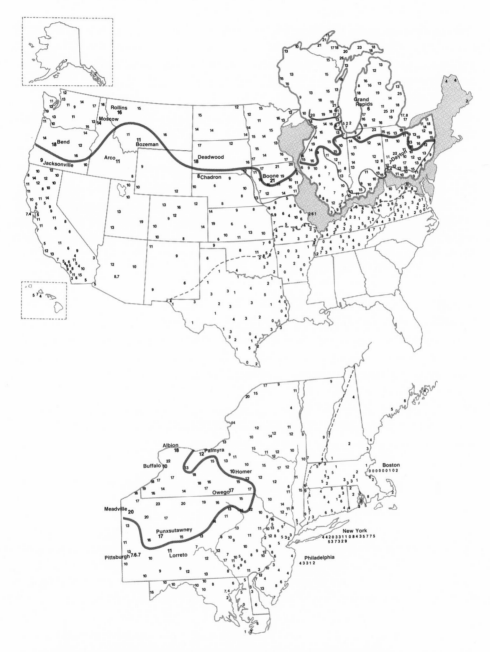

3.9. The Inland North Layer Based on 51 *DARE* Isoglosses. Primary, secondary, and tertiary boundaries.

native whose mention of it in his 1772 diary provides the earliest known example of the word. The Inland Upper North *friedcake* (= doughnut) may have succumbed to other, perhaps commercialized expressions in New England, such as *cruller,* which by the 1960s had spread throughout New England and the Northeast.

Stone fence is the Inland North counterpart of the Northeast *stone wall* or *dry wall,* the mortarless fence that farmers constructed from the unwanted rocks of cleared fields. The linguistic atlas showed the same contrast, with *stone fence* occurring almost exclusively in the "North Midland" area (New Jersey, Pennsylvania, and eastern Ohio). Oddly enough the earliest evidence (from *DAE*) shows that *stone fence* was current in Connecticut (1682) and Boston (1707). Washington Irving, a born and bred New Yorker, also used the expression in his writing (1819). But for some reason sometime after those dates, New Englanders and New Yorkers began to give preference to *stone wall.*

A similar thing happened with *crick* (= a small stream). This old variant of "creek" was first recorded in America by one of the original Yankees, Captain John Smith (1608, 1631). It appears again in the Rhode Island (1639) and Connecticut (1681) Colonial Records and again in a 1716 New England book about King Philip's War. *Crick* was in common use in colonial New England, and yet, after spreading into the Inland North and from there into the West, it died out in New England, probably in part because of speaker preference for *brook,* which is today most commonly used in the Northeast.

Some New England words were changed in their trek westward. *Bobsled,* which is used throughout the North including of course New England, was altered in the Inland Upper North to *bobsleigh* sometime in the latter half of the nineteenth century. *Thill,* which is in America confined to the Upper North but has been in English since the fourteenth century, is the shaft of a vehicle to which a horse is harnessed. But for some reason, either it was altered to be pronounced *fill* as it moved westward or else this variant, which survives in English dialect and thus may have come from England, died out in New England while surviving in the Inland Upper North.

Despite its influence on the Upper North, New England is clearly not its only dialect source. By the early nineteenth century, New England was in effect an insular region receiving little new linguistic blood from new settlers. The Inland North, on the other hand, was still being settled well into the nineteenth century by new arrivals from western New York and Pennsylvania, which is probably the seminal region for the Inland North layer. This is borne out by map 3.10, which simplifies the northeastern section of map 3.9 by generalizing the isogloss areas. The densest area of isoglosses occurs in western New York and northwestern Pennsylvania, the core region for this layer.

As the folk and rural population of the Inland North expanded, New England's was contracting into the urban centers. The economic and social vitality of the Inland areas soon contrasted with the more isolated and, to an extent, moribund rural world of New England. Inevitably the Inland North became a separate region with its own set of regionalisms, by contrast making New England a more distinctive speech area.

For many New Englanders when the wind dies down, it is *lulling down,* whereas

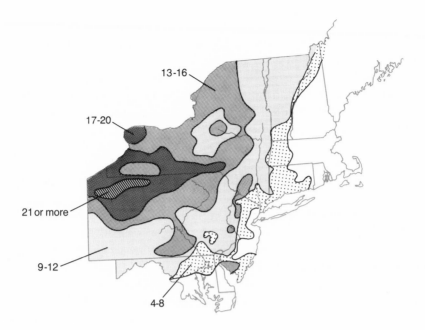

13-16

17-20

21 or more

9-12

4-8

3.10. Relative Isogloss Densities of the Inland North Layer in the Northeast

for the Inland Upper Northerners it is *going down*. To the Yankee, thin flexible ice that will just bear the weight of a man is *bendy bow ice* or simply *bendy bow* or *bendy*. But to the Inland speaker it is *rubber ice* or *rubbery ice*. The Inland resident speaks of *change work* or *exchange work* for the common rural practice of neighbor helping neighbor to raise a barn or to plow a field in return for a similar favor. After such a day's work the Inland farm wife might serve *cabbage salad* (= coleslaw) and *scalloped corn* with supper.

The West shares with the Inland Upper North a handful of expressions that are rare in the Northeast. A peach seed, for example, is called a *pit*. This may ultimately come from the Dutch in New York, who used *pit* in this same sense. In the same Inland region, marbles are called *migs;* a tagalong or someone who always follows or depends upon another is a *tag-tail;* and a bat-and-ball game for just a few players is known as *one-old-cat. Riled up,* that is, upset and agitated, is used throughout the North-and-West, but one is said to be *riley* primarily in the Inland Upper North-and-West. To be *churny* is an interesting but not often heard counterpart in non–Inland North areas and is based on the same underlying metaphor of an emotionally agitated and turbid stream.

The generally non–New England trait of creating and using slang expressions, many of them derogatory epithets, is very much a part of Inland North-and-West speech. In much of this area a cheap red table wine is sometimes called *dago red. Duck soup* is not necessarily a food in this region, but can also be something that is easily accomplished, a "cinch," or someone who is easily fooled, a "pushover." Both are probably twentieth-century coinages.

In the Inland Eastern North a *hunky* is an East European, especially one who is an unskilled laborer. Further West especially in the Northwest, such a person is called a *bohunk*. Without reference to nationality, any dull or stupid person is called a *goof* or *dolt* in the Inland Eastern North. In the same region, a Roman Catholic is (now anachronistically) called a *fish-eater*. With the same underlying logic this term had been applied in the early nineteenth century to various western Indians whose primary food was fish. It may have later been transferred to Catholics or, more likely, it was simply reinvented.

In the Upper North a nose is sometimes called a *schnozz*, but the full form, *schnozzle*, is primarily an Inland Eastern North usage. A cheap restaurant or "greasy spoon" is often called a *beanery* in the same Inland area. This is one of the older American colloquial expressions first recorded in the late nineteenth century in a San Francisco newspaper. A final example of Inland slang is the euphemistic exclamation *criminy* with the common variants *crimanently* and *crimanettly*. These can be heard throughout the Inland North-and-West.

The Inland Eastern North and Inland North-and-West are particularly rich with regionalisms, there being about twice as many as in the Inland Upper North (-and-West). Since the former sublayers received many of their dialect expressions from Pennsylvania and western New York, we would expect there to be a greater contrast between them and New England, than between the Inland Upper North (-and-West) and New England.

A *piece* or between-meal snack probably spread westward from Pennsylvania. Kurath calls it a "North Midland" form; *DARE* shows it in scattered use throughout the Inland North-and-West. Likewise, *sawbuck* (= a sawhorse, or rack with crossed end supports used to hold wood to be sawed) occurs in this broad region. It appears as a primarily "North Midland" form in *WG*, deriving from the Dutch of New York, *zaagbok*, perhaps coalescing with the German of Pennsylvania, *sagebock*.

Teeter-totter (= seesaw), which Kurath thinks was at one time common in Western New England, is now primarily an Inland North-and-West expression. A more recent children's game is *pom-pom-pullaway*, a fanciful Inland name for a kind of tug-of-war game. It was probably coined in the early part of this century and doesn't seem to have a counterpart in New England.

One expression that does have a strong New England counterpart is *quack grass*, the Inland name for the European couch grass, a weed naturalized throughout the United States. The New England name is *witch grass*. Other Inland terms with strong counter-parts are *raw fries* or *raw fried potatoes*, known in the Northeast as *home fries* or *pan fries; pop* (= a carbonated soft drink), known in the Northeast as *soda* and in Eastern New England as *tonic;* and *green onions*, known in the Northeast as *scallions*. *Pop* may have originated deep in the Inland North; early quotes place it in Wisconsin (1882), Arkansas (1893), and in the "midwest" (1920 in Sinclair Lewis's *Main Street*). The commercial distribution of the product and thus the name may have spread *pop* in an atypical way, but one that generally stayed within the cultural region, which to an extent corresponds to the economic and commercial region.

A similar situation may account for the regionalizing of *green onions* presumably by produce distributors and supermarkets. This notion of language spread is reinforced by the Inland North-and-West name for the most common vehicle used to distribute commercial products of all kinds, the *semi,* the giant trailer truck that is a familiar sight on U.S. highways. Similarly a fast train is often called a *flyer* in the Inland North. This word has climbed the technological ladder since its birth. First applied to race horses (1856), it was then transferred to fast vessels and steamships, and finally came to refer to a fast passenger train.

Most Inland Eastern North and Inland North-and-West expressions, however, are truly "down home" with roots in the folk speech. In the Inland North-and-West a gathering usually sponsored by the local church or sometimes another organization often to raise money for charity is called an *ice-cream social* or *ice-cream sociable.* The invention and popularization of ice-cream in the 1850s modified an old American custom and offered a new expression that, if the earliest citations are considered authoritative, may have originated deep inland in the Kansas (1873) and Oklahoma (1898) area.

Although the salt shaker has made the use of an open dish of salt on the dinner table old-fashioned, many Inland Eastern North informants still knew the expression *salt dip,* a once familiar sight on the family table. *Goose grease* is also an old-fashioned cough and cold remedy when applied as a poultice. It was still current enough in the late 1960s, at least in folk memory, to be seen as a clearly Inland Eastern North usage.

The remarkable linguistic construction *all the farther* using the comparative adjective *farther* or *further* as if it were a noun, is a common expression used in the Inland North-and-West by virtually all classes of speakers. It would not be unusual to hear the town banker, for example, say "That's all the farther we can go with your loan." Another formal regionalism has to do with the North word *mow* meaning to store hay in the mow or loft of a barn. In New England, this verb is usually used with *away* ("We mowed the hay away before noon"), whereas in the Inland Eastern North the preposition is rarely used ("We should mow the hay before it rains").

Grammatical regionalisms are relatively rare, but *run* is a case in point. In the North-and-West to have a splinter or something sharp thrust into the skin is to have it *run* into the skin: "He ran a thorn into his hand." But nearly all of the ninty-three informants who used *run* for the third person singular past (and present?) were Inland Eastern North natives: "He *run* a thorn into his hand." Interestingly the use of *run* in the third person singular past in its standard sense ("He run five miles yesterday") shows nearly the opposite regionality; it is used most commonly in the South and Lower North.

Other Inland regionalisms rooted in folk speech are to *pail* (= milk) a cow, to store grain in a *grainery* or *granary,* and to receive only a *skiff* or small amount of snow. This last expression is used side by side with *dusting* of snow, which is, however, especially common in the Northeast.

Finally, there are three additional colloquial expressions elicited from Inland North-and-West speakers. A narrow escape or "close call" is also known as a *close one.* If someone deliberately sleeps later than usual, he or she has *slept in.* And if someone sleeps in because he or she is very hungover or has the d.t.'s, then that unfortunate individual has *snakes in her (his) boots,* a relatively old (1877) and still vivid regionalism.

The Upper Midwest Layer

"Middle West," or more commonly "Midwest," is a popular but imprecise regional name. *Webster's Third New International Dictionary* defines it with magnificent vagueness: "regions lying somewhat to the west of a specified or implied point of orientation." This is perhaps more vague than is necessary, for there is in fact a general consensus of where the Midwest is located, though it covers a broad area roughly north of the Ohio and from the Alleghenies in Pennsylvania west to the Rockies.[2]

The Upper Midwest here refers to the region defined in map 3.11 by a composite of 17 isoglosses centered on Minnesota and including the Dakotas, most of Nebraska, northern Iowa and Illinois, all of Wisconsin, and western Michigan. This is a broader region than the "Upper Midwest" of Harold Allen's *Linguistic Atlas of the Upper Midwest* (*LAUM,* 1973–76), which only covers the portion of this region west of the Mississippi, an essentially arbitrary area defined more by the administration of the linguistic atlas project than by historical or linguistic forces.

The settlement of the area began in Iowa after the Black Hawk Purchase of 1832, which opened a strip of land on the western side of the Mississippi River, fifty miles wide and extending from Missouri's northern border to about Prairie du Chien in southwestern Wisconsin. Most of the settlers came from Illinois, Indiana, Ohio, Kentucky, and Tennessee, either by wagon train or more often by way of the Ohio and Mississippi rivers. In 1836 about ten thousand people lived on this fertile strip of bottom land. By 1840 the number had increased fourfold filling the southern half of the Black Hawk Purchase. News of the lush Iowa lands soon reached New England and New York and an even more mixed population began to flood into the territory, pushing the frontier northward and westward. By 1846 Iowa was settled enough to become a state.

Fur traders and then lumbermen were the first to settle the dense hardwood forests of central-eastern Minnesota, where the Sioux and Chippewa ceded the triangle of land between the Mississippi and St. Croix rivers. Most of these intrepid loggers came from Vermont and Maine, many via Wisconsin and Michigan. There were also a good number of Irish woodsmen. The high cost of getting food into the area soon beckoned farmers to move in and take advantage of the high food prices. Most of these new arrivals were from Wisconsin, Illinois, and Iowa. The 1850 census, however, showed that only 2,879 people lived in the St. Croix triangle. But during the 1850s an explosion of settlers moved to the Minnesota River Valley, most of them from New England or from New York, Pennsylvania, and Illinois of New England parentage. In 1852 Minneapolis was laid out. Six years later the territory had enough population, most of it situated in its eastern section, to become a state.

The Dakotas were first settled in the 1850s by Minnesotans and Nebraskans, who laid out the towns Flandreau, Sioux Falls, Vermillion, Yankton, and Bon Homme in the

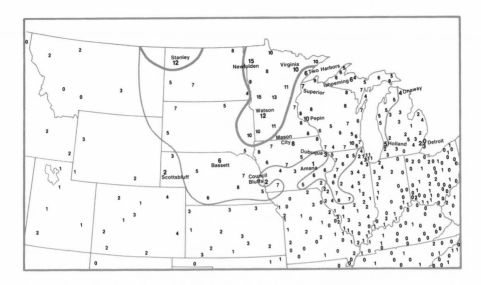

3.11. The Upper Midwest Layer Based on 17 *DARE* Isoglosses

southeastern corner. But it was not until 1868 when the Sioux Indians were finally
forced into reservations west of the Missouri River that the Dakotas began to be settled
in earnest. Most of the settlers came from the Mississippi Valley states, thus giving the
western section of the Upper Midwest a strong midlands influence. In addition, many
Europeans, particularly Scandinavians, found their way to this area. The advent of
railroads joining the prairie hinterland with Chicago's markets; the Homestead Act of
1862; the Black Hills gold rush of 1875; the "bonanza farming" in the Red River
Valley—all gave impetus to the settlement of the Dakotas. From 1880 to 1885 the
population increased 400 percent with five hundred fifty thousand persons living in the
Dakotas east of the Missouri River.

   This mixing of settlers from the midlands and North and the relatively recent
settlement create a dialect region that is difficult to define, especially the farther west
one goes. As Allen (1973–76) notes, the contrast between the Midland and Upper North
features is clearly maintained in the eastern half of the Upper Midwest, that is, through
Iowa, but the distinction blurs west of the Missouri River. When lines are used to
describe this region, its heterogeneous nature creates a confusing web outlining what
appear to be minor dialect areas (see map 3.13).

   The Upper Midwest layer of map 3.11 adds to this complexity by outlining a
subregion of the North with its own internal organization. The seventeen isoglosses of
the layer fall into two separate groups. Ten more or less cover the entire subregion,
while the other seven confine themselves to its northern area where a large proportion of
the settlers were immigrants from northern Europe. In the first census that kept track of
origin of birth (1860), the northern section of the Upper Midwest—Minnesota, Wisconsin, and northern Michigan—had a higher percentage (30 percent or more) of its

population born outside of the United States than most other parts of the country. And this was during the formative period of the region.

Lexicon

Because the largest group of foreign-born settlers were Scandinavians (though Germans made up the largest single nationality), we can expect there to be at least a couple of expressions relating to Norwegians. Like the other North layers that have nicknames and derogatory terms for persons of immigrant stock, *Norskie* is used to refer to persons of Norwegian heritage. It is also used in the Northwest, especially Oregon. *Lutefisk* is the name for skinned and deboned fish prepared by soaking in a lye solution, a procedure and term imported from Scandinavia. Its currency is restricted primarily to Minnesota and Wisconsin.

Other expressions that confine themselves to the northern portion of the Upper Midwest are the two recent coinages *boulevard strip* for the grass strip between curb and sidewalk, and *biffy* or *biff* for a toilet. Both are centered on Minnesota where they probably originated. A less urban term is *shining,* which is an old method of hunting, employed by frontiersmen like Daniel Boone. *To shine* deer one uses a lantern at night to stun or distract the animal so that an easy shot can be made. Despite its being made illegal, it is still a widely known method, called *jacking* or *jack lighting* in the Northeast, and *spotlighting* in the West.

Baga a shortened nickname for "rutabaga" probably originated in Michigan where it was recorded as early as 1854. *Juneberry* is an Americanism originating before the settlement of the region, but today it is used primarily in the northern sections of Minnesota, Wisconsin, and Michigan, for any of various trees and shrubs of the genus *Amelanchier* that have edible purple or red berries.

The remaining ten isogloss expressions have broader distributions. *Farmer matches,* for example, is the name for wooden friction matches in West Virginia and Upstate New York, but is most common in the Upper Midwest. *Machine shed,* the unremarkable term for an outbuilding where farm equipment is stored, is especially current in the Upper Midwest, but is also used in parts of the Lower North and the West. And although *prairie chicken* (= any of three species of grouse native to the prairie) is recorded throughout the Plains States as far south as Texas, it is most commonly used in the Upper Midwest.

The other names for flora and fauna, however, stay more strictly within the secondary boundary of the layer. Moneywort, which is a trailing plant introduced from Europe with yellow flowers, is called *creeping jenny* in this region. The common black grass bug with red markings that give it one of its names, *Canadian soldier,* would rarely be seen creeping on creeping jenny, since it prefers to feed on box elder trees: hence its Upper Midwest name, *box elder bug.* The tall grass that grows in low, wet land is called *slough grass* or *slough hay,* since it is often used as hay.

Among the regional names for foods are *American fried potatoes* or *American fries,* which are simply boiled potatoes sliced and fried, and *watermelon pickles,* which are made from the rind of watermelons. In other scattered parts of the country they are known by the fuller name *watermelon rind pickles*. A variant on this sweet condiment is *watermelon preserves*. Two regional pastries are the *long-john,* which is an oblong deep-fried cake usually with a frosting, and the *bismarck,* which is also a deep-fried cake but with a filling of jelly or custard.

The Upper North Dialect Region

Combined Atlas Boundaries

Like New England, sections of the North have been covered in some detail by the linguistic atlases, making it possible to compare their earlier results with the combined Northern layers derived from *DARE* fieldwork. Hans Kurath derived the Upper North boundary through Pennsylvania (see map 1.4) using the isogloss bundle method and fieldwork completed for the *Linguistic Atlas of the Middle and South Atlantic States (LAMSAS)*.

In the North Central states, Alva Davis in his important 1948 dissertation described the Upper North speech boundary based on two different sets of data. Using the grid method, he showed that the boundary roughly picked up where Kurath's description had left off in northwestern Pennsylvania. At the same time, Davis introduced the mail checklist to American dialectology and demonstrated its validity as a field method for gathering lexical data. He tested it against the direct interview fieldwork done by Marckwardt and others for the Linguistic Atlas of the North Central States (LANCS).

By making two grid count maps, one for each set of data, Davis found that the same 25 isoglosses bundled in essentially the same way. Map 3.12A is his map based on the LANCS material. As might be expected from the settlement history, a major bundle of isoglosses sets off the Western Reserve, cutting northwestward across Ohio to the Michigan border, which it follows closely through Indiana and into Illinois where the northeastern section of that state is separated from its lower central portion. A handful of isoglosses isolates Marietta, Ohio, and a strong bundle heads northward (cf. Shuy's boundary, map 1.5C), partitioning off the Galena area in northwestern Illinois.

Northern Illinois has several Upper North boundaries running through it, some primary and some secondary, reminiscent of the lines of the Upper North layer (see map 3.7). The tertiary boundary of that layer, for example, corresponds to Davis's line in central-west Illinois. Using Davis's grid method, Roger Shuy (1962) also defined the primary Upper North boundary in Illinois (see map 1.5C). Shuy found that the boundary turns almost due north in central-northern Illinois, then bifurcates in the northwestern corner of the state, much as Davis's does.

Of the 25 isoglosses counted in this map (3.12A), only 11 are Upper North terms: *angleworm, blat, fills* or *thills, evener, firefly, johnnycake, pail, quoits, shuck,* sick *to* one's stomach, and *whiffletree* or *whippletree*. The rest are a mixture of regionalisms: three from the Inland North (*drag, draw, friedcake*), three Midland (*cling peach, to hull, sook!*), four South I (*comfort, cherry seed, peach seed, pulley bone*), and four South II (*clabber, evening, nicker, sun-up*). Because of this mix of isoglosses, the boundary derived in map 3.12A must be shared by several different dialect layers. Not

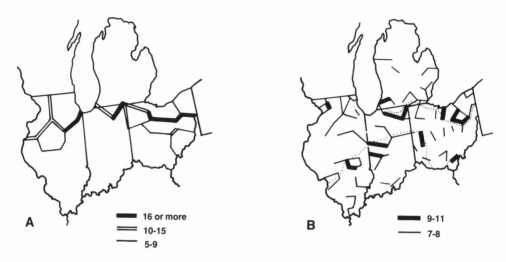

3.12. Two Versions of the Upper North Boundary in the North Central States. *A* is based on 25 isoglosses from the fieldwork for the Linguistic Atlas of the North Central States. Using the same grid-count method, *B* is based on the *DARE* versions of these same isoglosses, with only very roughly similar results. (Sources: *A*, Davis 1949; *B*, *DARE* data.)

only is it the southern boundary of the Upper North, for example, it may also be the northern boundary of the Lower North, Midland, and South I and II layers.

Using the *DARE* data, a grid-count map for the same isoglosses shows a different picture (map 3.12*B*). The *DARE* version has a much more uniform and apparently disorderly distribution of bundles that tends to mask the major boundaries of this region. Part of this uniformity is due to changes in the distribution of the terms in the twenty-year gap between the LANCS and *DARE* fieldwork. Five of the terms have virtually lost all of their boundary defining capacity: *firefly, cling peach, drag, sun-up,* and *quoits.* The informants using these terms, particularly the first three, no longer cluster in a neat distinctive pattern as they did in the 1940s. As Davis noted, "clear-cut distribution" is the most important factor in selecting an isogloss for a count map, and these terms have lost this (1948, 47). However, the rest of the isoglosses in this map do cluster distinctively and all are used in deriving the various major dialect boundaries in this and other chapters.

If we disregard the background noise in map 3.12*B*, we can make out the vague outlines of two major boundaries: the Upper North and the South (Davis's "Midland and South"). The Upper North line is present as a group of heavy but disconnected bundles situated in northeastern Ohio, northeastern Indiana and southern Michigan. Northeastern Illinois is roughly bounded by a set of lighter bundles. The Galena region is distinctly marked off. The other major grouping runs through southern Illinois into central Indiana and central-west Ohio (the so-called Hoosier apex) with the extreme southern portion of Ohio marked by a small but heavy bundle. This grouping of

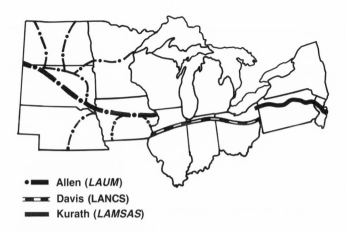

Allen (*LAUM*)
Davis (LANCS)
Kurath (*LAMSAS*)

3.13. The Upper North Boundary According to the Sectional Linguistic Atlases of the United States

isoglosses, as we will see in the next chapter, corresponds with the northern boundary of the South I dialect layer.

The third atlas study of the North is Harold Allen's *Linguistic Atlas of the Upper Midwest* (1973–76) and carries the Upper North boundary west of the Mississippi. His results are shown in map 3.13 in relation to the two other sectional studies done by Kurath and Davis. The major boundary through Pennsylvania, the North Central states, and the Upper Midwest is only roughly continuous, disjunctions occurring at the Ohio-Pennsylvania and Illinois-Iowa borders. The former discontinuity is not easily explained, especially since both Davis and Kurath used Guy S. Lowman's fieldwork for the atlas in the bordering counties of Ohio and Pennsylvania. In part, the break may be the result of the way Davis generalized this boundary from the results of the two grid maps. His checklist map, for example, shows the line beginning at a point farther north on this border in closer agreement with Kurath's.

The disjunction at the Illinois-Iowa border, however, is accurate and is the outcome of known historical forces. Settlement for a brief period stopped at the Mississippi River making it a naturally defining boundary. Moreover, the Mississippi facilitated south-to-north migration into Iowa, especially for settlers from the Lower Mississippi Valley who were diverted northward or to the Far West by the creation of the "Permanent Indian Frontier" in the 1830s and 1840s in Kansas and Oklahoma. This infusion of chiefly midland settlers into southern Iowa shifted the Upper North boundary nearly one hundred fifty miles northward in Iowa like a geological fault line along the Illinois-Iowa border (see Carver 1986).

The boundary across the Mississippi, however, may not be completely discontinuous. Shuy's definition (see map 1.5C), for example, has the boundary bifurcating in the northwestern corner of Illinois, the lower branch ending at approximately the same point on the eastern bank of the Mississippi as Allen's line on the western bank. This is more or less corroborated in the Upper North layer (see map 3.7), but the boundaries on the eastern bank are of a considerably lesser magnitude, than the lines on the western side. It would appear, then, that the discontinuity across the Mississippi is one of degree: a tertiary line in northeastern Illinois becomes a primary boundary in Iowa.

Combined Layers

To get a comparable and complete picture of the Upper North from the three North layers, it is necessary to combine the layers and show the areas of overlap. The area of the Upper North layer falls within both the North and Inland North layer areas and thus shares their lexicons in varying degrees. In other words, the speech of the Upper North has the greatest number of Northernisms, with its eastern section having additionally the lexicons of New England, the Northeast, and Upstate New York, and its western section having the Upper Midwest lexicon. Moving southward, the number of Northernisms decreases as we pass over layer boundaries and tiers of diminishing isogloss density.

The relationships among the boundaries of the layers are shown in map 3.14, which combines the primary and secondary boundaries from the North, Upper North, and Inland North layers (see maps 3.3, 3.7, and 3.9) in the northeastern United States. The boundary relationships vary from considerable coherence in the eastern half of their length through the Upper Susquehanna River Valley into New York outlining the Hudson Valley area, to considerable noncoherence in the western half where the strands diverge a good one hundred twenty miles between the primary boundaries of the Upper

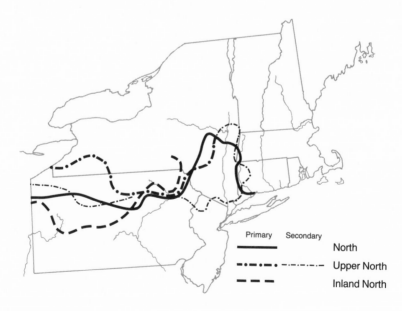

3.14. Combined Major Northern Boundaries in the Northeast (maps 3.3, 3.7, and 3.9)

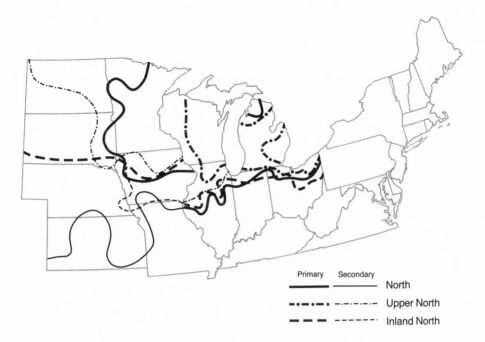

Primary   Secondary
━━━━━   ━━━━━   North
▬·▬·▬· ─·─·─·─ Upper North
▬ ▬ ▬   ------ Inland North

**3.15. Combined Major Northern Boundaries in the North Central States
(maps 3.3, 3.7, and 3.9)**

North and the Inland North. The primary North and secondary Upper North lines,
however, run through northern Pennsylvania relatively close together.

Map 3.15 shows the extension westward of the same layer boundaries. There is
considerable coherence of these lines through northern Ohio, Indiana, and Illinois along
a path very close to Davis's version. The fault line at the Mississippi River is particularly apparent in this map. The cord of major boundaries that leaves off in central-west
Illinois near the Iowa-Missouri border, resumes on the western bank a hundred miles or
so north in Iowa.

Also particularly noticeable is the dispersing of boundaries in the West. At the
Iowa-Missouri border two secondary boundaries (Inland North and North) run close
together westward to the Missouri River where they separate and go in different directions. The three strands through central Iowa likewise diverge near the Missouri River.
Just as the Mississippi marks a transitional point where boundaries are diminished or
shifted northward, so the Missouri River marks the furthest westward extension of
coherent Northern boundaries. West of the Missouri all of the lines that continued across
the Mississippi in a roughly parallel or contiguous manner fan out in all directions.
Allen discovered a similar situation in *LAUM* (see map 3.13).

Map 3.16 consolidates maps 3.14 and 3.15 and charts in a general way the
Upper North dialect region. It shows considerable agreement with the atlas version
(map 3.13).

3.16. The Upper North Dialect Region Generalized

Layers

North (maps 3.3 and 3.4)
  Eastern North
  North-and-West
Upper North (maps 3.7 and 3.8)
  Eastern Upper North
  Upper North-and-West
Inland North (maps 3.9 and 3.10)
  Inland Eastern North
  Inland North-and-West
  Inland (Eastern) Upper North
  Inland Upper North-and-West
Upper Midwest (map 3.11)

Regions

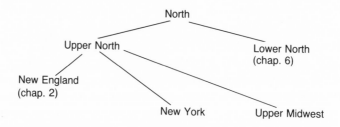

Fig. 2. Summary of the layers and regions of the North

The North speech region is one of the main dialect areas of the United States and can be analyzed into two important subregions: the Upper North and the Lower North (fig. 2). The very complex Lower North is dealt with in chapter 6, and the primary boundary of the North dialect region is treated more fully in the next chapter (4) in its discussion of the major North-South divide. Although the present chapter introduces the three North layers and their lexical features that define the North as a whole, it has also been concerned with deriving the Upper North boundaries from these layers.

NOTES

1. Thus, there are four Inland North layers: Inland Eastern Upper North, Inland Upper North-and-West, Inland Eastern North, and Inland North-and-West. To avoid the cumbersome name "Inland Eastern Upper North," it will be shortened in the text to "Inland Upper North."
2. See John F. Rooney et al., *This Remarkable Continent* (1982), maps 1.3, 1.21, and 1.29 for vernacular and cultural versions of the Midwest.

CHAPTER 4

The South

Southern English: An Overview

The South, like New England, is one of the best recognized dialect regions of the country. The so-called Southern drawl and the much parodied "y'all" are features on most of our "mental" dialect maps. As a single variety of speech, however, "Southern English" is a convenient fiction, for it is in fact a quilt-work of dialects. Even so, as a region, many unique traits unify and distinguish it from the rest of the country. Aspects of its cultural personality can be seen in its distinctive vocabulary.

The famous Southern cuisine, for example, provides a whole lexicon by itself. Bread has many dialect terms particularly when made with the New World grain, *corn* (itself an Americanism), one of the South's preferred basic ingredients. *Corn cake, corn pone, corn dodger, pone bread, fritters, hush puppies, awendaw, spoon bread, biscuit, ash* or *hoe cake, egg bread,* and just *bread* are versions of cornmeal breads. Wheat or white bread, especially store bought, is by contrast *light bread, biscuit bread, baker's bread, bought bread,* and *loaf bread.*

Like cornmeal, pork is a dominant ingredient in the culinary South; accordingly, there are numerous Southernisms for its various forms, such as *cracklins, souse, hasslet, breakfast bacon, middlins* or *middlin meat,* and *chitlins.* Similarly, food words distinguish the Southern subdialects: *gumbo, pralines,* and *jambalaya* in the Delta South; *Brunswick stew, hopping John,* and *liver pudding* in the Atlantic South.

Euphemism is alive and well in Southern speech and at times can be right prudish as when a Southerner prefers *male cow* to *bull* when speaking in mixed company, or says *woods colt* instead of *bastard, big* or *swallowed a pumpkin seed* instead of *pregnant,* and *bad place* instead of *hell.*

Although folk speech in general is characterized by metathesis or inversion, in America it seems to be a particular feature of the South, especially among the poorly educated and the working classes. Two classic examples of inversion are *peckerwood* for "woodpecker" and *hoppergrass* for "grasshopper." Both are indigenous to the South and were probably well known before the 1830s. An unrecognized inversion is the Southern phrase *hair nor hide* (= any trace or sign). The usual order since at least the early nineteenth century is *hide nor hair,* used in the negative: "I haven't seen hide nor hair of him." Of *DARE* informants, 568 scattered throughout the country gave this response as opposed to the 108 informants who gave the Southern version.

Inversion is also common in the Southern subdialects. In the Lower South, for example, a train boxcar is sometimes called a *carbox,* and in the Delta South an old or broken-down car is occasionally referred to as a *T-model* (from "model-T Ford"). Other examples of inversion that are occasionally heard in the South are *cook woman, dog-hanged, doll-baby, everwhat, everwhere, everwhich, everwho, pourdown, right-out,* and *tie-tongued.*

Although redundancy is characteristic of folk speech, it is an especially common feature among older Southern speakers with little formal education. Some examples: *boar-hog, brogan-shoe, brook-creek, generally-usually, granny woman, gully-ditch, hound-dog, might maybe, neighbor-people,* and *preacher-man.*

An unusual mixture of foreign loanwords is the spice in Southern English, a curry of French, Spanish, West African, and American Indian borrowings. Distinguishing it sharply from the Northern dialects, the Southern lexicon has few Germanic loans despite its considerable German settlements in Texas, Louisiana, Missouri, Mississippi, and the Carolinas. Instead, two romance languages are well represented: French in the Delta South, and Spanish in southern Texas and southern Florida. A few Indian borrowings survive, usually through French or Spanish (*bayou, lagniappe*). And English from the Ozarks to the Georgia coast is sprinkled with a handful of Africanisms (*juke, goober, cooter,* etc.).

The relative insularity of the South has given its language a number of distinctive features. Its lexicon has an unusually high number of regionalized terms, that is, expressions current at one time throughout the United States, but now used primarily in the South. It has also preserved a good sampling of obsolete British English or old dialect terms, especially from Scotland and northern England. In a sense, the South is (or was) the major linguistic relic area of the United States.

Although it is rapidly changing, it is the most rural region of the country, which in part accounts for its status as a relic area. Lacking the volatility of an urban society, its language tends to be conservative, preserving older forms of vocabulary and pronunciation. It is also characterized by many regional ruralisms, more than for any other section of the country. This aspect of the South is reflected in *DARE*'s sample of Southern informants, 47 percent of whom live in very rural areas (community type 5). The speech mapped in this chapter, then, is particularly characteristic of the South as a rural region. Its core dialect areas are in fact some of the most rural and underdeveloped sections of the South.

The Continental Divide: North-South

Because the North and the South are contiguous, we have already seen the northern limits of the South in the cultural and linguistic geography of the North. The primary boundary between these two major regions begins somewhere in central Delaware, extends westward near the old Mason-Dixon Line and continues approximately along the Ohio River. Map 4.1 shows two different interpretations of this cultural boundary as described by Zelinsky (1973) and Gastil (1975). Although their versions roughly follow each other to the Mississippi River, they diverge considerably in the cultural complexity of the Southwest. But in both cases east Texas is included in the Southern region. This

4.1. Cultural Geography of the South. Dashed lines are Zelinsky 1973; solid lines are Gastil 1975. (Source: Gastil 1975 and Zelinsky 1973.)

broad boundary, which in Gastil's version places all of Texas in the South, represents a cultural and linguistic continental divide separating the North (and the West) from the South. In the hierarchy of American dialects, these two watersheds are at the top.

Hans Kurath argues that dividing American speech in this way is naive. "The common notion of a linguistic Mason and Dixon's Line separating 'Northern' from 'Southern' speech is simply due to an erroneous inference from an oversimplified version of the political history of the nineteenth century" (*WG*, vi). But U.S. political history during that century was dominated by the differences between these two great regions, a reality of American history that came to be symbolized by the famous Mason-Dixon Line. The nation's politics were preoccupied with the struggle between the North and the South over, among other things, tariffs, slavery, and control of the emergent West. The same historical, social, and economic forces that divided the nation and led to the "Confederate War," as it is still called in the South (see McDavid and McDavid 1969), are the same forces that shaped the geography and character of the two major dialects.

To a great extent, the linguistic continental divide is a result of two broad streams of migration during the westward expansion of the United States (map 4.2). One stream of settlers primarily from the New England and Pennsylvania hearth areas fed into the northern watershed filling Upstate New York and flowing west through the narrows of Ohio, Indiana, and Illinois, then fanning north into the Upper Midwest and on into the broad expanse of the West. The South began in the Chesapeake Bay and

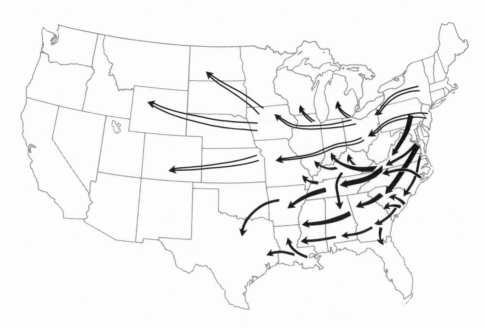

4.2. The Two Main Streams of Settlement in the United States

Charleston hearths and spread west and southwest, roughly confining itself within the crescent of the Ohio and Mississippi rivers. Of course the details of this migration are very complicated and the streams are not so neatly separated. But despite a few anomalous eddies, the tide of settlers swept westward in a broad two-part movement.

Climate was important in containing the settlement of the South in a way that does not seem to have operated in the westward expansion of the North, though many European immigrants favored climates and terrain reminiscent of their homeland. As the only semitropical region in the United States, the South attracted a distinctive population of settlers, fostered an agrarian economy, and helped shape a distinctive life-style, culture, and social structure. The cultural and linguistic South roughly corresponds with that section of the country where the rain is moderately heavy—forty to fifty-nine inches per year—and where the daytime January temperature seldom drops below freezing.

The two broad patterns of settlement established the cultural dividing line, but the national and ethnic origins of the settlers helped define the character of the two regions. This is especially relevant to language variation. After the first effective settlements, the South received very few foreign immigrants. Population maps of U.S. citizens born in other countries for the decades 1860–1900 (see Lord and Lord 1955, maps 174–76) show a sharp contrast between the South and the rest of the country, particularly the North. By the latter half of the nineteenth century, there were virtually no foreign-born residents in the South justifiably making it the most "American" region.

In the 1850s the large immigration of northern Europeans with their hatred for slavery helped swing the Old Northwest toward an alliance with the Northeast. At the same time the North became unified by a steel network. Before that decade the main trade route of the Upper Midwest was down the Mississippi River to New Orleans, but the rapid development of railroads in the North broke that tie to the South. Agricultural surpluses could be easily sent over the Appalachian barrier to the rich seaboard markets, uniting the Northwest with the Northeast. This important economic alliance helped unify the politics, culture, and ultimately the language of the North, in contrast to the South.

The Civil War and postbellum poverty, which until only recently has dogged the South, kept opportunity-seeking immigrants away. Even in the 1920s and 1930s when foreign immigration to the United States was at a high, less than 1 percent of the South's population, excluding Virginia, Louisiana, and Florida, were foreign born. This is in contrast to, for example, New York, New Jersey, Rhode Island, Massachusetts, and Connecticut, a quarter of whose populations were immigrants (Odum and Moore 1938, 533). This situation heightened the differences between the two speech regions. It enriched the distinctiveness of the Southern dialect by reinforcing its isolation and inbreeding, while Northern speech continued to feel the pressure of languages and cultures in contact as Europeans flooded its thriving industrial region.

The North-South Layer Boundaries

This bipartite national pattern is imprinted on the geography of the Southern lexicon, 78 of whose isoglosses are composited in map 4.3 (South I). The primary boundary that emerges approximates the cultural lines of map 4.1 beginning in Delaware and moving westward close to the Mason-Dixon Line to the Ohio River, which it follows into Indiana. There the familiar "Hoosier apex" juts up into central Indiana and east central Illinois. This area on the northern side of the Ohio River, which includes most of "Little Egypt" in southern Illinois, was settled by Upper Southerners mainly from Virginia and Kentucky. The Southern boundary then moves southward to include the bootheel of Missouri, all of Arkansas, the Ouachita Mountain area in the southeast corner of Oklahoma, and East Texas.

An important secondary boundary in map 4.3 shows the Southern influence extending even further northward in Indiana and creating another apexlike pattern in Missouri and extreme southern Iowa. Oklahoma (except for the panhandle) and Texas share to an important degree in this dialect layer, though three west Texas communities as well as those in the southern tip are exceptions. The furthest significant extension of this layer westward is into eastern New Mexico and a small adjoining area in southern Colorado.

If we compare map 4.3 with the maps for the North we can get a clearer picture of the linguistic divide between the North and South. Clarity in this case, however, does not mean neatly coinciding boundaries. The Northern region is simply not a jigsaw piece fitting tightly against the South; as implied in the cultural map (4.1) there is no clean line separating the two. All of the primary boundaries of the three Northern layers (North, Upper North, and Inland North; maps 3.3, 3.7, and 3.9) run considerably north of the South I layer leaving the Lower North "gap," about which we will have more to say in chapter 6.

4.3. The South I Layer Based on 78 *DARE* Isoglosses. Solid lines represent primary and secondary boundaries. Dotted lines represent relatively thin tertiary areas. Dashed lines enclose areas of high isogloss numbers.

Of all the Northern layers, the North's secondary boundary (map 3.3) comes closest to coinciding with the South I's contour (map 4.3). Map 4.4 superimposes the two layers' important boundaries. These run close together along the Mason-Dixon Line but part ways in Ohio where the southern boundary follows the river and the Northern wanders through central Ohio. The area where neither reaches is part of the core of the Lower North. In Indiana they cross each other's path making the tip of the Hoosier apex a complicated area of overlapping layers and mixed features.

Another Lower North island is created in southern Illinois where the two bound-

4.4. The Linguistic Divide Expressed in Terms of North (map 3.3) and South I (map 4.3) Boundaries. Parallel lines indicate on which side of the boundaries the individual layers lie.

aries again spread apart, the Southern line following closer to the river and the Northern wending in a more central direction. The primary Southern continues southward, while the secondaries again join at the Mississippi moving northwestward into southern Iowa and then dipping sharply southward to create a Missouri apex. This apex is also independently corroborated in Gastil's account of the cultural boundary (map 4.1). The western extension of the divide is marked in map 4.4 by the secondary lines that roughly follow each other into the Southwest, skirting most of Oklahoma and Texas into eastern New Mexico.

The implications of this major division between the North and the South are important for American regional dialectology. For example, it argues against the existence of a separate Midland dialect region, since the divide would cut directly across the region's center. At the same time it argues that the Lower North is a major region, distinct from the North and South because of its strong mixed and transitional nature.

The South I Layer

The dialect layer of map 4.3 unifies the South as a first-order linguistic region. Within this layer there are several boundaries where the isogloss numbers drop off suddenly and several differential areas where similar (low or high) isogloss numbers cluster. Secondary lines separate southern Louisiana and most of Florida from the main body of the layer. This is as might be expected given their very different settlement and cultural histories, which in effect have made them separate dialect areas.

A ridge of high isoglosses runs along the northern border of South Carolina and into Georgia near the Ogeechee River, a record left by one of the earliest settled areas of the South. In Georgia along the Chattahoochee River another high ridge is apparent, a line that also momentarily marked the furthest extension of the Old South (ca. 1830). As the plantation settlers pushed westward into Georgia from the south Atlantic piedmont, the Chattahoochee and the Creek Indians immediately to the west presented a natural frontier barrier that for a moment in history arrested the westward expansion (cf. map 4.11). As in the case of the Ogeechee River, the Chattahoochee became a linguistic boundary, a line of contrast between the older settlements east of the river and the new and more mixed settlements to the west in Alabama (cf. Wood 1971, 29). On the western side of the river in map 4.3, the isogloss density drops off sharply into a sparse, spade-shaped area (dotted line) covering central Alabama, a pattern we will see repeated in other layers and one which is also reflected in the early settlement (cf. map 4.11).

Another area of sparse isoglosses occurs in most of central Tennessee, with very low numbers in the western portion. This is in strong contrast to an adjacent area in western Kentucky (broken line), which is one of the densest areas of this layer. Another very dense area of isoglosses covers southern Arkansas, northern Louisiana, and small adjacent parts of northeast Texas. Eastern Virginia has a puzzling mixture of low and medium numbers that separate it as a unique speech area.

The South II Layer

Another layer with almost the same weight and extension as the South I of map 4.3, but with some important differences, shows the complexity of Southern dialect geography. Map 4.5 (South II) counts 84 isoglosses (6 more than its sister layer) that might be thought of as belonging to the traditional "South and South Midland" region. The primary boundary of this map essentially coincides with the primary in map 4.3, from east Texas to southern Illinois where they part ways.

Although the Ohio River plays an important role in shaping both Southern layers, it has a greater effect on this one. In the North Central states the boundary follows the entire length of the river but becomes less pronounced halfway along the Indiana border where it continues as a secondary line. Particularly noticeable is the way it completely cuts off the Hoosier apex, only the faintest of isoglosses hinting at the Southern presence in Illinois and Indiana. The "Southernness" of this apex area is real, but is only about one layer deep, once again illustrating the transitional and mixed nature of North Central speech.

The South II primary line cuts off the northeastern section of Kentucky and drops due south excluding all of West Virginia, Virginia, and North Carolina from the primary domain of this layer. Southern Louisiana and Florida are also excluded but in keeping with their separate dialect status already noted in map 4.3. South Carolina is again dense with isoglosses, a pattern we will see in other layers.

Unlike the Upper North boundary, which is relatively sharp and definable and is corroborated by the linguistic atlas, the Southern dialect boundary in the North Central states is more ambiguous. Robert Dakin in his voluminous dissertation (1966) on "The Dialect Vocabulary of the Ohio River Valley," based on the LANCS fieldwork, derives

4.5. The South II Layer Based on 84 *DARE* Isoglosses. Solid lines represent primary and secondary boundaries. Dotted lines represent tertiary isogloss areas.

a Southern, or in his nomenclature a "South Midland," boundary that at first glance seems to disagree with maps 4.3 and 4.5. His line (map 4.6*A;* Dakin 1966, 3:93) runs somewhere midway between the northern extreme of map 4.3 and the Ohio River line of map 4.5.

His boundary is generalized primarily from nineteen "South and South Midland" isoglosses counted and mapped (map 4.6*B;* Dakin 1966, 3:89) with the same participation method used throughout this book. In the *DARE* fieldwork, however, most of these isoglosses are significantly different and, as we saw for the Upper North boundary, when using the *DARE* versions of the LANCS isoglosses (map 3.12*B*), would not be effective in deriving the Southern boundary.

Only six of Dakin's nineteen LANCS isoglosses qualify to be counted in the South I layer (map 4.3): *lot, whetrock, branch, butter bean, light bread,* and *pallet.* A seventh, *middlins* or *middling meat,* might qualify except that only twenty-two *DARE* informants used it, a poor representation for such a large region.

The rest of the LANCS isoglosses are so different in the *DARE* fieldwork that they either qualify to be representative of other regions or else are not regional at all. Two of the nineteen are in the South-and-West layer (map 4.8): *clabber* and *hay shock.* There is one in the Lower South layer (*chitterlings* or *chitlins,* map 5.8), and one in the Midland (*rock fence,* map 6.5). Dakin also includes *breakfast bacon* and *gutters,* which according to the *DARE* fieldwork are more properly placed at the Atlantic South and Upper South respectively.

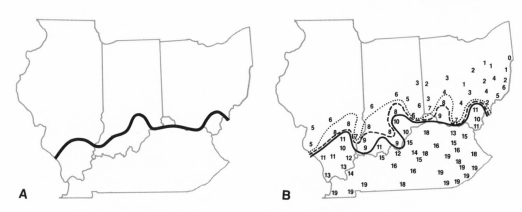

4.6. The Southern Boundary in the North Central States. *A:* generalized
"northern boundary of the South Midland" (Dakin 1966, 3:93). *B:* isogloss
count map (Dakin 1966, 3:89). (Source: LANCS as analyzed by Dakin 1966.)

He also uses *snack* (= food eaten between regular meals) as a representative
isogloss, even though he suspects that it was in more widespread use in the early 1960s
than the atlas data suggested (cf. *WG,* fig. 127; Dakin 1966, 2:346–48). The *DARE*
fieldwork shows that this term is virtually universal with some 85 percent of all its
informants giving it as a response.

The five remaining expressions that Dakin uses to derive map 4.6*B* either did not
have a *DARE* question to elicit them, as is the case with *you-all, you-all's* and *corn
shucks,* or else the question is general and is not intended to specifically elicit them, as
in the case of *waiter* (= a groom's best man) and *salad* (= greens).

Despite the considerable differences in the isoglosses from LANCS and *DARE,*
it is still possible to compare the boundaries derived from each, since, as we saw in the
diachronic picture of New England, a dialect boundary is more or less independent of
the individual isoglosses that at a given moment define it but that in time change and
shift drastically. The comparison, then, is not between the two sets of isoglosses, but
between the independently derived Southern boundaries of map 4.6*B* and map 4.5.

In map 4.6*B* Dakin draws three "possible boundary lines," his criteria being the
percentage of the nineteen terms that each community used, beginning with 42 percent
(eight of nineteen terms) and moving up by increments of 5 percent, to 52 percent (ten
or more of nineteen terms) represented by the solid line. But this is not the only possible
interpretation of this isogloss-count map and is probably not the best one. Map 4.7*A*
shows an alternative interpretation. Even though the isogloss numbers form a more or
less gentle gradient from high to low, south to north, a relatively large gap in the
gradation occurs generally along the Ohio River, marked here by a solid line. This gap
is presumably indicative of a measurable difference in speech and thus marks a clear
boundary. This boundary accords well with the boundary in map 4.5.

But perhaps more than anything else, Dakin's map illustrates the transitional
nature of this area. Unlike the relatively discrete Upper North, the South does not seem
to have a single sharply defined boundary. Instead of the Upper North's steep ridge, the

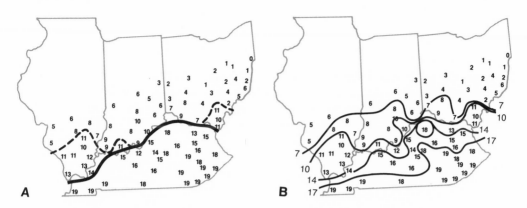

4.7. Dakin's Analysis Reinterpreted. *A:* the sudden drop in the numbers forms a primary boundary (solid line) along the Ohio River. *B:* isarithmic interpretation.

South is defined by a relatively gentle slope as interpreted in map *4.7B,* which is modeled on a topographical map using nearly equal intervals (three isoglosses) between lines. Even so, the closeness of the lines in this map along the Ohio River indicates a steep area or boundary.

Lexicon of the South I and II Layers

Combined, the South I and II layers broadly define the South dialect region (see maps 5.10 and 6.1). This lexicon is less old-fashioned, more current, and less rural than the lexicons of the Southern subdialect layers (e.g., Lower South, Atlantic South, Upper South, etc.; see maps 5.8, 5.2, and 6.2). Of the isoglosses in maps 4.3 and 4.5, only about one-third are used significantly more often by old speakers. And only about one-fifth of the lexicon is outright rural. Much of it is evenly distributed across the educational and social spectrum, with a small group of words, such as *rooter, give out, like to, paling fence,* and others, used primarily by poorly educated rural speakers.

The influence of black speech on these layers is relatively minor, especially in comparison with the Lower South layers. Only a handful of expressions (*before-day, harp, hoppergrass, jackleg, poot,* and *smoothing iron*) are used more often by blacks than whites.

As suggested earlier, the near absence of foreign immigration into the South left distinguishing marks on its speech. The South layers, for example, have relatively few non-English words and virtually no European loanwords. None of the 162 map words are of foreign (i.e., non-English) origin. Consequently most Southernisms are either new coinages or adaptations of old words.

Many of the minted forms are folksy and colorful: *snake doctor* for dragonfly, *pulley bone* for wishbone, *calling the hogs* or *sawing gourds* for snoring. Others are straightforward and homely: an *egg turner* is a spatula, *before-day* is predawn, *hind-part-before* means reversed or backward. Some are more cryptic: "those two never did *gee haw*" means they never got along well with each other. Others are graphic: a *cat's head* is a large biscuit, a *cooling board* is the plank or slab on which a corpse is laid out.

The adaptations made by Southerners of well-known English words are equally varied and characteristic. *Puny,* for example, almost universally means "weak or of inferior size or importance." But in the South, *puny* has taken on an extended or additional meaning: "sickly or in poor health." ("She was feeling right punylike and needed a tonic.") This sort of thing can catch a speaker of another variety of English off guard and create considerable confusion. If a Yankee overheard a young fellow asking a Southern belle if he could *carry* (= escort) her to the party, our eavesdropper might wonder if she were disabled. The nuance of her response that she'd be real *proud* (= pleased, happy) to go would also be missed. Our Yankee might also be a bit nonplussed if he heard that the beau were going to play the *harp* (= harmonica) as part of the evening's entertainment. And so on. Such minor confusions are always potential among speakers of widely different dialects, though they are seldom more than a nuisance. Southern English also has a relatively large group of unique regionalized expressions— words and phrases that at one time were widespread at various stages in the settlement of the country, but which have over two or three centuries' time eroded away in the North surviving only in the South. This regionalizing process occurs to some degree in every dialect layer. It is, however, particularly characteristic of the South, whose self-conscious cultural independence and isolation has preserved certain older forms, in many cases older English dialect expressions. This has created a distinctive lexicon that is both innovative and conservative, blending the new with the old.

Most of the regionalized expressions go back to the Elizabethan era or earlier and were in general use when the colonists arrived in the New World. Shakespeare, for example, used *free-hearted,* as do a large number of Southerners, to mean "generous or liberal." *Foxfire* (= a phosphorescent light caused by fungi on decaying wood), *kinsfolk* (now usually pronounced without the *s: kinfolk*), and *like to* (as in "He fell off the roof and liketa broke his neck") are all fifteenth-century expressions still current in the South. The old term *high sheriff* was used in England well before the fifteenth century and was widely known in the Maryland hearth as early as 1648 and in Boston at least by 1708. It refers to the chief executive officer of a district or county. Even though it can legitimately be considered a Southern term, it still has not quite become fully region-alized, for eight *DARE* informants in New England used the term.

Smoothing iron (= a flatiron for pressing clothes) and *weather boarding* (= clapboards or siding) were also common in New England by the end of the seventeenth century, but by the middle of the twentieth, they were rarely used outside the South. This historical linguistic connection with New England has by no means died out; on the contrary, as we will see in the next chapter, New England and the Lower South share a small lexicon.

Some regionalized expressions of the South are surprises because they are recognized in most parts of the United States, though are seldom actually used in the North or the West. The evocative sixteenth-century cant term *rogue* is still used in the South to refer to a thief. *Spew* meaning "to gush or spray forth" is anomalously limited to the South. Its earliest meaning "to vomit" reaches back to ninth-century England, but it wasn't until relatively recently that an Ozarker could say: "The wind blowed the line down, an' spewed maw's clothes all over the berry patch." There isn't a Northerner who wouldn't understand perfectly what this meant, though he would himself rarely use this verb. Finally, a *slouch* (= a slovenly person) may be one who *piddles around* (= wastes time in aimless activity) but almost never outside the South.

Not all regionalized Southernisms have their origin in the British isles. Some are Americanisms that were also current throughout New England and other Northern areas two hundred years or so ago. Around 1800, for example, *gallinippers* (= large mosquitoes) were nipping away at Philadelphians and Bostonians, but today this mysterious word for the *Georgia piercer* now lives only in the South. Another regionalized Americanism is *barlow knife,* which was in the late eighteenth century the coveted possession of every boy from New England to New Jersey, as well as the then settled South. Huck Finn a hundred years later in Missouri found just such a treasure, excitedly claiming it to be "worth two bits in any store." This single-bladed jackknife was originally designed and made by the British manufacturer, Russell Barlow. Today no more *barlows* are manufactured, but in the South older speakers still use the name to refer to any large pocketknife. Because the earliest citations using *firedogs* (= andirons) and to *fair off* or *up* (= of weather: to become clear) are from the Northeast, they are also probably Americanisms that have become regionalized to the South.

The Southern lexicon is seasoned with a good measure of English dialect, primarily Scotch-Irish and to a lesser extent, northern English dialect. These groups of speakers played a major role in the settlement of the South.

When Ulster immigrants began arriving in 1724 in the Delaware ports, they found William Penn's colony of Quakers and German Protestants too crowded for their independent ways. Most of the arrivals quickly moved inland across the Susquehanna River settling in Cumberland County, Pennsylvania, which became their New World cradle. After the peak years of immigration, 1772–73, the arrival of Ulstermen dropped off dramatically. From their new homeland in Pennsylvania, situated in the Appalachian valley system, they migrated southward down the Shenandoah Valley into the Great Valley of Virginia, then fanning out into the hills and piedmont of the Carolinas, and westward into Kentucky and Tennessee, where many settled in the Cumberland Valley. By 1800, one-sixth of the total European population of the United States was Scotch-Irish or their descendents.

The Scotch-Irish quickly adapted to wilderness America creating a hybrid culture that has contributed many unique features to the South, including the loghouse and single farm, and the extensive use of Indian crops and forest lore. Because they were predominantly frontier farmers instead of traders and adventurers, they made up a high proportion of the European farmers in America. This meant that they had a disproportionate influence on settlement patterns and land use, which in turn helped shape the cultural and linguistic geography of the region.

Although their influence on the language has long been noted, it has never been fully demonstrated (however, see Crozier 1984). They are, for example, thought to have given American English pronunciation its "r-fulness." It is easier, however, to show the lexical traces they left, particularly in the dialects of the South.

As might be expected many of the Scotch-Irish terms in the South relate to farming or rural life. If a cow or horse is scrawny and weak, it is said to be *poor*. The sound that a horse makes is a *nicker* (primarily in the Inland South) while a sheep *blates*. Other examples are *hippin* (= a baby's diaper), to *back* (= address) an envelope or letter, and to *pet a child to death* (= to overindulge or spoil a child). *Hants* are ghosts that usually live in *hanted*—often pronounced *hainted*—houses. The *Oxford English Dictionary Supplement* notes that these were "revived" in the 1930s as variants of *haunt,* but this seems doubtful at least in the South. Twain, for example, uses *hant* in *Huckleberry Finn* (1884) and *Dialect Notes* records it in 1904.

Other English dialect survivals in the South are *goozle* or sometimes *gozzle* (= throat or gullet), *plat* or *platting* (= to braid; braided hair), and *shackly* (= unsteady, rickety, dilapidated). This last, which derives from English dialect *shackle,* "to shake or rattle," has the variants *shacklety, shackledy, ramshackly,* and *ramshackledy.* Twain uses it figuratively to mean "loose-jointed" in *Following the Equator.* "A gaunt, shackly country lout six feet high . . . had on a hideous brand-new woolen coat." All of these Scotch-Irish and English dialect expressions still have remarkable currency (except *hippin*), another indication of the conservative nature of this speech region.

The South, of course, has its own unique set of phonetic rules that affect the way its vocabulary is pronounced. But there is a small body of words that have for one reason or another come to be pronounced in a distinctive and word specific way. For example, if something, say an apple, is dried up and shrunken, a Southerner might say that it is *swiveled up* (instead of "shriveled up") or that it is *ruint* (for "ruined"). He might describe its pulpy or "pithy" interior as being *pethy,* in which case it ought to be *chunked out,* that is "chucked" or thrown out. In the South, one is likely to say *counterpin* instead of *counterpane* (= a bedspread) and *dike out* instead of *deck out* (= to dress up). To *sull* means to "sulk" or pout (a back-formation of *sullen?*); to *squinch* is to "squint" (perhaps a blend of *squint* and *pinch*); and to *agg someone on* is to "egg" or incite someone. All of these terms seem to be almost idiosyncratic pronunciations or alterations of "standard" or generally used words.

Another unusual characteristic of this lexicon is the tendency to disregard the "standard" rules that govern verb conjugations. The reason for this, of course, is that the generally lower level of education in the South simply has not filtered out such regularized but "incorrect" verb forms as *know, knowed, knowed* and *wake, waked, waked.* The standard form of the participle of *rise* is *risen,* but in the South one can hear *rose:* "The dough has finally rose." Though with less frequency, *riz* is also used for both the past and participle forms. *Wore out* and *give out* meaning "tired or exhausted" are two more examples, the latter not even existing in a standard form. As might be expected, all of these examples were used considerably more often by *DARE* informants in the South who had little formal education.

So far we have dealt with the features of this layer primarily on a linguistic level.

But as with dialects in general, the words of Southern English give us a glimpse into the folkways of this region and outline an overriding and unifying culture.

There are numerous words, for example, that are generated by the distinctive religious structure of Southern culture. Except perhaps for the Mormon West, the religious South is more homogeneous than any other section of the country, though there are exceptional areas that are very mixed, such as the piedmont of North Carolina (see Ainsley and Florin 1973). But generally speaking, the South's limited denominational diversity exists within a basic evangelistic framework, one dominated by the Baptist and, to a lesser extent, the Methodist religious establishment. Indeed, the highest density of Baptist churches in the United States virtually outlines the South (see Gaustad 1976, 57).

The late European tide of immigration that brought new tongues and new religions to the North, left nearly all of the South untouched, reinforcing its linguistic and religious solidity. It stands in further relief by its notable scarcity of Catholics and Jews. The South defined in map 4.5 closely corresponds with the Southern religious region as derived by Zelinsky (1961, 193). Both Zelinsky's map and 4.5 for the most part exclude southern Indiana, which is very much a part of the South I (map 4.3) and Inland South (map 6.3) layers.

The Bible Belt, as H. L. Mencken aptly dubbed it, takes its religion seriously, conservatively, and literally. Its seriousness is reflected in an unusually high church membership. And its conservatism lies in its intense concern for getting back to the "fundamentals," stressing faith, morality, evangelism, and personal salvation. For most of the South, the Bible is an infallible document to be taken at face value. Where else would a group of people—to be sure a tiny, fanatical group—take Mark 16:18 literally and handle deadly snakes and drink poison to prove the strength of their faith?

Baptist (in the South frequently pronounced [bæb tɪs(t)] or [bæb dɪs(t)]) preaching began in North Carolina in 1755. Its evangelistic approach spread like wildfire with the settlement of the South. Because of the isolation of the frontier settlements, a preacher came round infrequently and people had to travel many miles to hear him. Revival meetings became marathons of preaching, prayer, and socializing, usually lasting several days. The popularity of these *protracted meetings* lay in their ability to satisfy both the social and religious needs of a scattered but gregarious people. Often the preacher was a farmer, self-taught, zealous, and at times even eloquent as he preached about the temptations of *Old Scratch* or the *bad man* and the everlasting fire of *torment*. Such unschooled evangelists, sometimes called *jackleg preachers,* were instrumental in the growth of the Baptist South.

The *big meeting,* as it was also called, required the construction of an *arbor* or *brush arbor,* which was usually a simple open-sided structure with a roof made of boughs to keep off the sun and light rain. Given its duration and the distance most people had to travel to get to it, a *camp meeting* (another synonym) usually meant staying several days, sleeping on the ground in a makeshift bed called a *pallet* and eating communal meals, which came to be called *dinner-on-the-ground(s). Pallets* were used in Chaucer's time (fourteenth century) and were usually made of straw, the earlier version of the word being French *paillet* (*paille* = straw). They were also known in Boston in the seventeenth century, though the term is little used in New England today.

Unlike the staid meetings of the typical New England church, revivalism was an outpouring of religious enthusiasm and meetings were often tumultuous, which fit well the temperament of backwoods converts who were naturally less restrained than their New England counterparts. The *amen corner* is in effect an outgrowth of this enthusiasm. Also called the *amen pew,* it is a front row section of church seats reserved for particularly zealous members who lead the responsive "amens." The amen corner is used throughout the South and in scattered parts of Pennsylvania and the North Central states, but it does not seem to have had a particular name until the middle of the nineteenth century.

Another special row of seats created by revivalist enthusiasm is the thoroughly Southern *mourner's bench,* which is a feature primarily of revival meetings and is reserved for the mourners. These mourners, however, are not lamenting the death of a loved one, but are those who publicly repent their sins. This use of *mourner* is also Southern. Despite its alternate name, *anxious seat,* those who availed themselves of it may have found something beyond anxiety, or as one writer put it in an 1848 issue of the *Ladies' Repository:* "She loves the mourner's bench, for there she found peace and pardon."

Such was the promise of the *altar call* or *invitation* which challenged the sinner to come to the anxious bench to be "prayed through to victory." Victory meant that you had *come through* or *gotten religion* and were *born again.* This intense personal experience of "salvation" is at the heart of much of the Southern religious experience.[1]

Because of the dominant rural character of Southern culture, a relatively large vocabulary of rural expressions helps regionally unify its speech. Not surprisingly, a major portion of this vocabulary relates to farming.

Though most farms in the South are small and run by a single family, some of the larger farms employ workers or *hands.* During the seventeenth and eighteenth centuries this term, which is also used on western ranches, was much more widespread. During slavery, *hand* usually referred to a black field slave, but after abolition it referred to any sharecropper or farm worker. Another legacy of antebellum labor is the term *overseer,* which referred to the man in charge of the field slaves. Today in the South and occasionally farther north, *overseer* is commonly used for the supervisor or boss of a group of workmen.

A farmhand's chores usually begin at *before-day,* often shortened to '*fore-day* or '*fo'-day,* when the sun is still below the horizon, and they may last until *evening,* that is, until mid to late afternoon, or even sometimes until *dusky dark* or twilight. *Feeding time* or "chore time" involves a variety of tasks, not merely feeding the *critters.* A citified linguist who, at least in the eyes of a hard-working *bottomland* farmer, probably never *hit-a-lick* in his life, would in no time have his notebook full of dialect words and his *brogans* full of manure ("Don't cut your foot," he might be warned) if he were to follow a hand around for a bit.

The itinerary might include *juicing* (= milking) the cows, then letting them out of the *cowlot* to feed in the pasture; then back to the barn to *mark* or castrate the young *male cow,* perhaps giving it a *lick* (= a hard blow) to make it cooperate; then out to feed the pigs, their *rooters* sniffing the air in anticipation, and the old *male hog,* kept in a separate pen, brandishing its *tushes* impotently. (The boar "whettez [= sharpens, whets] his whyte tuschez," our learned linguist might think to himself, quoting the fourteenth-century poem *Gawain and the Green Knight.) Sooey,* a word used to call hogs that even a Northerner might be familiar with, our note-jotting outlander would be surprised to hear used to drive a stray dog away.

After a substantial lunch washed down with a *cold drink* (= a carbonated soft drink), there would be some repair work to do on the *weather boarding* or wood siding of the house, though the broken pales of the white *paling fence* would have to be done another time. This latter term for a picket fence was current as far north as Pennsylvania and Ohio during the 1930s when the linguistic atlas collected data there, but thirty years later it had apparently receded southward, becoming even more regionalized to the South.

For at least two centuries beehives in the South have been made of hollow sections of gum trees. The association is so strong in fact that any beehive is called a *beegum* or *gum.* In this imaginary tour of a Southern farm, another farm hand might be constructing a *bee gum* to increase the harvest of honey. Having picked out a section of tree trunk that was suitably *doty* (= decayed) in the center and had none of the sticky *rosum* (or *rosin* = tree sap or pitch) of the living tree, he places it on a *sawrack* and saws off a two-foot section. He clears out the decayed wood from its nearly hollow interior and with a long chisel evens out the concave surface. Then near the middle he bores four holes at the compass points so that two sticks can be inserted through the gum at right angles to each other. When the log section is set up on one end, these horizontal sticks will act as supports from which the bees suspend their brood combs. The plank lid or "head," which is a square piece of plywood, is set on top and held in place. He then cuts V-shaped notches on one side at the bottom to serve as entrances. Although the name for this simple hive will probably survive for some time to come, this original construction is already virtually lost (see Wigginton 1973, 32–46).

In the meantime, another farmhand is forking a *piece of a load* of hay into the *scuttle hole* or hay chute of the *loft.*

The weeds along the paling fence need cutting, so the farmer's son is set to the task of sharpening the rusty *brush blade* or *mowing blade* (this use of *blade* being a Southernism) with a *whetrock* and then scything the knee-high weeds using an ancient but effective technique. This he does with some grumbling, however, for a friend is waiting to go *gigging,* a method of spearfishing known in the South at least since Lewis and Clark used it in their journals of their famous expedition (1803).

Children's play also has a considerable regional vocabulary. The farmer's son, for example, would undoubtedly know how to play *cat ball,* a bat-and-ball game with as few as four players and having numerous variations in the way it's played. In marble play, he would call the shooter marble—the marble that knocks the others out of the ring—a *taw* or *toy,* and the lag line used to determine who shoots first, the *taw* or *toy line. Mumble-peg,* also traditionally a boys' game, is the Southern and Western version of *mumblety-peg,* a game in which the blade of a jackknife is flipped so that it sticks in the ground.

Tit-tat-too is a variant name used in the South for "tick-tack-toe," just as *ring-around-the-roses* is primarily a minor Southern variant of the more widely used "ring-around-the-*rosy* (or *rosies*)." The common game of blindman's buff is usually called simply *blindfold.* In the universal game of hide-and-seek, children in the South and West call the place where "it" waits while the others hide, the *base.* Also in the South one is likely to hear *skin up* or *skinny up* a tree, instead of the more generally used "shin" or "shinny up." This expression meaning to climb (a tree) by holding alternately with the arms or hands and legs was used by Twain in the irregular past tense: "The beaver skun up a tree."

A toy, especially one for a young child, is often called a *play pretty.* A *poppet* or *corn shuck doll,* for example, is a play purty. At one time, children made, perhaps with the help of an adult, small toy merry-go-rounds called *flying jennies.* The full-blown versions, the elaborately decorated merry-go-rounds at carnivals and state fairs, were originally powered by a mule or *jenny* and were also called *flying jennies* or *jinnies.*

One of the most universal forms of children's play is to imagine or pretend they are heroines and heroes in distant lands. In the South, the usual way of saying this is to use *play like:* "Let's play like we're captured by pirates. . . ." This expression undoubtedly goes back at least to Chaucer's time when it meant "to act the part."

In addition to the numerous names of Southern foods already mentioned, there are many other terms for domestic items and comestibles. A bed cover, for example, filled with down or wool is usually called a *comfort* and the bedspread is a *counterpin* or very occasionally *county pin.* The round flat cover on an old-fashioned wood-burning stove is known as the *eye* and the handle used to lift the eye so that the stove can be stoked is, logically enough, the *eye lifter.* Not far from the stove and cooking area is a *slop bucket* used mainly for "edible" garbage or food waste.

In the old-fashioned *cook room* or kitchen, the Southern cook might be seen removing the *hulls* or outer covering of beans. *Hull* in the South-and-West also refers to a walnut shell. Lima beans are known as *butter beans;* sweet or green peppers are *bell peppers.* Though coleslaw is a widely known kind of cabbage salad, in the South it is frequently called simply *slaw.* Poaching eggs is also pretty universal, though the Southern cook is likely to say "*porching* eggs." In a properly porched egg, the *yellow* or yolk will still be liquid.

Eggs and milk are part of the ingredients of a favorite Southern dessert, *cobbler,* which is a deep-dish fruit pie with a thick biscuit crust on top. A good farm cook would always make sure that the fresh whole milk to be added in the cobbler crust did not taste like the weeds that cows occasionally graze on. Such milk is frequently called *bitter-weed milk* after the name of the plant that imparts the unwanted flavor. A rich peach cobbler can sorely test the unspoken rule of good manners that makes a person reluctant to eat the *manners piece,* the last piece of food left on a plate.

Because of the general Southern inclination for prohibition of alcoholic beverages, moonshining or the illegal manufacture of liquor has flourished and become a tradition, especially in the mountain South. In the South as a whole, moonshine is frequently called *white lightning,* which is apparently a very recent coinage probably not entering the lexicon before Prohibition. One who excessively drinks *white mule,* as it has also been called in the South since the late nineteenth century, is a *sot,* a term in use since the Old English period, but in America widespread only in the South. A sot or drunkard is said to *funnel* liquor *down* or *in.*

A significant part of the South lexicon relates to health, a fact that has important implications in the way patients, especially "folk speakers," communicate with their health-care providers. A doctor who knew only standard speech, for example, especially if he were a non-Southerner, might completely misunderstand a patient who said that she hadn't *come sick* last month, since that expression does not mean to become sick, but is a euphemism for menstruating. Obviously scenarios like this can be multiplied indefinitely. Clearly the effect of regional and folk speech on this kind of communication can be profound.

In the old days and perhaps even in some rural places today, an important health-care provider for pregnant women was a *granny woman,* sometimes also called a *granny doctor.*[2] She was a kind of gynecologist/midwife, usually an older woman who had considerable experience from *birthing* (= giving birth to) her own large family. Often her medical experience encompassed the entire village, having *grannied* or *birthed* (= to serve as midwife to) one or two generations of babies.

Often one of the effects on a woman of birthing a lot of children is *broken veins* or "varicose veins," also widely called in folk speech *very close veins,* since the veins are close to the surface, a good example of folk etymology. After a birth friends and relatives make a *sitting visit* to the new *mammy* (two expressions not much used anymore) and wonder out loud who the baby *favors* (= resembles). This sitting visit should not be confused with the final *sitting up* or *sitting up party,* which is a Southern wake when friends and family sit up with the corpse the night before burial.

In the South if a person sneezes, a sympathetic bystander is likely to say *scat,* the Southern equivalent of *gesundheit.* Both expressions are a wish for good health, the latter more or less directly from German (*gesundheit* = health), the former by way of folk mythology. It is a common and very old notion that spirits and demons can enter a person's body through the open mouth, especially when one yawns, which may be why it is "good manners" to cover the mouth. *Scat* is probably a command to stay away directed at those unseen *boogermen* and hobgoblins that may attack a person while vulnerable during a sneeze.

In the South if a person feels *wore out* (= tired, exhausted) and "ginerally" *bad* (= unwell), it may be because she or he *took sick,* perhaps with the *agers* (= ague, chills, and fever). This would make her feel pretty *puny,* and if it lasted a week or two and she was *running off* a bit (= had diarrhea), she might *fall off* some (= lose weight). She'd probably not feel like doing much but would just kind of *puny around* or go about in a dull and listless way.

Many Southern terms relating to health are very old and not much used anywhere else, and, despite their currency in this region, are approaching relic status. *Hurting,* for example, was used in Middle English to refer to an injury or hurt (the verbal noun of *hurten* = to injure or hurt), but did not stay in the mainstream of English, surviving primarily in the South.

In Southern English, any kind of pustular eruption of the skin, like eczema or impetigo, is called *tetter.* This word despite its regionally restricted usage is very old, having been in English since the eighth century and stretching its etymological roots even further back to the common ancestor of the Sanskrit version, *dadru.* The suppuration of such skin maladies is often still graphically called *corruption,* a term that the *Oxford English Dictionary* considers obsolete, having no record of it after 1642. Corruption may also exude from other kinds of ailments, such as a *rising,* which is a boil or abscess, or a *run-around,* which is a whitlow.

Given the very rural nature of the South, it is not surprising to find a large number of regional names for wild plants and animals. In the forests of Appalachia and the piney woods of the Gulf states a *misting rain* is perfect for growing mushrooms and *frogstools* (= toadstools) on the decaying matter of the forest floor. It also helps the growth of certain fungi on decaying wood that produce a ghostlike phosphorescent light called *foxfire.* This term arrived from England in colonial times when it had considerable currency throughout the country. It has since virtually died out in New England and the northern United States.

In contrast to a *misting rain* is the *toad-strangler,* a rain so heavy that, according to folk humor, it strangles the dryland critters like *toad-frogs* (= toads). A toad-strangler is more commonly called in the South a *gullywasher,* which can sweep away considerable debris and earth before the weather *fairs off* (= clears up). This latter term was also used in the Northeast in the nineteenth century, but today is primarily restricted to Southern speech. Even though the sky may *fair up* and the wind may be *laying,* a winter day in the South will usually still be *airish* (= chilly, cool). (A person who puts on airs and is remote and cool is sometimes said to be *airish* or *airy.*) But seldom will there be an actual *biting frost* (= a severe frost).

A rich spawning ground for Southern flora and fauna is in and along a *branch.* This shibboleth meaning a small stream or tributary of a creek or river was used from the beginning of the South's colonization, appearing in Virginia as early as 1624 and in North Carolina in 1663. The first choice of the Southern pioneer was to settle near a branch, which not only provided fertile bottomland, but was a limitless source of cold and pure *branch water,* a term Northerners usually associate only with bourbon. It was here that the settlers encountered *spring frogs* (= green frog or leopard frog), *terrapins,* and *crawfish.*

Turtles, which are not native to the British Isles, were an uncommon sight to the early colonists. It followed naturally that the early Virginians adopt a native, specifically Algonquian, name, probably *torope* from the Virginian dialect of Algonquian. The diminutive of this name produced *terrapin,* sometimes pronounced *tarrypin.* Also of early Southern colonial origin is *crawfish.* As early as 1624 when Captain John Smith mentioned crawfish in his Virginia journals, this crustacean was an intimate, albeit small part of the culture. It became, for example, a notable feature of Southern cuisine, such as *crawfish stew* which is well known in Louisiana. In most of the South, to *crawfish out* of something is to back out of an agreement or back down from a position, a reference to the peculiar retrograde movement of the crawfish.

The branch is also home to *minners, wiggle-tails,* and *gallinippers.* Wiggletails are mosquito larvae and grow up to be gallinippers, which when not feeding on people are in turn eaten by *snake doctors.* This odd name for the dragonfly did not appear in print until 1862 in a source which places it in Virginia, though Kurath (*WG,* 30) has reason to believe that it has been current since colonial times, having spread simultaneously from the Pennsylvania and Virginia hearths. The atlas map (*WG,* fig. 141) shows it to be confined to the Lower North and Virginia Piedmont regions. *DARE* evidence, corroborated in part by Wood (1971, map 16), shows that it has spread to all of the South, where it is generally current among most groups of speakers.

Other common kinds of insects with Southern names are the *green fly* (= the common green iridescent housefly or greenbottle fly), the *dirt dauber* (= any of various wasps that build mud nests), and the *chinch bug,* which is either the common bedbug or the small black and white insect (genus *Blissus*) destructive to wheat and corn.

The South also has many regionalisms for certain birds. *Didapper* is the name used for the dabchick or other small grebes. Variant pronunciation accounts for the Southernisms *thrash* (= thrush) and *killdee* (= killdeer). As with a majority of folk terms for plants and animals, some innate characteristic is the origin of the name. Thus, the ground-nesting meadowlark is best known in the South as the *field lark* and the swallow or chimney swift is called a *chimney-sweep(er)* from its habit of attaching its nest inside of a chimney. A *carrion crow* is not a crow (except in England) but a vulture, the carrion eater. Likewise, a *rain crow* is not a crow at all but is a yellow-billed or black-billed cuckoo. Its name comes from its supposed habit of becoming particularly noisy just before a rain. A cardinal is called a *red bird* for obvious reasons and the red-tailed hawk is often called a *rabbit hawk* from its propensity for dining on rabbits.

Chicken snakes have a supposed propensity for young chicks and eggs, but this variety of colubrid snake, also called the "rat snake," is probably more help than hindrance in its cleanup of the mice and rats that live in barns and other farm buildings. Even so, its name as well as its alternate, *egg snake,* testify to firsthand experience with the reptile's habits.

Among Southern names for plants is this mixed assortment: *old maid flowers* or *old maids* for zinnias, *dewberries* for any of several kinds of berries related to blackberries, and *multiplying onions* for winter onions. *Post oak,* any of several American oaks with moisture resistant wood suitable for fence posts, grows almost everywhere in the United States, but this name for it occurs primarily in the South.

The Southern lexicon is also characterized by a handful of unusual metaphorical or comparative phrases. A very mean or malicious person is often said to be *meaner than the devil.* Some people might even feel that he is not worth the *salt in his bread* or that he isn't worth *killing,* a particularly repulsive Southern expression.

If a Southerner says that there is a *dead cat on the line* he means that something "fishy" is going on, probably with reference to a catfish on a fishing line. If, for example, a couple *jumped the broom stick* (= married) secretly and the bride's mother suspected something, she might say that "there's a dead cat on the line." Formerly couples who were getting married literally jumped together over a broom handle as part of the ceremony, a symbolic rite of passage into domesticity.

In the "old" days (pre-1970s), the expectation was that the wife had charge of the house chores and if the house looked like a *storm hit it,* the husband might say that he had a *crow to pick* with her, the Southern version of the almost universal phrase, "to have a *bone* to pick with someone." If she did not take kindly to being *blessed out* (= scolded, rebuked), an argument or *fuss* might ensue.

If *fussing* became a regular thing between them, people might say that they just don't *gee* or *gee haw,* meaning that they don't get along well with each other. This last unusual expression derives from the calls used in the South to get a plowing team of horses, mules, or oxen to turn to the right, *gee,* and to the left, *haw* (see Jones 1973, 77). When the members of the team did not turn in unison at these commands, that is, when they did not "gee" or "haw," there was considerable disarray and commotion, not to mention the cussing done by the driver. It was a natural progression to transfer the reference of these terms to any sort of quarrel or fight.

A miscellany of Southernisms remains, but each is an expression of a small aspect of the South.

If someone is bitten by a dog or snake, he is said to be *dogbit* or *snakebit.*

If clothes shrink or a few people squeeze into a tight place, they *draw up.*

To splash or spill something is to *slosh* it, perhaps a canny blend of *slop* and *slush.*

A *johnny* and a *commode* are toilets; a *johnny house* is an outhouse. The barrel of a pen is a *staff,* earrings are *earbobs,* and little *boogers* are children.

An exclamation especially favored by old and rural speakers meaning "I vow" or "I swear" is "I *swanny,*" which the *OED* suggests derives from northern English dialect *Is' wan ye* (= I shall warrant you [that] . . .). "I *swan*" is also used in the South but by no means exclusively. Another kind of exclamation that is a favorite among many older Southerners connotes disgust or anger and begins with *dad,* a euphemism for "god" in such expressions as *dad blasted, dad burned, dad durned, -blamed, -shamed, -seized, -swamped, -snatched, -binged, -sizzled, -ratted, -rotted, -gummed,* and *-fetched.*

A common exclamatory greeting heard on Christmas morning in the South since at least the early nineteenth century is *Christmas gift!*

A person with piercing or sharp eyes has *keen-eyes* or is *keen-eyed.* If she closes and opens them rapidly, she is *batting her eyes.* This latter expression refers to the fluttering of a bird's wings and goes back to an Old French term used in falconry, *battre,* which means "to beat the wings impatiently and flutter away from the fist or perch."

Southerners often express a preference by *rather* or *ruther* as a noun: "If I had my rather I'd buy the blue parasol." And they usually say "quarter (or fifteen) *till* eight" o'clock. An unusual linguistic construction is the use of *all the* with an adjective functioning as a noun, as in "That's *all the far* or *fast* or *high* it can fly." (Compare the Inland North version of this that uses the quasi-comparative form, "all the farther.")

Generally speaking, then, the lexicon of the South I and II layers tends to be old, having very few recent coinages, virtually no slang and maintaining many terms that, despite their currency, are practically relics—old expressions that were once widely used but have died out everywhere but in the South where they continue to wane. In this regard, it is in contrast with the Northern layers except New England and has a more rural, folk flavor emphasized by certain usages, particularly verbs considered "nonstandard" and "uneducated." Also in contrast to the North, the lexicon has a sizable number of expressions relating to religion, has almost no foreign borrowings, and is replete with words of Scotch-Irish and English dialect origin. All this testifies not only to the uniqueness of the Southern lexicon, but to the linguistic division between the two major American regions.

The South-and-West Layer

Like the North, the South shares some of its lexicon with the West, though by comparison it is quite small. Every Northern layer, except those in the Northeast, extends well into the West (see map 7.3), whereas neither of the Southern layers we've discussed reaches much farther than New Mexico and southeastern Colorado. This is not too surprising given the insularity of the South prior to the twentieth century. Though this situation has changed considerably since the turn of the century, the effect of the South's historical isolation on the spread of language and on the creation of persisting speech boundaries was decisive.

While 88 of 195 isoglosses in the Northern layers also cover the West, there are only about 23 Southern isoglosses (out of 185) that extend significantly westward (map 4.8). Nine of these 23 isoglosses (listed in app. A) extend considerably north of the Ohio River, covering the area that Kurath calls "South and Midland," and are to a large extent responsible for a secondary line reminiscent of the Upper North boundary (map 3.16). These isoglosses—particularly *singletree, doubletree, hull,* and *seed*—are widespread except in the Upper North, which appears as a conspicuous blank space in their individual maps.

The primary line of map 4.8 approximates the primary boundary of the South except that it includes the extreme southern portion of Ohio and is disrupted by mixed numbers in western Illinois, suggesting a transitional area. The line is also disrupted somewhere in northern West Virginia but for a different reason. Here the distinct meandering ridge through southern Ohio and western West Virginia begins to fade into a gradually sloped plateau of numbers in Maryland and Virginia.

Lexicon

Except for one or two expressions like *sowbelly,* which is reminiscent of the common use of pork in Southern cuisine, this minor layer has little that is specifically Southern

4.8. The South-and-West Layer Based on 23 *DARE* Isoglosses. Primary, secondary, and tertiary boundaries.

about it. Even so, several of the expressions probably originated in the South and spread from there westward and sometimes northward. *Roasting ears,* for example, which are ears of sweet corn ripe enough to roast and eat, is a Southernism first recorded in Virginia (1650) and then in Kentucky and Alabama (1812 and 1854 respectively). It subsequently spread northward to the Upper North boundary (cf. *WG,* fig. 135) and throughout much of the West.

Likewise *calaboose* (= a jail) is also of Southern origin. The earliest printed example of it (1792) refers to the "Callebouse at Mobille," Alabama. Other references place it in New Orleans in 1840 (as a verb), Cincinnati in 1857, Nevada in 1866, and Oklahoma in 1898. Borrowed from the Spanish *calabozo* (= a dungeon) perhaps in Mobile, which was originally a Spanish town, it is one of the few European loanwords in Southern speech.

Early citations also suggest that *clabber* and *mash* originated in the South. *Clabber* or sour curdled milk is now the most common term for this food that has no nationwide or literary name. Shortened from the New England *bonnyclabber,* it ultimately derives from Gaelic *clabbar,* which means "mud" or "thick." *Mash* meaning to smash ("He mashed his thumb with the hammer") or to press or push ("She mashed the elevator button for the fourth floor") first appears in print in two Gullah sources, 1867 (coastal South Carolina) and 1880 (coastal Georgia). Moreover, the *Dictionary of Jamaican English* gives an 1862 citation. This sense, then, may have originated with black creole speakers, spreading into white Southern speech and into its present-day extension in the Lower North and the West.

Early records of *slough* (= an inlet or narrow stretch of backwater) locate it in Massachusetts (1665), Charleston (1714), and Virginia (1738). Today it is rarely used in Massachusetts or any other northeastern state, though its meaning is probably known in most areas of the country. Similarly *sultry* is an adjective that is probably known everywhere as referring to oppressively hot and humid weather, but is actually primarily used in the South-and-West. The historical record of this word, which goes back to Elizabethan English, is far too sparse to suggest its American place of origin.

Of course not all of the lexicon originated in the South. It is very likely that the Pennsylvania hearth had much to do with the spread of several of these isoglosses. *Belly-buster* in particular probably originated farther north with the other "belly" expressions that refer to the method used in children's sledding of taking a running start and throwing oneself onto the sled abdomen or belly first and riding downhill in this prone position. This term was later transferred to the kind of dive in which the front of the body hits flat against the water surface.

It is also likely that several of the terms were established simultaneously in the hearth areas south of New England. This seems to apply particularly to those words that are old but have strong dialect counterparts in New England and the Upper North. *Shock* (= a bundle or pile of hay) has been in English at least since the fourteenth century when it referred to bundled sheaves of grain. The Upper North counterpart is *cock* or *haycock. Singletree* (= the swinging bar to which the traces of a harness are attached), which was the standard term used in the Sears and Roebuck catalogues around 1900 and which is an alteration of the fifteenth-century-term *swingletree,* remains a regionalism by virtue of the rural Upper North's preference for *whippletree* or *whiffletree.*

The origins, geographical and otherwise, of much of the South-and-West lexicon are obscure. But it seems clear that this minor layer is predominantly Southern, though it shows little of the character that we associate with Southernness.

The Upper and Lower South

The South falls into two broad physiographic and cultural regions that have influenced the patterns of language on the land: the Highland or Upper South and the Lowland or Lower South.

The South's physical features are more varied than any other section of the country ranging from the highest mountains in the eastern United States—the Blue Ridge Mountains—to the swampy lowlands of the Louisiana bayous and the Florida Everglades; from the lush bottomlands of the Kentucky Bluegrass to the pine barrens of Georgia and the sand hills of South Carolina; from the Virginia and North Carolina tidewater veined with salt creeks to the ancient Appalachians and Ozarks with their coves and hollows.

This variform and pronounced topography (see map 4.9) was a major influence on the development of the South's human regions. Since the shape of the land naturally channels or impedes the flow of settlement, in a general way the dialect regions pattern after the land regions. To simplify things for a moment, the physiography of the South is divided into two major provinces—the highlands and the lowlands—that are closely related to the two-part division in the South's cultural and linguistic geography.

The *Highland South* covers the Appalachian and Ozark mountain systems and includes most of the piedmont of the Atlantic South. Appalachia reaches from Upstate New York to central Alabama, some nine hundred miles of rugged highlands lying roughly northeast-southwest. This broad region about two hundred miles wide has three parallel physiographic provinces of relatively high altitude each having a distinctive topography: the narrow eastern flank of mountains made up primarily of the Blue Ridge Mountains, the Appalachian Valley system, and the Appalachian Plateau extending from western Tennessee and Kentucky into West Virginia and Pennsylvania (see map 4.9).

Perhaps the most important of these provinces in terms of the settlement of the South is the Appalachian Valley, which is made up of a series of parallel ridges and valleys. The first of these valleys immediately to the west of the Blue Ridge is the Great Valley, which runs virtually the entire length of Appalachia and acted as a conduit to pioneer migration. Beginning in Pennsylvania as the Lebanon or Cumberland Valley and continuing as the Shenandoah in Virginia and the Tennessee Valley in Tennessee, settlers, notably Germans and Scotch-Irish, moved down the hilly Great Valley and established themselves on some of the best farmland in Appalachia. These hard working frontier yeomen, who also settled much of the piedmont plateau to the east, were relatively isolated from the tidewater aristocracy of eastern Virginia and the Carolinas.

The Appalachian Plateau, also known as the Cumberland Plateau in Tennessee and Kentucky and the Allegheny Plateau in Pennsylvania and New York, is the west-

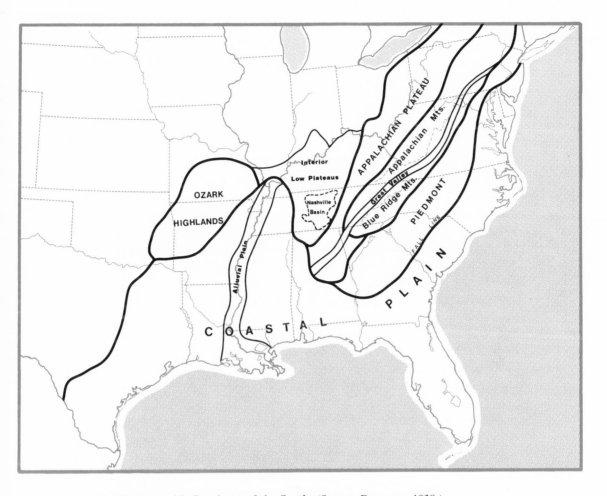

4.9. Physiographic Provinces of the South. (Source: Fenneman 1938.)

ernmost province of Appalachia. For the most part, level land is scarce here making it necessary for communities to squeeze into the small level spaces in the stream valleys.

The Ozark-Ouachita highlands are closely associated with Appalachia both in terms of topography and human settlement. In effect they mirror the provinces of the Appalachians, except that they run east and west instead of northeast and southwest. They also lack a counterpart to the relatively high Blue Ridge Mountains. Like the Appalachian Plateau, the Ozark section is an eroded plateau of hilly irregular land. The Arkansas River Valley is comparable to the Great Valley and the Ouachita Mountains to the south resemble the folded parallel ridges and valleys of the Appalachian Valley system.

Broadly speaking, the highland South corresponds to the Upper South cultural and speech region, though it is by no means homogeneous. As we will see, it is broken up by the inland plateaus, particularly the Bluegrass region of Kentucky and the Nashville Basin area of Tennessee.

The *Lowland South* is made up primarily of the tidewater of Virginia and North Carolina and the coastal plain, which extends from Maryland to Texas. This is only a portion of a very long physiographic province, the coastal plain that stretches from Cape Cod to Mexico, varying in width from less than a mile to over five hundred miles. Given its numerous rivers that facilitated settlement and trade and its attendant warm, moist climate, this was the natural province of the Old South, of cotton plantations and a culture that fancied itself aristocratic and genteel. Today it roughly corresponds to the Lower South cultural and linguistic region.

The boundary between the upland piedmont plateau and the lowland coastal plain is called the "fall line" (map 4.9). This "line," which varies in width and is perhaps better thought of as a narrow belt of transition, was the ancient shoreline of the geological past. As the sea receded depositing sand and other sediments it left the coastal plain with its own unique topography and composition that subsequently influenced the human geography. Running along the eastern edge of the fall line are the sand hills that further accentuated the division between the highlands to the west and the coastal lowlands.

The Mississippi floodplain interrupts the gulf section of the coastal plain. This area, whose rich alluvial land and river transportation was ideal for cotton plantations, is a belt of bottomland about fifty miles wide that is periodically flooded by the Mississippi. It extends from the confluence of the Ohio and Mississippi rivers southward to Louisiana where it flares out into a broad delta land. This physical province influenced the formation of the Delta South speech region (see chap. 5).

In eastern Texas the coastal plain continues until it meets the higher and arid interior plains, the southernmost section of the Great Plains province, which covers the entire middle section of the United States. This physiographic boundary marks the end of land and climate suitable to plantation agriculture and consequently closely corresponds to the western extension of the Lower South.

Influenced by the physiographic patterns, two broad streams of migration settled the South, one branch flowing from the Chesapeake Bay hearth into the *Upper* (or *Yeoman*) *South,* and the other spreading from the Carolina tidewater core into the *Lower* (or *Plantation*) *South* (see map 4.2). This general settlement pattern established the two major regions of the South whose differing cultural areas are shown in map 4.10.

The *Upper South* cultural region covers most of the piedmont area from Virginia to Georgia and includes adjacent Appalachia from West Virginia to northern Georgia. Kentucky and Tennessee are a complex part of the Upper South each being divided into three subareas. The Ozark Mountains of northwestern Arkansas, southern Missouri, and western Oklahoma are the farthest western extension of the Upper South. The speech of this region will be discussed in chapter 6.

The cultural *Lower South* includes the tidewater and coastal plains of Virginia, the Carolinas, and Georgia; the gulf plains of Alabama, Mississippi, Louisiana, and eastern Texas; and the lowland areas of Arkansas and western Tennessee. Southern Florida and southern Louisiana are separate culture and dialect areas. This quilt-work region is the subject of the next chapter.

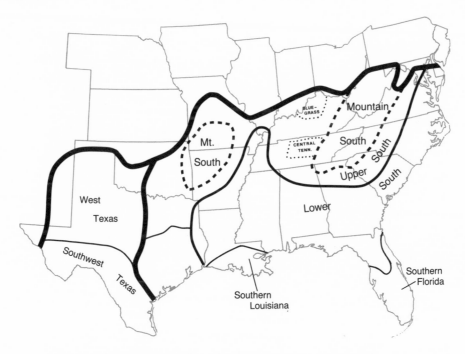

4.10. The Cultural Subregions of the South. (Source: Gastil 1975.)

The bipartite structure of the South is also evident in its overall settlement pattern, it being axiomatic in regional geography that settlement patterns affect human geography. Who settles which area to a great degree establishes the underlying structure of the culture. Map 4.11 shows the population density of the South for the first three decades that a U.S. census was taken: 1790, 1810, and 1830. In this map the "who" cannot be distinguished; only "how many" in an area is shown. But in a general way the rate at which a region is settled also affects the dimensions of that region.

We have already noted how the pause in the western expansion in Georgia first near the Ogeechee and later at the Chattahoochee established dialect boundaries along those rivers. Map 4.11 shows this in terms of population density for the years 1790 and 1830 respectively.

The map also reveals a portion of the Lower South boundary through North Carolina and Virginia. Earlier censuses, had they been taken, might have more accurately shown this boundary. Other Lower South speech landmarks evident here are the central island of population in Alabama and the crescent of settlement along the Mississippi delta in Louisiana.

In the Upper South we can also see the outlines of the Hoosier apex in terms of the 1830 population density. In addition, the map shows that the Upper South, particularly the Kentucky Bluegrass and Nashville Basin areas, which form minor Upper South subregions, was settled well before the Gulf portion of the Lower South.

Because the years of the censuses are arbitrary, at least with respect to accurately

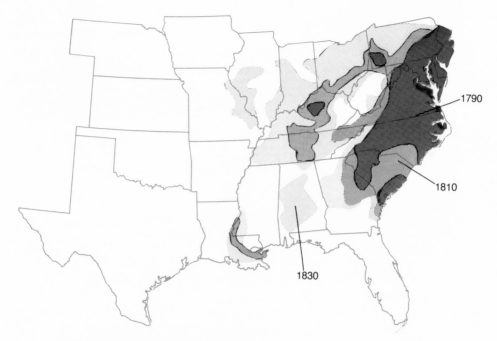

4.11. Settlement of the South, 1790–1830

measuring the geography of momentary pools of settlement, only some of the boundaries and regions are accidentally captured by this map. A more in-depth study of population expansion as it flowed westward and became momentarily dammed up is needed, one which is not so closely bound to the census years. The point of the map here, however, is that the South was settled in such a way as to create two general regions that correspond closely with the dialect regions: the Lower and Upper South.

Southern English is one of the most distinctive of American dialects and contrasts with the speech of the North both lexically and geographically (fig. 3). Its lexicon is replete with older expressions that are in effect relics, in widespread use in early America, but by the twentieth century almost completely gone in the North. Many regionalisms of the South are miniature windows into the culture and history: words relating to religion and cuisine; words of Scotch-Irish and English dialect origin; a lexicon that is generally more rural and euphemistic, with fewer slang expressions and foreign loanwords, than the North's.

This lexical contrast with the North is reflected in the geography that has characterized a basic division in American culture almost since colonial times, formalized in the Mason-Dixon Line. Some of the clearest linguistic boundaries defining this North-South divide are found in two strong layers, called here South I and II, which also reveal an internal structure that is important in the definition of the South's subregions, notably the Delta South, the Atlantic South, and the Lower and Upper South. Surprisingly like the North, the South also extends into the West, though to a much lesser extent.

Layers
South I (map 4.3)
South II (map 4.5)
South-and-West (map 4.8)

Regions

Fig. 3. Summary of the layers and regions of the South

Finally the South divides into two major dialect regions that roughly correspond to its physical geography: the Upper South and the Lower South, which are the subjects of the next two chapters.

NOTES

1. For an intimate look at the religion of the Southern folk, see Gillespie 1982.
2. For a firsthand account of granny women, see Wigginton 1973, 274–303.

CHAPTER 5

The Lower South

Unlike the Upper North's relatively unified sweep of migration originating from a single core area, the Deep or Lower South had three fountainheads of settlement: tidewater Virginia; coastal South Carolina, particularly the Charleston area; and New Orleans. As a result the Lower South is a patchwork of dialects.

The tidewater Virginia fountainhead is the earliest source of Southern speech and several of its varieties, such as Kurath's Virginia Piedmont and Delmarva subdialects, and to a lesser extent the Atlantic South. However, much of the evidence for the Mid-Atlantic dialects is indirect, appearing primarily in the internal structure of the major layers, such as the South I and II and Lower South layers. Consequently we will discuss Mid-Atlantic speech toward the end of this chapter.

The Atlantic South: Settlement

As the Virginia and Maryland tidewater colonies flourished, the Lower South's second cultural hearth was just beginning to take form (1670) at Charles Town on the South Carolina coast. Although it no longer holds the position it once did, Charleston was culturally and economically the center of coastal plain settlement from the Cape Fear area in North Carolina to central Georgia. Charleston was to this area of the Atlantic South, what Boston was (and is) to Eastern New England.

But it is a very different city from Boston. From its first boatload of English, Irish, and Welsh colonists, Charleston had a mixed company of settlers, unlike Boston. To non-Southerners it seems a foreign city with its "piazzas" and second-story balconies, its tiled roofs and stuccoed walls reminiscent of the West Indies and southern France, not to mention its striking dialect.

In 1670 through storms and shipwreck, the *Carolina* and two other ships made their difficult voyage from England to Charles Town. The trip by way of Barbados foreshadowed the close tie that later developed between the Carolina colony and the West Indies. Two waves of immigration some ten years later added to the unique mixture of colonists. French Huguenots fearful of Louis XIV's persecution of Calvinists were in the advance wave, followed by English dissenters, and a potpourri of Dutch from New Amsterdam and Holland, Baptists from Massachusetts, a handful of Quakers from Pennsylvania, and a few Irish Catholics and Sephardic Jews.

Tobacco did poorly in this climate, and there was at first little to support the colony except trade in deerskins, which were in rising demand in England. The colonists soon discovered that the low, semitropical tidewater was ideal for the cultivation of rice. By the mid 1690s the crop was bringing in tremendous wealth to the Carolina lowlands.

Rice, however, was not democratic. Large amounts of capital were needed to buy land and maintain the labor necessary to tend the finicky crop, making it virtually impossible for anyone but the richest families to share in the huge profits. Thus, it established two of the major hallmarks of antebellum Charleston culture: an aristocracy of planters and merchants with their attendant fine homes and elegant living, and the slave system with its profound and long-range effects. Almost from the beginning South Carolina was the largest mainland importer of African slaves. By 1708 there were as many black slaves as there were white freemen, and by 1724 there were three times as many slaves, giving plantation owners many sleepless nights, especially after the slave uprising in Santo Domingo in 1791.

Planters from Barbados seeking new profits laid out plantations north of Charleston on Goose Creek, establishing active trade with the West Indies and the influence of Barbados on the colony. Like eastern Virginia and Maryland, the entire region around Charleston was webbed with waterways, which allowed easy communication between the city and the plantations that spread along the Ashley and Cooper rivers.

With the exhaustion of the land, it was not long before the rice crops began to decline. Since England's war with Spain and France cut off the supply of most tropical products, indigo was in great demand and soon replaced rice as the cash crop of choice. Because indigo did not require flooding the way rice did, plantations could be located further upland, bringing thousands of new acres into Charleston's economic and cultural sphere. Plantation agriculture spread inland displacing the small farms and expanding the cultural influence of the tidewater. Farther inland, Charleston capital financed the early fall line towns like Augusta, Columbia, Camden, and Cheraw making them outposts of Charleston culture (see map 5.1).

Immigrants continued to arrive in the colony and move inland, adding to the ethnic mixture. These groups tended to congregate not only in certain colonies but in distinct areas within colonies. In 1735, for example, 220 German Swiss settled in Orangeburg, joining others in an area called the "Dutch Fork" between the Saluda and Congaree rivers (map 5.1). The Welsh, including Welsh Baptists from Pennsylvania, tended to gravitate to Society Hill, which was the center of the so-called Welsh Neck area on the upper Pee Dee River. The area north of the Santee River, however, was settled predominantly by Scotch-Irish from the coast, more or less forming a cultural continuum with the Highlander Scotch settlement in the Cape Fear Valley of North Carolina.

Up to this point the westward movement from Charleston was slow. The economics of lowland plantations and the need for defense retarded early rapid expansion. Indian tribes allied with the Spaniards occupied the area to the south and west, and hundreds of miles of wilderness lay to the north. Even by the mid-eighteenth century, settlement did not reach much farther than the fall line. But after 1761 the piedmont was opened to white settlement and new groups of settlers moved in adding to the population diversity of Carolina.

The settlers of the piedmont and Appalachians were mainly Scotch-Irish and

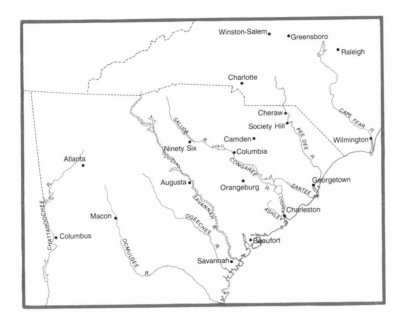

5.1. Important Colonial Towns in the Atlantic South

Germans from Pennsylvania and Virginia who came down the Great Appalachian Valley where they met westward moving settlers mainly of English descent from Virginia and the Carolinas. They established small farms without slaves and affected a life-style and culture quite different from that of the low country, which includes the coastal plain and tidewater. At the same time this difference was accentuated when the low country planters preferred to move into Georgia where new opportunities in rice cultivation and lumbering were opening up, instead of into the isolated piedmont area.

The influence of Charleston spread along the coast and westward into Georgia as the Indians were systematically dispossessed and plantations took their place. Several rivers in Georgia marked the Indian land cessions. The Ogeechee was for several decades in the late eighteenth century the farthest west the white man could legally settle until the Cherokee Treaty of 1805 opened the lands west to the Ocmulgee River in central Georgia (map 5.1). Because this river line was the boundary of Anglo civilization for some twenty-five years, it came to be a linguistic boundary long after white settlement had pressed westward.

By 1830 settlement had crept to the Chattahoochee River in Georgia, which was for a time used as another political borderline between the Indians and the white settlers. Again a linguistic boundary was established along a river which temporarily marked the limits of settlement by Atlantic pioneers. As settlement dammed up in Georgia establishing a base culture, central Alabama was momentarily a contrasting wilderness area. When the dam was finally released the settlers who poured into Alabama were a mixture of Georgians and Upper Southerners who rushed in to establish yet another cultural subregion.

5.2. The Atlantic South Layer Based on 45 *DARE* Isoglosses. Primary, secondary, tertiary, and quaternary boundaries.

The Atlantic South Layer

Map 5.2 documents the Atlantic South in terms of 45 isoglosses. The domain of the region extends from the southeastern corner of Virginia, across the North Carolina coastal plain, includes all of South Carolina and Georgia, and covers most of the western half of Florida. Gordon Wood (1963, 246–47) described essentially the same region, which he calls "coastal Southern." In map 5.2, the area enclosed within the tertiary boundary is the least uniform of the three subareas of the layer. This is particularly noticeable in southern Georgia along the Chattahoochee and Florida border where relatively high numbers properly belonging to the secondary area are isolated by a band of low numbers running through the center of the state.

    This layer unexpectedly ignores some of the important contours of the land. For example, although the line through North Carolina roughly approximates the division we have come to expect between the highlands of the piedmont and Appalachians and the lowlands of the coastal plain, in South Carolina the boundary separating the culturally distinct low country from the up country is at best only partially present. The Chattahoochee in eastern Georgia, however, once again coincides with a distinct linguistic boundary, and roughly marks the western extension of this layer.

    South Carolina is the heart of the region. Although it is not divided as we might expect along a line parallel to the fall line, a strong boundary divides the state into northern and southern sections, with the densest area of isoglosses in southern South Carolina. This primary boundary follows the Santee and Congaree rivers, north of which was the area heavily settled by the Scotch-Irish primarily from the lowlands and by the Scotch Highlanders farther north in the Cape Fear Valley. Surprisingly Charleston is outside of the core area of southern South Carolina. But this is probably more the result of the rural slant of the data, than a true reflection of the position of Charleston speech in this region.

Lexicon

The influence of the colonial ethnic mix is faintly evident in several words of the Atlantic South lexicon. German settlers, especially those from Pennsylvania, left their imprint in words like *outen* and "sick *on* one's stomach." The German *ausmachen* is probably the ultimate form responsible for *outen* meaning "to put out a lamp or light," though it may also be a version of the English dialect verb, probably Scotch-Irish, *out* meaning to extinguish or put out.[1] Not surprisingly, the *DARE* isogloss is densely concentrated in both Pennsylvania and South Carolina (see map 5.4).

The use of *on* in the phrase "sick on one's stomach" meaning to be nauseated or queasy is probably a direct translation or calque of the corresponding German idiom, *etwas auf dem Magen haben* (*WG*, 78). As the atlas isogloss shows, this expression is in use both in Pennsylvania and the Atlantic South (*WG*, fig. 152) and the *DARE* version essentially agrees.

The French—first the colonial Huguenots and later refugees from the French Revolution—left very little trace in American speech, but *batteau* (= a small, flat-bottomed boat) is probably a remnant. Likewise, the Dutch who seemed to be ubiquitous in colonial America may have bequeathed *dope* to the lexicon, which in this area refers to a carbonated, usually cola, soft drink. This may derive from the Dutch word *doop* (= sauce), though if true it happened in a roundabout way, since this particular sense is very recent (ca. 1910) and originally applied, and often still does, specifically to Coca-Cola, first concocted in Atlanta, Georgia.

The African influence is also present, primarily by way of Gullah, a relic African-English creole still spoken by old residents of the Sea Islands along the Carolina coast. *Cooter* (= turtle) is a classic example. It was probably brought to the New World by slaves from West Africa and is related to or derived from Bambara and Malinke *kuta* or Kongo *nkudu,* which mean turtle (see Turner 1949, 197). Voodoo and black magic brought with the slaves from the West Indies echoes in the Atlantic Southern usage *conjure* (= to cast a spell on someone). Most of the informants who knew the term were rural and middle aged, and a significant number were black. Where much of the rest of the country might colloquially call a penny a "copper" or a "red cent," many Atlantic Southerners also use *brownie*. Early written evidence suggests that originally this was a Gullah usage, though not of African origin.

Unusual for a Southern dialect is the Atlantic South's relatively large number of slang expressions, though it is unlikely that more than one or two originated here. From the beginning, *cracker* (= "poor white") was confined to the Atlantic South and probably coined in Georgia, hence the common combination of *Georgia* or *Florida* *cracker. Cracker* originally referred to a backwoodsman who was a braggart and sometimes an outlaw (1766). Then it was extended to refer to any rustic lout or poor, uneducated white, often used in the compound *country cracker.*

A more recent slang expression is *tail* for buttocks. Although nearly everyone would understand this term ("Get your tail out of here!"), as suggested by the scattered informants in the North and South, most of the informants are concentrated in the Atlantic South.

In much of the South, but primarily in the Atlantic South, a large jackknife, especially if it is blunt and clumsy looking, is called a *frogsticker.* The earliest known written example of the word places it in South Carolina in 1836, though it may have come from the English dialect expression *stick-frog* with the same meaning. This English expression is probably also involved in the origin of the Atlantic South term for mumblety-peg, *stick-frog,* a game in which a jackknife is stuck into the ground. A frog also appears in the slang term *frog skin;* its green, patterned skin is likened in a bizarre way to a dollar bill. This too is probably widely known in the United States, especially in the South, but is used primarily in the Atlantic South.

Though *duck* (= cigar or cigarette butt) may not qualify as full-blown slang, it is the sort of colloquialism that is rare in New England and Southern dialects, which tend to insist upon a certain linguistic decorum. The same can be said of *bell a buzzard.* Used in contexts like "He hasn't sense enough to bell a buzzard," this odd Atlantic Southernism has considerable currency. It humorously refers to belling or attaching a bell to the carrion bird, the reason for doing so being as ridiculous and stupid presumably as the person referred to. Occasional variants on this theme are *bell a bull* or *cow* or *cat,* and a curiously redundant folk etymology *bell a buzzer.*

Although map 5.2 suggests that southern South Carolina or the Charleston hearth is the origin and core of the layer, the Virginia hearth doubtless played a role in the development of this speech area. For example, *lightwood* (= dried pinewood used for fuel and kindling) almost certainly originated in Virginia in the late seventeenth century. And *Brunswick stew* gets its name from Brunswick County, Virginia, from where it spread as far as William Faulkner's rural Mississippi. In its original version it is made with wild game, particularly squirrel and rabbit. Oddly, no South Carolina informants gave it as a response to the *DARE* questionnaire.

Like other regions, the Atlantic South has its share of culinary, domestic, and farming terms. A farmer calling *co-wench* to his cows is using a survival from British dialect, a shortened version of *come* plus *wench,* the latter term according to the *English Dialect Dictionary* referring not only to a woman, but in rural England to a cow. If the cow were hornless, she would be called a *butt-head* or be described as *butt-headed,* an Atlantic South ruralism with considerable currency.

Two formerly common types of plows the Atlantic South farmer would be likely to use are the *turn plow,* which is a standard moldboard plow, and a *sweep,* which has flat narrow wings adapted for shallow cultivation of row crops. As the 1842 edition of the *Cotton Planter's Manual* suggests, these were especially used in the cultivation of cotton and at one time were probably in use throughout the cotton belt.

A horse that has plowed the fields hard and is short of breath is said to be *bellowsed,* an extended meaning from the old (1615) use of "bellows" to refer to the lungs. The sound that a horse makes is known in the Atlantic South as a *whicker,* which is also used as a verb. The atlas evidence (see *WG,* figs. 34, 97) shows *whicker* in Eastern New England and the Atlantic states from southeastern Pennsylvania to South Carolina. But this classic isogloss has changed considerably, remaining stable only in the Atlantic South. The wider view from *DARE* shows its use also in Florida and the Georgia piedmont, with scatterings in Alabama and Mississippi.

Speakers in the United States universally say an "armload" or "armful" of wood, except in the Atlantic South where it is a *turn* of wood or a *turn* of anything else carried in one load. This word has been around since at least 1800 and is still widely current in this region, the isogloss having changed very little since the atlas fieldwork of the 1930s (see *WG,* fig. 73).

Two important crops are peanuts or *ground peas,* as they have been called in the Atlantic South since colonial times, and fruit trees, which thrive in the warm, moist climate. The fruit seed or stone, especially of peaches, is frequently called the *kernel,* a specialized use that ultimately comes from the Old English term *cyrnel* for grain or seed. Though by far the densest occurrence of this term in the *DARE* fieldwork is in the Atlantic South, it is also scattered into Louisiana, Mississippi, and southern New Jersey.

Another plant that likes the Lower South climate is cowage, or as it is known in the Atlantic South, *cowitch.* Less climatically fussy plants are the weeds whose seeds stick to clothing and skin, such as burr grass. These seeds are often called *sandspurs* in the Atlantic South. Although the Lower South term *mosquito hawk* (= dragonfly) is well known in the Atlantic South, it more commonly comes out as *skeeter hawk.* Another insect with its own regional name is the *dog fly,* a biting stable fly that resembles the common housefly.

In addition to Brunswick stew, *catfish stew* (= a thick soup made with catfish) and *hopping John* (= meat, usually pork, cooked with peas and seasoned with red peppers) are popular dishes in the Atlantic South, especially in South Carolina, where they have been around since at least the early nineteenth century. *Liver pudding* is also a well-known food made of ground liver and pork trimmings, reminiscent of German "braunschweiger." *Syrup candy* is a popular candy homemade from cane syrup that is boiled until thick, then cooled and often pulled like taffy.

Among the utensils in an old-fashioned Atlantic South kitchen is the *key* or *stove key,* the handle used to remove the lids of an old "chunk stove" or wood-burning stove. Also in the kitchen, perhaps in a corner, one might find a long-handled broom or *stick broom.* If potatoes are on supper's menu, there are usually plenty stored in the *potato hill,* which is a heaped mound of root vegetables, mainly potatoes, covered with straw and earth as protection against the weather. These were also called *potato banks* in most of the Lower South, though this method of storage is rapidly waning.

To carry the potatoes one might use a *crocus bag* or *crocus sack,* Atlantic South terms for a gunny sack. *Crocus* is a coarse, loosely woven material once worn by slaves and laborers and common in colonial New England. It probably took its name from the sacks in which crocus or saffron was shipped (see Avis 1955). By the end of the nineteenth century, however, the name was obsolescent in New England. *Crocus bag* survived in New England into the 1930s primarily on Martha's Vineyard (*LANE,* map 150; *WG,* fig. 71), and by 1965 it was virtually a relic in New England with only one *DARE* informant in Maine and one in Rhode Island.

The Atlantic South and New England

Like many of the terms of this lexicon, *crocus bag* illustrates the linguistic kinship of the Atlantic South with New England. The relationship, however, is primarily historical, with a large part of their shared lexicon, like *crocus,* now virtually extinct in New England. Even so, a handful of expressions are still current in both regions.

Piazza exemplifies this pattern (see map 5.3). Borrowed into English in the sixteenth century from the Italian word for marketplace or square, it was later "erroneously" (*OED*) used to refer to a roofed gallery or colonnade. In America, specifically in Virginia (1699) and then in Boston (1771), it was stretched even further from its original sense and came to be the everyday word for a porch or veranda. However, this usage never took root in Pennsylvania, but remained viable in New England and the Atlantic South. *Belly-girt* or *belly-girth* (= the band of a harness that goes around the abdomen of the horse), has a similar pattern.

The remaining living examples of this bipartite pattern vary in unique but, given the settlement patterns, predictable ways. *Bush hook* (= a hand tool for cutting underbrush), for example, is still clearly an Atlantic South term, but its appearance in the Northeast is sparse and concentrated primarily in Upstate New York. *Spider* (= iron skillet), which is well known in the Atlantic South, is spread even farther westward in the North, from New England to Wisconsin (map 5.3). The isogloss for *adder* (= snake) is just the reverse; it is solid in New England and to a lesser degree in Upstate New York, but in the Lower South is spread from North Carolina to east Texas.

Similarly *hog('s) head cheese* is densely distributed in the Lower South from Maryland to Texas and in northern New England. This isogloss, at least in New England, has changed little since the atlas fieldwork (*LANE,* map 305; *Handbook,* 11).

Some of the forms that came very early to America, to root in Virginia and Boston, failed to spread into the rest of the Atlantic South, but remained primarily in Eastern New England and eastern Virginia. This pattern is most clearly seen in the atlas isoglosses of *corn house* (= corn crib; *WG,* fig. 57) and *breeze up* or *on* (= to become windier; *WG,* fig. 45), though the former only faintly appears in South Carolina and the latter hugs the coast closely.

These isoglosses may be remnants of a proto-American English, presumably the relatively homogeneous speech of seventeenth-century America that in time broke up, first into three major dialects, then into many subdialects. English colonists along the entire seaboard used these expressions, but with the large and continuous influx of immigrants into the Mid-Atlantic area (southeastern New York, New Jersey, eastern Pennsylvania), the terms soon died out there while persisting in the more conservative New England and Atlantic South regions. It is interesting to note that the layer most directly influenced by the Mid-Atlantic hearth, the Midland layer, especially as epito-

5.3. Selected *DARE* Isoglosses Shared by the Atlantic South and New England

mized by isoglosses like *coal oil* (= kerosene), is the reverse or negative of this New England–Atlantic South pattern.

Several extant isoglosses testify to the essential unity of colonial speech. One of the first things that the tidewater colonists encountered was the numerous saltwater inlets along the coast, which from the beginning (1608 in Virginia) they naturally called *creeks*, the oldest and standard English sense of the word. Later, *creek* took on its uniquely American reference to any small stream, but the original sense was preserved along the entire Atlantic coast (see *WG*, fig. 92) at least into the 1930s. (There was no *DARE* question to elicit this response.)

Freshet is another old word surviving primarily in the Atlantic states from Maine to Georgia. Originally the name for a small freshwater stream, in America it refers mainly to incidental streams caused from flooding or heavy rains. Oddly enough, in the *DARE* fieldwork this expression is not used in South Carolina. Also in the Atlantic states and in scattered parts of the Lower South, a pancake is called a *fritter*, although Kurath shows it only in northeastern New England (*WG*, fig. 11).

A wind blowing from the northeast has been called a *northeaster*, or with a more nautical flavor, a *nor'easter*, since the eighteenth century. The *DARE* fieldwork shows it in use along the Atlantic coast and in the Upper North especially around the Great Lakes (see map 5.3). An isogloss with the same sparseness in the Mid-Atlantic that may account for the New England–Atlantic South bipartite pattern is *tabby cat* or *tabby* (= a domestic cat with mottled and striped fur). This name is probably widely known but is a part of the active vocabulary primarily of Atlantic states speakers, and specifically of New England and Atlantic South speakers.

In general, the New England–Atlantic South pattern seems to be fading, primarily because much of the shared lexicon, like *crocus bag*, is obsolescent or has died out altogether in New England, while continuing to be current in the Atlantic South. This process, which has deposited much of the Atlantic South lexicon, has been going on since colonial times but is best documented in the years between the atlas and *DARE* fieldwork.

The atlas isogloss for *haslet* or *harslet* (= the edible internal organs of a hog), for example, is solid in both regions (*WG*, fig. 103), but in the *DARE* fieldwork, only one eighty-three-year-old informant in New Bedford, Massachusetts, knew the term, while most of the remaining thirteen informants were in the Atlantic South. In this case the low number of informants nearly all of whom were over sixty-five years of age, compared to the widespread usage in the atlas, strongly suggests that though *haslet* hangs on in the South, it is a dying expression.

A similar process has affected *whicker* (= neigh). The atlas isogloss in New England is concentrated in western Connecticut, Rhode Island, southeastern Massachusetts, and Maine (*WG*, fig. 97), while in the *DARE* fieldwork there were only two New England informants, one in Maine and one in western Connecticut. The remaining sixty-one informants are concentrated in the Atlantic South, essentially echoing the atlas distribution from Maryland to South Carolina, with the addition in the wider *DARE* sample of Georgia, Florida, and a handful of occurrences in Alabama and Mississippi. Unlike *haslet*, however, *whicker* does not appear to be dying out in its southern domain.

It is the same story for *lulling down* (= a subsiding of the wind), though the atlas evidence in the Atlantic South has not been published. *LANE* (map 92) shows this expression in use primarily in coastal New Hampshire and Maine, whereas the *DARE* isogloss wholly confines it to the Atlantic South, though in sparse fashion.

It seems clear, then, that New England and the Atlantic South, and to a much lesser degree their derivative dialect regions, the Upper North and the Lower South, are related in ways that have persisted even as they have become individuated and distinct. Perhaps the best known feature of this kinship is the dropping of postvocalic *r*. But the two regions have continued to drift apart since the development of colonial American English, leaving only fossil evidence of a shared dialect layer.

Much of the drift is due to New England's tendency to drop expressions in the shared lexicon, while the Atlantic South has just the opposite tendency to retain them. As we've seen, New England speech, like Southern speech is conservative; but in this case, the Atlantic South seems to outdo its northern cousin. Along with the Upper South, it is perhaps the most conservative major speech region in the United States, its lexicon being a repository of relic or old-fashioned expressions and of regionalized terms—terms that at one time had currency outside the Atlantic South, but which receded from use in the surrounding areas, becoming more and more the sole usages of the Atlantic South. We have seen this phenomenon in the Atlantic South's relationship to New England, but it also occurs with relation to the South itself.

The evidence for the regionalizing of Southern expressions in the Atlantic South comes from early written sources and so is less reliable than atlas fieldwork, which at this time is either not available or else, like the *Linguistic Atlas of the Gulf States,* was undertaken at approximately the same time as the *DARE* fieldwork, precluding a diachronic analysis. Even so, we can get a clear impression of this process in Atlantic South speech from such words as *firedogs* and *find*.

The first American record of *firedogs* (= fireplace andirons) occurs in the Boston paper *Massachusetts Spy* in 1792; but evidence since 1900, particularly in *Dialect Notes,* suggests that the term was used throughout the South from Arkansas to Texas to Virginia. The *DARE* isogloss also suggests a much wider distribution, with informants scattered throughout much of the country. However, the greatest concentration by far is in the Atlantic South.

When a cow or mare has offspring, the rural Atlantic Southerner is likely to say "she *found* a calf" or "the mare will *find* her colt soon." Again, the written evidence all recorded in the twentieth century shows this expression in use throughout the South. The *DARE* map faintly corroborates this distribution with one or two informants in Missouri, Oklahoma, Texas, and Kentucky, but with the preponderance of informants in the Atlantic South.

The Atlantic South and Pennsylvania

Just as the Atlantic South has a historical and linguistic connection with New England, it also has an important link with Pennsylvania, particularly southeastern Pennsylvania. But while there were virtually no New England settlers in the Atlantic South,[2] Pennsylvania settlers, notably the Scotch-Irish and the Germans, founded much of the cultural background of the up country. In addition, there was considerable trade between Philadelphia and Charleston (see Ernst and Merrens 1973).

As noted earlier, German settlers left their imprint in the language with the expressions *outen* (= to put out a lamp or light) and "sick *on* one's stomach." The isoglosses for these (map 5.4) illustrate geographically the connection between the two

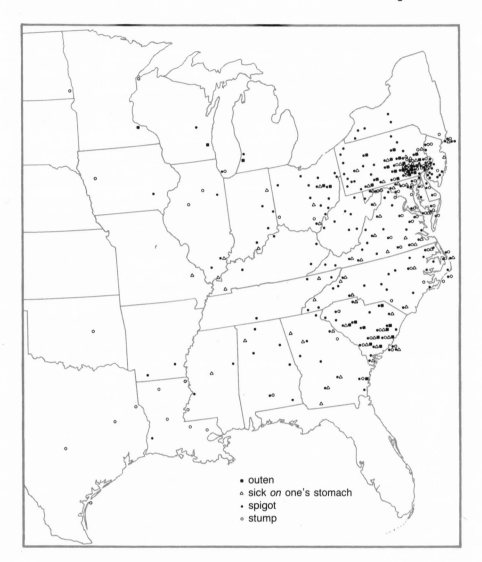

5.4. Selected *DARE* Isoglosses Shared by the Atlantic South and Pennsylvania

regions. In the Atlantic South *outen* is the more restricted of the two, staying entirely within South Carolina, except for a single informant in Midway, Georgia. The high density of responses in the Pennsylvania German area and the German backgrounds of the informants in Ohio, Minnesota, and Wisconsin, support the German pedigree of *outen*.

"Sick *on* one's stomach" shows a similar spread, but is additionally used throughout much of Virginia and parts of North Carolina. The distribution of this response in the North, however, does not follow the German settlement areas as closely;

nor do the informants have a particularly strong German background, suggesting that it may not be of German origin after all.

In the Pennsylvania–Atlantic South region, if coffee is taken without cream or sugar, or liquor is drunk undiluted, these drinks are said to be *barefoot*. Like the two previous expressions, *barefoot* probably originated in the southeastern Pennsylvania hearth and spread southward with settlement, though there is early written evidence that it was also known in parts of New England. Today it is used primarily by old speakers in Pennsylvania and the Atlantic South (except in South Carolina), and in eastern Kentucky and Tennessee.

The old word, *spigot,* which originally referred to the peg that stoppered the hole in a cask (fourteenth century), is used throughout this region to refer to the modern indoor faucet (map 5.4). Usually pronounced with the unvoiced velar consonant, [spɪkət], this isogloss, unlike *outen, on,* or *barefoot,* probably did not spread from Pennsylvania southward. Instead the scattering of the word in the Lower South and in eastern Ohio, West Virginia, and along the Ohio River—the settlement areas of the Lower South and Pennsylvania hearths—indicates that it probably originated in the southern and middle colonies simultaneously.

Stump (= a cigar or cigarette butt) has a similar distribution (map 5.4), though it stays closer to the coastal plain from New Jersey to Georgia. In the Pennsylvania German area, its currency was probably reinforced by the German cognate *stumpf.*

Speech in the Atlantic South as typified by its dialect layer is varied and complex, reflecting a unique and mixed regional history and culture. Not only does it have a clearly defined characterizing lexicon, but it shares a small set of features with New England and Pennsylvania. It tends to be one of the most conservative of speech regions harboring terms that have died out or become obsolescent in other areas. At the same time its lexicon has representative examples of slang and colloquial usage and of recent coinages.

The Delta South

The Delta South, the third hearth of the Lower South, centers on culturally unique southern Louisiana, whose focus is New Orleans. Its topographic core is the fertile strip of floodplain extending fifty or so miles on either side of the Mississippi River from southern Louisiana to the Arkansas border and the valley of the Red River that cuts catty-corner across the central and northwestern part of Louisiana (see map 4.9). Unlike the other two hearths—tidewater Virginia and Charleston—this one has had relatively little influence on the surrounding region, barely extending beyond the borders of Louisiana. Having remained relatively insular with little out-migration, a small but distinct speech region has developed from a melting-pot history and culture.

In 1717 Jean Baptiste, Sieur de Bienville, began construction of an outpost at the site that is today New Orleans. But few Frenchmen were eager to become settlers of the subtropical locale infested with malaria-bearing mosquitoes. Four years later only four hundred people lived in the struggling colony. Even when offered freedom in exchange for settling there, most convicts preferred prison. To meet the need for colonists, the French government even resorted to transporting prisoners, vagrants, beggars, and prostitutes.

John Law's Company of the Indies, which held the proprietorship of the colony from 1717 to 1731, tried a new tack by seeking settlers outside of France. It offered land, tools, and a year's provisions to anyone willing to go and farm. Many Germans who were suffering and displaced from the wars of Louis XIV were happy to seek opportunity in the New World. They settled along the Mississippi River just west of New Orleans in St. Charles and St. John the Baptist parishes. This area is still called the "German Coast," *coast* being a Louisiana expression for the fertile shoreland along the Mississippi.

Their hardworking temperament was successful in helping the colonial economy, but not in preserving their own heritage in the face of a French culture that had the remarkable ability of absorbing the other nationalities that settled there. Even many of their German names were frenchified. Trischl was changed to Triche, Himmel to Ymelle, Meltenberger to Mil de Bergue, and so on. Consequently, the contribution of the German language to the regional tongues is limited to a few place-names and one or two words.

Slaves from Africa and the West Indies were also imported. By 1744 there were about two thousand making a total of some fifty-eight hundred inhabitants, indicative of the impoverished and slow growth of the colony under French rule. Colonial Louisiana never achieved the prosperity or population of the Atlantic colonies. Economically it was a failure costing the near bankrupt French government more than a million dollars a year to maintain. When Spain took over in 1766, there were only about seventy-five hundred souls to be governed.

In 1765, the first Acadians—about six hundred and fifty—arrived from Acadia, or as it is called today, Nova Scotia. Expelled by the British beginning in 1755, these Canadian French settlers eventually found their way to hospitable Louisiana where they settled along the Mississippi and adjoining bayous in what is sometimes called the "Acadian Coast" (St. James and Ascension parishes). They brought with them a modified provincial French language and culture, adding a new dimension to the French dominated culture. The arrival of the Acadians, or Cajuns as they came to be called, almost doubled the population of the colony by 1770.

Under the Spanish, who had a generous land policy, the colony grew rapidly. Most of the growth came through immigration, the Acadians representing the largest single group. The American colonies supplied the next largest group of immigrants during and after the Revolutionary War. Oddly enough, very few Spaniards settled in Louisiana. The black population increased almost as fast as the white, including emancipated slaves who numbered some thirteen hundred in 1803.

When the Spanish gave up the colony in that same year, they left little of their culture, except architecture introduced after the great fires of 1788 and 1794 virtually leveled French-built New Orleans. Louisiana continued to be New World French well after the Americans took over the colony. Even today it is the continuing French element that gives the Delta South much of its unique regional status.

After the English defeated the French in 1763, British colonists were soon farming the bluff lands of the Felicianas and pushing into the Florida parishes north and east of the Mississippi as it flows by New Orleans. Anglo-Americans began to pour into the area after the Louisiana Purchase (1803), arriving from the Atlantic South by sea and from the Upper South and North Central states by way of the Mississippi. Soon the alluvial lands along the river and the hilly country of northern Louisiana were settled, dividing the cultural landscape into two general regions (see map 4.10): northern Louisiana dominated by an Anglo-Saxon, Protestant culture, including Scotch-Irish settlers, and southern Louisiana based on a French, Catholic heritage.

The Delta South Layer

The north-south division of Louisiana is mirrored in the linguistic geography, one version of which is composited from 15 *DARE* isoglosses (map 5.5). The heart of this layer covers southern Louisiana and much of the Red River Valley, while its domain of influence extends into southwestern Mississippi and up the Mississippi river to the Arkansas border but excluding most of northern Louisiana.

This linguistic picture is corroborated and supplemented by the fieldwork done by Babington and Atwood (1961; also Atwood 1962). Map 5.6 shows another version of the Delta South using 14 isoglosses (see app. A) individually mapped in Atwood's

5.5. The Delta South Layer Based on 15 *DARE* Isoglosses. Primary and secondary boundaries.

5.6. The Delta South Layer Based on 14 Isoglosses from Atwood (1962).
Primary and secondary boundaries.

The Regional Vocabulary of Texas (1962). The core in this version is southeastern Louisiana, and the domain extends northwestward up the Red River Valley and into the north-central part of the state. It also reaches into a tiny portion of southeastern Texas. Except for a single community in southwestern Mississippi, Atwood's fieldwork is limited to Louisiana and southern Arkansas making it impossible to see what happens along the river border between Mississippi and Louisiana.

The two maps (5.5 and 5.6) are not composed of entirely identical isoglosses, which would in part account for the differences in their boundaries. Those of map 5.6 are weighted toward southeastern Louisiana expressions, creating a denser pattern there. *Banquette,* for example, could not be used in map 5.5 because there was no *DARE* question for regional synonyms of "sidewalk." The same is true for *shivaree* as a noisy, good-natured hazing of newlyweds *when remarriage is involved.* This semantic nuance simply was not built into the *DARE* question for this item.

In the *DARE* fieldwork, too few informants used the southeastern Louisiana term *cush-cush* (= cous-cous, a dish made with cornmeal or semolina) to make it a representative isogloss for map 5.5. The same is true for the Louisiana expression used to request getting off a bus. Atwood found a tight cluster of southeastern Louisiana speakers who said "I *want to get down,*" which may be a translation of the French *descendre.* But *girdle* (= the bellyband that attaches the harness to the horse) presents a different problem. Atwood found ten communities where this word was used, seven of which were in southeastern Louisiana. *DARE* fieldworkers, on the other hand, found it in widely scattered parts of the eastern United States, but not in Louisiana.

5.7. Combined Delta South Layer Boundaries (maps 5.5 and 5.6)

In total, there are 5 of 14 isoglosses included in map 5.6 that are not in map 5.5. Contrariwise, 6 of the 15 isoglosses in map 5.5 are not available in Atwood's study and so were not used to derive map 5.6. These are *coon-ass, gaspergou, jambalaya, neutral ground,* and *poule d'eau.* Thus, the two maps share a total of 9 isoglosses.

Though differences between Atwood's and *DARE*'s fieldwork make it difficult to compare specific isoglosses, the boundaries they measure when composited are complementary. This is shown in map 5.7, which combines and generalizes the boundaries of the two composite maps. Major and minor lines tend to bundle together north of New Orleans creating a strong boundary that runs roughly parallel with the Mississippi River. To the west another bundle of lines runs along the Sabine River, the Texas-Louisiana border, forming a major layer boundary.

Lexicon

The Delta South is one of the most linguistically varied regions in the country. It has the only non-English-based creole, the French Creole spoken by the descendents of slaves imported from West Africa and the French West Indies. And it is the only region where a French dialect—the speech of the Cajuns—can still be heard. Inevitably these languages influenced in distinctive ways the varieties of English that evolved.

Louisiana French has given the lexicon much of its distinctiveness. Over half of the expressions whose composited isoglosses make up map 5.5 are French in origin. For example, a large, usually ornate wardrobe or clothespress is often referred to by its French name, *armoire,* a common loanword in the English dialect since at least the early nineteenth century. Commercialization may be spreading it to other parts of the country, but the isogloss shows it tightly clustered in Louisiana and southern Mississippi (cf. Atwood 1962, map 50).

Although *gallery* was borrowed from French *galerie,* it became an English word at two different times and places: sixteenth-century England and eighteenth-century Louisiana. Its meaning, "porch or veranda," is first recorded in America in one of George Washington's numerous diaries (1784). He was using the word as it came directly from England. But this sense of "gallery" did not catch on in the Atlantic South. In the meantime, Louisiana French had either outright provided the loanword for English or else reinforced the already existing English "gallery." In this region it survived and spread into Texas, Arkansas, Mississippi, and parts of Alabama, becoming part of the Delta South dialect.

Lagniappe (= a small gift or bonus given with a purchase) had an even more circuitous etymological route that traces a part of the history of the land. The trace begins in South America with the Quechuan word *yapa,* which had essentially the same meaning in the Indian language as it does in English today. The Spanish conquistadors and colonists adopted the word, adding the definite article *la* and converting it into *la ñapa.* Perhaps it was during the Spanish rule of New Orleans that the word was then borrowed into Louisiana French and then sometime in the early nineteenth century into Louisiana English where it has stayed (cf. Atwood 1962, map 18).

Bayou is also of Indian origin. The French adopted the Choctaw word for a small, slow moving stream, *bayuk,* sometime in the seventeenth century. A century later it passed into English, where it has stayed in common use in Louisiana, southeast Texas, and southern Arkansas (cf. Atwood 1962, map 53).

In order to move about in the bayous, the Louisiana frontiersmen and settlers adopted the Indian practice of making canoes from large hollowed-out tree trunks. These the Spaniards called *piragua,* a word they probably took from the Carib Indians of the West Indies. The French of Louisiana in turn borrowed the Spanish word and in time *pirogue* became the common English word in the Delta South for a dugout canoe or any kind of crude open boat.

Like the British colonists of the Atlantic coast, the French colonists encountered many natural phenomena, such as bayous, which are especially characteristic of the Gulf Coast but for which they had no ready-made words. However, they were able to adapt old words for new purposes, so that today a swamp is often called a *marais;* a marshy prairie is a *flottant;* alluvial land is *batture;* a hummock or tree-covered low ridge is a *cheniere;* and a small stream or a ravine is a *coulee.*

Among the critters of this low wetland, one could find a *gaspergou* and a *poule d'eau.* A *gaspergou* is a freshwater drum or croaker (see Read 1945), while a *poule d'eau* or *pooldoo* is a coot or mudhen. The latter is usually pronounced [pʊl du]. All of these words for natural phenomena have become fully naturalized in English while remaining close to the Louisiana hearth.

Given the French reputation for fine cuisine, it is hardly surprising to find a substantial number of Louisiana French culinary words in the English lexicon, the most widely known being *praline, gumbo,* and *jambalaya.* A *praline* is a rich candy made with pecans and brown sugar. The original French word was taken from the name of a seventeenth-century field marshal, Count Plessis-Praslin, whose cook—so the story goes—invented the confection. Today commercialization has placed the word in the latent vocabulary of a large number of Americans, but it remains a term and recipe in common use only in the Delta South.

Gumbo is also a widely known name for a stewlike dish containing okra, vegetables, and meat or seafood, though it originated in New Orleans (ca. 1805) and is actively used primarily in the Delta South. It probably derives from French Creole *gombo,* which took it from a West African word meaning okra, perhaps from Bantu or Umbundu (e.g., Umbundu *ochinggombo*).

Jambalaya is a rice dish made with tomatoes and herbs and with ham, chicken, shrimp, or oysters. Also known outside this region but not used with any frequency, it derives from French Provençal *jambalaia,* a stew of rice and fowl.

Other Louisiana French foods less well known outside the region are *brioche* (= a kind of coffee cake); *bisque* (= a cream soup); *boudin* (= a kind of sausage); *courtbouillon* (= a dish made with redfish); and *pigeonnier* (= a pigeon roast).

Only a handful of expressions in the lexicon do not have their origins in the French, Spanish, Creole, or Indian cultures that played an important part in the development of Louisiana speech. The regional term for bacon, for example, is *salt meat,* and cottage cheese is often called *cream cheese,* a name that would cause considerable confusion outside this region (see Atwood 1962, maps 47, 52).

The median strip dividing a highway into lanes of opposing traffic is called *neutral ground,* as if the highway were a battle zone. Wood (1971, 371n) notes that this is also the expression sometimes used for the grass strip between the sidewalk and the street. Except for a single informant in Arkansas, the isogloss is confined to Louisiana and southern Mississippi.

Coon-ass is a name of uncertain origin that refers to Cajuns or persons of Acadian French heritage. It is not necessarily considered a derogatory name and seems recently to have become a point of pride among Cajuns to be recognized as a coon-ass. Not recorded until the early 1960s, the word is doubtless much older. Not surprisingly, since the Cajuns live only in this region, the use of this name is restricted to Louisiana and southeastern Texas.

The Delta South layer, then, reveals a compact region whose focal point is southeastern Louisiana and whose lexicon is dominated by French loanwords.

The Gulf States

Settlement of the Gulf region came largely from the Atlantic South along the national highways built after 1815. The Great Valley Road carried settlers through Knoxville into northern Alabama and on into central Mississippi. The Upper Road and the Fall Line Road were migration conduits passing through the Carolinas and into Georgia where they converged at Columbus. From there the federal roads through southern Alabama opened the stream to the southern Gulf plains.

Just as climate affected the settlement of the South as a whole, it also set general guidelines for the expansion of the plantation culture dependent on cotton. The Lower South lies within a broad warm band running from the Virginia tidewater through the piedmont of North Carolina and westward into Texas. The average January temperature of this band is forty to forty-nine degrees Fahrenheit. The western limit of the climatic boundary is formed by the curtain of heavy annual rainfall that stops in eastern Texas and runs northward.

Any isolating force—sociological, economic, geographical, even climatic—will be a factor in the creation of a region, in part, because such forces are intertwined with settlement and cultural definition. The importance of cotton, and other agricultural products best grown in the warm, wet climate of the Lower South, such as tobacco, rice, and indigo, had a great deal to do with the way the South was settled and developed.

Maps of cotton production for virtually any year to about 1950 show the "cotton belt" region to be essentially identical with the Lower South's cultural and dialect area (see Lord and Lord 1955, 145–46). The rural nature of this region is also reflected in the geography of its agrarian economy. For example, the percentage of farm tenancy (see Lord and Lord 1955, 155–56) and the mule-horse ratio (see Zelinsky 1951a, 177) also roughly mark off its general boundaries.

With the expanding cultivation of rice and cotton, civilization gradually spread from South Carolina inland and southwestward into Georgia. But prior to the 1830s the powerful Cherokee, Creek, and Choctaw tribes in Alabama and western Georgia discouraged settlement west of the Ocmulgee River. As a result, western Georgia, Alabama, and Mississippi lagged by about thirty years behind the settlement of Kentucky and Tennessee in the Upper South (see map 4.11). In 1812, there were only about twenty thousand white settlers in the Mississippi Territory, the broad block of land between the Mississippi and Chattahoochee rivers. After the removal of the Indians from Alabama in 1814–16, the scramble for cotton-growing farmland began. By the end of 1819 nearly two hundred thousand settlers had moved into the Gulf plains.

The Lower South Layer

Map 5.8 shows the Lower South as measured by 61 counted isoglosses. A relatively steep ridge of numbers forms a primary boundary marking off an area where 17 or more expressions from the lexicon occurred. This core includes all of South Carolina and most of Georgia, Alabama, and Mississippi except for their extreme northern sections, which are part of the Upper South. The boundary through these states and into southern Arkansas, a small portion of eastern Texas, and southern Louisiana is very distinct with a large difference between numbers on either side of the line. A portion of western Florida is also distinctly excluded from this area.

But in southern Mississippi and the rest of Florida the distinctiveness is blurred by a gentle gradation of numbers. Moreover, the core is by no means homogeneous, particularly in central Alabama, which presents a special case. Although the line in northern Alabama remains distinct by virtue of the relatively large difference on either side, the group of numbers to the south of the boundary are lower than the cutoff point

5.8. The Lower South Layer Based on 61 *DARE* Isoglosses. Primary, secondary, and tertiary boundaries.

of seventeen. This thin area of isoglosses, marked off in map 5.8 by a dotted line, extends into southern Mississippi and indicates a Lower South subregion whose historical causes lie in the relatively late and homogeneous settlement of Alabama.

Additional subregions inside this boundary appear as numbers clustering within certain ranges. South Carolina, for example, again has the highest isogloss numbers, forming a core and seminal area, as well as a speech island harboring regionalized and relic expressions. Remarkably low numbers define southeastern Louisiana as a distinct subregion. And most of Florida is marked off by relatively low numbers.

Another important but secondary line more closely approximates the usually accepted cultural and linguistic boundary of the Lower South. However there are important differences. In Virginia this boundary (map 5.8) runs closer to the tidewater than either Kurath's (see map 1.4) or Gastil's (see map 4.10). And instead of following or even running parallel to the fall line as we might expect, the secondary diverges westward through North Carolina into the Appalachian province completely skirting South Carolina. Through northern Georgia and Alabama it more closely follows the cultural boundary (map 4.10), but the curve northward into Tennessee is cut short of the alluvial lands along the Mississippi where the cultural boundary runs as far north as southern Illinois. Instead, the linguistic boundary runs close to the Tennessee border into central Arkansas and east Texas where it again more closely resembles the cultural boundaries.

Lexicon

As with most of the Southern layers, the distinctive cuisine provides the lexicon with a substantial number of terms. *Grits* (= coarsely ground grain, especially corn) is perhaps the best-known Lower South food term. In fact its isogloss could almost as easily have been placed with the lexicon of the South II layer (map 4.5) since scattered informants in the Upper South used it. However, by far the greatest concentration of *DARE* informants giving it as a response were in the Lower South where the word has been used since the eighteenth century, though it is much older, going back to the Old English period.

Equally well known, though not much eaten outside of this region is *chitterlings,* usually pronounced ['čɪt,lɪnz] or occasionally ['jɪt,lɪnz]. This is deep-fried hog intestines, a delicacy also eaten in old England at least as far back as the thirteenth century. In the Lower South, but also in most rural areas of the country, everything but the pig's squeal is used. The jowls, feet, brain, and other scrap parts of the hog are chopped, cooked, and allowed to congeal into a loaf, which can be sliced and fried. In the Lower South and New England it is known as *hog's* or *hog headcheese,* while in the North-and-West it is usually called simply *headcheese.*

Among the many kinds of corn bread, fried cornmeal cakes are often called *fritters* in the Lower South. In a typical older kitchen, these along with other breads and pastries are stored in a *safe,* a cupboardlike container. It is also called, depending on how specific you want to get, a *bread safe, kitchen safe,* and *cake* or *pie safe.*

Formerly, cottage cheese was commonly called *curd* in the Lower South; but because nearly all of the twenty-five informants were old and none were young, this word, first recorded in America in 1697, is now probably obsolescent. Kurath showed that *curds* and *curd cheese* were extensively used in the Chesapeake Bay area with scattered instances in Virginia and the Carolinas. But none of these expressions were used by *DARE* informants in Virginia, North Carolina, Alabama, or Florida, further evidence of the decline of these terms.

Collard greens (= a smooth-leaved kale) is a popular food in the Lower South. Peaches, however, are universal and have several regional names for the two general kinds. A clingstone peach, the variety whose flesh adheres to the stone, is known as a *press peach* in the Lower South, while a freestone peach is known as a *clearseed* or less commonly a *clearstone* peach. The basket or container used to store and transport peaches is often called a *hamper* in this region.

String beans, another universal food in the United States, are frequently called *snap beans* probably because the young pods snap when broken before cooking. This name has been current in the Lower South since the mid-eighteenth century. In the rural parts of this region, root vegetables such as potatoes and sweet potatoes are often stored by covering a mound of them with straw and earth. These are called *potato banks* or *potato hills.* Root vegetables are also often stored and transported in *croker sacks* (= gunnysack), an alternate name for the Atlantic South *crocus sack.*

A hand-held broom that is often used for small jobs in the home is sometimes called a *Swiss broom,* a folk etymology of "whisk broom." Outdoor sweeping is done with a *yard broom.*

As usual there is a sizable body of farming terms. Instead of saying that he is going to "plant" corn or cotton, a Lower South farmer might say that he is going to *drop* corn this year. Before doing so, he would have to plow the field with a *middle buster* or double moldboard plow that throws earth to both sides. A *middle* is an uncultivated strip of earth between rows of a crop. To clear a patch of weeds and grass he might use a *sling blade,* which he has first sharpened with a *grinding rock* or *grind rock,* a circular stone with a flat edge. He would not be likely to say that the tools were stored in the "shed" if it were a separate structure, since in the rural Lower South a *shed room* is usually a room added on to the ground floor of a house.

A grumpy, angry person is known colloquially in much of the United States as a *sore head,* but to many Lower South farmers sore head is also a poultry disease. Chickens having this disease, also known as "fowl pox," might be described as being a *sorry* lot, too poor in quality to be fit for market. In the South, *poor* is also used to describe weak and sickly livestock, but in the Lower South it is additionally used of humans. A thin cow that is *poor* might also be described as *rawboney,* the Lower South version of the Elizabethan "rawbone" or "rawboned."

Also typical of rural regionalisms are names for the sounds made by farm animals. In the Lower South, a cow or calf *lows,* a word that goes back to Old English *hlowan.* A calf also *blates.* Though speakers from all parts of the country would say that donkeys *bray,* some Lower South speakers also use it of horses.

Among the terms for wild plants and animals speakers in the Lower South call the gray squirrel a *cat squirrel;* the massasauga or pygmy rattlesnake a *ground rattler;* and the small tree frog or spring peeper a *rain frog.* All of these names have been in use here since at least the early nineteenth century. Chiggers, the tiny red blood-sucking insects, are best known as *red bugs,* and the dragonfly is usually called a *mosquito hawk* after its propensity for preying on mosquitoes. In the Atlantic South *mosquito hawk* originally (ca. 1700) referred to the nighthawk, which also feeds on flying insects, and may have been humorously transferred to the dragonfly.

In the Lower South a fisherman often uses mosquito larvae as bait, and calls them *wigglers* or, if they are particularly big ones, *Georgia wigglers.* One of the preferred freshwater fish to catch are *bream,* usually pronounced [brɪm]. This old name, first recorded in America in New England (1634), refers in the Lower South primarily to the bluegill or warmouth.

Chestnut trees in this region are known as *chinquapins.* Originating early in the seventeenth century in Virginia, it was borrowed from an Indian tribe of Algonquian stock and is akin to the Indian word *chechinkamin* or to the Delaware words *chinqua* (= large, great) and *mihn* (= berry, nut). Pine needles, especially dried ones, are called *pine straw,* an old Lower South word that also probably originated in the Virginia hearth.

Kindling wood from trees with a high resin content is called *fat pine* in the Lower South. By contrast, Kurath classifies it as a Midland term (*WG,* 29, 51). None of the *DARE* informants, however, were from the midlands. Because the earliest citation (1674) places the term in New England, it is possible this Americanism was at one time widespread, including the Midland of the 1930s, but has recently become greatly re-gionalized, with special concentration in the Gulf states. Moreover, given the relatively small number of *DARE* informants (twenty-four) none of whom were young (under thirty-five years old), it appears that *fat pine* is becoming a relic. However, if fat pine disappears, Lower Southerners will still have *splinters* to use for kindling.

In the children's lore of the Lower South, the game of hopscotch is often called *hop scot*. A somersault is a *tumbleset*, and stilts are *Tom walkers* or *Tommy walkers*. In the Lower South a *ball* is not always a toy, but is often a hair bun. To go "skinny-dipping" or swimming in the nude is to go in the water *buck naked*. The best swimming holes are calm and not too deep and don't have any *suckholes* or whirlpools. In England and colonial America, a "suck" was a whirlpool. Now obsolete, it survives in *suckhole,* a primarily rural usage.

To throw something is to *chunk* it, the counterpart to the Northeastern *chuck*. But unlike chuck, the Lower Southernism does not require naming the object being thrown. The earliest citation (1835) illustrates this: "His dog stole my bacon . . . and . . . I chunked the varmint." In the Northern usage to "chuck a varmint" would be to throw the dog itself. However, in the South if one "chunks a fire," one is probably neither throwing the fire nor throwing something at the fire, but is instead feeding it with chunks of wood.

The odd expression, "He doesn't know *B from bull's foot,*" indicating that someone is stupid or ignorant, is part of the general euphemistic tendency of Southern speech. An equally colorful expression indicating that one absolutely does not know someone is a variation on the familiar phrase about the unknown Adam: "I don't know him/her from *Adam's housecat.*"

Two Lower Southernisms related to illness are *squirts* and *mulligrubs*. The former is slang for diarrhea, a very real physical ailment. *Mulligrubs,* on the other hand, is not physical at all, but is a general feeling of discomfort akin to the "blues" or melancholy. This word, which the *OED* calls "a grotesque arbitrary formation," was used in sixteenth-century England and still has considerable currency in the Lower South.

Hey is the common greeting in this region equivalent to "hello" or "hi." To walk very quietly is to *tip* ("No one noticed when he tipped out of the shed room").

To forget something is to *disremember* it. In the nineteenth century this expression had wider currency including in many parts of the North and in English dialects, but has since become regionalized to the Lower South. Surprisingly a disproportionate number of the *DARE* informants who gave it as a response had a college or high school education and, given its nonstandard status, were probably using it self-consciously or facetiously.

The Lexicon and Black Speech

Many of the words of this lexicon are miniature essays on particular aspects of the culture of the Lower South. For example, the prevalence and importance of cotton is evident in the coy expression used to tell a woman that her slip is showing: *the cotton is low,* which has several variations that allude to the economic origin of the phrase, including *the cotton's below the market, cotton's below price,* and *cotton's getting cheap.*

Some expressions of the lexicon, such as *high yellow,* hint at the position of blacks in this society. This expression, which refers to a mulatto or a black person of light skin color, is one of many names for nuances in skin color and suggests the importance that has historically been placed on this feature. The African heritage itself is encapsuled in *pinder* (= peanut), brought from east Africa (Kongo *mpinda*) first to the West Indies where it is recorded in Jamaica in 1696, and then to the Lower South, where it is still current but primarily among older speakers.

Two Lower South expressions commonly used by black speakers are *big daddy* and *big mamma* for grandfather and grandmother respectively, and *beau dollar* for a silver dollar. This latter term may have originated with the trappings of the Southern dandy, formerly called a *beau;* or perhaps it is the French *beau* meaning "beautiful" with reference to the shiny surface of the coin. In either case a bit of culture and history is conveyed in the expression.

But the importance of the black subculture to this region is only hinted at in these expressions. Its impact on the distinctiveness of Lower South speech is considerable. The black slaves were, after all, among the first settlers of the Lower South and inevitably contributed many features to its regional character. The distribution of slaves naturally conformed closely to the limits of the cotton culture. As late as the 1930 census (see Lord and Lord 1955, 111), the black population density still showed the early settlement pattern, its densest area roughly outlining the linguistic and cultural Lower South.

This picture has changed considerably since World War II with the migration of Southern blacks into the urban North. But the early Afro-American subculture, the product of social isolation and an almost forgotten African heritage, has left a lasting influence on the Lower South on many levels—religious, artistic, linguistic.

The African slaves brought to America did not know the language of their captors and masters. Nor did they usually know the language of their fellow captives, since the slavers intentionally mixed together members of different tribes and villages, there being many different languages and dialects in West Africa. By the time they arrived in the American slave markets usually by way of the West Indies where additional influences modified their speech, the slaves spoke an expedient and simplified form of English—a pidgin—with elements of African syntax, pronunciation, and vocabulary.

When the children learned this pidgin as their native or first language, it became a "creole" that over time gradually absorbed more and more features of English. This process, known as decreolization, in which a creole language moves closer in its structure and lexicon toward a standard language—in this case American English and particularly early Southern American English—continued down to the present. The relic Gullah along the coasts of Georgia and South Carolina is testimony of an early American black creole. Moreover, traces of such a creole still exist in the vocabulary of the Lower South in particular, and in American English in general.

The contribution of black speech to the Southern dialect can be easily seen in such terms of African origin as *cooter, goober, gumbo, juke, juju, okra, pinder, poor joe,* and *tote.* Many of the African words brought to the South by the slaves have spread well outside the South, such terms as *banjo, bogus, boogie-woogie, chigger, hep* or *hip, jazz, jitter, jive, mumbo-jumbo, phoney, voodoo, yam,* and *zombie.* The creative influence of black speech, especially on the lexicon, is still very much alive, but instead of being confined to the South, it is national and primarily urban.

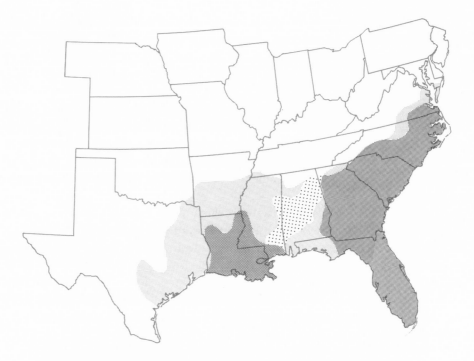

5.9. Combined Lower South Layers (maps 5.2, 5.5, and 5.8). The
darker shade represents the overlap of two layers. The dotted area represents the
region of fewest isoglosses within the Lower South.

Black and white Southern speech, of course, mutually influenced each other.
The effects were bidirectional (see, for example, Feagin 1979, 266). Given the close
relationship between the two groups over a three-hundred-year period, their speech
varieties inevitably modified each other in mutual and specific ways. As the black creole
moved toward standard white English, the whites for their part adopted many of the
black forms—phonological, morphological, syntactic, and lexical.

In no other section of the country were the races so closely in contact. The
members of the typical small family farm worked side by side with one or two slaves.
On the large plantations, the black mammy raised the white children, whose playmates
were apt also to be black. When these white children reached adulthood, their contact
with black servants continued. Though isolated socially and educationally so that their
subculture maintained its identity, the blacks were an integral and interdependent part of
white culture. It is this unique and complex relationship that undoubtedly created part of
the distinctiveness of Lower South speech.

How and in what specific ways this happened has only begun to be studied in
detail.[3] But that it happened is supported by (1) the currency of Africanisms in American English and particularly Lower South English, (2) the close historical relationship
between Southern blacks and whites, and (3) the coinciding of black population with the
Lower South linguistic region.

Combined Layers

Map 5.9 combines the three Lower South layers we've discussed so far: the Atlantic South (map 5.2), the Delta South (map 5.5), and the Lower South (map 5.8). Each layer is simplified by treating the area of its secondary boundary as a relatively unified speech region and is superimposed on the same base map. The area where two layers overlap is given a darker shade in map 5.9. The dotted area in central Alabama and eastern Mississippi represents the thin isogloss count in the Lower South layer.

The Lower South, then, is a patchwork of about four broadly defined subregions. These include the Atlantic South and the Delta South separated by the Alabama–eastern Mississippi speech region. Eastern Texas, northern Louisiana, and southern Arkansas also form the Outer Delta subregion. These in turn can be broken down into minor subdialect areas.

To get a more detailed picture we need to take into account the Southern layers from chapter 4 that overlap the Lower South. To show the interrelationships of the layer boundaries, the primary and secondary boundaries of five Southern layers are combined in map 5.10: the three Lower South layers (Atlantic, Delta, and Lower South—maps 5.2, 5.5, and 5.8) and the South I and II layers (maps 4.3 and 4.5). The boundaries of

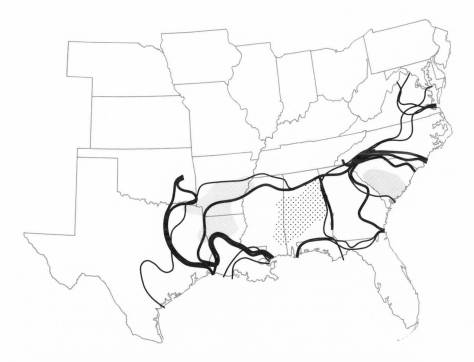

5.10. Combined Boundaries of Five Southern Layers (maps 4.3, 4.5, 5.2, 5.5, and 5.8). The shaded portion of northern Louisiana and southern Arkansas is an area of high isoglosses in the South I layer. The shaded section in South Carolina represents the overlapping of four layer cores. The dotted area is the region of fewest combined isoglosses.

these layers coalesce and bundle in various combinations at different places. Especially noticeable are bundles in eastern Texas, central and southern Louisiana, northern Florida, northern Georgia, and along the border between the Carolinas.

The Atlantic South Dialects

In every Southern map except the Delta South, South Carolina—particularly its southern half (represented by a shaded area in map 5.10)—has some of the highest number of isoglosses and thus forms a core area of Atlantic South speech. Three roughly coinciding primary boundaries from the South II, Atlantic South, and Lower South layers run along its border with North Carolina. They form one of the strongest boundaries in the Lower South and divide the Atlantic South into upper and lower regions.

The Lower Atlantic South extends from this bundle near the Carolina border to the Atlantic South's western boundary along the Chattahoochee River[4] and includes all of South Carolina and most of Georgia. Within this area a minor division occurs in eastern Georgia where another bundle of boundaries runs roughly parallel to the Ogeechee River, which as we've seen was for some time the western extension of settlement (see map 4.11).[5]

Although Florida, particularly its eastern half, participates in the Lower and Atlantic South layers, most of the state is an area of very sparse isoglosses, so much so that two secondary boundaries coalesce to mark off nearly the entire state as a separate speech region (map 5.10). The infrequent use of the lexicons is particularly true for the Atlantic coast, which in the last hundred years or so has steadily received much of its population from the North and from the Spanish-speaking Caribbean, notably Cuba. Moreover, most of Florida was set apart from the Lower South by its relatively late settlement even though the Spanish had very early on established a handful of coastal settlements.

The Upper Atlantic South, sometimes called "Mid-Atlantic" (*WG, DARE*) is just as complex and includes most of Maryland, southern Delaware, and eastern Virginia, and North Carolina. The influence of the Atlantic and Lower South layers on this area diminishes as we proceed northward away from the Charleston hearth until we reach northern Virginia and Maryland where few expressions from these lexicons can be heard and the influence of the Virginia tidewater hearth dominates. Here the bundles are relatively weak (map 5.10) indicating a diminished affinity with the Lower South. The Upper Atlantic South, then, is a distinctive speech region in its own right, which has been well documented by the atlas fieldwork. The area as a whole first came under the immediate influence of the Virginia tidewater hearth, the oldest in the New World. A little later the outer coastal settlement of North Carolina had its own independent influence on the southern portion of the Mid-Atlantic. The overall effect is that certain words and phrases have been deposited in relatively small areas creating pockets of isoglosses and tight subdialect regions.

Because of the broad scope of the *DARE* data, these subareas of Lower South speech are difficult to measure. Even so, it is possible to define some of the more prominent boundaries that can profitably be compared with the results of the older data from the atlas.

Kurath described a first-order boundary separating "the clearly defined sectors of . . . the Midland and the South" (*WG*, 11) running through western Virginia and central North Carolina (see map 1.4). In map 5.10 the two secondary lines of the South I and II layers (maps 4.3 and 4.5) vaguely hint at a portion of Kurath's boundary in northwestern Virginia. The secondary boundaries of the Atlantic South and Lower South layers in map 5.10 more or less continue Kurath's Midland-South boundary through south-central Virginia and central North Carolina. But these lines form at best a minor boundary not at all approaching the magnitude of Kurath's version.

The Virginia Piedmont

The indirect evidence in maps 5.9 and 5.10 generally corroborates Kurath's description (map 1.4) of the Atlantic South subdialects. Despite the tangle of lines in map 5.10, which suggests a very complex linguistic region, we can make out a three-part division of Virginia. The state is first divided into a western and eastern half, with the eastern half again divided somewhere in the southern portion. The western half is considerably larger than Kurath's description, though this picture will be modified when we take into account the Upper South and Midland layers in the next chapter. Southeastern Virginia is essentially a part of the tidewater and coastal plains speech region of North Carolina.

The northeastern section roughly corresponds to Kurath's Virginia Piedmont subregion (number 15 in map 1.4). The extremely mixed isogloss numbers in this area in most of the South layers, including the extension of the North layer (map 3.3), indicate a distinctive and somewhat heterogeneous Lower South subdialect.

The direct evidence is equally compelling. Kurath was able to present numerous representative atlas isoglosses for this region, several of which are corroborated by the *DARE* data, others of which have changed and lost their representative status. Map 5.11A charts four expressions from the *DARE* fieldwork that have more or less remained Virginia Piedmont isoglosses. As we've seen, *corn house* (= a building for storing corn), is also used in New England and in South Carolina (cf. *WG*, fig. 57). Because of its strong and continuing presence in South Carolina, it is representative of the low country of South Carolina (see *WG*, fig. 2).

Batter bread, yet another Southern version of cornbread, one made with eggs and milk, is used throughout most of Virginia and seems to have changed little in its distribution since the 1930s (map 5.11A; cf. *WG*, fig. 33). A *hovel* or *hover* for a "chicken house" or "chicken roost" originated in tidewater Virginia and spread inland to the fall line and into Kentucky where four *DARE* informants knew it. The Virginia Piedmont call to chickens *coo-chee* or *coo-chick* has dwindled in currency since the atlas fieldwork (*WG*, fig. 106), but remnants in the *DARE* materials still partially outline this subregion (map 5.11A).

The *DARE* fieldwork shows *garden house* (= an outdoor toilet) as having a sparser and broader distribution than the atlas showed (see *WG*, fig. 55). Because the

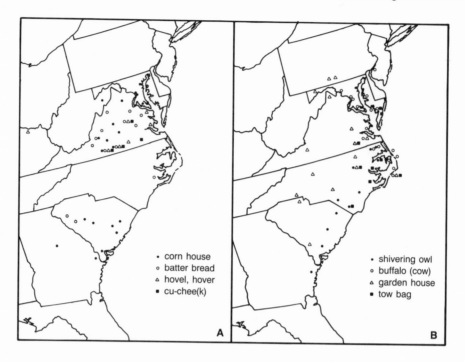

5.11. Selected Mid-Atlantic *DARE* Isoglosses

DARE informants are spread from central south Pennsylvania to southern South Carolina (map 5.11*B*), this isogloss has lost its status as representative of the Virginia Piedmont but gained as a representative of the Upper Atlantic South as a whole.

Most of the dozen or so remaining Virginianisms that Kurath used as defining isoglosses have changed drastically, most being obsolescent in the *DARE* fieldwork. *Cow house* (= cow barn) and *cuppen* (= cow pen) have been in use for a long time, the former since the early seventeenth century in New England; both were still strong dialect expressions in the 1930s (*WG*, fig. 31). But by the 1960s, only one South Carolina informant knew *cow house*, and only two informants, one each in Virginia and the District of Columbia, knew *cuppen*. Likewise, only a single Virginia informant knew *old-field colt* as an expression for an illegitimate child, an "old-field" being a worn-out or overcultivated piece of land presumably where colts of unknown paternity were conceived (cf. *WG*, fig. 150).

In the *DARE* fieldwork only a South Carolina and an Arkansas informant knew the expression *lumber room* (= store room; cf. *WG*, fig. 33), while only one Florida and one Georgia informant knew the term for a man's vest, *wesket* (cf. *WG*, fig. 86). Four informants used the Virginia expression *soft peach* for a "freestone peach" (cf. *WG*, fig. 130), two in Virginia and one each in Ohio and Missouri. Only two New Jersey informants knew the command *way!* or *yay!* used to stop a horse (cf. *WG*, fig. 108). All of these expressions have become obsolescent and are no longer representative isoglosses for Kurath's Virginia Piedmont.

A different situation applies to several other Virginia words that the *DARE* fieldwork shows to be by far more common outside of Virginia, though none of these has any great currency. Among these are the call to pigs, *chook* (*WG*, fig. 104); the name for the horse on the driver's left side, *wheel horse* (*WG*, fig. 110); and the name for a gunnysack, *sea-grass sack* (*WG*, fig. 71).

Chook was used by seven informants, only two of whom were in Virginia. No informants knew the full expression *sea-grass sack* but twenty-six, most of whom were in Kentucky, Louisiana, and Virginia, used the shortened version *grass sack*. Half of the twenty-six informants who used *wheel horse* defined it "incorrectly" as the horse on the driver's right side, a semantic confusion that may indicate the obsolescence not only of these expressions but of the practices they refer to. All twenty-six of the informants were widely scattered, only three of whom were in Virginia, while three California informants gave the variant *wheeler*. A single Louisiana informant gave the Virginia synonym, *line horse* (*WG*, fig. 110).

Despite the changes in the use and geography of these expressions, the Virginia Piedmont remains a viable and important subdialect of the Altantic South. But because of the broad nature of the *DARE* fieldwork, it is difficult to define precisely the boundaries of this relatively small speech area, though what evidence we can extract seems to agree essentially with Kurath's definition.

Eastern North Carolina

The coastal plain of North Carolina, and, according to Kurath, southeastern Virginia and northeastern South Carolina (numbers 16 and 17 in map 1.4), form another subdialect region of the Atlantic South. This is also the approximate region marked off by the various layer boundaries in map 5.10.

Map 5.11*B* shows a few *DARE* isoglosses that offer more direct evidence of this region. Of these only one is mentioned in *WG* as being a representative isogloss: *shivering owl* (*WG*, fig. 37). The *DARE* isogloss of *shivering owl* (= screech owl) has approximately the same distribution, except that it appears as far south as southeastern Georgia (map 5.11*B*). Although *tow sack* is widely known in much of the South, *tow bag* is primarily an Eastern North Carolina expression (map 5.11*B*).

As with the Virginia Piedmont, most of the isoglosses that Kurath uses are no longer useful in defining this subdialect. According to the *DARE* fieldwork, for example, *clabber cheese* (= cottage cheese) and *johnnycake* (= a corn griddle cake) are just as well known outside of North Carolina, although neither has much currency. No *DARE* informants gave *breakfast strip* as a response to the question referring to "bacon," although twenty-one primarily Atlantic South informants used the related form *breakfast bacon*. Other expressions like, *woods colt* (*WG*, fig. 150) for an illegitimate child, are completely absent in the *DARE* informant responses.

Many of the isoglosses that Kurath uses to define this region are features of the Lower South or Atlantic South layers, for example, *press peach, piazza, whicker*, and *mosquito hawk* (*WG*, figs. 34, 35). These he apparently uses to define the northern boundary of the region. The *DARE* isoglosses of these can serve the same function.

With so few representative *DARE* isoglosses for this region, the primary evidence is indirect. Map 5.11A, for example, hints at the distinctiveness of the Eastern North Carolina subdialect negatively; that is, except for a single occurrence of *batter bread*, North Carolina is conspicuously blank. As with the subregions of New England, most of the individually defining isoglosses of Kurath's Upper Atlantic South subregions have changed considerably, while the boundaries themselves have remained relatively stable, indirectly evident in the South and Lower South layers and directly in a handful of old and new isoglosses.

The Delta South and Outer Delta

The primary South II boundary coincides with the primary boundary of the Delta South layer to divide Louisiana into northern and southern sections (map 5.10). Southern Louisiana includes the Red River Valley and is itself subdivided. French-influenced southeastern Louisiana appears as an area of low isoglosses in three layers: South I and II and the Lower South.

To the north and west is the Outer Delta subdialect that includes northern Louisiana, eastern Texas, southern Arkansas, and northwestern Mississippi loosely held together as a speech region by the boundaries and relative isogloss densities of the overlapping South I and II and Lower South layers. But the density of the layers varies in three or four general areas.

Northwestern Louisiana and southwestern Arkansas form a core where the density of all three layers is very high. Because it is within the primary boundary of the Lower South layer, and because it is also within the densest area of isoglosses in the South I layer (the shaded area in map 5.10), the speech of this small area is characterized by the extensive use of the terms in this particular combination of lexicons.

The rest of southern Arkansas is on the other side of the Lower South primary boundary, though still within the dense, shaded area of the South I layer. This area has fewer Lower South regionalisms in its speech. Just the reverse holds for northeastern Mississippi: fewer South I regionalisms but a high number of Lower South terms. Much of Mississippi, however, seems to be a transitional area between the Outer Delta to the west, the Delta South to the southwest whose secondary boundary crosses that part of the state, and the Alabama subdialect to the east. East Texas is outside of both the Lower South primary boundary and the shaded area of dense South I isoglosses and so is characterized by the lowest proportion of the two lexicons in its speech.

It is not clear from this map (5.10) just how coherent a subregion the Outer Delta really is, though we can say that it is unified insofar as it is the only area in the Lower South that shares only the three layers (South I and II, Lower South). But there is a small group of regionalisms that more or less congregate in this area. Twelve of these are mapped in map 5.12.

The numbers tend to be sporadic, but the densest collection covers southwestern Arkansas, northwestern Louisiana, and the area along the Sabine River in eastern Texas and western Louisiana. The words of this tiny lexicon are an odd mixture of the traditional and rural, such as *slide* (= a flat sledge used to drag stones from a field) and

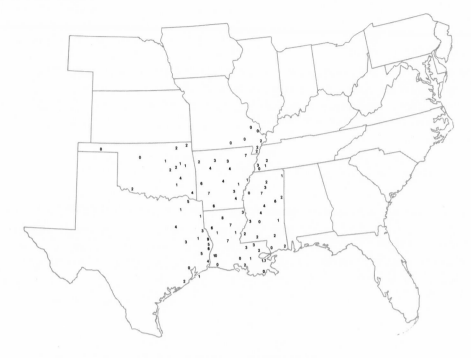

5.12. The Outer Delta Layer Based on 12 *DARE* Isoglosses

net wire fence (= a fence made from woven wire); of the old-fashioned (*earscrews* = earrings with a screw fastener) and mundane (*storm house* = an underground shelter); and of the colloquial and slang, such as *urp* for vomit and *cannonball* for an express train.

In this area, a *butcher calf* is a veal calf, and *low-quartered shoes* are oxford or low-cut shoes, an expression formerly current in other parts of the Lower South. Many of the Outer Delta expressions at one time had wider currency, as the scattering of informants outside the region suggests. Several informants in Virginia, North Carolina, and South Carolina, for example, knew *slide,* and a handful of informants in Iowa and Michigan used *urp*.

Grindle (= a bowfin or mudfish) is one of the few German borrowings in Southern speech (*grundel* from *grund* = bottom or ground) and, because first recorded in North Carolina (1709), may be known in other localized German settlement areas. A sunfish, especially a warmouth or rock bass, is frequently called a *goggle-eye* in this region. Cone flowers are often called *niggerheads* or *nigger navels*.

The Alabama Subdialect

One of the most surprising things to emerge from the combined layer map (map 5.10) is the disposition of Alabama. It is outside of both the Delta South and Atlantic South layers and though the other three layers overlap here (Lower South and South I and II), the isogloss count in each is remarkably low over an area stretching from the north-eastern corner of Alabama diagonally across the center of the state down to Mobile and into eastern Mississippi (the dotted area in map 5.10). To the east is the strong boundary running along the Chattahoochee River. In other words, speakers in this area use fewer Southern regionalisms than anywhere else in the Lower South.

Virginia Foscue (1971) corroborates this from a different point of view. She found in Alabama that national terms are replacing regional expressions, and the North, especially Lower North, influence on the vocabulary is increasing, emphasizing an existing situation. The difference between Alabama speech and that of the surrounding Lower South ultimately lies in its relatively late settlement pattern.

Map 4.11 shows the spread of population at three different points in time. Alabama was only sparsely settled when the Atlantic South and Upper South were already well founded. By 1830 the spread of civilization into Alabama from the Upper South, especially Tennessee and the Appalachians, and from the Atlantic South, amounted to a thin island in the central and northern portions of the present state, which roughly corresponds to the modern dialect area. The mixture of Upper South yeomen and Lower South plantation owners established the beginnings of a speech variety distinct from that of the surrounding regions.

Gordon Wood comes to essentially the same conclusion, though his description is in terms of the penetration of the "Midland" or Upper South vocabulary into Ala-bama and eastern Mississippi. He uses the isogloss for *tow sack* as a paradigm of this phenomenon (Wood 1963, 244–45). This term for gunnysack probably originated in North Carolina[6] and was carried west into Tennessee and then into Alabama and Mississippi. The complementary distribution of the synonym *croker sack* supports the notion of an Upper South corridor in the Gulf states. It spread westward from South Carolina on either side of the corridor, into Georgia and southeastern Alabama, and into northwestern Mississippi and Louisiana. The *DARE* isoglosses essentially agree with Wood's checklist results.

A more localized expression hinting at an Alabama lexicon is *Yankee dime,* which means a kiss. The *DARE* isogloss covers most of Alabama, with scattered informants in northern Georgia, Tennessee, and Kentucky. Why a kiss would be called a "Yankee dime" is obscure, but it likely has something to do with the Confederate South's attitude toward the North.

Two major Indian barriers discouraged early mass movement into the territory and are in part responsible for the dimensions of the Alabama corridor. Before the War of 1812, the Creek Indians occupied the country between the Ocmulgee River in central Georgia and the Tombigbee River in western Alabama. The Choctaw and Chickasaw tribal lands extended westward from the Tombigbee. A series of scandalous treaties from 1816 to 1821 forced these tribes from their ancestral lands, gradually clearing the rich plains of Alabama for land hungry cotton planters.

During the period of first effective settlement from 1815 to about 1830, the land available was essentially the broad strip between the Creek Indian barrier east of the Coosa River and the Choctaws west of the Tombigbee, the approximate area of the subdialect (map 5.10). The ruthless and final removal of these tribes during the 1830s soon obliterated the boundaries of this strip as land grabbers swarmed into western

Layers
Atlantic South (map 5.2)
Delta South (map 5.5)
Lower South (map 5.8)
Outer Delta (map 5.12)

Regions

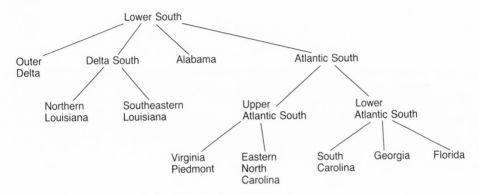

Fig. 4. Summary of the layers and regions of the Lower South

Georgia, eastern Alabama, and Mississippi. Traces of those early Indian boundaries, however, remain in the geography of Lower South speech.

The Lower South dialect region, then, is anything but uniform (fig. 4). It is made up of five important layers (South I and II, Lower South, Atlantic South, Delta South) that divide it into four general subregions: the Outer Delta, the Delta South, the Alabama subregion, and the Atlantic South. Marked off by bundles of layer boundaries and isogloss ridges, there are within these four subregions four smaller dialect areas: Southeastern Louisiana; Northern Louisiana; the Upper Atlantic South, which further subdivides into the Virginia Piedmont and Eastern North Carolina speech regions; and the Lower Atlantic South, which falls into the three subdivisions nearly corresponding to the states of South Carolina, Georgia, and Florida.

NOTES

1. It may also be a use of the *-en* suffix that forms verbs, usually from adjectives (e.g., *darken, deepen, harden, moisten*). Or it may be a combination of these, one version more responsible than another, depending on the region. The German calque, for example, is likely to have had a greater influence in Pennsylvania where *outen* is commonly used in folk speech.
2. Exceptions to this are the tiny New England settlements of Cane Creek and New Garden, North Carolina; Dorchester, South Carolina; and Midway, Georgia.
3. For a detailed treatment of African-American creole and the development of black English see

Cassidy 1980; L. Davis 1983, 114–27; Dillard 1972; Fasold 1981; Hancock 1980; McDavid and McDavid 1951; Stewart 1967; Stewart 1970; Turner 1949; Williams 1970; Wolfram 1971; Wolfram and Clarke 1971.

4. This linguistic line is formed by the primary and secondary boundaries respectively of the South I and Atlantic South layers.

5. This bundle is made up of the primary Atlantic South boundary and a secondary boundary in the South II layer.

6. Note that the variant *tow bag* survives almost exclusively in North Carolina, see map 5.11*B*.

CHAPTER 6

The Midlands: The Upper South and Lower North Dialects

The traditional division of American dialects set down by Hans Kurath calls for three major regions: the "North," "Midland," and "South." This division, however, is not completely accurate. Chapter 3 of the present work dealt with the Upper North, which roughly corresponds to Kurath's "North," and chapter 5 was concerned with the Lower South, the rough equivalent of Kurath's "South," though he defines these regions only for the Atlantic seaboard. But as we've seen, the Upper North and the Lower South do not have the same weight; that is, three major layers (the North, Upper North, and Inland North) define the Upper North dialect region, whereas only the Lower South layer defines the Lower South region.[1] Instead, defined by three strong layers in chapter 4, the South, which Kurath recognizes only as a composite region ("South and South Midland" or "South and Midland"), more properly matches the weight of the Upper North.

Moreover, as we will see in this chapter, the broad expanse between the Upper North and the Lower South—Kurath's "Midland"—is not a true unified dialect region. And although a small set of features, the Midland *layer,* characterizes the area as a whole, Kurath's "Midland" is split by the North-South linguistic divide into two dialect regions: the Upper South and the Lower North.

As was argued in chapter 4, the first division of American dialects is into two parts: the North and the South. Then, based on the relative weights of the regions, the hierarchical arrangement is, like Kurath's, tripartite, but is made up of different regions: the Upper North, the Lower North, and the South.

It is for these and other reasons that the term *Midland* is used here only as the name for the single layer, or in some cases, as designating the area without special reference to speech. In addition, Kurath's labels, "North Midland" and "South Midland," are abrogated here, because they misleadingly imply subdivisions of a nonexistent Midland dialect, when in reality they exist at a higher level than the Midland layer. Thus, "Lower North" and "Upper South," which correctly imply subdialects of the North and South, have been adopted.

The Upper South Dialects

The land-locked northern section of the South, known variously as the "Upper South," the "Yeomen South," the "Hill," "Highland," or "Mountain South," the "Southern

Uplands," and the "South Midlands," extends in a broad westward sweep from the southern Appalachians to the Ozarks of Missouri and Arkansas. Despite its close relationship with the Lower South, there are many historical and geographical differences that separate these two subregions. In chapter 4 (map 4.9) we saw the main physiographic features that distinguish the two: the low coastal plains and tidewater of the Lower South, and the mountains and highland plateaus that dominate the Upper South.

But the Upper South landscape is not all highland. It is interrupted by a peninsulalike projection of the coastal plains into western Kentucky and Tennessee, southeastern Missouri, and eastern Arkansas (map 4.9), which cultural geographers usually include with the Lower South (map 4.10). But the geography of Upper South speech, at least as revealed by the *DARE* data, includes this alluvial peninsula.

In contrast to the Lower South, the Upper South tends to be more homogeneous culturally and linguistically. Where the Lower South had three widely separated sources of settlement, the Upper South sprang essentially from the Virginia and Pennsylvania hearths.

When the first colonists arrived in the tidewater frontier of eastern Virginia, they found low, swampy land veined with rivers and saltwater inlets. The flat countryside extended 50 to 150 miles inland and received heavy rainfall in warm temperatures. Its climate and thin layer of rich soil was ideal for the newly discovered cash crop, tobacco, the economic base on which the early colonies, Jamestown (1607) and St. Mary's (1634), flourished. By 1670 the two tobacco colonies had spread throughout the Chesapeake Bay area, filling the Rappahannock and Potomac river valleys to the west, and the Nansemond and Blackwater river valleys to the south. This was the first fountainhead of future Southern settlement.

Soil exhaustion and cheap, easily obtained land soon had the tidewater colonists pushing into the Old West, the hilly, forested piedmont region between the fall line and the eastern edge of the Appalachian Mountains. In the 1730s two new groups moved into the western valleys: the Palatine Germans from southeastern Pennsylvania into the Shenandoah Valley, followed by the Scotch-Irish into the Great Valley of Virginia and the Appalachian valleys of North Carolina, overflowing into the Carolina piedmont.

These two groups—but especially the Scotch-Irish—played a major role in the establishment of the regional culture, leaving traces of their language in the dialects of both the Upper South and the Lower North. A partial list would include from the Scots dialect *brickle* (= brittle), *fornent* or *fernent* (= near to, opposite), *scoot* (= to move or slide something), *muley* (= a hornless cow), *piece* (= snack), and *redd* (= to clear off or clean up), which characterize various layers. And from German came *smearcase* (= cottage cheese), *hot potato salad,* and *spatzie* (= sparrow), which are all features of the Lower North.

By 1760 Germans, Scotch-Irish, and others had filled the piedmont and western valleys. The need for new land and the relatively easy route through the Cumberland Gap drew the settlers into eastern Tennessee and then into the Kentucky Valley, establishing the frontier on the western side of the Appalachians. By 1776 several thousand settlers, mostly from Virginia and North Carolina, lived in eastern Tennessee and central Kentucky. Throughout the Revolutionary War settlers continued to arrive in the heartlands of the Upper South. In 1779 James Robertson led a group of pioneers from North Carolina into Tennessee and during that winter founded Nashborough, later called Nashville. Harrodsburg and Boonesborough had been founded a few years earlier in the Kentucky Bluegrass region. And Louisville sprang up virtually overnight in 1780 with settlers arriving on the Ohio River.

Migrants continued to pour into the rich lands of "Kaintuck" leaving the exhausted soil of Virginia, Maryland, and North Carolina behind. Migrating Virginians took the Great Valley road down the Shenandoah Valley or the Richmond Road across the piedmont to the Cumberland Gap, then onto the Wilderness Road across Kentucky to Louisville and Frankfort. North Carolinians were apt to move due west to Knoxville and then along the Nashville Road to Nashville. By 1790 the valley of eastern Tennessee, the Nashville Basin, the Kentucky Bluegrass region, and the Ohio River lowlands were well settled (map 4.11).

Most of the settlers were humble farmers who had sold their farms and "old fields." Some were Scotch-Irish from central and southern Pennsylvania. Some were aristocrats like the Virginian, Colonel David Meade, who sent his slaves ahead to Kentucky to prepare a plantation for the arrival of his family. Thousands poured across the Cumberland. In a two month period in 1795, twenty-six thousand crowded the frontier highway leading to Nashville. In 1796, the year Tennessee was admitted to the union, there were seventy-seven thousand people living there. The 1800 census shows two hundred twenty thousand people in Kentucky. In a matter of one generation the heart of the Upper South had gone from wilderness to civilization.

Missouri was not seriously settled until after the War of 1812, but by 1821 an eighty mile wide strip along the Mississippi and Missouri rivers had enough population for Missouri to become a state. Most of the settlers came from Kentucky, Tennessee, and Illinois. Arkansas grew more slowly, with a steady trickle of settlers from the Upper South, Tennesseeans being especially heavily represented. By 1836 Arkansas had achieved statehood. Settlers continued to push into Oklahoma and central and eastern Texas, where traces of Upper South culture and language can still be found today.

Except for a few cultural islands like the Bluegrass region of Kentucky, the Nashville Basin, and the alluvial lands along the Mississippi, the Upper South was not a plantation culture. Instead, small single family farms usually without slaves dotted the countryside. Indeed, the fact that the Upper South has always had a very small black population, sets it in contrast perhaps more than any other single factor to the Lower South.

The ruggedness of the mountain South—specifically the Appalachian and Ozark highlands—and its relatively poor land that could support only small farms of twenty-five to fifty acres were important factors in the growing isolation of this region. Roads were difficult to build and even the well-established trails such as the Wilderness Road from the Cumberland Gap to the Bluegrass region were winding and difficult and to be avoided whenever possible. Prior to 1930 there was still no network of paved roads to the back country.

The effects of this isolation were long range and profound. The economic impact, for example, was considerable: markets were distant and commerce was virtually nonexistent. This in turn retarded urban growth. Without cities or plantations, and with few resources and relatively poor soil, very few new immigrants were willing to settle in this region. Thus, with no new blood added to the population pool, the area's ethnic background remained that of the early Scotch-Irish, English, and German settlers, strongly conservative and thoroughly Protestant in religion. As the isolation of these people increased over time, their attachment to their locality grew and their society became increasingly inbred and conservative.

While surrounding regions changed, the mountain South became more distinctive by not changing. Its speech tended to harbor old-fashioned and relic expressions. Some linguists even claimed that Ozark and southern Appalachian mountain folk spoke a form of Elizabethan English, the language of the first settlers (see, for example, Combs 1916). Though that claim is perhaps more poetic than true, that the Upper South is linguistically conservative is undeniable. The lexicons of the layers of the Upper South are replete with archaisms and relics. Moreover, given the generally poor economic status and little formal education of the speakers (see Gastil 1975, 117–21), particularly in the rural and mountainous areas, lower class or "poor white" social dialects probably dominate a good part of the everyday speech of the Upper South.

The relatively cohesive migration westward from the Appalachians spread Southern features from the coastal hearth into the Upper and Lower South forming three unifying layers (the South layers) and establishing the northern limits of Upper South speech. At the same time, it laid down additional features within the early Upper South settlement area, analyzable as the Upper South and Inland South layers, over which yet another layer of dialect features was deposited: the Midland layer.

Before dealing with the individual layers of this region, we can at this point define the Upper South in terms of the layers already discussed. Map 6.1 shows the Southern substratum of the Upper South by superimposing the two major South layers (maps 4.3 and 4.5) onto the Lower South (map 5.8). In other words, map 6.1 defines the Upper South as the shaded region between the northern boundaries of the South and the Lower South.

This definition approximates very closely the settlement pattern of the Upper South. Nearly all of the southern Appalachians, Kentucky, eastern Tennessee, northern Alabama, and northern Arkansas are the heart of this region, with peripheral areas in southern Indiana and Illinois, almost all of Missouri, Oklahoma, and much of northeastern Texas.

Several subareas are not shown in map 6.1: the light isogloss density in central and eastern Tennessee, and the heavy isoglosses in southern Arkansas and western Kentucky (primarily from map 4.3). The darkest area of the map combines the two cores of the South (South I and II, maps 4.3 and 4.5); the next darkest a core (map 4.3) and a domain (map 4.5); and the lightest area is a single core (map 4.3). In the southern portion of the Upper South is a transitional strip where the domain of the Lower South overlaps with the cores of the two South layers.

Kurath observed that "contrary to widespread belief," the Upper South (which he calls "South Midland") "has rather few unique regional and local expressions" (*WG*, 36). Moreover, many of those expressions cannot be used as representative isoglosses

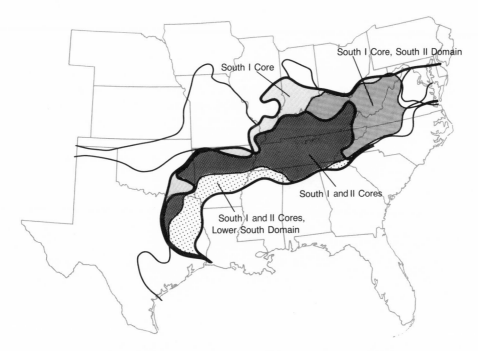

6.1. The Upper South as South I and II (maps 4.3 and 4.5) minus the Lower South (map 5.8)

because they tend to be old-fashioned or relic expressions with little currency. For example, only two *DARE* informants, both in Kentucky, gave *brought-on* as a response to the question, "What do you call a piece of clothing not made at home?" Other evidence, primarily written, establishes that the expression is uniquely Upper South. But *brought-on* has so little currency that it gives no useful information for describing boundaries. Even so, enough isoglosses can be gleaned from the *DARE* fieldwork to define two relatively minor Upper South layers.

The Upper South Layer

This layer is defined by 34 isoglosses (map 6.2) centered on the early Upper South settlement areas of southern Appalachia, eastern Tennessee, Kentucky (except the Blue-grass region), and the Ozarks of Arkansas. There are one or two anomalous details in this layer that hint at minor dialect areas. Most of central and western Tennessee is skirted completely, as is all of Missouri. The layer is thinnest or else completely absent in much of central and northern Kentucky, one of the earliest areas to be settled, and misses the Upper South settlement in northeastern and central Texas.

This layer is relatively faint and has less prominence in the speech of the Upper South than the South layers. Not only is its lexicon less than half the size of either the South I or II, its terms have a lower frequency of usage. An average of only 23 percent of the Upper South informants gave half of the thirty-four responses conflated in map

6.2. The Upper South Layer Based on 34 *DARE* Isoglosses. Primary and
secondary boundaries.

6.2. For the Lower South layer (map 5.8) the average frequency is about 28 percent,
and for the South I layer (map 4.3) it is approximately 35 percent. In short, the words of
the Upper South layer have relatively low currency.

In addition, even when we take into account that the *DARE* informants, reflecting this region's general demography, are more rural and less educated than in any other
section of the country, the lexicon is used overwhelmingly more often by speakers who
are rural, old and/or not educated beyond the sixth grade. In other words, the dwindling
currency of these terms and the social profile of their users indicate that this is an
obsolescent layer, a fading aspect of the Upper South dialect.

Lexicon

Not surprisingly the lexicon has a strong old-fashioned, folk flavor. If it weren't for the
genuineness of its expressions we might consider them mere caricatures of the speech of
mountain folk, the kind we might find in the old "Lil' Abner" comic strip, or in
"Snuffy Smith." The greeting *hidy* (= hello), a blending of "hi" and "howdy," is an
example of this, as is the use of *ever* to mean "every" in combinations like "everwhere," "ever direction," "everway," and so on.

Some of the "folksiness" comes from the old-fashioned or relic nature of many
of the expressions, such as *brickle* and *brickly* meaning brittle or fragile. These variants
of *bruckle,* which still has currency in Scotland, probably came to America with the

Scotch-Irish. Similarly, *fornent* (= opposite, near to, against), usually pronounced *fernent* or *ferninst,* is also originally Scots. Only nine informants, all well over sixty-five years of age, used this term indicating that it is probably much less current than in 1835 when Davy Crockett wrote: "I walked with them to a room nearly fornent the old state-house" (*An Account of Col. Crockett's Tour to the North and Down East* 1835, 123).

Some of the expressions concerning illnesses equally have a folk resonance to them, though they are not necessarily relics. A momentary feeling of weakness accompanied by a rapid heart beat and difficulty in breathing is sometimes called a *smothering spell,* an expression known by a surprising number of middle-aged and young informants. This condition, which might be eased with a *dram* (= a small amount) of brandy, would not qualify as being *bad sick,* a term reserved for acute or chronic illnesses. One would be said to be bad sick if the symptoms included the *flux,* or worse, the *bloody flux,* an especially severe case of diarrhea.

As might be expected, many of the terms are rural in nature, dealing with farming and down-home cooking. Calls to farm animals are highly distinctive of rural regional speech. The Upper South is distinguished by *co-sheep(ie)* or *cu-sheep(ie),* used to bring sheep in from the pasture, and *cope* or *kwope,* the corresponding call to horses. Both expressions have the nearly universal, abbreviated form of "come": *co-, cu-* or *kwo-,* the latter call, *cope,* probably deriving from *come up.* Similarly the names for the udder of a cow are also frequently characteristic of rural dialects. The Upper South has the rather homely version, *sack.*

When a farmer plants his fields, he is liable to say that he is going to *set* a crop. Two types of plows he might use in setting his crop are a *double shovel plow,* which is simply a plow with two shovels or blades, and a *bull tongue plow,* which has a shovel shaped something like a tongue. Both terms have been in use since the early nineteenth century. When hitched to a draft animal, the leathers or ropes used to guide it are often called *checklines,* in standard usage "checkreins."

The hay chute in a barn is sometimes known as the *scuttle hole,* a landlubber extension of the nautical term for a covered hole or hatchway in the deck of a ship. The extended meaning, however, referring to.any lidded hole in a roof or wall is an early development (ca. 1700), but came to refer specifically to a hay chute only in the Upper South.

Among the common types of grasses a farmer may use for pasturage are *fescue* and *orchard grass.* The *DARE* fieldwork shows *fescue* in use almost exclusively in the Upper South and scattered areas of the Atlantic South coastal plain. *Orchard grass,* on the other hand, is more widely known, especially in the North, though the greatest concentration of informants are in Kentucky, eastern Tennessee, and in the western portions of North Carolina and Virginia.

A grove of sugar maple trees has been called a *sugar orchard* in the Upper South, specifically in Kentucky, since at least 1833. However, many *DARE* and atlas informants in New England, famous for its maple syrup, also knew this expression (cf. *WG,* fig. 145). In the Upper South the *DARE* informants are concentrated in the Appalachian province.

Fruit orchards in this region of the South often produce *plum peaches,* the regional name for the clingstone peach (cf. *WG,* fig. 128). In the garden *half-runner beans* (= a firm white pea bean) might be planted, and in certain cultivated fields *goober peas* (= peanuts) may be set. Although *goober* is known throughout most of the South, the Upper South often uses the fuller form, *goober pea,* which first appeared in print in an 1833 Louisville, Kentucky, newspaper.

Most of this produce would at one time or another appear on the dinner table. Other foods one would be likely to see are *corn dodgers* and *redeye gravy.* The former is yet another Southern version of corn bread, this one usually in the form of small cakes. *Redeye gravy* is a simple unthickened gravy made from ham or bacon drippings, the grease forming small eyelike globules. Although probably inherently salty, if one were to add more to it, one would use the *salt shake,* a container found on most American tables for sprinkling salt.

At breakfast, pancakes or *flitters* are often served, a variant of *fritter* and in use in this region since at least 1848. Over a stack of flitters, *sorghum,* or in full, *sorghum molasses,* is sometimes poured, a syrup made from the juice of the sorghum plant.

If milk is sour it is called *blink* or said to be *blinked,* the latter term used interchangeably with the Inland South, *blinky.* These expressions may have their origin in the old folk belief that milk is turned sour through witchcraft and the "blinking" of the evil eye. Another version has it that the flashing or "blinking" of lightning is the term's origin, since thunder and lightning were thought to blink or sour milk.

In the Upper South the mantel above a fireplace is often called a *fireboard,* a transferred sense of the older usage referring to a cover over the front of a fireplace. Kurath calls this a South Midland term (*WG,* fig. 27) and Atwood (1962, map 73) shows its use scattered over central and eastern Texas, the southeastern corner of Oklahoma, and southern Arkansas. The main log placed toward the back of a fireplace is called a *backstick,* a variant of the more universal "backlog."

The locution *to feel of* meaning to examine something by touching it ("The Delaware drew near, felt of the wood, examined its grain," Cooper, *Deerslayer* 1841, xii) was at one time used in New England and New York, but seems to have died out there sometime in the nineteenth century. Today it survives primarily in the Upper South where a surprising number of Upper South informants were young or middle aged.

Upper Southerners, especially older and rural ones, are likely to call an argument or verbal fight a *cuss fight.* Sandstone is often *sandrock,* and the noisy cicada is frequently a *jar fly,* perhaps so called because of the jarring noise it makes.

Delirium tremens, which afflicts chronic users of alcohol, is sometimes known as the *jake-legs* in the Upper South. During Prohibition, this expression applied more specifically to a paralysis of the legs caused by drinking Jamaica ginger—*jake* for short—which was an alcohol extract of ginger cut with methyl alcohol to discourage its consumption. So drinking *any* adulterated liquor, particularly bad moonshine, or, according to some sources, drinking "sterno," will give one the jake-legs. With the repeal of Prohibition and the decline in the consumption of bad liquor, the term survived by more loosely applying to the d.t.'s.

Except for one or two expressions, then, the lexicon of the Upper South layer has dwindling currency, even among old and rural speakers. Accordingly, it is characterized by a strong folksy flavor, enhanced by a majority of old-fashioned and decidedly rural expressions.

The Inland South Layer

Map 6.3 shows the geography of an even fainter layer, with only 22 isoglosses (see app. A), though it has a fairly well-defined boundary. The isogloss numbers show considerable strength in the highlands of Virginia and North Carolina, in most of South Carolina and Texas, and in scattered parts of Alabama, Mississippi, and southern Louisiana.

This suggests a close relationship with the South I layer of map 4.3. That is, not only does the northern extension of this layer closely mimic the South I layer, complete with Hoosier and Missouri apexes, but the general area virtually covers the entire South except for most of the coastal plain. Indeed a few of the isoglosses might just as easily have been counted with the South I lexicon, notably *house shoes, ambeer, nicker,* and *saw.* It seems probable, then, that the Inland South layer is essentially an aspect of the same historical forces that created the South as a whole and is merely a minor subdivision of Southern speech.

At the same time, but to a much lesser extent, it also resembles the Midland

6.3. The Inland South Layer Based on 22 *DARE* Isoglosses. Primary and secondary boundaries.

layer, covering the core of that region and generally excluding the coastal plains. However, only one isogloss counted here, *scoot* (= to move something over), is sufficiently ambiguous that it could arguably be placed in the Midland layer. At any rate, the crucial difference between the two layers is that the Inland South stays below the North-South divide.

The core of highest isoglosses, set off by the heavy line in map 6.3, covers all of Kentucky, which is the heart of the region. Tennessee is also included, but as in the South I and II layers (maps 4.3 and 4.5), central and southwestern Tennessee has very low numbers essentially excluding it from the core area. The northern portions of Georgia, Alabama, and Mississippi are a part of this core, the boundary through this region roughly coinciding with the Lower South boundary. The Outer Delta is also neatly outlined and is the only portion of the Lower South included in this layer.

Lexicon

Although the lexicon does not give many clues to the precise origin of this layer, what information we can glean from the histories of many of its expressions, suggests that it originated primarily outside the Lower South. Put another way, the layer for the most part was not formed by a regionalized vocabulary, one that originally had widespread currency in the South, but subsequently died out in the Lower South, while surviving in the Inland South.

The citations of several of the expressions further suggest that the vocabulary came with settlement west and southwest from the Virginia tidewater and Pennsylvania hearths. The earliest citation for *careless grass* (= any of various weeds of the genus *Amaranthus*), for example, indicates that by 1807 it was established in Maryland and Delaware. Likewise *carrion crow* (= vulture) was quite current in North Carolina in the 1790s. Originally a sixteenth-century English term for a species of crow, by late the next century it also referred to a vulture. The first record of it in America comes from William Bartram's travelogue of the Carolinas (1791), noting that "the inhabitants called [the coped vulture] the carrion crow."

Unlike these expressions, there is no early documentation for *saw!*, a command that Inland South farmers sometimes use to make a cow stand still during milking. However, the atlas fieldwork for the Atlantic states shows it in heavy use in Virginia and to a slightly lesser degree in western Maryland, central-south Pennsylvania, West Virginia, and North Carolina (*WG*, fig. 101). The *DARE* isogloss essentially agrees, but shows the term to be rare in the coastal plain of North and South Carolina, and in most of Georgia and Florida. In any case, these distributions suggest a Virginia origin.

Pennsylvania, however, seems to have had a greater part in the creation of this layer spawning the largest number of traceable expressions, even though today most of these have little currency in that hearth. *Cur dog* (= a mongrel or worthless dog) is a good example. Although it appears to be a redundant folk term, since "cur" also means a mongrel, both words can be traced back to Middle English *curre-dog*, derived in part from *kurren*, which means to growl. It shows up in America first in Pennsylvania (1791) and then in Massachusetts (1830). *Dog-irons* (= andirons) is also first cited in Pennsylvania (1790) and then in Kentucky (1836). Except for one informant who used "dog-irons," no other *DARE* informants in Pennsylvania used these expressions.

The original sense of *hydrant* as the well-known street fixture is first recorded in Pennsylvania (1806). This Americanism, an invented form using Greek *hydor* (= water), next shows up in a work by the New York writer James Fenimore Cooper (1846). Sometime during its migration into the Inland South, it began to be used with its regional meaning of "water faucet."

Two expressions from the lexicon probably came from Pennsylvania with the Scotch-Irish. The humorous sounding *bumfuzzled* meaning "confused, perplexed, or flustered" may be related to Scots "bumbazed" (= stupified) or else may derive from English dialect "dumfoozle" (= to bewilder or nonplus).

To slide something over or to move oneself so as to make room for someone else is to *scoot over* or *down*. The original Scottish sense of *scoot* was "to eject or squirt" something. Although this sense does not seem to have come to America, the meaning "to slide something" did and is first recorded in Pennsylvania (1837) and New England (1838). It seems to have had a certain amount of currency in nineteenth-century New England—it is used in *Moby Dick,* for example—but today it is rarely used there (no New England *DARE* informants gave it as a response) and is well known throughout the Inland South and West.

It seems likely, then, that this layer is primarily the result of the sweep of Upper South settlement from Pennsylvania and the Virginia tidewater hearth. The histories of the remaining words of the lexicon are too sketchy to draw any further conclusions about the origins of this layer. However, they do fill in the cultural picture of the region.

Crawfish, for example, is a familiar name for a well-known feature of Southern culture and cuisine. As early as 1842 it was used metaphorically in Georgia to mean "to move or crawl backwards." It was further extended figuratively to mean "to back down from a position or commitment" ("You got me into this blamed mess, and now you want to crawfish." Eggleston, *Hoosier Schoolmaster* 1899, 108). Today it is used in this sense throughout the Inland South, and surprisingly enough, in the Pacific Northwest.

Although terms relating to food usually play a significant part in the lexicons of every dialect layer, this one is notably lacking them. The only exception is *blinky* meaning "sour" with reference to milk. And one of the few domestic terms that is regional is *house shoes,* which is both a recent and widely current term for slippers worn indoors.

The lexicon, however, is well represented by rural and farming terms. A hay wagon is often called a *hay frame,* and the common moldboard plow is a *turning plow* or *turn plow* since it turns over a furrow slice. In this region, a horse *nickers,* and a short distance is referred to as a "short or little *piece.*"

A right smart piece is the distance veteran tobacco chewers can spit their *amber* or *ambeer* (= saliva colored by tobacco), "chewing" being primarily a pleasure of rural folk and baseball players who have common access to wide-open spaces for depositing their ambeer. This last oddity was also used in Britain in the eighteenth century and derives from the color "amber," which has been altered to include the connotations of "beer."

Calf-rope has nothing to do with roping calves, but is instead a children's cry of surrender, synonymous with the more universal "I give up" and "uncle." Children's pastimes in this region include playing a *French harp* or harmonica, the isogloss of which is a paradigm for the Inland South.

Perhaps a more common pastime, especially among boys, is *town ball,* a bat-and-ball game resembling baseball but with fewer players. This game is actually a forerunner of baseball and probably did not originate in the South. *DeWitt's Base-Ball Guide* for 1878 noted that "nearly forty years ago [this] species of base-ball . . . was in vogue in Philadelphia" (15). It was called town ball because it was played whenever a town meeting was held. Though it has become regionalized to the Inland South, even there it is less well known than the similar game, *cat ball,* and is probably dying out.

Hunting and fishing are also common boys' pastimes. In this region the *catalpa worm,* the larva of a large American hawk moth, is a favorite bait to use. Among the edible freshwater fish to try for is *shad,* which is probably a crappie or sunfish. When a novice hunts game he may get "buck fever" (= extreme nervousness at the sight of game), but only in the Inland South does he get *buck ague* or *buck ager.*

The Inland South layer, then, is a relatively faint one, originating in the Virginia tidewater and Pennsylvania hearths, even though Pennsylvania, Virginia, and North Carolina are almost completely excluded from it. In addition, it reinforces the major North-South boundary through southern Illinois, Indiana, and Ohio, and adds another dimension to the Upper South dialect.

Combined Layers

Map 6.4 generalizes boundaries and areas from four different layers: the Upper South layer (map 6.2), the Inland South layer (map 6.3) and the South I and II layers (maps 4.3 and 4.5). The general outside boundary essentially corresponds with map 6.1, with some important exceptions.

The Upper South layer reinforces the boundary through the Atlantic South, from Virginia to northeastern Alabama, while the Inland South layer strengthens it through the Gulf states, Georgia to Mississippi, and in eastern Texas reinforces the already strong Southern boundary. But in northern Louisiana, the Inland South layer adds another level of complexity to the transitional Outer Delta subregion (the dashed line, map 6.4).

A relatively strong internal boundary running north and south cuts through the Appalachians and is generalized from the primary boundaries of the South II layer and the Upper and Inland South layers, which form a very loose strand that winds erratically through the mountains. The isoglosses immediately to the west of this boundary are considerably denser than they are to the east. That is, speakers in parts of eastern Tennessee utilize more of the lexicons of these layers than do speakers in parts of western North Carolina.

Two striking areas of very low isogloss density occur in the Bluegrass region of northeastern Kentucky and the Nashville Basin, including a section to the southwest, in

**6.4. Combined Layers: Upper South (map 6.2), Inland South (map 6.3),
South I (map 4.3), and South II (map 4.5)**

Tennessee. These two subregions, however, are not characterized by the same layers.
The relatively low isoglosses in Kentucky occur in the South II and Upper South layers,
while in Tennessee the thin densities occur in all four layers, though the South II layer
is the least distinctive.

The situation in Tennessee is a complex one and needs closer analysis than is
possible with the wide-meshed *DARE* data. The evidence here suggests that Tennessee
is divided into two general speech regions: eastern and western Tennessee, the latter
being characterized by considerably fewer South and Upper South features. This accords
with aspects of the early settlement pattern. The Cumberlands, for example, for a long
period formed a barrier between eastern and middle Tennessee.

Tennessee, however, has historically been divided into three sections: east,
middle, and west. In the early days there was a land office and a treasurer for each of
these. Today the Supreme Court still sits in rotation among these three districts (Vance
1935, 36–37). The physiography of the state also corresponds with this three-part
division with the Mississippi lowlands in the west, the Nashville basin in the middle,
and the Appalachian system of plateaus and highlands in the east.

The Ozark highlands, which have a distinctive culture and history, dominate the
Missouri apex formed by the South I and Inland South layers, a pattern reinforced by
the North layer extending southward on both sides of the apex.

The Midland Layer

Even with the four layers combined and generalized in map 6.4, the picture of Upper South speech is not complete without an account of the Midland layer. Map 6.5 shows the Midland layer as a composite of 40 isoglosses, 14 of which extend into the West (see app. A), while the other 25 more or less confine themselves to the western limits of the Upper South.

A primary boundary encloses a core area of high numbers (13 or more) in Kentucky, West Virginia, southeastern Ohio, and the so-called Hoosier apex in southern Indiana and southeastern Illinois. The secondary boundary runs along the Appalachians, through the northern portions of the Gulf states, meandering westward through southern Arkansas and northern Texas where it is not always sharply defined. In the North Central states this boundary wends through central and northern Ohio in an erratic manner, on into northern Indiana and Illinois, reaching the Mississippi fault line and continuing in Iowa at a more northerly point. A clear tertiary boundary runs across central Pennsylvania and includes small sections of northern Ohio and Illinois.

Map 6.6 shows the relationship of the Midland layer to the Upper South by superimposing its primary and secondary lines on the Upper South boundary of map 6.4. In general, the Midland layer is slightly displaced farther north, with its core occupying all of the northern section of the Upper South and its southern boundary from Virginia to Arkansas running parallel to the Upper South line (the dotted line).

The Midland layer, however, with only 40 isoglosses has considerably less weight than the Upper South, which is derived from several different layers. Because it is relatively faint, and because it is roughly coterminal with the Upper South, it is essentially part of the Upper South itself. At the same time, it is a transitional layer between the Upper South and the Lower North, which it overlaps. The Ohio River threads through the center of the Midland core suggesting that this major waterway of migration from the east played a greater role in the formation of this layer than it did for the other Upper South layers whose cores in Kentucky suggest the dominance of the Cumberland Gap–Wilderness Trail migration route.

The penetration of Midland terms into Indiana and Ohio reinforces the apex patterns already established in the South I and Inland South layers. The term *apex,* and specifically *Hoosier apex,* is one of those catchy nicknames that dialectologists are sometimes fond of giving to distinctive or unusually shaped dialect patterns on the land.[2] Albert Marckwardt was probably the coiner of "Hoosier apex" (Marckwardt 1957, 7). Using early preliminary fieldwork for LANCS, he noticed the prevalence of certain characteristics of Southern speech in Indiana, notably the [z] pronunciation of *greasy* and the use of *granny woman* for "midwife." What made this remarkable was that these features were essentially absent from the speech of the sister states to the east and west, the result of the early migration of Southerners across the Ohio River, reaching "a point farther north in Indiana than in either Ohio or Illinois" (Marckwardt 1940, 139).

The deep northern extent of the apex is evident from map 6.6. As a mixture of features primarily from the South, Inland South, and Midland layers, it reaches into

6.5. The Midland Layer Based on 40 *DARE* Isoglosses. Primary, secondary, and tertiary boundaries.

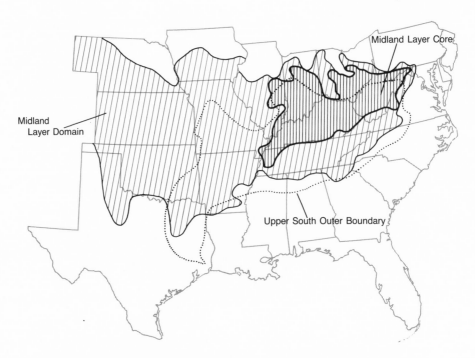

6.6. The Relationship between the Upper South Layers (map 6.4) and the Midland Layer (map 6.5)

northern Indiana, and central and southeastern Illinois. Similarly a corresponding, if somewhat smaller, apex covers southern Ohio.

The Appalachians

With their conduit valleys, the Appalachians played a large role in the formation of the layers of the Upper South, spreading features southwestward and forming the eastern edge of the region. A handful of isoglosses suggest the importance of the Appalachians to the Upper South.

Spring houses were probably invented by the resourceful yeomen of the Blue Ridge mountains and valleys of western Virginia early in the eighteenth century. By building a small house over a spring or brook, perishable foods could be kept cool and safe from spoilage. Despite the widespread use of refrigerators, spring houses were still widely known in the Appalachians, as the one hundred and three *DARE* informants testify (map 6.7).

Poke suggests a historical connection and geographical closeness between the Midland layer and the Upper South. This term for a bag or small sack usually made of paper—the same "poke," by the way, that is in the widely known phrase "a pig in a poke" (or the Scotch version "a cat in a poke")—is used throughout the Appalachians from Pennsylvania to Alabama (map 6.7), a distribution reminiscent of the eastern limits

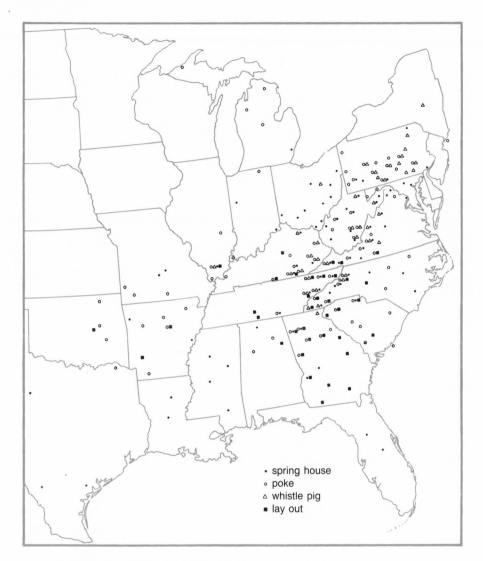

6.7. Selected Appalachian Isoglosses

of the Midland layer. From there the isogloss breaks off and reappears in southern Illinois and in the Ozarks, settlement areas of the Upper South.

The isogloss for *whistle pig,* the name given to the groundhog or woodchuck, is virtually exclusive to the Appalachians from New York to northern Georgia. To *lay out* of school (= to play truant or hooky), however, is an expression found almost exclusively in the southern Appalachians from western Virginia and eastern Kentucky to the piedmont of Georgia and South Carolina.

All of the isoglosses in map 6.7 suggest that the Appalachians have a viable if small regional lexicon, perhaps a remnant of a much larger vocabulary that diffused throughout the Upper South, sometimes, as in the case of *poke* and perhaps *whistle pig,* moving northward up the mountain province into the domain of the Midland layer in Pennsylvania, later to be carried westward into Ohio.

The Midland Layer Lexicon

Because the Midland layer originates from the southeastern Pennsylvania and tidewater Virginia hearths, it is reasonable to expect the histories of the words of the lexicon to reflect this. But only two expressions, *sugar tree* (= sugar maple) and *papaw* (= a North American tree), can be reliably traced to the tidewater, and only two, *muley* (= a hornless cow) and *donsie* (= ill, sickly), are traceable to southeastern Pennsylvania, brought to America from the Scotch dialect. The rest of the vocabulary is very poorly documented in America, since less than one-third of the Midland layer words are Americanisms. The remaining two-thirds have not drawn the special attention of scholars, word lovers, or historical dictionaries concerned with American English, and so their histories in America are extremely sketchy.

The most remarkable thing about the Midland lexicon is that it is rather unre-markable; for the most part it does not have the uniqueness or flavor we've come to expect of a regional lexicon. It does not have, for example, the relic quaintness of the Upper South lexicon, nor the ethnic flavor of many Lower South words. Most Midland words would probably not give a speaker outside of the region much pause; words like: *armload* (= armful; cf. *WG,* fig. 73); *bedfast* (= confined to bed due to illness), which is not recorded in American English prior to an 1890 Louisiana citation; *coal oil* (= kerosene) and *coal bucket* (= container for coal); *blinds* (= roller shades; cf. *WG,* fig. 16), which is first recorded in a Harriet Beecher Stowe story of 1875; *strand* (= necklace); and the expression requesting to disembark from a bus, *want off* (cf. *WG,* figs. 15, 159). All of these terms are well known throughout the Midland-and-West.

The largest group of words and perhaps the most colorful are the expressions for certain plants and animals. Four North American trees have Midland names. The orna-mental Osage orange is often called a *hedge apple,* while the basswood tree or linden is called a *lind wood.* Both *sugar tree* (= sugar maple) and *papaw* (= a North American tree with purple flowers and large edible fruit) were known in colonial Virginia, as the writings and diaries of Robert Beverley and George Washington testify. The latter tree's name is probably an alteration of *papaya,* a tropical American tree that bears large yellow fruit, whose name was adopted by the Spaniards from an Indian language probably of the Carribbean.

The woodland plant with its distinctive cuplike flower, known most often as jack-in-the-pulpit, has been called the *indian turnip* in the Midland area since at least 1806. As early as 1819 *smartweed* was used in Missouri for any of various knotweeds so named because they have an acrid "smarting" juice.

The ubiquitous dragonfly, with its many regional folk names, is known by users of this lexicon as the *snake feeder* (cf. *WG,* figs. 15, 141). First recorded in mid-nineteenth-century Illinois, the name shares in the popular myth that has dragonflies attending snakes—hence also the Southern version, *snake doctor*. Another insect with several regional names is the wasp that builds a mud nest with cells into which it lays its eggs along with a provision of paralyzed prey for the future larvae. In the Midland-and-West lexicon these various wasps, which might actually be from different genuses, are *mud daubers*. Primarily in the eastern portion of this layer, any of numerous small short-tongued bees are known as *sweat bees,* perhaps because they are attracted by sweat.

Earthworms in this latter region are often called *fishing worms,* for the obvious reason that they are used as bait. A *woolly worm,* however, is not a worm at all, but is any of various large hairy caterpillars, also sometimes used as fishing bait. One of the edible water animals that one might fish for but not with a line and hook is a *crawdad* or *crawdaddy,* a fanciful variant of the Southern *crawfish.*

Farming expressions make up the next largest group of the lexicon. When a Midland farmer wants to call his cows he is likely to shout *sook* or *sook cow* (cf. *WG,* figs. 4, 15, 99). This is probably an alteration of *suck* with reference to suckling or feeding and has been used at least in the Upper South since the 1850s. To call sheep the farmer, especially if he were from the eastern portion of the Midland layer, would simply use *sheep* or *sheepie* (cf. Dakin 1971, 41).

In the Midland-and-West a hornless cow is called a *muley* or *muley cow.* The earliest American citation for *muley,* however, is from New York (1838), and for the variant *mooley* from New England (1838; see *DAE*). Nevertheless, because it derives from the Scots and Anglo-Irish word for "hornless," *moiley* (ultimately from the Irish or Welsh word for "bald," *maol* or *moel*), it was probably in earlier use in Pennsylvania and the Appalachian Valley. Also in the Midland-and-West, a calf is said to *bawl* when it cries for its mother.

A *hedge fence,* the unremarkable Midland term for a hedge used as fencing, probably would not restrain even a small herd of cows, but would be used to mark property boundaries and provide a certain amount of privacy. The term was first used in colonial New England (1662 in Rhode Island, 1778 in Massachusetts), and so must have been widespread, but in time became regionalized to the Midland area. A much stronger fence, known in the Midland lexicon as a *rock fence,* is made from the stones removed from the fields by means of a drag or *sled.* This large and heavy sled, however, was quite unsuitable for children to do *belly-busters* with, that is, to do a running dive onto a coasting-sled and riding it downhill lying on the stomach.

In this lexicon a haycock or stack of hay is a *rick* or *hayrick* (cf. *WG,* 54, fig. 60). This is the very old English word, *(hreac),* in use prior to the tenth century. This earliest form, however, also referred to stacks of other farm crops, such as grain and peas. *Horse corn* in this lexicon is field corn and is usually considered livestock feed. Although it may be fed to mules, in some parts of the midlands it is also used to make *white mule,* that is, moonshine, which is both white or clear and has a mulish kick to it.

Among the more domestically oriented words are *fourteen-day pickles,* cucumbers soaked in brine for two weeks before processing; *sop,* a Midland-and-West term for gravy; and *fat meat* for bacon, also sometimes used as a poultice. Bacon is usually smoked, a process that, before modern techniques of chemical preservation and re-frigeration, was done in the *meat house,* a small building for curing and smoking fish or meat. To remove the hulls of beans and peas is to *hull* them (cf. *WG,* fig. 132).

One of the oddest Midland usages is *mango pepper* or simply *mango* for the large sweet pepper or bell pepper. Since a mango is a tropical fruit with a juicy pulp and taste quite unlike a pepper, it is a puzzlement why this name has been transferred to the New World capsicum. Nevertheless, it is probably here to stay, since 112 *DARE* informants throughout the Midland layer area used the expression. While shopping for mangoes, one might carry them in a *poke* or sack (cf. *WG,* figs. 17, 70). This old term, the diminutive of which gives us the standard "pocket," is tightly restricted to this lexicon, except in the common expression "to buy a pig in a poke." Given the currency of *poke* in the Scotch dialect, especially formerly, it seems probable that this term entered the lexicon via Scotch-Irish immigration (cf. Crozier 1984, 325).

One expression that was almost surely brought to America by the Scotch-Irish is *donsie* or *dauncey,* ultimately deriving from Scotch Gaelic *donas* (= evil, harm, bad luck). Its earliest Scotch and northern English meaning (1717) is "neat and trim," which seems at odds with its other early senses (1786) "unfortunate, unlucky" and (1802) "dull, duncelike." The Midland usage followed later and is an extension of the last two senses: "ill, sickly, feeble, low-spirited." With only twenty-six *DARE* informants, its use in the Midland lexicon appears to be dwindling and is probably headed toward obsolescence.

One notable feature of the Midland layer is its lack of terms for children's games and play. Except for *belly-buster,* there are no other children's expressions in this lexicon, at least as the layer is defined here.

The Nonexistent Midland Dialect

The features of the Midland layer have led linguistic geographers to conclude that there is a strong Midland dialect on the same order as the other major dialects such as Lower South and Upper North. Hans Kurath first developed the notion of a Midland dialect in *WG,* but he presented only twelve representative isoglosses (*WG,* 28–30). Eight of these are also used to derive the Midland layer (map 6.5) in the present work: *snake feeder* (= dragonfly), *sheep* or *sheepie* (= a call to sheep), *sook* (= a call to cows), *want off* (= to want to get off [a bus]), *bawl* (= the cry of a calf or cow), *armload* (= the amount that can be carried in the arms), *hull* (= to remove the outer covering of beans), and *blinds* (= roller shades). The atlas distributions of these eight essentially agree with the *DARE* data, their geography having changed very little in the period between the two sets of fieldwork, except that their full western extension can be seen in the *DARE* versions.

The other four isoglosses that Kurath uses have either changed or probably should have been assigned to a different layer. Since he was using the atlas fieldwork that included only the Atlantic states, his view of the country was incomplete and could not reveal, for example, that *till* in expressions of time ("It's quarter till nine") is used throughout the South (map 4.3), or that *piece* (= a certain distance) more properly belongs to the Inland South layer (map 6.3).

Likewise the *DARE* view of *spouting* (= rain gutters or downspouts) places it in the Lower North layer. *Skillet* (= a heavy frying pan), however, has probably expanded its province. It has invaded the Northeast and the Atlantic South where the regional counterpart, *spider,* once held ground. "Skillet" is now well known throughout the country, though the *DARE* isogloss still hints at denser usage in the Midland layer area.

If we were to use only these twelve isoglosses from the *DARE* fieldwork, it would be possible to outline a region very similar to that of the Midland layer. Indeed Kurath's definition of Midland (see map 1.4) essentially agrees with the Midland layer's tertiary line. But the fact that it is a tertiary line implies that he gave too much weight to these few isoglosses. They are important but they represent the outer limits and not the main body of the layer, which as we've seen, is closer kin to the Upper South than to any dialect region unto itself.

One reason that Kurath placed more emphasis on the Midland layer than it deserves can be attributed to his not detecting the North-South divide, in part because of the limitations of the area of his fieldwork that did not extend south of central South Carolina or west of the Appalachians (except in eastern Ohio). In his study there is no boundary corresponding to the northern limits of any of the three South layers (cf. map 1.4). Nor did he discover the boundaries of the North layer. Without an awareness of these important boundaries, the first-order North-South linguistic divide eluded him, which in any case he dismissed out of hand as an oversimplified conception.[3] If he had been aware of this divide he would not have been as likely to posit a major Midland dialect straddling it. Instead, taking the strong Upper North and Lower South boundaries as primary, he divided American speech into North, Midland, and South.

Not only does the linguistic divide preclude a Midland *dialect,* but there is very little in the cultural geography that corresponds to a Midland region. Factors such as physiography, climate, religion, economics, historical institutions (e.g., slavery), or the patterns of material folk culture (see Glassie 1968, fig. 9, p. 39) contradict the existence of such a region.

Because Kurath cut the dialect pie into North, South, and Midland, which roughly correspond in this study to the Upper North, the Lower South, and the Midland *layer,* he gave them all essentially equal weight as dialect regions and set the pattern of thinking in American linguistic geography into a tripartite classification. His approach further classifies the Upper South as a subregion of a Midland dialect and accordingly labels it "South Midland." Likewise the northern portion of his Midland region he calls "North Midland," which resembles the Lower North layer.

This difference in names—*Upper South* versus *South Midland* and *Lower North* versus *North Midland*—is an important one; more is at stake in this opposition than mere nomenclature. At issue is how to classify the major dialect regions, which is itself a problem in understanding how the dialects relate to each other and has numerous implications for the cultural and historical geography of the area.

Ironically the first person to question the classifying of the Upper South as a subdialect of Midland was Kurath himself. "It may well be that the South Midland, which has few distinctive terms of its own but shares some of its vocabulary with the North Midland and some of it with the South, may have to be regarded in the end as a subarea of the South rather than of the Midland" (*WG*, 37). Despite his reservations, he treats the Upper South as the "South Midland" subdivision of Midland, thereby establishing what has become virtually doctrinal in American dialectology.

One of the most profound effects of this approach has been to classify a large body of regionalisms as being "South and Midland" or "South and South Midland" as if these lexicons did not present evidence of a separate and unified dialect area. Instead their areas are usually conceived in terms of the three-part division. But as we saw in chapter 4, the South I and II layers (approximately equivalent to Kurath's "South and Midland" and "South and South Midland" respectively) form a first-order dialect region that has one of the largest characterizing lexicons of any region. It is a misconception to treat this primary region in terms of the relatively minor Midland layer.

Charles-James Bailey (1968) was one of the first linguists to seriously question Kurath's tripartite division. Although his paper is impressionistic and offers virtually no objective evidence, relying primarily on the test of his own Upper South speech, his intuition about the position of the "South Midland" in the hierarchy of dialect regions is basically correct. He maintains, for example, that "the boundary separating the alleged 'North Midland' and 'South Midland' dialects [i.e., the North-South boundary] is of far greater importance than the one separating the latter from 'Southern' [i.e., Lower South] speech" (Bailey 1968, 1) and therefore "South Midland" properly belongs with the South and not with the so-called Midland dialect.

In other words, it is a matter of attending to the weight or relative importance of two boundaries, the one dividing the North from the South and the one dividing the Upper South from the Lower South. As we saw in chapter 4, the North-South boundary, although difficult to pinpoint precisely, forms the primary linguistic divide in the United States. Certainly this boundary far outweighs the line separating the Lower and Upper South.

Because there has been no unified collection of data covering the country as a whole, American dialectology has not recognized this first-order boundary and so has persisted in speaking of a Midland dialect region. Because this boundary is at the top of the hierarchy of regional dialects, there cannot be a dialect which overlaps this line the way the traditional "Midland dialect" is supposed to do. It follows that any subregions that fall south of this line are subdivisions of the South, and those that fall to the north are subdivisions of the North.

Bailey goes on to argue that "the two Northern dialects [i.e., the Upper and Lower North] and the two Southern dialects [i.e., the Upper and Lower South] have more linguistically significant resemblances to each other than the resemblances that obtain between the currently styled North Midland and South Midland dialects" (1968, 1).

The relatively close linguistic kinship that Bailey claims exists between the Upper and Lower South is evident from the South I and II layers (maps 4.3 and 4.5)—three if we count the South-and-West (map 4.8)—that the two subregions share. Moreover, the boundary separating the Upper and Lower South in map 6.1, especially in southern Arkansas, northern Mississippi and Alabama, and in western North Carolina and Virginia, is relatively minor, particularly in contrast to the northern boundaries of the Upper South. Even when we take into account the two minor dialect layers, Upper and Inland

South, because they are based on relatively few isoglosses that tend to be obsolescent or relic forms, there is still no strong contrast with the Lower South. This suggests that like the Lower South, the Upper South is properly a subdialect of the South and not of the Midland.

Indeed "Midland" refers to a single relatively minor layer that is really only a variation on the Upper South theme. Given its relatively small number of isoglosses, and its great overlap with the Upper South, it simply does not have the primary status in the dialect hierarchy that Kurath assigned to it. Nevertheless, the Midland layer is an important one for it contributes to the great complexity of the Lower North.

The Lower North Dialects

Pennsylvania

Although Pennsylvania, the last coastal hearth to be settled, played an important role in establishing the Midland layer and the Upper South as a whole, notably through the influence of the Scotch-Irish and Germans from the southeastern corner of the state, it played a greater part in the foundation of the Lower North. At the same time, it formed at least one distinctive speech region of its own.

Pennsylvania was not colonized until the 1680s when William Penn established a Quaker community in what is now the greater Philadelphia area. From the beginning it was a sanctuary for Europe's oppressed. The Thirty Years' War and the unsettled political, religious, and social conditions in Europe, particularly in southwestern Germany, which was ravaged by Louis XIV in 1688–89, condemned a large number of Germans to a wretched life of hardship. Because Penn's colony had the best farmland in the North and was liberal and open to all religions, it attracted large numbers of immigrants. Penn himself visited Germany to tell the persecuted minorities about the promise of his New World colony.

Four groups dominated the early settlement: Quakers and other English and Welsh colonists, who for the most part remained in the urban area of Philadelphia, and German and Scotch-Irish settlers, who moved immediately into the back country. Most of the German immigrants had a strong pietistic Protestant bent, most apparent in the large number of Moravians, Mennonites, and Amish.

After the initial establishment of the colony by the English, Palatine Germans began arriving in 1710. By 1717 mass migration from Germany, often via England, was under way. Most arrived as indentured peasants, who, after working for seven years to pay off the cost of their passage, pushed into the interior, where, because they were too poor to buy land, they simply squatted. By 1726, about one-hundred thousand of them had carved out farms that were eventually recognized as legitimate claims to the land.

The first Palatines settled along the Delaware valley as far as Bethlehem, which was established by a group of Moravians in 1741, and along the Schuylkill River as far as Reading, which was founded in 1748 by people from Württemberg and the Palatinate. The Tulpehocken area in western Berks County was first settled in 1729 and became an important German settlement area whose cultural centers were (and are)

Womelsdorf and Stouchsburg. The Susquehanna Valley, however, which resembles the Rhenish Palatinate, was the promised land that attracted most of the settlers. Gradually these areas filled up, until settlement reached the less fertile lands around the Juniata River. At this point the stream of German settlers turned southward and began moving down the accessible Great Valley of the Appalachians.

Close on the heels of the Germans were the Scotch-Irish. Beginning around 1720, a repressive series of Parliamentary acts induced thousands to leave Northern Ireland and to settle in New England or the New York frontier. Most, however, headed for the peripheral lands of the Pennsylvania colony. Because the Germans occupied the best lands, the Scotch-Irish were forced farther afield into the hillier country along the Juniata as far west as the frontier outpost of Bedford. It was not long before they turned southward, especially after 1738 when Virginia and North Carolina promised religious freedom for Presbyterians.

By the 1740s, while most of Pennsylvania was virtually empty, settlement filled the southeast corner stopping at the foot of the Appalachian Mountains, which form a broad crescent impeding westward movement but facilitating southwestward migration. The result is that southeastern Pennsylvania is a dominant cultural region distinct from the later settled areas.

Because of the Appalachian block to migration, western Pennsylvania did not begin to be settled in earnest until the 1760s. Virginians considered the southwest corner of Pennsylvania—present-day Greene, Fayatte, Westmoreland, Washington, and Allegheny counties—to be part of their state. Consequently, during the early 1750s most of the settlers in this area were from Virginia. Despite Indian treaties forbidding settlement west of the Appalachians, by 1763 several hundred houses surrounded Ft. Pitt, which was to become Pittsburgh, and scattered settlements lined the upper Monongahela River. Nearly all of these early settlers were from Virginia and Maryland.

Problems with the Indians were not resolved until the Treaty of Fort Stanwix in 1768 opened the entire territory south and east of the Ohio River. Virginia still holding claim to the southwest corner of Pennsylvania continued to supply most of the settlers, until about 1785 when the Scotch-Irish began flooding into the area after the state of Pennsylvania completed improvements on the Forbes' Road ultimately connecting Philadelphia and Pittsburgh. Prior to this, Pennsylvanians migrating to this area had to travel first southward and then westward along the trails used by the Virginians.

In the decades that followed, the southeastern section continued to expand north and westward, while the southwestern section filled up and expanded north and eastward. It was not until the 1790s that the northwestern part of the state began to be settled in earnest.

These settlement patterns to a large extent shaped the persisting cultural and linguistic geography of Pennsylvania. Its long history and varied ethnic origins, as well as its seminal position in the settlement of the Lower North and the Upper South, have made Pennsylvania an important and complex cultural area, whose unique characteristics fortunately lend themselves well to field research, making it one of the best-documented regions in the country. Geographers have used at least seven types of cultural elements to define the area: farmstead characteristics (Glass 1971), town mor-

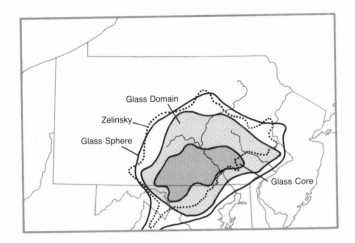

6.8. The "Pennsylvania Culture Region." Glass core, domain, and sphere (1971) and Zelinsky (1977). (See also Rooney et al. 1982, 15.)

phology (Zelinsky 1977), urban street patterns (Pillsbury 1970), material folk culture (Glassie 1968), folk housing (Kniffen 1965), religion (Zelinsky 1961), and of course speech (Kurath 1949).

Joseph Glass (1971) using the physical characteristics of barns, farmhouses, and other farmstead elements and employing an arithmetic analysis of these features that he recorded at regularly spaced grid points, was able to define a core, domain, and sphere of the Pennsylvania Culture Region, as the southeastern section shown in map 6.8 is sometimes called. Wilbur Zelinsky, focusing on the same general region, achieved similar results based on common morphological features of towns, such as the presence or absence of row houses, duplexes, stucco, stone construction, painting of brick buildings, the use of trees, and several other features. The results of his fieldwork (map 6.8) defined a region that closely followed the western and northern line of the cultural sphere of Glass's study, with boundaries also running closely parallel to the Allegheny Front. In the south and southeast, however, Zelinsky's line differs considerably. Even so, both studies were able to outline a distinct cultural region.

Not surprisingly a similar picture is seen in the geography of the language. The Pennsylvania German region, for example, falls within Glass's domain though it does not extend into Maryland. But coinciding more closely to the Pennsylvania Culture Region as a whole is the Southeastern Pennsylvania dialect layer that in map 6.9 is made up of 15 isoglosses. The outer boundary, which is quite distinct, closely follows the domain in Glass's description (see map 6.10). Because Glass used farming and farmstead elements, his boundary naturally corresponds more closely to *DARE*'s rurally biased fieldwork than, say, to the town or urban morphology.

Pennsylvania German is to the region of this layer as Dutch is to the Hudson Valley. Half of the isogloss terms are adopted directly from Pennsylvania German, particularly from the Pennsylvania German kitchen. *Thick milk* (= sour clabbered milk) is still a common usage, a calque from *dichemilch*. In both Pennsylvania German and

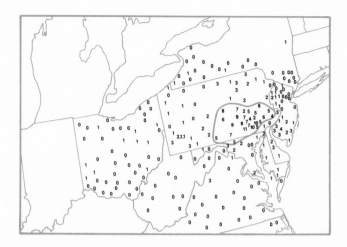

6.9. Southeastern Pennsylvania Dialect Layer

Pennsylvania English, *pannhas* or *panhas* is headcheese or scrapple and can be analyzed into the German forms *Pfanne* (= pan, skillet) and *Hase* (= hare, rabbit), there apparently being in the Pennsylvania German imagination, at least formerly, a connection between pan (fried) rabbit and sliced scrapple, which is often fried.

A deep-fried cake or fritter is often called a *fastnacht,* though this formerly referred only to *Fastnacht Kuchen,* cakes made on Shrove Tuesday (German *Fastnacht* = fast night). Bacon is sometimes referred to as *flitch,* especially by older speakers. This is actually an old Germanic word used in Old English before 700 A.D. (*flicce*), as well as in Old Norse (*flikki*) and Middle Low German (*vlike* or *vlieke*), the latter being

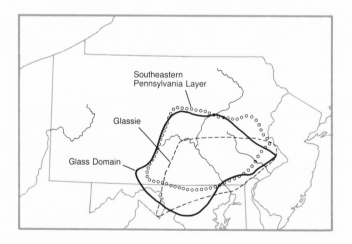

6.10. Combined Southeastern Pennsylvania Boundaries. Glass (1971) domain (map 6.8), Glassie (1968), and Southeastern Pennsylvania layer (map 6.9).

the source of the Pennsylvania Dutch *flitsch*. Despite its possible English credentials, the Southeastern Pennsylvania *flitch* probably entered American speech via Pennsylvania German since it survives nowhere else in American English.

A recipe that may have come from a German kitchen is the one for *chicken corn soup*, which, according to the *American Heritage Cookbook*, is made with chicken, corn, and egg-and-flour dumplings and was a picnic favorite in Lancaster County, a Pennsylvania Dutch county.

When someone says "The potatoes are all" meaning they are finished or all gone, he or she is probably from a community settled by Germans and one probably in Pennsylvania. This usage is a direct borrowing of German *alle* (= all gone) and was first noticed by the American lexicographer William Bartlett in 1859, who observed that it was a Pennsylvania usage.

Among some Pennsylvania English speakers, a rubber band is a *gum band*, which may have its origins in or been influenced by German *Gummi* (= rubber) and *Gummiring* (= rubber band). However, nearly all of the twelve informants were located in western Pennsylvania. Another expression that may derive from the German dialect is the preterite form *got awake* (= woke up), perhaps a calque of *wacker warre* (or *wocker waare*) or *mach wocker*. Atwood in his analysis of the verbs in the linguistic atlas fieldwork noted that this idiom was "very common" in this region (1953, 25, see fig. 20).

The remaining seven terms in map 6.9 apparently do not have their origin in Pennsylvania German. *Baby coach* is the usual term for a baby carriage here, and as Kurath also discovered (*WG,* fig. 20), is confined primarily to southeastern Pennsylvania, southern New Jersey, Delaware, and eastern Maryland. A *caretaker* in much of the state, though not the southeast, is neither a baby-sitter nor a keeper of grounds, but is a highway superintendent. In most of the state, except the Philadelphia area, the median strip that runs down the center of a highway is called a *medial strip*.

Other equally recent regionalisms characteristic of Pennsylvania are *viewing* (= a funeral wake), *washboard* (= a baseboard or mopboard), and the expression for a wooden friction match, *barn burner,* which has pyromaniac overtones. Finally, *dressing* or gravy, is recorded in the *American Dialect Dictionary* as having been "in best educated use" in Lebanon, Berks, and Lancaster counties in the 1930s, all three counties having relatively large Pennsylvania German populations.

Pennsylvania Subregions

The so-called Pennsylvania Culture Region, as we've seen in the discussion of settlement, is an important source area for the country to the west (the Lower North) and to the southwest (the Upper South). In Pennsylvania itself, the spread outward from its southeastern focal area created three subareas that geographers have charted using several criteria. Map 6.11 combines the boundaries from four different regional studies, each based on a different type of data for the most part obtained from fieldwork.

Richard Pillsbury's study (1970) maps the distribution of geometric ("rectilinear" and "linear-r") and nongeometric ("linear" and "irregular") street patterns of

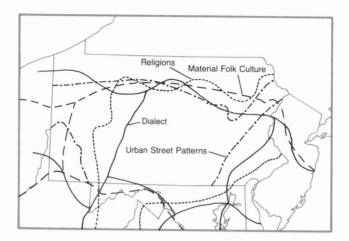

6.11. Cultural Region Parameters of Pennsylvania. Religions: Zelinsky (1961), material folk culture: Glassie (1968), dialect: Kurath (1949), and urban street patterns: Pillsbury (1970).

358 Pennsylvania towns. He found that the state is divided into four sections. The largest section is central and western Pennsylvania that is dominated by geometric street plans, as well as other incidental features such as the Pennsylvania German barn and certain house types (442). Nongeometric town plans dominate the northern and southeastern sections of the state, which have, however, quite different cultural features. Finally, the southwestern corner of the state has a mixture of geometric and nongeometric street patterns and, as Pillsbury notes, "probably is not a separate culture area . . . but rather a transition zone which contains elements of both the Pennsylvania [i.e., Southeastern Pennsylvania] and Chesapeake Bay cultures" (443). We have already seen the source of this transitional area in the settlement history.

Henry Glassie's more inclusive work (1968) is based on the material folk culture of the Eastern United States. He too divides the state into four general areas: southeastern (see map 6.10), northern, central, and southwestern. The first three are clearly marked off by such things as types of spinning reels, or the folk art of "sgraffito," which is a type of pottery decoration (46), or the presence of central or external chimneys on houses. The southwestern area, however, again appears to be transitional, "characterized by the irregularity of the cultural landscape," a patchwork of Yankee, Southern, and Pennsylvanian elements (157).

Wilbur Zelinsky in his study of cultural regions (1961) used church membership records to plot the distribution of the members of twenty-two different religious denominations. Because each denominational group has one or more regional concentrations attributable to the cultural and settlement history, it was possible for Zelinsky to derive a general map of the religious regions of the country. Because of the unusually open and free policies toward religion in the Penn colony, the Pennsylvania hearth became notably diverse in its religious makeup. The best represented groups were the Quakers, Methodists, Presbyterians, Dutch Reformed, Lutherans, and various Germanic

groups (Zelinsky 1973, 98), such as the Brethren (popularly called "Dunkards"), Mennonites, and Moravians. Based on the geography of these churches and on other factors,
Zelinsky outlines a major subregion in Pennsylvania that he calls Pennsylvania German
and that covers nearly all of central and southeastern Pennsylvania (see map 6.11).

Finally, the most relevant study for our purposes here is Kurath's (*WG* 1949),
which is based on the linguistic atlas fieldwork. He divides the state into four regions
(see map 1.4): the Delaware Valley (the Philadelphia area), the Susquehanna Valley,
northern Pennsylvania, and the Upper Ohio Valley (western Pennsylvania).

The boundaries of all four of these studies have been conflated in map 6.11
where they bundle in a very general way. The tightest bundle not surprisingly occurs in
the North, indicating a primary linguistic and cultural boundary, the same boundary
derived in map 3.16. This by now well-established line is remarkably sharp, ranging
from only ten to forty miles in width. Given the diversity of the data and its span over a
hundred-fifty-year period (from about 1800, when the street plans were established, to
1952, the approximate year of the church membership census), the spatial variations
among the Upper North boundaries are minor.

The story in the southeast and especially in the southwest is quite different.
There is a strong bundle separating the Philadelphia and Pennsylvania German area of
the Lower Susquehanna Valley, but it is not as coherent as the Upper North boundary
(cf. maps 6.10 and 6.11). We would expect this boundary to be more transitional in
nature, since Philadelphia is the source of the Pennsylvania Culture Region. The distinction between these two subregions is probably primarily attributable to the German
settlements of the interior, which additionally are distinguished along rural-urban lines.[4]
The boundaries in southwestern Pennsylvania are even more scattered, clearly indicating
a transitional zone that essentially lacks definition as a single, generalized line.

The dusty but no less true maxim of dialectology that "every word has its own
history" applies to the larger divisions of culture. Each element of a culture—religion,
architecture, speech—has its own history and regional geography, but one that generally
stays within certain broad parameters or boundaries. The distribution of the language
through space (its geography) and time (its history) changes less on the macroscopic
level than on the individual level of specific features (phonemes, words, syntax).

The *DARE* fieldwork (1965–70) reveals little change in the macroscopic dialectology since the 1930s. Map 6.12 combines various boundaries from the North, Lower
North, Midland, and Southeastern Pennsylvania layers. The Susquehanna Valley is
marked off from the Philadelphia area; boundaries coalesce approximately along the
border with Maryland; the Upper North bundle is reaffirmed; and the primary line of the
Lower North layer hints at the transitional west.

The Lower North: Settlement

The Upper South and Upper North boundaries (maps 6.4 and 3.16) run east and west in
a roughly parallel manner (except for the Hoosier apex) and in the process leave a large
gap between them—the shaded area in map 6.13—indicating a unique speech region
whose lexicon is not characterized by Upper North, South, or Upper South words.

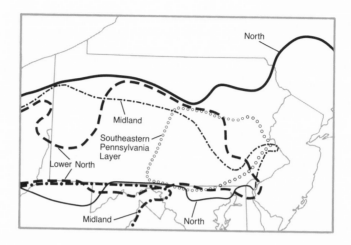

6.12. Combined Dialect Layers in Pennsylvania. North primary and secondary (map 3.3), Midland primary and tertiary (map 6.5), Lower North primary (map 6.15), and Southeastern Pennsylvania layer (map 6.9).

Particularly complex and difficult to describe, this region roughly corresponds to the cultural geographies outlined by Gastil (1975) and Zelinsky (1973), who call it the "Middle West," though they don't entirely agree on its dimensions (see map 3.1). Caught between the strong opposing cultural forces of the South and the Upper North, this is naturally a region of transition and mixture.

Three different streams of migration channeled in the relatively small space between the Great Lakes and the Ohio River made this an extremely complex linguistic area. Not only was it a crossroads of migration, a conduit from the East to the West, but it was and still is a transitional corridor between the two major cultural regions, the North and South.

There were four main entryways to the Lower North. The earliest was through the Cumberland Gap. Settlers who took this route traveled up the Wilderness Trail settling in north-central Kentucky or continued westward on the Cumberland River or northward on the Kentucky River, eventually reaching the Ohio Valley. Later, particularly after the War of 1812, these routes extended across the Ohio into what is now southern Illinois and Indiana bringing a flood of immigrants primarily from the uplands of Kentucky, Tennessee, Virginia, and North Carolina. Once across the great river, they continued along the territorial roads to Lafayette and Vincennes in Indiana, or to St. Louis and Alton on the Mississippi River, pushing Southern culture deep into the North.

The Ohio River itself was an early major entryway into the North Central states, carrying settlers primarily from the Northeast, including Pennsylvania and Maryland, who settled such river towns as Marietta, Massie's Station, Columbia, and Cincinnati in Ohio and North Bend in Indiana. Later these settlers moved into the back country of central Ohio soon to be joined by land seekers from Pennsylvania, Virginia, and Kentucky.

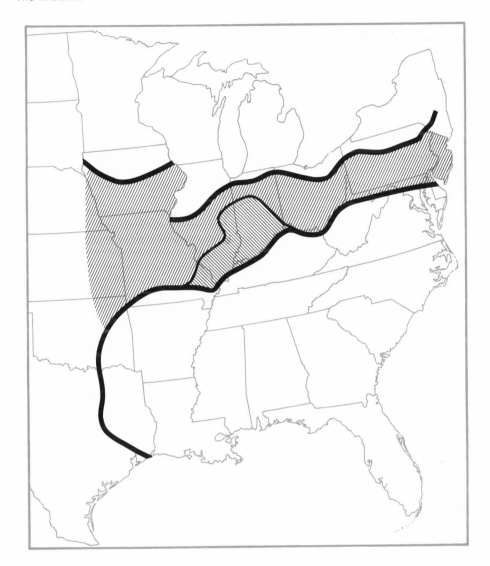

6.13. The Lower North as the Upper North minus the Upper South

This westward river route was later supplemented by the National Road (see map 3.6), which in 1818 extended from Cumberland, Maryland, to Wheeling, West Virginia, on the Upper Ohio, giving greater access to that river. Eventually the road was extended to Columbus, Ohio (1833), and on to Indianapolis and Vincennes, Indiana, eventually ending at Vandalia in southern Illinois, some seventy-five miles short of its intended terminus in St. Louis. Settlers primarily from Pennsylvania and Maryland followed this highway, settling along its length or moving into the back country along territorial roads. The National Road lives today as U.S. Interstate 70.

As we saw in chapter 3, the Great Lakes and the Erie Canal were another major

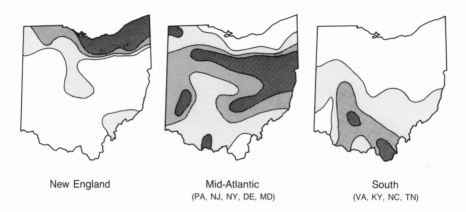

New England   Mid-Atlantic   South
                    (PA, NJ, NY, DE, MD)   (VA, KY, NC, TN)

6.14. Percentage of the 1850 Population in Ohio from Three Eastern Hearth Areas. Darkest to lightest shading represents: over 75%, 51–75%, 26–50%, and less than 26% of the population born in another state. (Source: Wilhelm 1982.)

entryway conducting settlers from New England and New York into the northern parts of Ohio, Indiana, and Illinois, as well as into Michigan and Wisconsin. This route also funneled European immigrants into the Upper North who landed at New York City, the principal port of entry.

The four entryways served migration streams from three distinctive sources— Upper Southerners by way of the Wilderness Road and the Ohio River; Pennsylvanians and Marylanders by way of the Ohio River and the National Road; and Yankees and New Yorkers by way of the Great Lakes. All three streams tended to remain separate as they continued westward, creating a three-tiered settlement pattern in Ohio, Indiana, and Illinois (cf. maps 1.1 and 3.2). Map 6.14 shows this pattern in Ohio in terms of the percent of immigrants from the three source areas in 1850.

Predictably, the various cultural features were distributed in a similar pattern. Alva Davis (1948) using the lexical features from the Linguistic Atlas of the North Central States, Henry Glassie (1968) using elements of the material folk culture, and Wilbur Zelinsky (1973) using the distribution, among other things, of religious organizations, each found that Ohio, Indiana, and Illinois are divided into three fairly well-defined regions.

The linguistic geography of the Lower North, however, is not as neat and simple as these studies might lead us to believe. Despite the generally discrete settlement pattern in Ohio shown in map 6.14, it is evident that there is also considerable mixing, overlapping, and anomaly. There are, for example, sizable percentages of Northeasterners in central and southeastern Ohio, Mid-Atlantic settlers in southern Ohio, and Southerners in central Ohio. Nevertheless a dialect layer unifies a good portion of the region, giving it its own lexicon, and at the same time mirrors the general tripartite scheme of the settlement history.

The Lower North Layer

A version of the Lower North layer is shown in map 6.15 made up of 53 isoglosses. Its outer limits marked by a relatively faint secondary boundary include northern Maryland, Delaware, all but a northern sliver of Pennsylvania, virtually all of Ohio and Indiana, central and southeastern Illinois, and a small area in southeastern Iowa. It also includes a small section of western Virginia and eastern West Virginia, a trace probably left by settlers moving down the Great Appalachian Valley from Pennsylvania.

The numbers tend to drop off rapidly north to south, but from east to west the general trend is a gradual decline from the densest isoglosses (15 or more) in southern Pennsylvania, the source or hearth of the region, and central Ohio, the earliest settled area. The isoglosses scattered in Ohio are reminiscent of what Albert Marckwardt calls the "Ohio wedge" (1957, 8), historically the result of migration from Pennsylvania. Fourteen isoglosses are particularly representative of this wedge pattern (see app. A); that is, their distributions are concentrated in the eastern portion of the Lower North. The historical evidence for at least two of these, *bank barn* (= a two-story barn built into a hillside) and *smearcase* (= cottage cheese), suggests a Pennsylvania source.

Map 6.16 shows the layer in terms of two generalized areas of isogloss densities. When the Upper North and Upper South boundaries are superimposed on this map it is easier to see the dimensions of the Lower North and its relationship to the two adjacent primary dialect regions (map 6.17). The denser area along its northern edge roughly corresponds to the Upper North boundary, while the entire layer is essentially contained within the "gap" created by the two boundaries.

So far the Lower North appears to be a relatively clearly defined region, unified by nonlinguistic cultural evidence and by a dialect layer whose boundaries essentially coincide with the adjacent major speech regions to the north and south. This picture, however, is incomplete. We also need to take into account at least two other layers.

On the one hand the Lower North is strongly unified, and on the other, the edges and boundaries of several dialect layers overlap here, cutting it into a patchwork of apparent disorder. The series of isoglosses that Albert Marckwardt (1957) derived from the LANCS fieldwork shows essentially the same thing. Strands of isoglosses cross east and west, paralleling each other, spreading north and south from the Michigan state line to the Ohio River, loosely "coalescing" in hundred-mile-wide bundles.

This relatively unusual jumble of boundaries and isoglosses indicates that the Lower North is a broad and complex transitional zone. Caught between the strong opposing pulls of the cultures to the north and south, the transition takes some two hundred miles to complete. It is through the heart of this region that the linguistic divide cuts, though it is by no means a sharply defined line, as we've seen in map 4.4 where the primary South I and secondary North boundaries meander together, cross, part, and recross.

Map 6.18 gives another picture of the divide and the complexity of the Lower North, particularly in Ohio and Indiana. It combines the secondary boundaries of three important layers: the North (map 3.3), the South I (map 4.3), and the Midland (map

6.15. The Lower North Layer Based on 53 *DARE* Isoglosses. Primary and secondary boundaries.

6.16. Relative Isogloss Densities of the Lower North

6.5). The shaded areas represent various permutations of overlapping layers. It is apparent that the linguistic divide is not a monolithic boundary, but is a broad band of mixture and transition that wends its way across northern West Virginia, southern Ohio, central Indiana, and Illinois. In a sense the Lower North is itself a very broad boundary, the great divide between the North and South.

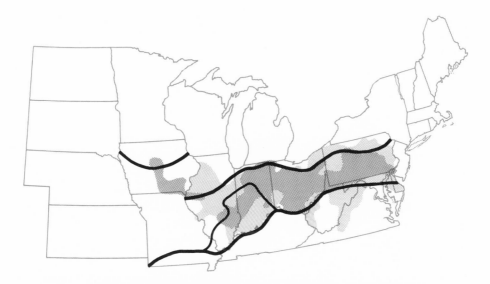

6.17. The Relationship of the Lower North Layer to the Upper North and Upper South. Shading represents the core and domain of the Lower North (map 6.16); bold lines are the Upper North and Upper South boundaries (cf. map 6.13).

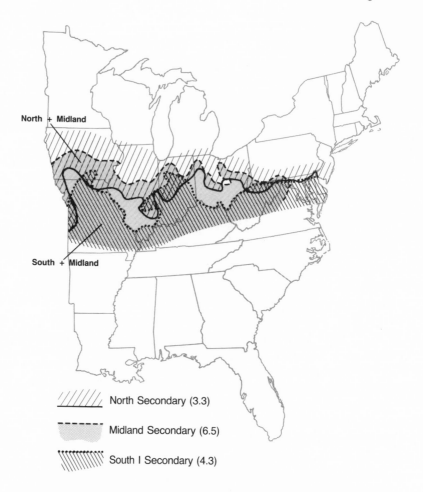

North + Midland

South + Midland

/////// North Secondary (3.3)

- - - - - Midland Secondary (6.5)

\\\\\\\ South I Secondary (4.3)

6.18. The Linguistic Divide in Terms of the Secondary Boundaries of the North (map 3.3), Midland (map 6.5), and South I (map 4.3) Layers

This raises a taxonomic problem, one that is more than just an exercise in classification, since in linguistic geography to delineate the hierarchy of regions is to understand the geographical relationships of the component layers. Ultimately it is to understand how the dialects themselves relate linguistically and historically to each other. The problem is this: is the Lower North a subregion of the North?

Just as the Upper South is generally contained within the area of the South I layer, so the Lower North is subsumed by the North layer. But how far does this analogy go? Because of its strong transitional character, the Lower North is a very different kind of region than the Upper South. Map 6.19 superimposes the three general isogloss densities of the North layer (from map 3.3) on the outline of the Lower North layer. A gradient of Northern terms, from high to low frequency, north to south, covers the Lower North, though the densest areas of the North layer do not generally overlap with the densest Lower North areas.

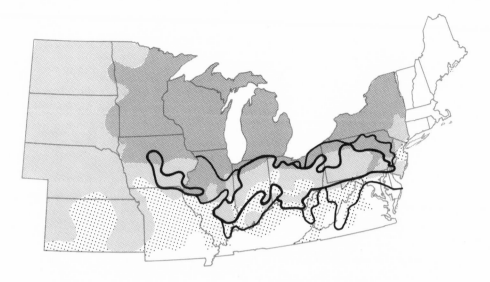

6.19. The Relationship of the Lower North to the North Layer. Shading represents the relative isogloss densities of the North layer (map 3.4); the bold lines are boundaries of the Lower North (map 6.16).

The way that the North layer overlaps the Lower North differs in an important way from the way the South I and II layers overlap the Upper and Lower South. Where the latter are almost completely contained within the primary boundaries of the South layers, the Lower North is outside the North primary boundary, which is essentially the same as the Upper North boundary. The secondary boundary of the North, however, subsumes much of the Lower North layer except in Indiana and Ohio (map 6.19) where it creates a kind of apex. The Inland North layer (map 3.9) covers the Lower North layer in much the same way.

Although the Lower North shares features with the South layers, primarily in southern Indiana and to a lesser extent southern Ohio, it clearly has a greater affinity with the North than with the South. For this reason, the Lower North is treated in this book as a subregion of the North dialect region.

At the same time, however, because the Lower North straddles the divide, it can be argued that it is not a subclass or subregion of either the North or the South, but a unique transitional region between the two, a region of mixture and gradient. Moreover, it is remarkably unified, having a distinctive and fairly large lexicon and being separated off by the strong primary boundaries of the Upper North and South. There is reason, then, to consider the Lower North as a dialect region unto itself, at approximately the same hierarchical level as the Upper North and the South.

The Lower North is physically homogeneous—very flat and ideal for farming. Indeed one of the greatest unifying forces is the rural economy. The first settlers grew wheat for eastern markets; but as the soils quickly wore out, farmers turned to corn for animal feed. Because the entire plant was usable, it yielded very large quantities of feed. It was the perfect plant ecologically and economically, and established the corn-based farming system, which used plant and animal in a very efficient, high-yield way. By the 1830s Cincinnati was known as "Porkopolis" and the formation of the "corn belt" was well under way.

Not only is the Lower North, especially the western section, unified by the corn and livestock economy, but the farming methods themselves have spread with the settlers. Settlers from southeastern Pennsylvania, for example, used a crop rotation system that is the origin of the basic three-year crop rotation practiced in most of the Lower North (see Hart 1972a, 266). This usually involved the alternate planting of corn, small grains, and hay, though between the two world wars, it increasingly became an alternating rotation between corn and soybeans.

This economy and the resulting life-style established a culture steeped in the work ethic. The belief that the limits of success were bounded only by one's capacity to work hard was passed down, along with the farm itself, from generation to generation. This and its general isolation from forces of change contributed to the remarkable stability of the Lower North culture and to its tendency to resist change. In this it strongly resembles the Lower South.

Lexicon

Though there is the usual contingent of farming terms in the speech of this layer, surprisingly almost none of them have any reference to the role that corn has played in the economy and culture of the region.[5] In fact two of them refer instead to maple syrup production. *Sugar grove* or *sugar maple grove* is the regional term for an orchard of sugar maple trees. When a speaker wants to refer to the grove together with the facilities for producing syrup (boiling house, arches, etc.), he or she would be likely to use the expression *sugar camp*. This latter expression was also used in New England as early as the 1770s, though it has virtually died out there (see *WG,* 76, fig. 145).

One of the rotation crops, hay, is piled into small stacks or *hay doodles* (often shortened to *doodles*). This may be another example of folk nicety, a euphemized version of *haycock,* since *cock* is also a name for penis. Grain is stacked into bundles or shocks and covered with a top bundle or *cap sheaf.* A hay pasture might be fenced off with a *stake-and-rider fence,* which typically has a top bar or "rider" supported on crossed stakes. Such a fence, however, might not be strong enough to prevent the accidental or unintentional breeding of a mare, the foal of which would be said to be *pasture bred.*

The fields in olden days were cleared of large stones by means of a *mud boat,* the Lower North name for a drag or sledge. The stones themselves might be referred to as *dornicks,* though this term usually signifies hand-sized stones small enough to throw. This unusual word probably comes from the Irish *dornog,* a small round stone. However, it seems unlikely that it arrived with the Irish, who did not come to America in significant numbers until the later nineteenth century, by which time the word was already well established in Missouri (1840) and Arkansas (1853). Instead it probably came with the Scotch-Irish, even though they used few purely Irish terms.

The harvest's root vegetables were often stored either in a natural cave or in a dug out cellar; both were called a *cave*. The cellar of course was where you retreated in severe weather, especially in this flat, tornado country. Accordingly forty-five *DARE* informants said that an "underground place to go in case of a violent windstorm" was called a *cave*.

Houses in the Lower North, as in other regions, have a metal trough along the roof edge to carry off rainwater, but here it is called *spouting* (cf. *WG,* fig. 54). A privy or toilet is also pretty universal but in this region it is sometimes called a *stool,* a name that goes back to early-fifteenth-century England, where the fuller form was the "stool of ease."

Many farm houses have a *summer kitchen,* a small building adjacent to the house, or more recently, an additional room on the house itself. During the hot months most of the cooking, which naturally increases the indoor temperature, is done in this kitchen isolated from the rest of the house. This Lower North feature has been around since at least the mid-nineteenth century.

Two potato dishes have Lower North names. *Hot potato salad* is probably a regional recipe brought to America from Germany, while *fresh fried potatoes* or *fresh fries* (= sliced and fried potatoes) are probably indigenous to America, though this is a Lower North term. *Scrapple* is the name in the eastern Lower North for headcheese, which is made from "scraps" of meat boiled with cornmeal and allowed to set into a loaf.

Smearcase is also used primarily in the eastern Lower North, having spread there from the German settlement area of southeastern Pennsylvania. The German word for cottage cheese, *Schmierkäse,* refers to its softness and ability to be smeared on something, preferably on other foods such as bread or lettuce. If you were to smear a bit of this cheese on a cracker and eat it between meals, you'd be eating a *piece.* This too comes from southeastern Pennsylvania, but probably from the Scotch-Irish. It is short for "piece of bread" and is a Scotch expression for a snack of bread and perhaps jam or other topping. Another Scotticism is *redd* or *redd up,* which means to clear an area ("redd the dinner table") or to clean or straighten up a space ("redd up your bedroom"; see Crozier 1984, 311).

The Lower North has three different regionalisms for the syrup or sweet sauce poured on ice-cream or sometimes pudding. *Dressing* is usually used in combinations like "chocolate dressing" or "raspberry dressing." *Dip* has been in use in America since at least 1846. *Dope* is especially common in Ohio and probably derives from Dutch *doop* meaning sauce. The earliest American English use of dope (1807), however, refers to gravy.

Among the terms for certain flora and fauna are *hedge tree* for Osage orange, *umbrella plant* for mayapple, and *Johnny-jump-up* for any of various pansies or American violets. In the Lower North stag beetles are often called *pinch bugs,* a name Mark Twain used more than once (see *DA*). A sparrow is sometimes called a *spatzie,* another term borrowed from German (*der Spatz* = sparrow). Since at least the early nineteenth century, minnows have been called *minnies,* and a stream where one can find minnies, is often called a *run.*

Run has been used in America since the colonial beginnings, the earliest citation coming from a 1605 source. It was established early in New England and Virginia, where it was still of sufficient currency in the late eighteenth century that George Washington could use it in his diaries unself-consciously. But by the twentieth century the term is found almost exclusively in the eastern Lower North. In the Old World it seems to have been primarily a Scottish usage sometimes pronounced and spelled "rin."

Among the children's games played in this region, a form of tag is called *black man*. In this version, played since at least the late nineteenth century, there are safety bases, and if one is caught by "it" or the "black man," then the one caught also becomes a "black man." The game in which a ball is thrown over a house between two players is called *andy-over*, while a somersault or handspring is called a *flip flop*. A belly-flop on the water is known as a *belly-smacker*.

In much of the Lower North an infected, suppurating ear is said to be *gathered*, but in the eastern portion of the region it is also said to be *bealed*. Similarly, an abscess or boil, especially if it is in the ear, is called a *bealin'*, these two latter terms being variants of *boil* (= pustule).

To walk quietly or tiptoe is to *sneak*. In standard American English "to sneak" connotes a furtive or stealthy act, whereas among the Lower North *DARE* informants it was used in a very nonfurtive context: "She came sneaking to the baby's bed." *Wakened* is a common past participle form of "wake": "I have wakened from a nightmare" (cf. Atwood 1953, 25, fig. 20). A know-it-all or smart aleck is also known as a *smarty*, which is sometimes used as an adjective, as when Twain writes in *Life on the Mississippi:* "In the old times, the barkeeper owned the bar himself, and was gay and smarty and talky" (370).

Like the Upper North, this lexicon has expressions that are slang in nature. Thus, we could expect a Lower Northerner to say of someone who is considered very dull or stupid, "He (or she) hasn't sense enough to *pound sand down a rathole*." Illegible handwriting is called *chicken tracks*, and a cigar or cigarette butt is called a *snipe*, a rather long-lived slang term, first recorded in an 1889 New York source, which probably comes from the hobo expression "to shoot snipes" meaning to pick up stubs on the sidewalk or street.

Two other expressions perhaps more colloquial than slang are *goose drownder* for a heavy or steady rainfall, and *peanut heaven* for the upper balcony of a theater, possibly a blend of *nigger heaven* and *peanut gallery*.

Such words as *bank barn, smearcase, spatzie, hot potato salad, piece, redd, run,* and perhaps *dornick* suggest that Pennsylvania, particularly the southeastern section with its German and Scotch-Irish influence, is the hearth of the Lower North. At the same time the lexicon also shows mixed American origins. *Belling* (= shivaree), *meat platter* (= a dish for serving meat at table), *stake-and-rider fence, run,* and *sugar camp* were in very early usage in New England, and *dope, scrapple, snipe,* and *cap sheaf* were first recorded in New York, both regions being sources of the Upper North. This affinity with the Upper North is additionally strengthened by the handful of expressions that are slang in nature.

The Lower North, then, is a complex transitional region straddling the broad divide between America's two most dominant subcultures: the Upper North and the

Layers
Upper South (map 6.2)
Inland South (map 6.3)
Midland (map 6.5)
Southeastern Pennsylvania (map 6.9)
Lower North (map 6.15)

Regions

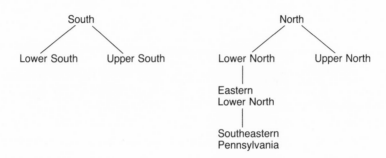

Fig. 5. **Summary of the layers and regions of the Upper South and Lower North**

South. At the same time it has an underlying unity of its own, the outcome of settlement primarily from the Pennsylvania hearth, but also the result of economic and other factors.

One of the guiding principles of this book has been that a dialect region is not fully defined by a single set of characteristic features, but is analyzable into many sets that partially overlap one another (fig. 5). Put another way, a given community of speakers will know various proportions of several regional lexicons and use them with varying frequency in contrast to the usage of every other speech community. Thus, to approach a fuller description of the regional speech of the American midlands, we must take into account the proportions and interrelationships of the layers discussed so far.

Map 6.20 combines the major boundaries and layers of the great midland section of the country. Each of the twelve layers is represented by a symbol whose size signifies a primary or secondary aspect of a layer. Thus, a combination of symbols roughly approximates the qualitative and quantitative lexical composition of the speech for selected localities. However, as already noted the weights of the layers are not neces-sarily equivalent. There are two broad categories of equivalency. The first category has more than twice the weight of the second and includes the Upper North, North, Inland North, Lower South, and South I and II layers. The second includes the Lower North, Midland, Inland South, Upper South, South-and-West, and Atlantic South layers. In this way we get a broad qualitative definition of regional speech in terms of the relative quantities of specific lexicons.

This chapter has shown that the traditional North, Midland, and South is an inaccurate description of the major regions east of the Mississippi. At the same time, a

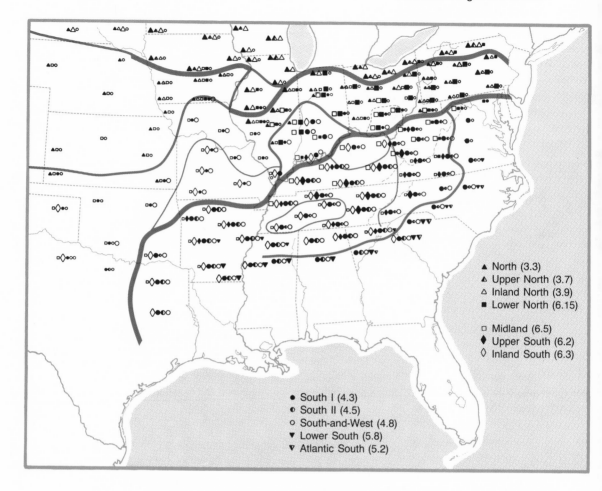

North (3.3)
Upper North (3.7)
Inland North (3.9)
Lower North (6.15)

Midland (6.5)
Upper South (6.2)
Inland South (6.3)

South I (4.3)
South II (4.5)
South-and-West (4.8)
Lower South (5.8)
Atlantic South (5.2)

6.20. Dialect Layers and Boundaries Summarized. Symbols represent localized areas not informants or specific communities. Southeastern Pennsylvania
and the Outer Delta layers are not included.

three-part dialect division has emerged: the Upper North, the Lower North, and the
South. From map 6.20 we can see that the Upper North is a relatively distinct region
defined almost exclusively in terms of the three northern layers with very little interposi-
tion of other layers.

The Lower North by contrast is very mixed. Southern features intermingle in
varying degrees with Northern features, the former dominating in southern Illinois,
Indiana, and southern Ohio, and the latter Northern features being strong in central
Illinois, northern Indiana, and central Ohio. This region is unified by a single minor
layer and by virtue of its position between the strong primary boundaries to the north
and south. This weak cohesiveness becomes even more tenuous west of the Mississippi
in Missouri, southern Kansas, and Oklahoma, where (except in southern Missouri) it is
difficult to discern any unified pattern at all.

The South, specifically the Upper South, is also mixed but in a very different way. It is a region of diversity in unity. Like the Upper North, three layers (South I and II, South-and-West) strongly unify it. But unlike the Upper North, several other layers (the Upper South, Inland South, Midland, and Lower South) in various combinations and degrees provide marked diversity.

The speech of the American midlands, then, is divided into two very different regions: the transitional Lower North, largely the result of the mixing of three different settlement streams, and the older and more unified Upper South. They are aspects of the complex but relatively clearly defined dialect regions east of the Mississippi, where time has sharpened the differences. As we will see in the next chapter, the situation west of the great river is quite different.

NOTES

1. The Atlantic South layer, however, helps define the Lower South boundary along the southern Appalachians, and the South I and II layers help define it through Texas.

2. One of the earliest and most famous examples of such a name is "Rhenish fan," which German linguists used to label the fan-shaped bundle of isoglosses separating Low from High German.

3. In *The Pronunciation of English in the Atlantic States*, however, Kurath and McDavid (1961, vi) detected the linguistic divide in terms of phonetic isoglosses. They write:

   > The relative importance of the phonetic boundaries between subareas often differs notice-ably from that of the lexical boundaries. The most striking instance is the boundary between the North Midland (Pennsylvania) and the South Midland (West Virginia), which is relatively unimportant in matters of vocabulary but very prominent in features of pronunciation.

4. Pillsbury (1970, 445) made an additional field survey stressing folk architectural forms and found that it agreed more closely with the word usage and street patterns, than the religions. But cf. Glassie's material folk culture line in map 6.10.

5. This may not be as unusual as it seems, however, when we consider the paucity of cotton terms in the Lower South lexicon (but cf. *the cotton is low*).

CHAPTER 7

The West

Excluding the early Spanish settlement of the Old Southwest, the West is barely a hundred years old, one-third the age of the Atlantic states. It was not until the 1870s and 1880s that the "New West" or "Far West" emerged as a recognizable region in contrast to what increasingly became known as the "Middle West." Consequently the language of this newest region, especially when reckoned with the dating of the atlas and *DARE* fieldwork, has barely gone through two or three generations, little time to distinguish itself clearly as a separate dialect. If American English as a whole is a youth compared to the European national languages, western American speech is a mere infant. And like an infant, its personality and features are not yet well formed.

In effect the settlement of the West is still in progress. As late as the 1950s and 1960s, migration to this vast region continued at a remarkable rate, particularly to the Pacific states, as well as Arizona and Colorado. And even in the 1970s and 1980s economic conditions were encouraging families in the industrial North to seek better fortunes "out West." Thus, Western speech is both extremely young and still undergoing the modifications and leveling processes of a region in social flux. But this in itself contrasts its speech with that of the rest of the country.

The Greater West

The West is often conceived as being "half" of the nation in contrast to the East. Some of its most obvious contrasts with the East are its very different physical environment, a great expanse of rugged, relatively empty territory once known as the "American desert"; its distinctive mix of people including Indians, Mexicans, Chinese, Mormons, cowboys, miners and others; and its insular settlement pattern, in which the primary cultural areas are separated from each other by great distance and harsh country, unlike the East whose settlements were relatively comprehensive and "integrated into a generally contiguous pattern" (see Meinig 1972, 160).

This East-West division is also present in the language in two widely distributed sets of dialect expressions. One set forms the West layer that lies wholly west of the Mississippi. The other set of a dozen or so terms can only be loosely considered a "set." These terms cover all of the West but additionally spread east of the Mississippi in various patterns, some extending as far as the Appalachians, sometimes including the Inland South, sometimes not. This group of isoglosses is so diverse in eastern extensions that it is questionable whether it legitimately forms a layer. In any case, it covers

7.1. The East-West Division as Represented by the *DARE* Isoglosses for Gunnysack and Burlap Bag. Both Alaska communities used *gunnysack;* two Honolulu, Hawaii, communities used *burlap bag* and one used *gunnysack.*

what might be called the Greater West and is an aspect of the somewhat ill-defined dichotomy between East and West.

The distribution of *gunnysack* (= a rough, loosely woven cloth bag) shown in map 7.1 illustrates one common pattern in the Greater West. In America, *gunny bag* occurs as early as 1820 in Massachusetts and was apparently a common form in the nineteenth century, the version with *sack* not appearing for another fifty years. *Gunny* came into English from Hindi and traces back to the Sanskrit *goni,* which means "sack," one of those circuitous semantic routes that gives the contemporary *gunnysack* an oddly redundant meaning, at least etymologically. In the course of that route the Hindi loanword took on a new referent, since English already had a perfectly good word meaning "sack," but lacked a word for the coarse material that these sacks are made of (*burlap* originally being a finer fabric used for clothing).

If *gunny bag* or *sack* began in New England or perhaps the Northeast as suggested by the faint persistence of the term in those areas (map 7.1), it quickly spread westward probably in the North-and-West pattern and then died out in the East, particularly the Northeast where the counterpart, *burlap bag,* became the preferred form. Although concentrated in the Northeast, *burlap bag* is used throughout the states east of the Mississippi, but with less currency in the South where *tow sack* is the usual form.

Mud hen (= American coot), an Americanism first recorded in Pennsylvania in 1813, has a similar Greater West distribution and shows the North-and-West pattern even more clearly than *gunnysack.* Similarly the isogloss for *cottonwood* (= any of various poplar trees) has aspects of this same distribution, but it is also common in the Gulf states, except in Florida. Unlike *gunnysack* and *mud hen,* however, *cottonwood* probably originated in the Mississippi Valley (1802), which suggests that its Greater West distribution has some other underlying pattern than the North-and-West.

Several other isoglosses have strong distributions in the South and the North Central states, as well as the West, and clearly delineate the East-West distinction. Two cover all of the West and reach eastward as far as the Appalachians where a relatively sharp line separates them from the Atlantic states: *baby buggy* (= a small four-wheeled carriage for a baby) and *shivaree* (= a noisy, prankish wedding celebration).

Baby buggy is the usual term west of the Appalachians, while *baby carriage* is usual east of the mountains. However, in the area between the Mississippi and the Appalachians, but to a lesser degree in the West, the Eastern term, *baby carriage,* is commonly used alternately with *baby buggy.* In other words, *baby carriage* is less sharply regional, perhaps in part because it is the older expression. On this matter, eastern Pennsylvania, southern New Jersey, and surrounding areas insist on their own expression, *baby coach.*

Shivaree extends to the Appalachians in Kentucky and Tennessee, but it is relatively rare in Ohio where *belling* is the usual term (see Meredith 1933, and A. Davis and McDavid 1949). It is also rare in the Gulf South where there does not seem to be a regional expression for this folk custom. *Shivaree* derives from French *charivari* with a similar meaning, in turn deriving from the Medieval Latin word for "headache," an appropriate enough designation for this cacophonous, sometimes drunken celebration. The custom was well known in Indiana where it is first located in print (1843). The Hoosier writer Edward Eggleston describes a "shivareeing" at length (in *The End of the World,* 1872) giving a detailed picture of a good-humored and noisy hazing of new-lyweds, who were expected to provide refreshments or other placating compensation to silence the "serenaders." Except in New York and Connecticut, the most common Eastern counterpart is *serenade,* which is used in the Atlantic states, especially in the Appalachians themselves.

A soft, homemade candy made with egg whites, apparently considered by some to be heavenly, is known throughout the Greater West as *divinity.* This too is used primarily west of the Appalachians, but is also known in scattered fashion in the Atlantic states. It is a relatively recent term (1913) and probably a recent recipe, also cited by *DA* in Washington in 1921.

The remaining Greater West terms have a more restricted distribution. *Gumbo* is rarely used east of the Mississippi River Valley to refer to heavy soil that is sticky and waxy when wet. Given their rich clay soils, the prairies, of course, have a need for such a term. By the same token, the arid and sandy Southwest and most of California have little use for it. The prairie-land novelist, Sinclair Lewis, gives a vivid sense of the quality and effects of gumbo in this tongue-in-cheek description from *Free Air:* "The car shot into a morass of prairie gumbo—which is mud mixed with tar, fly-paper, fish glue, and well-chewed, chocolate covered caramels. When cattle get into gumbo, the farmers send for the stump-dynamite and try blasting" (1919, 4).

Because *gumbo* is a transferred meaning from the Delta South term for thick okra soup, okra itself having a sticky, slippery texture, it is likely that this newer usage spread from the Lower Mississippi Valley into the prairie and Western states. The earliest written record, however, is in an 1881 article of the *Chicago Times* that refers to Nebraska soil. Other early citations place it in Wyoming (1894) and more vaguely in the West (1898). The closest Eastern counterpart is *muck,* which is especially common in the Northeast and Florida. *Black wax* is an alternative form in Texas, Oklahoma, and Arkansas.

Adam's off ox never got stuck in prairie gumbo, because it is an imaginary beast that one wouldn't know even if one saw it. This is a folk-embellished version of the "Adam" that one emphatically does not know in the expression "I wouldn't know him/her from Adam." An *off ox* is the ox in a team of oxen on the driver's right side (the left ox is the *near* or *nigh ox*). Thus, to not know or recognize someone from Adam's off ox is even more emphatic and less clichéd than the widely known unknown "Adam," which has been around since at least 1784 in England. A further embellishment on this theme of Adam is the Lower South's *Adam's house-cat* and the equally jocular *Adam's apple.* The Greater West version, which seems to have come into use late in the last century, is virtually unknown east of the Appalachians, and is particularly common in Texas, Oklahoma, Arkansas, and Louisiana.

An even more recent but clearly nonfolk regionalism is *ethyl* (= premium grade gasoline), which is in solid use west of a line from Michigan and Indiana to Georgia. Shortened from "tetraethyl lead," it is a tradename for an additive in gasoline that prevents engine knock. In the 1970s for environmental reasons, ethyl was gradually phased out as an additive; but the term is likely to remain as the generic name for high octane gasoline. The Eastern counterpart *high test* is in general use throughout the Atlantic states inland to Ohio, Kentucky, and Tennessee. It overlaps extensively with the *ethyl* region as far as a line from Minnesota to Louisiana. But west of this line *high test* is (or was, as of 1965–70) virtually an unused expression.

The three remaining Greater West terms to be discussed here have to do with children's games. The exclamation *king's ex* is used in chase games like "tag" to claim momentary immunity from being caught or to call a brief suspension of the game. Probably derived from *king's excuse,* it is an American regionalism used almost exclusively west of the Appalachians, except in Michigan, Kentucky, Tennessee, and Louisiana. The usual term in these latter four states and in all of the Atlantic states including Georgia and Florida is *time out,* an expression that does not have very strict regionality, since it is also known if less used throughout the West.

In the game of marbles the line that determines the order of play, the player whose shot is closest to the line going first, is called the *lag line* or *lagging line* in the Greater West. "To lag" is also the technique used in other games, such as billiards, to determine the order of play. Though there doesn't seem to be a single Eastern counterpart, in the South this line is called the *taw* or *toy line,* and in other scattered areas it is known as the *starting line.*

One of the numerous versions of a bat-and-ball game for a few players is *work-up.* It is played in the Greater West though almost exclusively west of the Mississippi, except for Wisconsin, Michigan, and scattered places in the northern sections of Illinois, Indiana, and Ohio.

All of these Greater West expressions have considerable currency and are relatively recent additions to American English, except for *cottonwood, mud hen, gunnysack,* and *shivaree,* and even they are early-nineteenth-century coinages. Moreover, none of the terms were the responses of a disproportionate number of old *DARE* informants; indeed, half were given by a notably young group of informants.

Although all of these expressions are pure Americana, nearly all being coined in America, none have the flavor of the West proper. They are more generic and less culturally specific than the West lexicon and define only in the loosest way a true subarea of American culture.

The West Layer

Map 7.2 is a composite of 17 isoglosses that restrict themselves to what is traditionally thought of as the West. Although this is one of the faintest layers we have dealt with, it clearly defines this nascent region, the largest in the United States. A single line

7.2. The West Layer Based on 17 *DARE* Isoglosses

emerges as the eastern edge of the region running southward through the Dakotas, into Nebraska veering eastward, then into Kansas where the line is less well defined, and finally skirting all of Oklahoma and Texas, which is surprising at least given the popular image of the history and culture of these two cowboy states. Texas, however, is a very complex mosaic of linguistic and cultural regions and will be examined in detail in a separate section.

Like most layers this one has "holes" in it, that is, nonconforming areas indicated by low, apparently anomalous numbers. There are such holes in central Colorado, in the Puget Sound area of Washington, the Willamette Valley in Oregon, and in parts of California near San Francisco and Los Angeles. It is tempting to hypothesize that these areas participate less in the layer as a whole because they are the cultural cores of regions within the West itself and have their own distinctive lexicons. But given the sparseness of the data this hypothesis cannot be adequately tested here.

The presence of nearly half of the lexicon (*frontage road, lug, bull snake, sourdough bread, bear claw, catch colt, parking* and *parking strip,* and *civet cat*) in the Upper Midwest, specifically western Wisconsin, northwestern Illinois, Iowa, and southern Minnesota, suggests a close linguistic connection between the West and the Upper Midwest.

Lexicon

The words of this layer, unlike the Greater West terms, are redolent of the so-called Wild West, evoking its history and culture. *Corral* (= a pen or fenced enclosure for livestock), for example, evokes the whole ethos of cowboys and cattle ranges so important to the early development of the West. Borrowed from Spanish by the early American settlers (1829), *corral* is reminiscent of the influence of the Mexican vaquero, who had centuries of experience at raising cattle in this arid, harsh country. The pioneers of the West also used the word to refer to their innovative technique of self-protection as they crossed the open plains. To create a defensive encampment against Indian attack, they drew up their wagons into a circle known as a "corral."

Although Easterners were familiar with the gentle gorges and hollows of the Appalachians, they had never encountered the Western mountain versions that were steep sided and cut deep by swift streams. These required a new word altogether, and once again Spanish was raided in the early nineteenth century for such a word: *canyon.* Like *corral, canyon* is also known in the East, but is rarely used there.

During the nineteenth century, the North American panther or cougar ranged throughout most of America, but as settlement pushed west, it quickly retreated to the less-populated areas. Because its retreat usually sent it to the mountainous areas, Westerners naturally called it the *mountain lion,* though very occasionally they referred to it as the *California lion.* The former name probably originated in the Colorado Rockies sometime in the 1850s and spread from there throughout the West.

A less fearsome animal but one no less to be avoided is the *civet cat* or *civvy cat,* which is the Western name for a skunk. First applied to the racoonlike mountain cat or "cacomistle" (a Nahuatl word meaning "half mountain lion"), *civet cat,* with the emphasis on the odorous "civet" (ultimately an Arabic word), was loosely applied to the spotted skunk and more generally to any skunk.

The large colubrid snake known in some parts of the country as the *bullhead, gopher,* or *pine snake,* is in the West called the *bull snake.* This name first appearing in Kentucky in 1784 and in other parts of the South as late as the mid-nineteenth century, is today almost exclusive to the West, except that it is also current in southeastern Wisconsin, western Illinois, and all of Iowa.

As with most layers there were several distinctive expressions referring to food. Two are particularly evocative of the West: *jerky* and *sourdough bread. Jerky* is thin strips of usually spiced or salted beef preserved by drying and was at times an important source of protein in the diet of early Westerners. It is another borrowing from American Spanish, *charqui,* which in turn is a borrowing from Quechua, an Indian language of Peru. It seems to have entered American English in California around the time of the 1849 gold rush and spread from there throughout the West. More recently it has been commercialized, which is probably why it is widely known throughout the country, even though as a response to the *DARE* questionnaire it is solidly a Western usage.

Sourdough also probably had its American beginnings in the California gold rush. Sour or fermented dough has been used since at least the fourteenth century as a leavening agent. Typically a bit of the fermented dough from a batch of bread is saved for use in the next baking. This method was so widespread among the early miners in the West that prospectors were often called "sourdoughs." Although *sourdough bread* was used almost exclusively in the West when the *DARE* fieldwork was done, commercialization has probably given it wider currency.

The same may be true of a *bear claw* or *bear paw,* which has nothing to do with bears, except that this pastry remotely resembles the paw of a bear. A relatively recent bakery product usually made with raisins and chopped nuts, it probably originated in California, perhaps San Francisco in the 1940s or so, and spread throughout the Pacific states where its use is most common. The Linguistic Atlas of the Pacific Coast (LAPC) field records also confirm its currency throughout California and Nevada (see Bright 1971, 177).

Unlike these foods, commercialization has had little or nothing to do with the spread of *mush,* the preferred Western term for cooked cereal. Mush is thoroughly American, coming into use as early as 1671; but back then it usually referred to a porridge made of cornmeal, also called "hasty pudding." It had numerous variations including cooling it so that it congealed, then frying slices of it and serving with maple syrup, often as a dessert. This use of mush is generally foreign to the West. There the term usually refers to cooked wheat or oat cereal eaten with milk and sugar for breakfast.

If someone is causing a disturbance by being rowdy or acting wildly, behavior reputedly common in the rough frontier towns of the West, he or she is said to be *raising cain.* This rather tired expression coined about a century and a half ago is primarily current in the West, including all of Texas.

The West's *catch colt* refers to the offspring of a mare that is unintentionally bred. Both the *DARE* and linguistic atlas fieldwork (see *WG,* fig. 150) found isolated instances of this in central New York. Moreover, the earliest citation (1901) also places it there. New York, of course, contributed substantial numbers to the settlement of the West, as well as to northwestern Illinois and western Wisconsin where this term is also used according to the *DARE* isogloss. Like the Southern *woods colt* and the Upper Atlantic South *old-field colt, catch colt* was transferred to refer to a child born out of wedlock. Both senses, however, are particularly rural and seem to have diminishing currency.

Before the so-called sexual revolution, if a woman did give birth to a "catch colt," she would have been considered a woman of loose morals, or in the slang of the day, a *chippie*. A prostitute is also a chippie. This dated expression at one time had much wider currency: it is recorded in New Orleans in 1886, Colorado in 1890, and in New England in 1896. In the late 1960s it was still current throughout the West, though only in scattered fashion in the Southwest. It was also current in scattered parts of the Lower North.

Equally obsolescent is the term for a person who divines water usually using a forked stick. Such a stick in the hands of a genuine *water witcher* would jostle and point to the ground where water could be found. In the arid West, this method was perhaps as reliable as any.

The three remaining isoglosses used to define this layer are of recent coinage and are less dated. A *lug* is a Western term for a crate or box used for shipping fruit and came into use in the 1920s or 1930s. It is also current in Wisconsin, western Michigan, and northwestern Illinois.

By the middle of this century the concrete sidewalk had become almost universal. This mundane amenity created a need for a term referring to the grass strip between the sidewalk and curb. In the West this is often called the *parking strip*. The predecessor of the parking strip was the *parking,* which came into use before sidewalks were commonplace. This form was recorded in Virginia in 1885 (three of the few non-Western *DARE* informants were located in Virginia) and Idaho in 1918 and referred to any area turfed and treed and adjacent to a building. According to the LAPC (see Bright 1977, 167) and the Linguistic Atlas of Colorado (see Hankey 1960, 60), *parking* is still common in those sections of the West.

Like the sidewalk, the road that runs parallel to a highway giving access to businesses is also commonplace wherever there are highways. Except in most of Washington and Oregon, Westerners call this a *frontage road,* a term also current in Wisconsin, Illinois, and Iowa.

It would be possible to cite many more Westernisms. But the words used to map this layer are sufficient to illustrate, as representative isoglosses, both the geography and the distinctive color of the West, hinting at several characteristic Western aspects: its unique natural dimension in *canyon, bull snake, civet cat,* and *mountain lion;* its history in *sourdough* and *jerky;* and its Spanish heritage in *canyon, corral,* and *jerky. Corral* is evocative of the cowboy and his culture, and *frontage road* and *parking strip* are linguistic echoes in a vast land where the scattered population has, even more than most Americans, a love for the automobile.

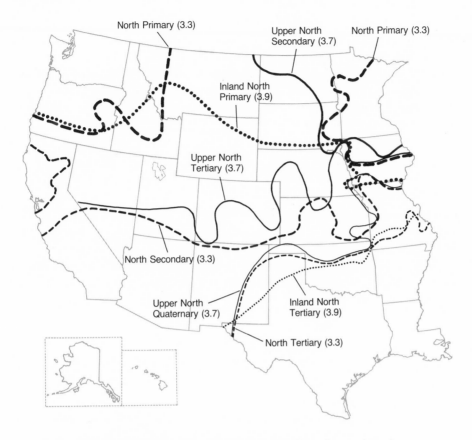

7.3. The Extension of the Boundaries of the Northern Layers into the West. This map conflates the boundaries of the North (map 3.3), Inland North (map 3.9), and Upper North (map 3.7) layers.

The Extension of Northern Features into the West

Not only is the West often conceived in terms of its apposition to the East, but, as D. W. Meinig observes, it is also thought of as part of a triad, in which "a South and a West are seen as existing in some degree of subservience to a North/East long dominant in political, economic, and social power" (1972, 159). The West, however, has many more connections with the North than it does with the South.

Just as Northern settlers dominated the population, so Northern features dominate Western speech, although primarily in the northern two-thirds of the West and, of course, with other distinctive features mixed in, notably from the Midland and Southern layers. Map 7.3 shows the three major Northern layers in the West: the Upper North (map 3.7; the solid, secondary through quaternary lines); the North (map 3.3; the dashed, primary through tertiary lines); and the Inland North (map 3.9; the dotted, primary and tertiary lines).

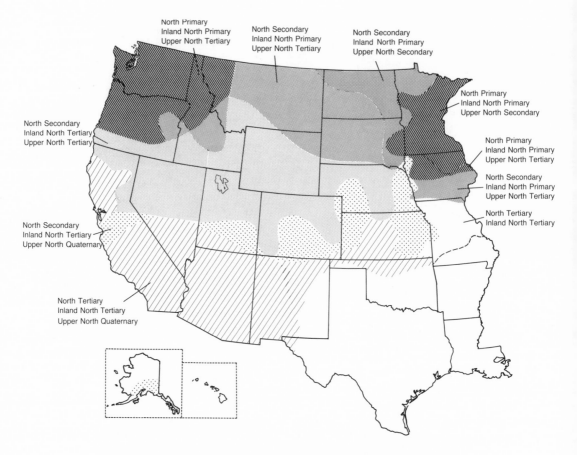

North Primary
Inland North Primary
Upper North Tertiary

North Secondary
Inland North Primary
Upper North Tertiary

North Secondary
Inland North Primary
Upper North Secondary

North Primary
Inland North Primary
Upper North Secondary

North Secondary
Inland North Tertiary
Upper North Tertiary

North Primary
Inland North Primary
Upper North Tertiary

North Secondary
Inland North Primary
Upper North Tertiary

North Tertiary
Inland North Tertiary

North Secondary
Inland North Tertiary
Upper North Quaternary

North Tertiary
Inland North Tertiary
Upper North Quaternary

7.4. The Areal Interpretation of the Northern Extension into the West.
North (map 3.3), Inland North (map 3.9), and Upper North (map 3.7).

Instead of a linear interpretation, map 7.4 expresses the overlapping of layers in terms of shaded areas, which often makes the relative weights of the layers easier to interpret. The darkest shading (the diagonal lines) represents the overlap of one secondary and two primary layers (except in northwestern Iowa and in the Northwest where the secondary has become a tertiary); that is, the areas of the highest isoglosses in two layers—the areas within their primary boundaries—overlap each other, as well as overlap the area within the secondary boundary of a third layer. The next lightest area in map 7.4 in northwestern Minnesota and northeastern North Dakota represents two secondary and one primary portions of the three layers. The next lightest areas represent one tertiary, one secondary, and one primary layer, and so on. Although this method reveals the relative weights of the layers, it does not account for the specific proportions.

The map shows a steplike gradation north to south outlining several of the major regions. The densest area of isoglosses is the Upper North extending almost due west, with a large "valley" or an area of lighter density between the eastern Dakotas and the

Northwest. The Northwest clearly emerges as a region, characterized by relatively heavy use of North and Inland North features and a smattering of Upper North terms, slightly fewer than Minnesota.

The next lower gradation or plateau of features, the Central West, extends from Nebraska across most of Wyoming, the northern sections of Colorado, Utah, and Nevada, northeastern California, and the far southern sections of Idaho and Oregon. This broad region tends to use a moderate (secondary) number of North features and only a handful (tertiary) of Upper North and Inland North words. Along the southern edge of the Central West is an irregular transition belt differing in its tendency to use fewer (quaternary) Upper North terms.

The lowest plateau of Northern features defines the Southwest as the high arid country of western New Mexico, southwestern Utah, the southern portions of Nevada and California, and all of Arizona. Here the relative weakness of the Northern influence distinguishes it from the Central West, but just the reverse holds true for the area to the east: the strength of Northern usage in the western portion of the Southwest separates it from eastern New Mexico, Texas, and Oklahoma. We will see other aspects of this east-west division in the discussion on the Southwest.

The Central Plains area—southern Nebraska, Kansas, and northern Oklahoma—is a very mixed transitional zone, while northern and central Missouri is probably a dialect region in its own right, characterized here as having only a handful of North and Inland North features.

Since New England and New York form the general hearth or source area for the North as a whole, we can get a fresh angle on the influence on Western speech by looking at the New England and New York words scattered in the West. Of the 45 isoglosses from the hearth region (map 2.4), 28 were recorded in one part or another of the West, never more than 3 in one community. Their sparse western distribution is shown in map 7.5.

Except for urban southern California, the Southwest lacks New England terms. Northern and Southern California are separated as two, completely different clusters of isoglosses (except for the peripheral overlapping of *side-hill plow,* the symbol t on the map). We will see this north-south division in more detail in the section on that complex state.

Adder and *belly girt* are New England (Upper North) and Atlantic South (Lower South) distributions: hence the concentrations in east Texas, northeast Oklahoma, and Arkansas in the South and scattered occurrences in Minnesota, Iowa, the western Dakotas, and eastern Montana.

The North-South Linguistic Divide in the West

The extension of the Midland and South-and-West layers (maps 6.5 and 4.8), each only about half the "weight" of any one of the Northern layers, are very difficult to interpret in the West. In the eastern half of the Midland and South-and-West layers, regions within these layers are relatively easy to define because boundaries are formed by steep declines in the magnitude of the numbers. But this is not the case in the West. Instead

7.5. The New England Layer (map 2.4) in the West. *a,* adder; *b,* belly-
bumper; *c,* belly girt; *d,* brown bread; *e,* corn chowder; *f,* cow corn; *g,* creepers;
h, dressing; *i,* flea in one's ear; *j,* frankfurt; *k,* grinder; *l,* hatchway; *m,* kittens;
n, matterating; *o,* mow it away; *p,* notch; *q,* pea bean; *r,* pug; *s,* rotary; *t,* side-
hill plow; *u,* snap-the-whip; *v,* swale (hay); *w,* tedder; *x,* tenement; *y,* titman; *z,*
tunnel; *A,* ugly; *B,* witch grass. (See app. A for glosses.)

the numbers vary, either gradually staying within a relatively narrow range or else
forming a "checkerboard" pattern of juxtaposed high and low numbers, as in southern
California. Where the numbers do align themselves into ridges of sudden change, it is
almost always for short distances, failing to enclose an area.

As a result these two layers, which have significant representation in the West,
tend to obscure rather than clarify the regions, with two exceptions: the Midland layer
faintly outlines the eastern boundary of the Northwest, and both layers reveal the
extremely mixed nature of regional speech in California.

But the influence of Southern speech on the West is not at all negligible, as is
apparent in map 7.6, which combines the 185 isoglosses of the three Southern layers:
South I (map 4.3; 78 isoglosses); South II (map 4.5; 84 isoglosses); and South-and-West
(map 4.8; 23 isoglosses). The result is a wavelike pattern spreading west and northwest-

7.6. The Extension of the Southern Layers into the West. This map totals
the number of isoglosses in the South I (map 4.3), South II (map 4.5), and
South-and-West (map 4.8) layers. Lines are used here to separate relatively
uniform groups of numbers (in parentheses). The widths of the lines are keyed
to the relative magnitudes of the numbers that they bound.

ward from a core area in Arkansas, east Texas, and northern Louisiana across the entire
West, gaining a slight increase in the Northwest, but fading rapidly in the Upper North.
From its core, the numbers of this composite layer drop precipitously. By the time the
wave reaches west Texas, northern Oklahoma, and central Missouri, its intensity (iso-
gloss density) has dropped 20 to 50 percent. It drops another 50 percent across New
Mexico, Arizona, and southeastern Colorado, and continues to fade across the Central
West. In California the numbers tend to be erratic, again suggesting that settlement is
still too new to have created relatively uniform speech areas.

Perhaps more than any other factor, the North-South linguistic divide defines the
general nature and geography of Western regional English. Map 7.7 compares the
Northern (map 7.4) and Southern (map 7.6) extensions, and shows how their reciprocal
relationship in the East extends into the West, where, however, Northern features gain
considerable ground.

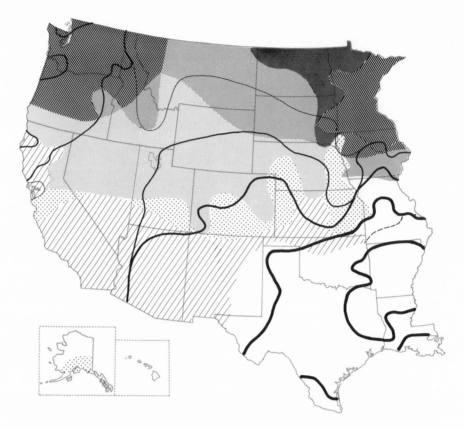

7.7. The Northern and Southern Extensions Compared. The shaded sections represent the presence of the Northern isoglosses (cf. maps 7.4 and 7.6).

The North-South divide takes its strongest expression in the differences between the Northwest and the Southwest, the two best-defined Western regions. Map 7.8 shows selected isoglosses from each region.

All three representative Southwest isoglosses are fully naturalized forms borrowed from American Spanish, a pervasive influence in this region that coincidentally and uniquely emphasizes the North-South split in the West. All three isoglosses tend to cluster in the wide strip of land that once belonged to Mexico from southern California to southern Texas. From there in rapidly diminishing usage they radiate northward especially in California and Colorado. The four representative isoglosses of the Northwest radiate southward and eastward blending with the Southwestern terms in the southern portions of Utah and Colorado which, as we saw in the Northern layers (maps 7.3 and 7.4), form a transitional zone.

The West, however, is not merely a product of the "divide" with its Spanish-influenced variation. A look at its unique overall settlement and cultural patterns will give some insight into its speech regions.

7.8. Selected *DARE* Isoglosses of the Northwest and Southwest

The Regions of the West

The close relationship that we have come to expect between settlement patterns and dialect regions is more difficult to assess in the West. The biggest obstacle is the sparsity of linguistic data. Except for the Pacific states and Colorado, most of this vast region has not been surveyed at all or surveyed in a preliminary or tentative way. The coverage of the *DARE* fieldwork is also noticeably thin, especially in the Southwest and Rocky Mountain states where hundreds of miles separate the few communities investigated. Only two communities were investigated in Nevada, only three in Wyoming, four in Idaho and New Mexico, and five each in Montana, Utah, and Arizona.

The newness of the West adds to the difficulty. A large portion of the population of any given Western state was born somewhere else making the communities mixed and difficult to describe in terms of dialect divisions, a situation especially evident in southern California (though, of course, there is nothing sacred about clearly bounded dialect regions). Because the West is passing through a development stage that the East long ago completed, fieldwork done in the mid-twentieth century captures the early processes of dialect mixture and leveling that generally occur prior to the formation of new dialect types. Moreover, the rural population, in contrast to the East, is sparsely distributed, so that the cities have grown up without the usual hinterlands, which adds to the geographical heterogeneity of Western speech and the concomitant difficulty of doing an adequate linguistic survey.[1]

Because it is vast and generally arid, the first effective settlements of the "American desert" were insular in character. Settlement leapfrogged across wide areas that were only much later and often less permanently settled. The Mormons, for example, moved from Nauvoo, Illinois, to the Great Salt Lake Valley; settlers from the Mississippi and Ohio river valleys settled in Oregon and Washington; and New Yorkers and Missourians settled in California, all without leaving any permanent intervening settlements. Thus, during the nineteenth century (much earlier in the Southwest), concentrated pockets of settlement sprang up, creating distinct cultural areas usually isolated by great empty distances. By contrast the colonization of the East was relatively uniform and comprehensive, spreading in more or less even waves from the coastal colonies or up river valleys and outward from there.

Because the centers of settlement and culture in the West were for a time discrete units, only recently becoming linked and integrated into the nation by new transportation and communication systems, the cultural regions often stand out in relief. Map 7.9 shows the major nuclei (as described by D. W. Meinig 1972) and their associated regions as they existed sometime in the latter part of the nineteenth century when they were particularly distinct. Insofar as the dialect picture can be pieced together from the meager evidence available, these isolated settlement areas appear to underlie the geography of the language.

The Northwestern settlement area, centered on the Willamette Valley and Portland, corresponds with a dialect region. California is divided into northern and southern sections as is its speech. And Colorado speech is distinguishable from Utah's by its concentration of Midland isoglosses (see map 6.5), which corresponds to the cultural and settlement boundary between the two states shown in map 7.9 (see also Hankey 1960).

But Utah and its distinctive Mormon history, which clearly makes it a cultural and settlement region (see Meinig 1965), is not so clearly a separate dialect area, at least based on the very sparse fieldwork available. More problematic is the Southwest with its distinct settlement areas in southern California and New Mexico. Again, the lack of a regionwide, detailed language survey makes it very difficult to confirm or deny some of the patterns suggested in map 7.9.

The Southwest

The dry mountainous land of the Southwest, extending over a thousand miles from southern California to west Texas, was from the beginning of its European colonization dominated by Spanish culture. For numerous reasons, such as the continued influx of

Hispanic borderland

7.9. Settlement Regions of the West. When the political border between
Mexico and the United States was drawn, a borderland was created that had a
significant Hispanic population and that increased and expanded considerably.
The Hispanic borderland shown here is defined using 1960 statistics (Source:
Nostrand 1970). The areas marked off in Texas are cultural regions (Source:
Meinig 1969, 93; see also Rooney et al. 1982, 13). (Source: Meinig 1972, 169.)

Mexicans, the Hispanic culture and language have resisted assimilation. In map 7.9 the
diagonal lines delimit the area of strongest Hispanic-American influence based on population and other data collected in the 1960s (see Nostrand 1970). This area is one
definition of the Southwest and to a certain extent mirrors the three Southwestern
isoglosses of map 7.8.

   Not surprisingly all three of these isoglosses are Spanish loanwords. *Frijoles* are
beans, usually kidney beans, which are frequently cooked, spiced, and mashed to a
paste consistency, and often served with *enchiladas* (= a tortilla filled with meat or
cheese, often covered with chili sauce and baked) or *tacos* (= a tortilla shell filled with
meat, cheese, chopped lettuce, etc.). Although these dishes and their names were
clearly Southwestern regionalisms in the late 1960s when the *DARE* fieldwork was
being done, commercial interests have spread them as both ethnic and fast-food items
throughout most of the United States, greatly diluting their original regional status.

Arroyo also from Spanish, however, is still a Southwesternism with a relatively broad semantic range extending from a "creek or small stream" to a "gully, dry wash, or streambed," to "small valley." It stays closer to its Southwestern origins (southern California, southern Arizona, New Mexico, southern Colorado, and west Texas) than the food terms *enchilada* and *taco* (see map 7.8), which in the late 1960s were beginning to spread northward in California and Colorado and into other areas such as Kansas City and east Texas.

These and the many other loanwords that characterize the dialect of the Southwest and its subareas are primarily old borrowings from the colonial period. *Arroyo,* for example, occurs in American English as early as 1806, and *frijoles* appears in 1759 in an English translation of a Spanish work on the history of California. Indeed, the English of the Southwest has been very little influenced by immigrant Spanish, that is, by the language of noncolonial, recent Hispanic immigration to this area (outlined in map 7.9; see Sawyer 1957, 1959). This is particularly true for the phonology, morphology, and syntax (see Weinreich 1954b).

Subregions of the Southwest

Although the strong Hispanic cultural strain is one of the unifying factors of the Southwest as a single general region, its history divides it into two subregions, one centered on southern California and the other on New Mexico and southern Texas.

Late in the sixteenth century the Spanish established colonies in the upper Rio Grande Valley in what is now New Mexico. Santa Fe was established as the capital of this isolated region whose primary connection for two and a half centuries with the outside world was a burro trail to Chihuahua. Its mixed population—mestizos, Pueblo Indians, Mexicans, and Spaniards—and the attendant plural culture were eventually subjected to an influx of "Anglos." The impact of Anglo settlement was profound and permanent. It not only altered the three-hundred-year-old culture, but it revolutionized the regional economy when in the 1880s railroads opened up new commercial possibilities, as well as new integrative ties with the nation.

It was not until the mid-nineteenth century that the eastern portion of the Southwest came more and more under the influence of "imperial" Texas. Eastern New Mexico, for example, was tied to Texas with railroad lines well before connections were made with Albuquerque. First cattlemen, then railroads, reinforced by periodic surges of migration and investment well into the middle of the twentieth century, consolidated the Texas influence and spread it as far as central Arizona and southern Colorado (see Meinig 1969, chap. 6, esp. map 17). At the same time, from neighboring Mexico the Hispanic culture continued to be an important, even growing, element in the Texas Southwest.

The general Southern penetration of lexical features of map 7.6 corresponds to the wavelike spread of Texas culture and economic influence, the last significant wave dying out in Arizona, southern Utah, and Colorado, creating a vague linguistic boundary between the Texas Southwest and the California Southwest. This boundary is

likewise reinforced by the Northern features of map 7.3 but in just the reverse concentrations. The veil of Northern features in the western section disappears altogether in
the eastern or Texas section.

Just as Texas forms an eastern hearth of influence on the Southwest, so California forms a western hearth. Like New Mexico, southern California was first a Spanish
colony later dominated for centuries by Mexican ranching families. Anglos began arriving in the 1850s, but not until the boom of the 1880s were the gates opened to a flood of
immigration primarily from the "Middle West." Centered on Los Angeles this land of
irrigated subtropical crops soon became a distinctive and famous place of wealth and a
free-and-easy life-style, but not before its influence had spread eastward into Arizona
and the southern parts of Nevada and Utah.

The dichotomy between these two Southwestern hearths is best illustrated in one
of the important and distinctive occupations of the West: cattle ranching. The pervasive
Spanish-Mexican influence distinguishes the Southwest from most other American versions of handling cattle. A large proportion of the methods and lore suited to an arid
region were imported whole from Spain and perfected by the Mexican *vaqueros*, including roundups in the spring and fall, branding and ear cropping and the *reata* or lariat. In
dress it was the broad-brimmed hat and spurred boots. The saddle with a horn and a
single cinch set to the front, as well as the ornate spurs and *chaparajos* or *chaps,* were
unique to the early Southwest.

But as the Southwest became Americanized, first in Texas and later in southern
California, two subregions soon emerged. Beginning in the 1820s settlers primarily
from the South moved their families and livestock into the semiarid Texas ranges. They
brought with them the cattle traditions of the piney-wood South, which were in turn an
inheritance of English colonial practices. As a result, the American tradition of cattle
raising, in contact with the ranching methods and lore established by the Mexican
vaqueros, created a hybrid tradition. By contrast California ranching remained more
purely American Spanish in nature. The Easterners who bought land there and took up
ranching often had little or no background in caring for range cattle (see Kniffen 1953).

Naturally these differences in approach to raising cattle led to differences in the
culture and language. In California a ranch hand or cowboy was often called a *buckaroo*
(Bright 1971, 193), a name rarely heard in Texas (Atwood 1962, 53). It derives from
vaquero,[2] which as late as the 1950s was current in southwest and central Texas
(Atwood 1962, 53, map 2), but only in scattered parts of California (Bright 1971, 193).
In both areas *cowhand, cow puncher,* and *cow poke* are still used, but in Texas one also
commonly hears *wrangler* or *horse wrangler,* an Anglicized form of the American
Spanish *caballerango,* which refers to the cowboy whose duties included caring for the
riding horses.

The typical California buckaroo differed from his Texan counterpart in that he
was more often than not a family man who had grown up on the ranch where he
worked. The Texas wrangler, by contrast, was typically a bachelor and worked with
several different outfits over the course of his hard career.

The California cowboy could be distinguished by his single-cinch saddle, usually called a *center-fire saddle* or *California saddle*. The Texan used a *double rig* or *double barrel saddle*, which had two narrow cinches, and analogous to its counterpart was also called the *Texas saddle*.

Other accoutrements that consistently differed were the spurs and bridle reins. Californians preferred the Spanish great-rowel spur, and braided the ends of their bridle reins to form a *romal* (Spanish *ramal* = strand of rope), which was used as a *quirt* or small whip (American Spanish *cuarta* = horsewhip, from Spanish *cuerda* = cord). The Texans favored the blunt rowel and split reins held loosely together with a *keeper*.

One of the most important tools of the trade that has numerous regional names is the *reata*, a rope originally made of rawhide and usually kept on the saddle horn for ready access. This term from Spanish *reata* (= rope) was still current in the 1950s in scattered parts of California and western—especially southwestern—Texas (Bright 1971, 174; Atwood 1962, 50). It usually meant the same thing in American Spanish, but in Spain it was more specific, referring to the rope used to keep animals in single file, a usage that also probably survived in America (see R. Adams 1944).

Reata, however, has largely given way to other terms for a leather, hair, or fiber rope usually having a sliding loop and used primarily for catching and tying cattle and horses. *Lariat,* also from Spanish *la reata*, is the most frequent usage in Texas, according to Atwood's survey, with *lasso* running a distant second. Just the reverse seems to be true in California and Nevada. *Lasso* from Spanish *lazo* (= noose, snare) is additionally regionalized in California. In northern California it is frequently pronounced with [u], whereas in southern California the pronunciation is more often with [o] (Bright 1971, 174).

Two other terms for the reata are apparently geographically unique. In California *lass* or *lass rope* is sometimes heard, a shortened version of *lasso,* and does not seem to be used at all in Texas. On the other hand, *roping rope* is not used in California, but forms a neat isogloss in central Texas (Atwood 1962, map 40) where German settlement is particularly strong and may account for its somewhat anomalous non-Spanish origin.

Two obsolescent terms that also show the California-Texas split in the Southwest are *maguey* and *mecate* both referring to nonleather lariats. The former, sometimes altered to *McGay,* was probably most common in the Texas side of the West and was made of fibers from the maguey or century plant indigenous to Mexico and the Southwest. The *mecate* was also often made of these fibers, or else sometimes of braided horsehair, and was probably used primarily in California and the Far West. The Spanish borrowed the word from Nahuatl *mecatl* (= cord, rope). By the late nineteenth century the American cowboy had anglicized it to *McCarty.*

The California buckaroo could also be distinguished from the Texas vaquero by his use of *dallies* or *dally weltas*. To avoid strain on the reata that, especially when it was made of leather, had a tendency to break, the cowboy would wrap it around his saddle horn and then, as the animal pulled and jerked at the other end, he could let it slip slowly reducing the effects of the jerks on the rope. These turns of the rope around the saddle horn were called *dallies* or *dally* or *dolly weltas* from the Spanish imperative *dale vuelta* (= give it a twist). A cowhand that used them was a *dally welter*. Texas cowboys preferred to tie the rope fast to the horn and so were generally not *dally men*.

The California cowboy is apt to call the bag containing feed that is strapped to a horse's head to prevent spilling a *feed bag* or *nose bag* (Bright 1971, 173). The Texan is just as apt to refer to it as a *morral* (Atwood 1962, 50), a Spanish loanword rarely heard in California. The familiar spotted or piebald Western pony is known in both regions as a *pinto* or *paint*, but the latter term is the more common usage in Texas, while *pinto* is by far the more frequent usage in California (see Atwood 1962, 55; Bright 1971, 169). Both terms entered English in the mid-nineteenth century as adjectives in the combinations *paint horse* and *pinto horse* (or *pony*, *colt*, *bronco*, etc.), the latter influenced by the former (Spanish *pinto* = painted).

A final example of the California-Texas distinction is in the names for a group of saddle horses kept as a supply of remounts. Although both names are known and sometimes used in both regions, *remuda* (American Spanish for a spare horse or remount, from Spanish *remudar* = to exchange) tends to be more common in west Texas, and *caballado* (from Spanish *caballo* = horse) is used primarily in California. Atwood found only a few old informants in Texas who knew *caballado* and indeed the earliest record of it is from Texas. But by the mid-nineteenth century it had been largely replaced in Texas by *remuda*. *Caballado* was a difficult term for the Anglo cowboy to pronounce, and it accordingly underwent several transformations, first to *caviada*, then to the folk-etymologized *cavalry yard*, *cavy yard*, and *calf yard*.

Texas

Because Texas was a significant factor in the genesis of the Southwest, as well as in the definition of the West as a whole, both in the popular mind and in certain aspects of Western speech, it deserves a closer look. This would not be possible, however, if it were not such a well-documented state.[3] It is also a complex region in itself, having several cultural and linguistic subregions.

Two cultural subregions emerged in Texas during the Spanish and Mexican period lasting until 1836. The oldest was centered around San Antonio where typical colonial Spanish towns flourished in an area of ranching. Traffic and tradition tied it to Coahuila and Mexico beyond. In cultural and physical contrast was Nacogdoches far to the northeast in an area of thick forests and swamps. It was a military and missionary outpost of the poorly defined border of Spanish territory. Unlike San Antonio and nearby Goliad (La Bahia), the population of Nacogdoches was heterogeneous and oriented toward Louisiana, with no firm allegiances to Mexican or Spanish authority.

In 1821–22 a third subregion was born between San Antonio and Nacogdoches when, with permission of the Mexican government, Stephen Austin led three hundred Anglo-American families to the Colorado and Brazos river valleys in central east Texas. Most of the settlers that Austin recruited were from west of the Appalachians and south of the Ohio River, particularly from Louisiana, Arkansas, Alabama, Tennessee, Kentucky, and Missouri, and most were Catholic in accordance with the Mexican government's stricture. Austin's colonies grew rapidly. By 1828 there were over two thousand colonists and twice that many three years later. Slavery, too, came to Texas in that first Anglo-American decade. In 1830 there were approximately one thousand slaves in a total population of about twenty thousand.

The faint beginnings of yet a fourth subregion could be seen in the 1830s along the Red River Valley and the rolling hills and small prairies to the south. Most of these settlers came from the Upper South, particularly Arkansas, Kentucky, and Tennessee. This area based on a kind of loose kinship network instead of centralized towns was formed as a county of Arkansas Territory until 1836 when Texas became an independent republic.

After independence, immigration primarily from the South accelerated considerably in two general streams. Upper Southerners particularly from Missouri, Arkansas, Tennessee, and Kentucky came to the northeast and north-central part of the state; and Lower Southerners moved into the eastern section (see map 7.10). Most of these settlers came from long distances rather than progressively infiltrating across the borders.

European immigrants came in significant numbers to central and coastal Texas. In the 1830s German settlers established Oldenburg, Weimar, and New Ulm in central Texas, and infiltrated the nearby characteristically American-named towns of Cat Spring, Round Top, and Columbus. New Braunfels was established at the base of the hill country as a jumping off point for later German settlement and soon became an attractive and thriving town. Thousands of German settlers, many shepherded by the Society for the Protection of German Immigrants, continued to settle in the hills of central Texas until by 1860 nearly a quarter of the population of this area was German. In the 1850s Slavic immigrants—Bohemians, Czechs (Moravians), Sorbians, Poles— added to the European mix in the Brazos, Colorado, and San Antonio river valleys.

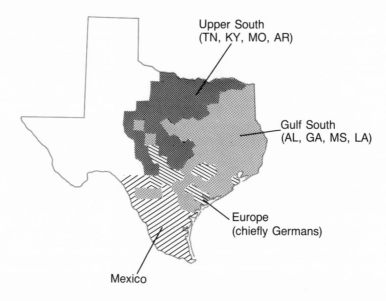

7.10. Texas Population Origins, 1880. (Source: Jordan 1967.)

From 1860 to 1900 the population of Texas increased fivefold. North Texas continued to receive settlers from Missouri, Arkansas, and Tennessee, while immigrants largely from Alabama and other Gulf States continued to pour into east Texas, emphasizing the contrast between the two regions (see map 7.10). Essentially an extension of the older Deep South, east Texas was a rural society with agrarian ideals whose economy was based on cotton, corn, hogs, cattle, and slavery, slaves making up one-third of the population. North-central Texas by contrast had few slaves and a more diversified agriculture in which cotton played a small part. It was also less rural, towns being vital to the organization of its society, and there was less contrast between rich and poor.

West Texas developed late and very slowly, substantial immigration not coming to the area until after a decisive military campaign in 1875 removed the Indians. Much of the new settlement was an extension of the older north-central region. In 1876 some four hundred thousand persons moved into north-central and west Texas, over half of these coming from states north of Arkansas and Tennessee. Perhaps more than any other factor, cattle ranching provided the impetus for the expansion of north Texas westward.

These population regions (map 7.10) are the underlying source of the cultural geography of Texas, and are an important consideration in defining its major cultural subregions shown in map 7.9. This orderly patchwork of settlement also allows us to make greater sense out of the sometimes confusing picture presented in isogloss counts and overlapping layer boundaries.

Map 7.11 combines the boundaries from the Lower South (secondary), Midland (secondary), and Inland South (primary) layers, the latter two having slightly less weight than the first. This map corresponds to the settlement and cultural areas in

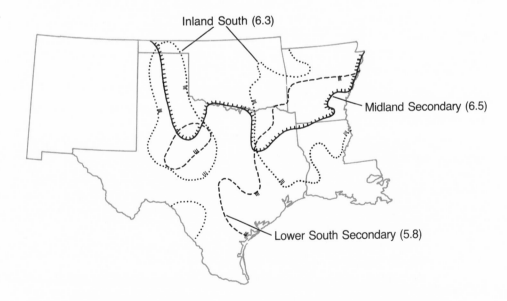

7.11. The Midland (map 6.5), Inland South (map 6.3), and Lower South (map 5.8) Layers in Texas

several details. The Lower South layer, for example, falls where we would expect it to in east Texas and along the coast. The island of Lower South features in the central west, overlapped by the Inland South layer, is the linguistic residue left by settlers from the Gulf and Upper South (cf. map 7.10). In the northwest the Upper South influence is represented by the Inland South layer, overlapping with its kindred Midland layer. The Inland South segment in southwest Texas may in part be the outcome of the island of Gulf South settlers shown in map 7.10, the Inland South layer, as we've seen, being partially influenced by the Lower or Gulf South.

Perhaps the most unexpected outcome of these conflated dialect layers (map 7.11) is the gap in the north-central portion of the state. Given that settlers from the Upper South were particularly heavily represented in this area, especially in the north, we would expect to see the corresponding layers. Instead it is an area defined by the absence of these layers. Some of this, especially in the area that Jordan defines as "mixed" (see Rooney et al. 1982, map 1-10), may be the result of the leveling effect that this very mixing of cultures and settlement origins has on language.

Using the isoglosses from Atwood's finer meshed survey (1962), it is possible to outline the smaller yet distinct dialect subregions of Texas.

South Texas

One long-range effect of the Austin colonies and continued settlement from the north and east was at first to dilute then replace the original Spanish culture and thus to divide Texas into two first-order culture regions: the area dominated by Anglo-Americans north of approximately the San Antonio River, and the Hispanic cultural region south of the river. Map 7.12 shows the resulting dialect layer of South Texas as defined by thirteen of Atwood's representative isoglosses. Although it is not possible to draw a clean boundary around the isogloss numbers, the region nevertheless is generally defined as lying south of the San Antonio River.[4] It extends westward close to the Rio Grande and fades out more gradually along the northern "edge" in West Texas than in South Texas where the core and hearth of the region is located.

Not too surprisingly every one of the isogloss terms of this tiny layer is a Spanish loanword (see app. A). Two, as we have already seen (map 7.8), are used throughout the Southwest: *frijoles* and *arroyo*. Several others are probably widely known, though very rarely used outside of the Southwest, especially those terms related to cattle raising, such as *toro* for bull and *hacienda* for the main ranch house. Likewise, cowboy stories and movies have probably spread *vaquero* (= cowhand) and *reata* (= lariat, lasso) into many other parts of the United States. The same is probably true of *chaparral,* which is a common thicket-forming shrub or shrubby tree that grows in this wide open region. Though these terms may be familiar in many other parts of the country, they remain genuine usages primarily only in the Southwest.

But few English speakers outside of South Texas would know what a *resaca* (= a dry water channel; a backwater; a body of water stored for irrigation) or an *acequia* (= an irrigation ditch) is. The same can be said for *olla,* an earthenware crock or pot, and for *pilon,* which is the South Texas version of the Louisiana *lagniappe,* something

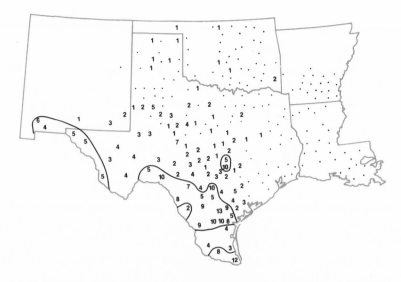

7.12. The South Texas Layer Based on 13 Isoglosses from Atwood (1962)

given as a bonus or in addition. Similarly, few but South Texans would know or use *pelado,* a contemptuous term for a Hispanic or Latin American person, a term that has been used in Southwestern English since the early nineteenth century when it referred more specifically to a poor, ignorant person of low social class, especially a Mexican peon.

Finally, when American English came to Texas it had no name for the broad treeless plains and arid prairies of much of the state and so adopted the indigenous Spanish term *llano.* This barren land form was forbidding to newcomers and inhibited the settlement of much of west Texas prior to the discovery of oil. One of these high arid plateaus called the Llano Estacado, "the Staked Plain," covers forty thousand square miles of western Texas and eastern New Mexico (due west of Lubbock). In 1834 a visitor to this plateau captured the trepidation it inspired when he wrote: "The Llano Estacado, on whose borders we then were encamped, and which lay before us like a boundless ocean, was mentioned with a sort of terror" (see *DAE*).

Central Texas

Just as Spanish loanwords distinguish South Texas, so German features characterize Central Texas, making for a sharp contrast between these adjoining regions. Map 7.13 combines 11 isoglosses from Atwood's study that tend to cluster in central Texas, including the German Hill Country defined in map 7.9. But reflecting the settlement of this area that was dominated by Anglo-Americans, the German influence is proportionately less prominent than the Spanish influence in South Texas.

Of the 11 isoglosses (see app. A), 4 are of German origin: *clook, smearcase, kochcase,* and *cook cheese.* None of these, however, are unique to Central Texas, but

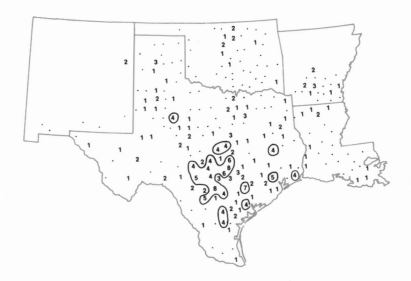

7.13. The Central Texas Layer Based on 11 Isoglosses from Atwood (1962)

are also found in the other German settlement areas of the United States, especially in Pennsylvania and other parts of the North. The Germans brought with them their word for a broody hen, *die Glucke* or *Klucke* (*Gluuk* in Pennsylvania German), which was adopted into English as *clook*. In Texas the high back vowel /ʊ/ of the original German word is apparently retained, while in the Inland North, where the term is still current, it is usually *cluck* with the central vowel /ʌ/, the difference in pronunciations probably indicative of independent borrowings.

As we saw in chapter 6, *smearcase* (= cottage cheese) is first recorded in American English in Pennsylvania, where English borrowed the German word *Schmierkäse* (literally "smearing cheese") and from whence it spread throughout most of the Lower North. At about the same time, but independently, the Germans brought their word to Central Texas.[5] They also brought *kochcase,* which refers to a soft cheese similar to cottage cheese but which is cooked and poured into containers. The anglicized version is the calque *cook cheese.* These forms are also found in obsolescent use in Pennsylvania and other German settlement areas, but because few people now make homemade cheese, these terms in the late twentieth century doubtless are relics.

The other 7 isogloss terms are similarly not unique to Central Texas, with the possible exception of *roping rope. Roping* was coined in the Southwest (earliest citations are from Arizona) probably sometime in the 1880s and is the common term for lassoing stock, which is now probably more common in rodeo contests than on the range. A *roping rope,* then, is the rope or lariat used in roping.

The other terms are clearly not unique to Central Texas. According to the *DARE* data, three of the eleven are in use in much of the United States. The least common of these three is *tool house* for a small building where tools and machinery are stored, *tool shed* being the more common form.

Settee, a widely used term, refers to a medium-sized sofa and is most likely an altered form of *settle.* It is originally British, but came to America, probably initially to the urban Northeast, sometime in the mid-eighteenth century (it first appears in New York in 1773). The other term in use throughout much of the United States is *lunch* meaning a snack or food taken between main meals. Atwood suggests that this usage probably indicates German influence, since "the Germans had, and still have, the practice of eating a light meal in midmorning and midafternoon, to which they applied the term" (1962, 94).

Grass sack (= burlap bag), according to the linguistic atlas fieldwork (*WG,* fig. 71), is regionally confined to eastern Virginia, Maryland, Delaware, and southern New Jersey, and is probably a shortened form of *sea-grass sack,* perhaps because its original function was to hold sea grass that may have been used as hay or fodder. The *DARE* fieldwork shows the term scattered in the central South, from Indiana to Mississippi.

Like *grass sack, plunder room* also seems to have migrated to Central Texas from a section of the South Atlantic states. The atlas shows it occurring throughout Virginia, and the Carolinas (*WG,* fig. 52). The *DARE* isogloss, however, suggests that the term is dying out and survives primarily in linguistically conservative South Carolina. *Plunder* is a Southernism, perhaps originating in Virginia, for personal effects, baggage, household goods, and the like. A *plunder room,* then, is a room for plunder, that is, a storage room.

The influence of the North is also present in the Central Texas lexicon. The preference for *house* instead of *shed* in the expression *tool house* also occurs in *wood house.* This latter expression, although not very common according to the *DARE* fieldwork, is chiefly a Northern term for a building or shed for storing wood. Likewise, *tarvia* and *tarviated road* for a paved road are primarily Northern, and are taken from the name of the old commercial firm Tarvia. Atwood speculates that the concentration of these two expressions in Central Texas, especially in the vicinity of Austin, must have resulted from transactions with the Tarvia company sometime in the past (1962, 93).

West Texas

Several isoglosses in Atwood's study also delimit the West Texas region (1962, maps 12, 21–25). Although *mesa* (= a high plateau) and its synonym, *plains,* are West Texas terms in part because they are features of the regional landscape, the other four or so isoglosses are more closely linked to the region's culture and economy: *remuda* (= a small herd of riding horses), *morral* (= a feed bag or nose bag), *wrangler* (= a cowhand), and *maverick* (= a motherless calf). The cattle industry in West Texas was a blend of the Anglo experience with relatively small herds, and the Hispanic tradition, which had perfected the management of large herds of half-wild cattle on arid open ranges. Consequently, these terms clearly show the influence of colonial Spanish. Not surprisingly, the handful of isoglosses that cluster in the central and northern part of West Texas away from the Spanish colonial areas of the south (Atwood 1962, maps 9, 11, 13) are not part of the Hispanic tradition. Indeed, they show a very different heritage. *Shinnery* (= land covered with scrub oak), for example, emigrated from Louisiana and is the anglicized version of Louisiana French *cheniere,* ultimately from French *chene* which means oak. *Chenier,* incidentally, is still current in Louisiana, where it refers to a clump of scrub oak on open ground, somewhat different from the vast thicketlike terrain of the Texas shinnery.

Similarly, *sugan* testifies to the distant Scotch-Irish heritage of northwestern Texas. A sugan is a coarse blanket or comfort, often made of scraps of material patched together. In the Gaelic areas of the British Isles a *suggan* (recorded as early as 1722) was a primitive kind of saddle made of straw or rushes. In time it also referred to a thick bed coverlet, which in the rough past may also have been made of straw. It was this latter usage that the Scotch-Irish probably brought to America, specifically to the southern Appalachians, from where it eventually found its way into Texas and Oklahoma with Upper South settlers and their descendants (see Pearce 1958, 103–5). The word was especially common among cowboys who also called sugans, *camp quilts.* It may have been the cowboy who carried the term into the western areas of the Dakotas and Nebraska (see *LAUM*) and even into Montana and Idaho where *DARE* informants used it.

Two other northwest Texas isoglosses cited by Atwood are *draw* (= a usually dry streambed or gully) and *surly* (= a bull). According to the *DARE* isogloss, *draw* is used in many other parts of the country, but has its main concentration in Texas. This term appears in American English with reference to a site in the Rocky Mountains toward the end of the nineteenth century, and may derive from the older *draught* or *draft* (= a narrow valley or stream course) or perhaps it refers to the notion that this natural drainage ditch "draws" the water off the land.

Surly (= a bull) may be the absolute use of the adjective *surly* (= irritable, threatening) with reference to a bull's disposition. *DARE* evidence also shows its use in Kentucky, and *Dialect Notes* finds it in the Ozarks. This suggests that like *sugan, surly* came to Texas with the Upper South settlers, whose prudishness supplied them with plenty of euphemisms for such things as bulls and other stud animals.

The relatively late settlement of West Texas was part of the increasing influence of the older, wealthy Texas on New Mexico, southern Colorado, and eastern Arizona in the latter half of the nineteenth century, an influence that was a major factor in the two-part cultural and linguistic division of the Southwest.

The Pacific and Rocky Mountain Regions

After the Civil War the culture and lore of these two nuclear regions of the Southwest rapidly spread outward. Diffusion from southern California was northward across Oregon into central Washington and eastward into western Idaho, most of Nevada, and southern Arizona. From southern Texas the diffusion was much broader covering all of the Plain and Rocky Mountain states except western Idaho (see Kniffen 1953, fig. 2). In this latter region a continued influx of Eastern settlers who turned to small-scale cattle production strengthened the divergence from the Mexican pattern.

This dichotomy in the West has been discussed for the Southwest in terms of the culture surrounding cattle raising—to be sure a distinctive and important feature on the

Western landscape—but inevitably the dichotomy exists in other terms not directly related to ranching or its diffusion from the two hearths. Other historical forces, some still in progress, contributed to the separation of the Pacific states, especially California, from the Rocky Mountain area.

Mineral wealth and mining and the attendant economies they created were perhaps the most powerful attractions to settlers of the West. Miners were willing to inhabit thousands of square miles of mountain and desert that were initially avoided by the farmer pioneers. The California gold rush of 1849 brought the first large influx of mining settlers, eventually establishing a major economic and cultural center in the West focused on San Francisco. After the gold rush many of the miners moved from California eastward in the opposite direction of the general settlement trend, such as those who flooded into the area of Virginia City, Nevada, with the discovery of the Comstock Lode in 1859.

The "miner's frontier" (see Billington 1956, chap. 11) expanded south into Arizona and New Mexico, and north into Idaho, Montana, and Canada. Boom towns often blossomed and died, but for every ghost town that haunted the West, a living and durable community was established somewhere else, such as Tucson, Arizona, or Denver, Colorado.

As is usually the case, a handful of isoglosses can be gleaned that reflect the history of a region, in this case the dichotomy between the Pacific and Rocky Mountain areas. *Bunkhouse,* for example, according to the *DARE* fieldwork, is most commonly used in the Far West or Pacific states, including Nevada, Arizona, and New Mexico, though doubtless it is known elsewhere. It was originally used in mining camps and designated the miners' sleeping quarters, according to the 1876 eighth annual report of the *Statistics of Mines and Mining in the States and Territories West of the Rocky Mountains* (see *DAE*). Later it referred more broadly to the sleeping or living quarters for groups of workers such as ranch hands, loggers, and railroad crews.

Battens, the wood strips or clapboards used to cover the exterior of houses, is also used primarily in the Pacific states. It is recorded as early as 1684 in Rhode Island, when it meant "a bar or stout strip of wood," being closer to its original form *baton.* Once established in New England, it was just a matter of time before it found its way to California and the Pacific Northwest.

Three isoglosses likewise distinguish the Rockies. A *barrow pit,* sometimes shortened to *bar pit,* is a ditch alongside a graded road, the excavated dirt being used or "borrowed" as landfill. The term is common in Utah, Colorado, Idaho, Wyoming, and Montana, with scattered occurrences throughout much of the West. This distribution contrasts with that of *barrow* or *bar ditch,* which is common in Texas, Oklahoma, eastern New Mexico, and the southern parts of Utah and Colorado. *Barrow ditch* is apparently the oldest form. The *English Dialect Dictionary,* which defines it as "a small ditch" and labels it obsolete, cites it as early as 1752. In America all four versions are very recent usages, none recorded before the 1920s.

Even more tightly confined to the Rockies is the term for a newly weaned calf or pig: *weaner.* An old term (1579) that originally applied to the person, such as a nanny or nurse, who weans a child, it later in Australia referred to a hand-fed calf, the equivalent of the American *dogie* (see Greenway 1958). It seems to have come into Rocky Mountain use only in the present century, perhaps imported from Australia.

Another expression that originated in the Rockies is *camp robber,* known else-where in the North as the *Canada jay.* This plucky bird earned its name from its habit of stealing provisions from camps. As map 7.8 shows, the term is used throughout the Colorado Rockies northward. Given that the earliest (1893) citation for the name is from Colorado, *camp robber* may have originated there and migrated into Wyoming, Montana, and westward into eastern Washington and Oregon.

Although these few isoglosses do not prove the existence of the two regions as having full-fledged distinctive dialects, they suggest the lines along which they may exist or eventually develop.

California

Like Texas, California, the most populous Western state, had considerable impact on the development of the Southwest and on the West as a whole. And like Texas, it is complex culturally and linguistically, having several definable subregions. It also re-sembles Texas in that it had three periods of settlement: the Spanish period beginning with the first mission at San Diego in 1769 and ending with Mexican independence in 1821; the Mexican period, which secularized the Spanish missions scattered from San Diego to San Francisco and lasted until 1846 when California became United States territory; and the American period that exploded into being with the discovery of gold at Sutter's Mill in 1848.

Two years after that fateful discovery the population had climbed from a handful of mountain men and a few hearty settlers to ninety-two thousand souls. By 1860 the population had quadrupled and was concentrated in and around San Francisco whose raison d'être was to provide supplies and financing for the mines and miners and an outlet for the mined gold. The discovery in 1859 of the Comstock Lode added new impetus to settlement of both California and Nevada.

The booming mining economies also encouraged the development of better transportation to the West. Before the Civil War access to the Far West was primarily by way of two or three major trails: the California Trail extending from St. Louis to Salt Lake City to northern California; the Oregon Trail that branched off from the California Trail along the Snake River and fed settlers into Washington and Oregon; and the Santa Fe and Old Spanish Trail from St. Louis to Santa Fe through southern Utah and on to southern California. The latter line was supplemented by the Gila Trail running from central Texas through the extreme southern portions of New Mexico, Arizona, and California. Migration to California via these trails was long and arduous, which discour-aged large numbers of settlers from traveling to the Far West. The railroads soon changed this.

In 1869 the Transcontinental Railroad was completed ending California's long isolation and opening the floodgates of emigration, at first primarily to northern Califor-nia. It took over a decade more before southern California was opened to rapid settle-ment with the completion of the Santa Fe Railroad line from Kansas City to Los

Angeles in 1887. Thus, it was not until the last quarter or so of the nineteenth century that permanent settlement came to large areas of California establishing the beginnings of a new regional culture and language.

While northern California was growing rapidly, southern California remained a pastoral Hispanic region. Not until the decade of the 1880s did the southern California land boom begin to increase the population significantly. Indeed, by the end of that decade the numbers had increased fivefold, making Los Angeles a larger urban center than San Francisco. With the development around the turn of the century of irrigation and an extensive aqueduct system, the Imperial Valley blossomed and the farm population increased dramatically. But this region was fated to be primarily urban. A combination of year-round sunny weather and an attendant "laid-back" life-style captured the imagination of twentieth-century America. Real estate development dominated the economy of the region. By 1950 Los Angeles was almost three times the size of San Francisco. Today it continues to attract large numbers of emigrants, making for an unsettled and heterogeneous dialect situation.

New Yorkers made up the single largest emigrant element in California and were spread throughout most of the state (see map 7.14), though by 1930 their numbers had dropped to fourth place behind settlers from Illinois, Missouri, and Iowa. In the mid-nineteenth century, discontent, overcrowding, and lack of open land for new settlement in the Indian country across the Mississippi River accounted for the large number of

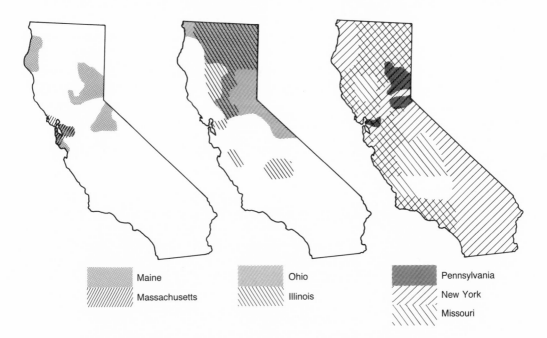

7.14. Settlement of California (1870) by Place of Origin. Shaded areas represent 10 percent or more of the population as being from the indicated Eastern state. (Source: Bright 1971.)

emigrants from the Mississippi Valley frontier who peopled Texas, Oregon, and California (Billington 1960, 481). Missourians, for example, have always been the second or third most common group in California. Their concentrations are primarily in the western and northeastern parts of the state (map 7.14).

New Englanders came in far fewer numbers although there was significant emigration, especially from Massachusetts and Maine, in the San Francisco area and other parts of northern California. Also confined to the northern areas of the state were settlers from Illinois, Ohio, and Pennsylvania (map 7.14). These and the Yankee settlers helped to separate the cultures of northern and southern California. During the depression of the 1930s, the north-south divide was further emphasized by the arrival primarily in southern California of disenfranchised farmers from Oklahoma and Texas, the so-called Okies.

As one would expect, the historical division also appears in the linguistic geography of California. David Reed first suggested the presence of such a division and cited the isogloss for *chesterfield* (= sofa) as a possible paradigm for the Northern California speech region (1954, 5). The *DARE* isogloss essentially agrees. Elizabeth Bright's *A Word Geography of California and Nevada* (1971), however, gives the most detailed analysis of California speech to date. It is based on numerous isoglosses from the field records of the Linguistic Atlas of the Pacific Coast, which were completed in 1959 and contain three hundred interviews in California and Nevada.

One of the first things we learn from her careful study is that a majority of the isoglosses one might choose to map do not cohere, but are mixed and jumbled. Very few reveal clear regionality. And this is consonant with the rather mixed and unfinished settlement of the region as a whole. There are, however, three sets of isoglosses that are reasonably coherent, namely, those that segregate to one degree or another northern California and northwestern Nevada. She bases these isogloss sets, which she labels Patterns VIII, XIII, and XIV (her maps 31, 38, and 39), on the distributions of nineteen, twenty-eight, and twenty-three words respectively.

Northern California

Map 7.15 conflates Bright's three layers.[6] All three overlap from the San Francisco Bay area northward, including northwestern Nevada. That is, this is the area where the lexicons of all three layers are used. As in many of the layer maps for the older Eastern sections of the country, the density of usage tapers off as we move southward.

The representative isoglosses that make up these layers that Bright has selected are a mixed bag of rather ordinary terms very few having more than 10 percent currency among the three hundred informants of the study. Indeed only a handful of these seventy words are unique to the area or are extensions of Eastern dialect regions. A majority of the terms are widely known, though their preferred usage in Northern California imparts a regional dimension to them.

Chesterfield (= sofa) is perhaps the clearest cut example of a regionalism unique to Northern California. First recorded in British use in 1900 as referring specifically to a couch with upright armrests at either end, it was probably named after a nineteenth-

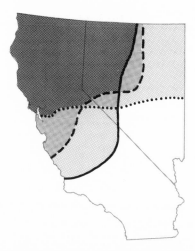

7.15. Composite of California-Nevada Isogloss Boundaries. The three boundaries Bright designates with roman numerals are VIII (dotted line), XIII (dashed line), and XIV (solid line). (Source: Linguistic Atlas of the Pacific States fieldwork as analyzed by Bright 1971, 64, 79, 81.)

century Earl of Chesterfield, for reasons that are obscure. It is still occasionally heard in England. But in Canada, where it came into use at about the same time (1903), it is a widely used generic term for any kind of sofa. Perhaps coming from Canada, in America it is almost exclusive to Northern California, according to the *DARE* data.

Other possible Northern Californianisms are *letter carrier* for postman, *corked* meaning tired, *rustic siding* for a kind of clapboard exterior on houses, *the City* with reference to San Francisco, and *coast* when referring to a swim at the beach ("We went for a swim to the _____."). The folk-etymologized form of "wheel barrow," *wheel barrel,* may also be unique to this region.

Tules and its compounds, *tule land* or *tule swamp,* is also probably a Northern Californianism, at least in its origins. The Spanish borrowed from the Indians of Mexico and Central America the Nahuatl word, *tullin,* which means bulrush. The Americans then borrowed it from the Spanish early in the nineteenth century and used it to refer specifically to two large New World bulrushes that grow in marshy areas. By the mid-nineteenth century the meaning of *tules* was transferred to refer to the marshy or swampy land itself. Today this sense is primarily used in Northern California and adjacent areas, though it is probably known elsewhere in the West.

Some of the terms that Bright uses to define the Northern California patterns are imports from other dialect regions. *Nigh horse* (= the horse on the left side) is an Upper North term (map 3.7) known to some rural speakers in Northern California (6 percent of the LAPC informants). *Danish pastry* (= a kind of sweet roll), which is used throughout the North (map 3.3), is also used in the California subarea. In parts of the Upper North and Upper South a mountain pass or notch is known as a *cut,* a term that has found its way into the speech of some Northern Californians.

The Upper South is also represented in the terms *janders* or *yellow janders,* a pronunciation variant of (*yellow*) *jaundice*. Surprisingly, the influence of the South is present in the term *snake doctor* (= dragonfly), which was known to 5 percent of the informants. These were rural informants, however, which may indicate, though on a much smaller scale, a similar rural-Southern/urban-Northern opposition as is found in the Lower North, notably in Illinois (see chap. 6). An alternative folk term for the dragonfly in Northern California is *ear sewer* (Bright 1971, 75), which is also known in other scattered parts of the country. It captures one of the several folk beliefs that surround this well-known insect, namely, that it has the power to sew up one's ears if it catches a person off guard or sleeping outdoors.

Pourdown for a downpour of heavy rain is also a Southernism occasionally found in the northern part of the state. A South-and-West expression also found here is *slough* for a swamp or backwater. The West layer's *catch colt* (= an illegitimate child) was also recorded by the atlas fieldwork in Northern California though only 3 percent of the informants knew the expression.

The Northwest term for the warm southwest wind that sometimes blows in this part of the country, *chinook,* was known to 15 percent of the informants. But as Bright points out "in most of the responses in California, the word was admittedly unfamiliar or associated with other places such as Oregon, Alaska, Montana." Moreover, there was little agreement on the meaning of the word: "of the responses given, 4 stated the wind came from the south, 3 from the north and 2 from the west; similarly, 6 said it was a dry wind, 5 that it was moist" (Bright 1971, 142). Nevertheless, it is clear from this that Northern California is to a degree in the Northwest's sphere of influence.

Most of the rest of the terms used to derive map 7.15 are not regionalisms at all, but are known virtually everywhere. However, they are preferred forms, expressions that easily come to mind and that Northern California speakers commonly use; whereas in other parts of the West, different but synonymous terms would be used. As isoglosses they still have the power to define a dialect layer. In a sense, then, the vocabulary whose distribution is mapped in 7.15 is as much a measure of certain lexical preferences, as it is a unique "lexicon" proper.

For example, Northern California speech is in part characterized by a preference for the mild intensifier *fairly* in the sentence "It's _____ cold," whereas speakers of other areas, but including this one, would use *kind of, pretty,* or *a little.* Other examples are: *powerful* or *muscular* in referring to a strong person; *roustabout* or *chore man* for a hired farmhand; *peeved, excited,* and *hot* (*around*/*under the collar*) meaning angry or irritated; *tied the knot* for married; *notion store, novelty store,* and *fifteen-cent store* for a store where all kinds of small or cheap goods are sold; and *garret* for attic.

Central Western and Coastal Southern California

Two other subregions of California speech stand out in Bright's isogloss patterns. In map 7.15, a wedge shaped subdialect area in central west California, formed by the overlap of Bright's patterns XIII and XIV is reinforced by isogloss pattern VI (1971, 59) shown in map 7.16. The boundary of pattern VI, however, outlines an area of absence, one that generally lacks the thirty-eight or so terms of the pattern.

7.16. Composite of Isogloss Boundaries in Southern and Central California. Note that the bundle of isogloss boundaries excludes coastal southern California. (Source: Bright 1971, isogloss boundaries I–IV and VI, 49, 51, 53, 55.)

A similar absence defines the southern California coast as a subregion. Map 7.16 reveals this area by conflating Bright's patterns I through IV (1971, 49, 51, 53, and 55).

Southern California

Although there is clearly a north-south divide in California, there is no strong southern counterpart to map 7.15. That is, we would expect there to be at least one or two layers filling the blank area of that map in southern California and Nevada. Surprisingly, except perhaps for the frequency distributions of the Spanish loanwords, none of Bright's isogloss patterns isolate Southern California as a dialect region in its own right with its own characterizing (English) lexicon.

One explanation may be that it is not as unified a speech region as the north. The North and Midland layers, for example, have very mixed isogloss numbers in Southern California (maps 3.3 and 6.5), a situation also evident in the records of the Pacific Coast atlas, which show "a curious overlay of Northern and Midland forms" (Reed and Reed 1972, 137). The leveling process that must take place in the evolution of a dialect region simply has not had time to run its course here (see Metcalf 1972). Moreover, the coastal subarea of map 7.16 splits off part of the southern region, showing at least one other way the area as a whole is divided.

The one unifying lexical factor, however, is the pervasive Spanish influence. Map 7.17 shows the area of greatest frequency of Spanish borrowings based on Bright's analysis (1971, 101–8). These frequencies are given in terms of forty-nine possible loanwords used in California. They fall into three general referential categories: ranching, topography, and domestic and social relationships. We have already seen several of the terms in the first category, like *corral, reata, morral, vaquero, buckaroo, toro,*

7.17. Currency of Spanish Loanwords. (Source: Bright 1971, map 48 on p. 101.)

pinto, lariat, and *lasso.* Others here are *comun* or *casita* (= outhouse), *bronco* (= an unbroken or wild horse), *burro* (= a small donkey), *latigo* (= a cinch), *rodeo* (= a public show that features cowboy contests, such as cattle roping and bronco riding), *bracero* (= a migratory worker), and *ranchero* (= a cowboy).

The topographical and related terms include *mesa* (= a flat elevated area of land), *potrero* (= a pasture or meadow), *hoya* (= a mountain valley or basin; a park), *rincon* (= a secluded valley; park), *barranca* (= a gully or ravine), *arroyo, adobe* (= sun-dried clay), and *Santa Ana* (= a warm northern or eastern wind). Among the domestic and social terms are *patio* (= a court usually paved and adjacent to a dwelling), *ramada* (= a porch or covered walk), *tortilla* (= a thin flat cornmeal cake), *carne seco* (= chipped beef), *frijoles* (= beans), *langosta* (= crawfish or spiny lobster), *madre* (= mother), *tata* (= grandfather), and *nana* (= grandmother). With varying degrees of derogation, there are several terms of Spanish origin for a Mexican or Hispanic American: *vecino, paisano, hombre, peon,* and *cholo,* the last two having the greatest currency. Two miscellaneous terms are *embarcadero* (= wharf) and *pachucos* or *pachukes* (= impudence, nerve).

Of course a majority of these terms have little currency and can be heard only occasionally and almost exclusively in Southern California. Nevertheless they were all used by American English speakers in an English context. The Spanish influence alone, however, does not fully account for the features that set this region in apposition to the more unified Northern California region.

Until a more detailed study can be done, Southern California can be considered a region separate from Northern California for three reasons. It is excluded from the Northern California lexicon. It has the highest number and frequency of Spanish loanwords. And it is an area of greater mixture of forms and isoglosses, because the stage of linguistic leveling has been prolonged by a very late and continuing influx of settlers. There simply has not been time for the speech community to select and strengthen certain popular lexical variants, to make certain compromises among vowel variants, and to merge unnecessarily contrasting phonological elements (see Metcalf 1972, 33).

The Northwest

The Northwest is a separate dialect region of the West and can be defined in two ways: in terms of isoglosses that are more or less unique to the area, and in terms of the dialect layers that overlap here. The handful of isoglosses characteristic of the region approximate the domain of the first effective settlement core shown in map 7.9, which includes all of Washington, northern Oregon, and northern Idaho, though the sphere of linguistic influence can extend into northern California and western Montana.

Chinook is perhaps the most famous of these, and is known from northern California and northern Nevada (Bright 1970, 91) to eastern Minnesota (map 7.8). The term actually refers to two different types of regional winds, which accounts for some of its relatively wide geographic dispersion. The earlier reference still very much in use in Washington, Oregon, and eastern Idaho, is to a warm moist wind usually blowing from the southwest. According to the *Dictionary of American English,* the English fur traders of the Hudson's Bay Company quartered at Astoria at the mouth of the Columbia River named the wind Chinook because it blew from the direction of an encampment of Chinook Indians. In any case, the term is borrowed from the name of that Northwest Indian tribe. In the northern Rocky Mountain states and in the Dakotas, a chinook is a dry warm wind that blows from the north. This is a transferred usage from the original Northwest term.

The ubiquitous ring-necked pheasant is known in the Northwest as the *chinese pheasant* or *china pheasant,* which refers to the genetic precursor from Asia of the North American hybrid. This isogloss (map 7.8) confines itself much more closely to the northwestern corner of the West and best approximates the settlement pattern of map 7.9.

A popular pastry in the Northwest is the *maple bar,* which is oblong or barlike and has a maple-flavored frosting. Although its isogloss (map 7.8) is primarily clustered in Washington, Oregon, and northern Idaho, maple bars are also known in parts of California, Nevada, and Utah.

One of the important ethnic groups to settle in the Northwest, primarily in Washington, northwestern Oregon, and central-west Montana were the Scandinavians (see Zelinsky 1973, 30). As in the Upper Midwest, they have left a unique trace on the regional speech, as well as connecting it culturally to the primary Scandinavian settlements in Minnesota, Wisconsin, and surrounding states. This connection is evident in two or three *DARE* isoglosses. The distribution of the somewhat derogatory *Norskie* (= a Norwegian-American), for example, mirrors the settlement pattern in Washington, Oregon, and throughout the Upper Midwest.

Without having direct reference to members of this ethnic group, *snoose* (= snuff; a snuff user) gives a clearer picture of the Scandinavian connection between the two regions. Most users of the term are doubtless unaware that it is a Scandinavian (Danish, Swedish, Norwegian) loanword, *snus,* short for *snustobakk,* (*snusa* and *snuse* being the Swedish and Danish/Norwegian terms respectively meaning "to sniff"). The

American version *snoose* is used throughout Wisconsin, Minnesota, and the Dakotas westward to Washington, Oregon, and northern California.

Most of the Scandinavian settlers, however, arrived relatively late, primarily toward the end of the nineteenth century. The British were the first Europeans in the Northwest, followed closely by the Americans. The earliest Americans there were chiefly New Englanders, who dominated the fur trade and controlled the Oregon coast at the end of the eighteenth century. So prevalent was their influence and presence that the Indians called all white men "Bostons." The British, however, dominated the interior and by 1828 had successfully settled the Puget Sound area in Washington.

In 1843 the first large group of settlers, about a thousand men, women, and children, came to the Willamette Valley in northwestern Oregon, establishing the hearth site of the Northwest. Most were from the Ohio Valley states and Tennessee. Two years later another three thousand emigrants arrived in the Valley giving it a booming population long before Washington drew its first large groups of emigrants. In general the largest infusions of settlers to Oregon were from Missouri with Illinois and Iowa also contributing a good share. The 1880 census shows that Missourians continued to predominate in Oregon, whereas Upper Northerners formed the majority in Washington and Idaho.

The preliminary linguistic survey of the Northwest, completed in the early 1950s by Carroll Reed, as might be expected, corresponds to the settlement patterns of the region. Reed found that Washington and Idaho are characterized by the highest frequency of Northern terms, while Oregon has a decided preference for "Midland" forms, and that strictly Southern terms are always very rare in the Northwest (C. Reed 1957, 86–88).

The *DARE* evidence reveals a similar picture but with some important differences. The Northern isoglosses of map 7.4 define the Northwest as encompassing all of Washington, central and northern Oregon, northern Idaho, and extreme western Montana. The midland influence is evident in the Midland layer (map 6.5) and to a lesser extent in the South-and-West layer (map 4.8). The Midland map shows minor or tertiary presence of the layer in most of Oregon, southern and eastern Washington, and northern Idaho, more or less in agreement with Reed's preliminary finding. But map 7.6 reveals that Southern isoglosses are surprisingly prevalent in the Northwest, throughout most of Washington, Oregon, and northern California. The West layer (map 7.2) is also very much present here, but least so in Oregon.

The Northwest, then, is a relatively well-defined region of the West, with its own small set of unique isoglosses. Moreover, several dialect layers combine in a singular formula to define its speech. The predominating Northern features of the region form a linguistic base, making it the heartland of Northern speech in the West. To this base are added a smattering of Midland features (least so in northwestern Washington), and surprisingly, a significant number of Southern features throughout most of the region including northern California.[7]

The West as a speech region is both continuous with the East, its most important link being through the Northern dialect layers, and discontinuous, being set off from the East by two groups of isoglosses: the Greater West isoglosses and the West layer (fig. 6).

Layer
West (map 7.2)

Regions

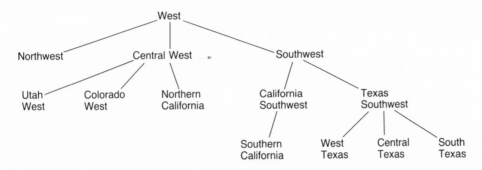

Fig. 6. Summary of the layers and regions of the West

Although the largest portion of this expansive region is dominated by Northern speech, Southern features also play an important role. Together they extend the North-South linguistic divide into the West, but with important variations on this theme. The strong influence of the Hispanic past, for example, has given the southern portion of the divide a unique character represented in the Southwest dialect. Almost as sharply differentiated, the Northwest is also a distinctive region.

Texas played an important role in the development of the Southwest, particularly the eastern section, and to a lesser extent, in the development of the West itself, especially the Rocky Mountain and Plains regions. This is most evident in the culture and life-style surrounding cattle ranching. Texas's complex history also created several subdialect regions within its own borders. In cultural and historical juxtaposition to the influence of Texas in the West is Southern California, which not only forms the influencing hearth of the western Southwest with its more characteristically Hispanic methods of ranching, but is also a separate speech region in contrast to Northern California.

The newness of the West is perhaps its single unifying feature, which at the same time is its most disunifying force, at least in terms of a dialectology that attempts to describe the geography of speech. Although nascent boundaries in the West can now be established not as lines but as tendencies, it will probably take a century or two before the language settles into more clearly definable areas.

NOTES

1. For a fuller discussion of the problems inherent in doing linguistic geography in the West, see Kimmerle et al. 1951.
2. See Mason 1960, Cassidy 1978, Hill 1979.
3. The discussion here is especially indebted to D. W. Meinig's seminal "essay" on the cultural

and historical geography of Texas (1969), and on Atwood's detailed study of the linguistic geography (1962).

4. Some of the "spottiness" or heterogeneity of the numbers is probably caused by the variation in the number of informants in each community. Thus, there was more opportunity to pick up a given isogloss term if a community had many informants than if it had only one or two. Austin, for example, had more than thirteen informants, and consequently it has a disproportionately large number of isoglosses in both maps 7.12 and 7.13, even though an isogloss was counted only once regardless of the number of times it appeared as a response in the community. This kind of distortion does not occur in the count maps based on the *DARE* fieldwork, because only one informant answered any given question. This, of course, may result in a distortion of another kind.

5. Atwood admits the possibility that "some of the Texas occurrences may be importations from farther north rather than independent borrowings from Texas Germans" (1962, 61). It seems less likely, however, that the few Lower North settlers in Texas, and specifically in Central Texas, should have brought the word instead of the concentration of Germans who so clearly marked the language of this tiny corner of the state.

6. She does not use the term *layer,* but presents her analysis as isogloss boundaries rather than as areas.

7. The Southern terms especially in the South-and-West layer are, of course, also current in much of the midlands, though primarily in the Upper South section. They represent the influence of "Midland" speech that Reed detected, though the distribution of these is somewhat more prevalent in Washington than Reed found.

CHAPTER 8

Conclusion

Let us stack the layers and summarize the regions that have emerged. Chapters 2 and 3 presented seven different layers that, when taken together, define the North dialect region and its subregions. The three largest Northern layers (discussed in chap. 3) can be analyzed into sublayers characterized by whether they extend into the West or not.

North (maps 3.3 and 3.4)
    Eastern North
    North-and-West

Upper North (maps 3.7 and 3.8)
    Eastern Upper North
    Upper North-and-West

Inland North (maps 3.9 and 3.10)
    Inland Eastern North
    Inland North-and-West
    Inland (Eastern) Upper North
    Inland Upper North-and-West

Four weaker layers add to the subregional complexity of the North: the New England (map 2.4), Northeast (maps 2.8 and 2.9), New York (map 2.7), and Upper Midwest layers (map 3.11), the former two have considerably more weight than the latter. These layers when taken together form the hierarchical arrangement of regional dialects as shown in figure 7.

Two other New England regions could have been included based on the *LANE* findings: the Boston area and central-eastern New England (eastern Massachusetts, New Hampshire, eastern Vermont, southern Maine).

Note that although the Northeast layer helps define the boundaries within the Northeast, it does not form a true dialect region. Just as the Midland layer straddles the North-South divide, so the Northeast layer spans the strong Eastern New England boundary. And like the Midland layer that belongs primarily to the Upper South, the Northeast layer is more akin to Western New England, New York, and Pennsylvania, than to Eastern New England.

Chapter 4 established the primary split in American regional dialects between the North and the South and defined the latter region in terms of three layers: the South I (map 4.3), South II (map 4.5), and South-and-West (map 4.8) layers. Four other layers

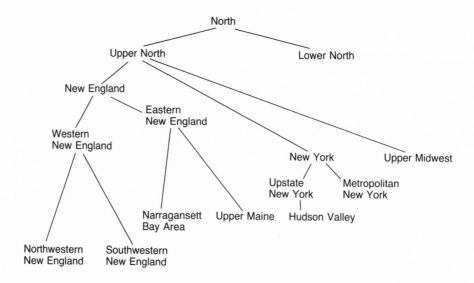

Fig. 7. Regions of New England, the Northeast, and the North

dealt with in chapter 5 combined to reveal the patchwork of one of the South's two major subregions, the Lower South. These layers are: the Atlantic South (map 5.2), Delta South (map 5.5), Lower South (map 5.8), and Outer Delta layers (map 5.12). They define the dialect regions as shown in figure 8.

Chapter 6 dealt with the traditional American midlands, the broad central section of the country roughly between the Mississippi River and the Appalachian Mountains. This general area is not only bifurcated by the North-South linguistic divide, but is covered to one degree or another by six other layers: the Upper South (map 6.2), Inland

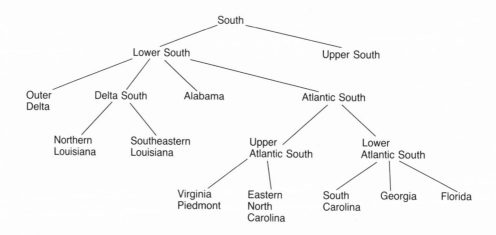

Fig. 8. Regions of the South

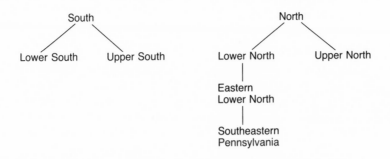

Fig. 9. Regions of the South and Lower North

South (map 6.3), Midland (map 6.5), Southeastern Pennsylvania (map 6.9), and Lower North layers (map 6.15). These yield the hierarchy of regions shown in figure 9.

Finally, chapter 7 discussed the largest American dialect region primarily in terms of the western extension of the three North layers (North, Upper North, and Inland North) and the relatively weak West layer (map 7.2). The extension into the West of the Midland, Inland South, and the three South layers also help define the regional structure of the West. Taken together the dialect regions of the West emerge as in figure 10.

Because of the newness of this vast region, the boundaries that separate the subregions of the West are hazy and necessarily more tentative than those in the East. That the West is primarily an extension of the North, however, is relatively clear and yields a general hierarchy of regions (fig. 11).

The geography of these general regional dialects is shown in map 8.1.

The regions "discovered" in this book, however, are by no means definitive. Indeed, there can be no "definitive" approach or description of regional varieties of American speech because of the elusive complexity of language variation and the inevitable distortion inherent in the fieldwork that tries to capture it. But it is possible to approximate a complete and adequate geography, one that can never be finished or final,

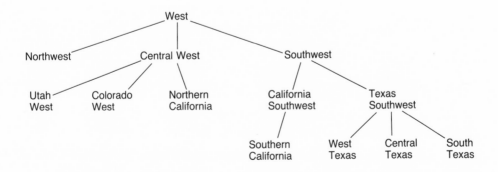

Fig. 10. Regions of the West

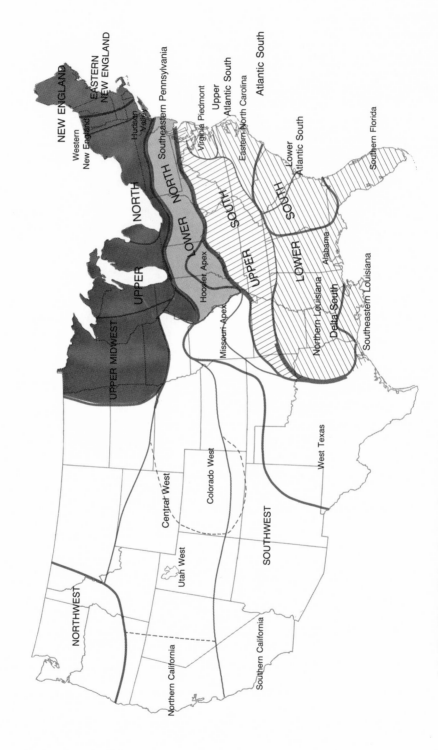

8.1. The Major Dialect Regions Summarized

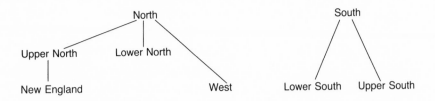

Fig. 11. General regions

but that will need repeated modification and refinement. This study has attempted to present a generalized overview of American regional dialects, a broad sketch whose details will have to be filled in with a finer analysis of the atlas and other data collections.

Appendixes

Lists of Map Words

The New England Layer (Map 2.4)

Eastern New England

belly-bump = a belly-flop (on a sled)

belly-girt(h) = the band used to cinch the harness

bulkhead = slanting cellar doors

bush scythe = a tool used to cut underbrush

dressing = manure

drop(ped) egg = poached egg

flea in one's ear = a hint, "bee in one's bonnet"

frankfurt = frankfurter, hot dog

gone by = (of root vegetables) old and tough

grinder = a hero or submarine sandwich

Indian pudding = a cornmeal pudding served with milk and molasses

kittens = soft rolls of dust that collect under furniture

nor'easter = a wind blowing from the northeast

notch = a mountain pass

open-and-shut day = a variably cloudy day

piazza = veranda

pug = a hair bun

pung = a horse-drawn sleigh often used to haul loads

rock maple = sugar maple

rotary = a traffic circle

rowen = a second growth of hay after the initial mowing; aftermath

tedder = to spread new-mown hay for drying

tenement = an apartment building

tunnel = a funnel

vum = to vow or swear

wheel harrow = an implement used to break up lumps after plowing

witch grass = couch grass or quitch grass

New England and Western New York

a-yuh = yes

adder = a snake

allie = a playing marble, especially a shooter or taw

brown bread = a steamed bread made of molasses, cornmeal, and rye flour

calling hours = a funeral wake or viewing

corn chowder = a thick soup made with corn

cow corn = field corn

creepers = metal cleats fastened to boot soles to grip ice

cross-lot(s), go = to take a short cut

hatchway (doors) = sloping cellar doors

matterate = suppurate

mow away = to store hay in the loft or mow of a barn

pea bean = a small white dried bean

side-hill plow = a plow with a reversible moldboard

snap-the-whip = a game played on the ice

swale (hay) = hay that grows naturally on wet land

titman = the runt (pig) of a litter

ugly = (of an animal) bad tempered

The Northeast Layer (Map 2.8)

brook = a small stream

buttonball, buttonwood = sycamore

can = buttocks

clapboard = wood slats used to cover the exterior of buildings

cobblestone = a small smooth or rounded stone

corn broom = a broom made of the panicles of broomcorn

cowboy = a reckless driver

cruller = a deep-fried sweet cake

double house = a house whose rooms are on each side of a main entrance hall; a duplex

dowser = a diviner (of water)

dowsing rod = divining rod

dry wall = a mortarless fence made of fieldstones

get a wiggle on = usually imperative: to hurry, go faster

grass = asparagus

guinea = a person of Italian heritage

hamburg = hamburger

hen hawk = any of several buteonine hawks, esp. red-tailed hawk

home fried (potatoes) = raw potatoes sliced and fried

hop-toad = toad

jacking = an illegal method of hunting deer at night with a jacklight

Jersey mosquito = a large mosquito

macadam = a road surface made of layers of broken stone; blacktop; a paved road

mackerel sky = a sky covered with cumulus clouds forming a pattern that resembles the markings on a mackerel

mud wasp = any of certain wasps that build mud nests

nanna = grandmother

nightwalker = earthworm

panfried (potatoes) = raw potatoes sliced and fried

peeper = any of certain small frogs (especially *Hylidae*), usually the small tree frog

pole = a wagon tongue

route [such and such] = a numbered or lettered rural road

rummy = a drunkard

scallion = a green onion often eaten raw

soda = carbonated soft drink

stone wall = a mortarless wall made of fieldstones

thank-you-ma'am = a sudden short dip in the road

wagon shed = a farm building usually used to house wagons

whiffletree = the pivoting bar to which the traces of a harness are fastened

The North Layer (Map 3.3)

Eastern North

babushka = a head scarf

basswood = linden tree

bobsled = a sled with double runners often used to haul loads

boughten = purchased rather than homemade

butter-and-eggs = wild snapdragon

chestnut = an old joke, cliché

coast = to slide downhill on a sled

creep = (of a baby) to crawl

croaker = a frog, especially a large one

dandelion (greens) = greens eaten raw

Danish (pastry) = a sweet, breadlike pastry usually frosted

divvy (up) = to share or divide with

douse (the glim) = to put out (a light or lamp)

duffer = an old man

dust kitten = dust ball

farmer = a rustic, countrified person, hick

flail = a hand tool used in separating grain from straw

flat = an apartment on one floor of a building

gentleman cow = a bull

grackle = a kind of blackbird

griddle cake = pancake

grind = someone who studies or works all the time

hairy woodpecker = any of various North American woodpeckers

mandrake = mayapple

once over, give it the = to do something superficially or lightly

perdition = hell

polack = a Polish person

rope = a cigar

snapper turtle = snapping turtle

snuffer = a snuff user

sweat like a butcher = to sweat heavily

sweetbreads = the pancreas or thymus (of a calf)

ted = to spread (hay) to dry

wetstone = whetstone

wild carrot = Queen Anne's lace

woolly bear = caterpillar

North-and-West

all in = tired, exhausted

baker's bread = bread purchased at a store

belly-flop(per) = (in children's sledding) a running dive onto a sled abdomen first, riding downhill in a prone position

belly-flop(per) = a dive into water in which the front of the body strikes first

coffin nail = a cigarette

comforter = a padded or filled bed cover

crazy bone = elbow

crow bait = a thin, broken-down cow or horse

Dutchman = a German

felon = an inflammation of a finger or toe, usually involving the bone; a whitlow

fried mush = cold cooked cereal, usually cornmeal, sliced and sautéed

gang plow = a plow with multiple shares operating as a unit

gesundheit = response to someone's sneeze

glassie = a marble

hay rack = hay wagon

hay mow or **mow** = storage area in a barn for hay

headcheese = a jellied loaf meat made of the edible parts of the head and feet usually of a pig

hubbard squash = a kind of winter squash

hull = the leafy cap of a strawberry

jag = a small quantity or load

jibe = to be in accord, agree with, fit in

knickknack shelf = a shelf for small, decorative objects

mick = an Irishman

nightcrawler = an earthworm

piccalilli = a relish of chopped vegetables and pungent spices

pie plant = rhubarb

pitch = tree sap

pod = the outside covering of peas

potluck (dinner or **supper)** = a social gathering to which one brings a dish to share

raised = (of bread dough with yeast) rose, risen—past and past participle

ran = past tense: to pierce or thrust (a wood splinter, etc.) into the skin

rapids = a place in a stream where the water descends rapidly and turbulently

riled (up) = upset; vexed; annoyed

root cellar = a cellar for storing (root) vegetables

sea cook, son of a = euphemism for "son of a bitch"

sinker = a doughnut

split = to laugh hard: "I thought I'd _____."

statues = a children's outdoor game

stiff neck = a sudden pain or crick in the neck

strung up (by the neck) = hung (by the neck)

sulky plow = a kind of plow, usually having a seat for the driver

sweet corn = corn high in natural sugar and good for table use

tainted = (of milk) tasting of something that the cow ate in the pasture

talkfest = a gathering where there is a lot of talking

timothy (grass) = a meadow grass used for forage

toad = toad (cf. *hop-toad* and *toad-frog*)

tugs = the traces of a harness

woody = (of root vegetables) old and tough

The Upper North Layer (Map 3.7)

Eastern Upper North

beet greens = the leaves and stems of garden beets often eaten cooked

blat = the sound made by a calf or cow

bloodsucker = leech

boiled dinner = a dinner of boiled meat and vegetables

bullhead (cat) = a freshwater, edible catfish

by guess and by gosh = (to do something) by hit or miss; unplanned and "by ear"

canuck = a Canadian

clear = (tea or coffee) without anything added

(devil's) darning needle = dragonfly

Democrat wagon = a light wagon usually having two seats

dirt, meaner than = very mean or ill-tempered: "He's meaner than dirt"

dog's age = a very long time

down cellar = in or into a cellar

eave(s) trough/spout = a trough or gutter along the edge of a roof to carry off rainwater

elastic (band) = rubber band

evener = singletree

ex = axle

for all of me = "for all I care"

four-corners = a crossroads

galley-west = crooked, out of plumb

get the best of = to get an advantage over (someone or something)

go = to be acceptable, put up with, like

goal = in hide-and-seek, the place where "it" waits

gooms = gums

guinea hen = guinea fowl

haycock or **cock** = a pile of hay

hitch = to get along well together (used negatively)

johnnycake = cornmeal bread

ko-day = a call to sheep

May basket (night) = the night of May first

milk snake = a harmless snake, *Lampropeltis triangulum*

milquetoast = a timid, ineffectual man

nigh horse = the horse on the left side of a team

on the fritz = in disrepair, broken

pitchforks = prickly seeds

popple = poplar

shuck = a walnut shell

skew-gee = crooked, out of plumb

souse = a drunkard

spider = a skillet

stump fence = a fence made of stumps

sugar bush = maple grove

swill = to feed (pigs)

thills = on a buggy, the two outer shafts

thorn apple = hawthorn tree or its fruit

whinner = neigh

whippletree = the moveable bar to which the traces of a harness are attached

Upper North-and-West

all the tea in China = anything: usually in the phrase "I wouldn't do that for ____."

angleworm = earthworm

blat = the noise made by a sheep

boss = a cow: usually used in calls

duck on a rock = a children's game

fussbudget = an overly fussy or finicky person

heave = to throw (something)

kitty-corner = diagonally, catercorner

mopboard = baseboard

nigger heaven = the upper balcony of a theater

no-see-um = a tiny stinging fly or midge

on the make = to pursue members of the opposite sex

polka = a dance

pollywog = tadpole

sick to (one's stomach) = queasy, nauseated

sliver = a small, sharp piece of wood

so-boss = an exclamation used to make a cow stand still

stoneboat = a wheelless vehicle or sled used to remove stones from a field

stove handle = the tool used to lift or remove the round lids on a wood-burning stove

yap = mouth

The Inland North Layer (Map 3.9)

Inland Eastern North

beanery = a cheap, usually poor quality, restaurant

close one = a narrow escape

dolt = a foolish or stupid person; a rustic or hick

fish-eater = a Roman Catholic

flyer = a fast train

goof = a dull and stupid person

goose grease = a cough and cold remedy

hunky = an east European immigrant

mow = to store hay

pickle = a cucumber

quack grass = couch grass

raw fries = sliced raw potatoes fried in a pan

run = to get hurt with something sharp

salt dip = an open dish for salt

schnozzle = nose

stone fence = a rock fence made without mortar

Inland North-and-West

bib overalls = work pants that have suspenders and an apron covering the chest

crick = a stream

crimanently = an exclamation (euphemism for "Christ")

criminy = an exclamation (euphemism for "Christ")

exchange work = a mutual exchange of help or work

farther, all the = as far as: "That's all the farther we can go."

grainery = a grain storage area in a barn

ice cream social = a social gathering often for the purpose of raising money for charity

pail = to milk (a cow)

piece = a between-meal snack

pom-pom-pullaway = an outdoor children's game resembling tug of war

pop = a carbonated soft drink

sawbuck = a rack to hold wood for sawing

semi = a large trailer truck

skiff (of snow) = a very light snowfall

sleep in = to oversleep in the morning

snakes = delirium tremens

teeter-totter = a seesaw

Inland Eastern Upper North

bobsleigh = a bobsled

bunter = a butting goat

cabbage salad = coleslaw

change work = a mutual exchange of help or work

fills = on a buggy, the two outer shafts

friedcake = a doughnut

going down = (of wind) decreasing

rubber ice = thin, flexible ice that will bear one's weight

scalloped corn = a corn dish

wheatcake = a pancake

Inland Upper North-and-West

duck soup = easily done, a cinch

mig = a playing marble

one-old-cat = a bat-and-ball game

pit = the stone or seed of a peach

porky = a porcupine

riley = agitated, upset, stirred up

tag-tail = a tagalong

The Upper Midwest Layer (Map 3.11)

Northern Upper Midwest

baga = rutebaga

biffy = a toilet

boulevard (strip) = the strip of grass and trees between sidewalk and curb

juneberry = any of various American trees or shrubs of the genus *Amelanchier* having edible purple or red berries

lutefisk = skinned and deboned fish, cured in lye water

Norskie = a person of Norwegian background

shining = hunting game at night with a lantern

Upper Midwest

American fried potatoes = boiled potatoes sliced and fried

bismarck = a deep-fried cake with a jelly or custard filling

box elder bug = a common red-and-black grass bug (*Leptocoris trivattatus*)

creeping jenny = moneywort

farmer('s) match = a wooden friction match

long-john = an oblong deep-fried cake, usually frosted

machine shed = an outbuilding where farm equipment is stored

prairie chicken = any of three species of grouse native to the prairie

slough grass = any of various tall grasses that grow in low, wet land

watermelon pickle = pickled watermelon rind

The South I Layer (Map 4.3)

agers = chills and fever

badman = the devil

barlow (knife) = a large jackknife

bat one's eyes = to close and open the eyes rapidly

biscuit bread = bread made with wheat flour

blate = the bleat (of a sheep)

blindfold = blindman's buff

booger = affectionate name for a small child

boogerman = hobgoblin, bogeyman

bottom(land) = level, low-lying land along a stream

branch = a small stream

bunch bean = a bean (e.g., kidney bean) of a nonrunning variety

butter bean = lima bean

calling the hogs = snoring

chimney-sweep(er) = chimney swallow

Christmas gift! = a Christmas morning greeting

comfort = a bed cover filled with down or wool

commode = a toilet

corruption = pus, suppuration

crawfish = a crayfish

crow to pick (with someone) = to have a dispute to settle, to have a bone to pick with someone

cuckleburrs = the prickly seeds of certain weeds

devil, meaner than the = very mean or ill tempered

dewberry = any of several berries resembling blackberries

doty = (of wood) decayed

draw (up) = to squeeze (oneself) into a tight place

entrails = internal organs

fair (off, up) = (of the weather) to become clear

far/fur piece = a long distance

feeding time = chore time

free-hearted = generous

funnel (in, down) = to drink greedily or habitually; to guzzle

fuss = an argument, quarrel, fight

gallinipper = a large mosquito

gee(-haw) = to agree or get along (with someone)

gig = to spear (fish) with a gig

give out = very tired, exhausted

green fly = greenbottle fly

gullywasher = a heavy rain, a downpour

hanted = haunted

harp = harmonica, mouth organ

hind-part-before = backward, reversed

hull = the outer covering of beans

hush-puppy = a deep-fried cornmeal cake

keen-eyed/-eyes = (having) sharp or piercing eyes

kinfolks = family, relatives

light bread = bread made from wheat flour and yeast, as distinguished from corn bread

male cow = a bull

paling fence = a fence made with pales or pickets

pallet = a temporary bed made on the floor

pethy = pithy

piddle (around) = to waste time, dawdle, trifle

platt = to braid or plait (the hair)

play like = to pretend

pulley bone = wishbone

puny = sickly, in poor health

rosin = tree sap, pitch

skin up = to climb or shinny up a tree

slaw = coleslaw

snake doctor = dragonfly

snuff dipper = one who uses snuff

sooey = an expression used to drive away
   animals

sot = a drunkard

souse (meat) = the pickled ears, head, and
   feet of a pig; headcheese

spew = to scatter liquid

terrapin = a turtle

tetter = a skin disease

till = (in phrases with reference to clock
   time) before: "fifteen minutes till eleven"

toad-frog = a toad

took = to become (ill): "He took pneumonia."

tush(es) = tusk(s)

waked up = woke up, awakened

weather boarding = clapboard, siding

whetrock = a stone used to sharpen tools

white lightning = moonshine

wiggle-tail = mosquito larva

woods colt = an illegitimate child

wore out = tired, exhausted

The South II Layer (Map 4.5)

agg on = to urge, incite

all the far = as far as, the farthest

amen corner = a front-row section in a
   church occupied by particularly zealous
   members

back = to address an envelope

bad = unwell, out-of-sorts

bad place = hell

bee gum = a beehive, especially one made
   from sections of a hollow gum tree

before-day = predawn or dawn

bit (dogbit, snakebit, fleabit, etc.) = (quasi-
   suffix): bitten by (a dog, snake, etc.)

blade = (in combinations, e.g., *bush blade,
   ditch blade, grass blade*) a hand tool for
   cutting underbrush

bless out = to scold, browbeat

blessing out = a scolding, reprimand,
   browbeating

brogan = a man's work shoe

broken veins = varicose veins

cackle (out) = to suddenly burst out laughing

chicken snake = any of various colubrid
   snakes; rat snake

chinch (bug) = bedbug

cobbler = a deep-dish fruit pie

cold drink = a carbonated soft drink

counterpin = bedspread, counterpane

dead cat on the line = a suspicous situation,
   something "fishy" or "behind one's back"

didapper = dabchick or other small grebe

diked out = dressed up

dirt dauber = any of various wasps that
   build mud nests

dogbit = bitten by a dog

draw = (of clothes) to shrink

earbobs = earrings

egg turner = a cooking spatula

evening = afternoon

eye = the round flat cover on a wood-burning
   stove

fall off = to lose weight, especially due to
   sickness

favor = to resemble (someone)

field lark = meadowlark

flying jenny = a homemade merry-go-round

foxfire = phosphorescent light on decaying
   wood

frogstool = toadstool

goozle = the throat

granny woman = a midwife

high sheriff = the executive officer of a
   county or district

hippin = a baby's diaper

hit-a-lick = a minimal amount of effort or
   work—used negatively: "He hasn't hit-a-
   lick all day."

hoppergrass = grasshopper

hurting = a pain

jackleg = (usually of a preacher or lawyer)
   unprofessional; unscrupulous; dishonest

lick = a hard blow

like to = nearly, almost

mammy = mother

manners piece = the last piece of food left
   on a plate

minner = minnow

misting rain = a light rain with fine drops

mourner's bench = a front seat at a revival

or camp meeting reserved for those who publicly repent their sins

old maid flower = zinnia

parasol = an umbrella

peckerwood = woodpecker

pet (to death) = to pamper, indulge, spoil (especially a child)

piece of a load = a portion or part of a load

play pretty = a toy

poor = lean, scrawny; feeble

poot = to break wind from the bowels

porch = to poach (an egg)

post oak = a kind of oak suitable for making posts

rising = an inflammation, swelling, or abscess

rogue = a thief

rooter = a pig's nose

run-around = a felon

salt in one's bread = something of no value: "He isn't worth the salt in his bread."

saw gourds = to snore

scat = an exclamation said after someone sneezes

shackly = unsteady, shaky, rickety

sitting up = a funeral wake

slop bucket = a container for garbage or food waste

slosh = to splash or spill (a liquid)

smoothing iron = a nonelectric iron for pressing clothes

squinch = to squint; to screw up (one's face) as in pain, etc.

staff = the barrel of a pen

storm, like a = simile for untidy, messy: "The room looks like a storm hit/struck it."

sull = to sulk or pout

swallowed a pumpkin seed = pregnant

swanny = an exclamation: "I swear," "I vow."

swiveled = shrunken and dried up

tittie = a woman's breast

torment = hell

tow sack = gunny sack

toy = (in marble play) the shooter or taw

trace chains = a harness strap or tug

yellow = egg yolk

The South-and-West Layer (Map 4.8)

base = in hide-and-seek, the place where "it" waits while the others hide

bell pepper = green pepper

belly-buster = belly-flop (on the water)

blackleg = a disease of cattle

calaboose = a jail

clabber = sour, curdled milk

doubletree = the crossbar on a wagon to which two whiffletrees are attached

hay loft or **loft** = a hay storage area in a barn

hull = the shell of a walnut

juice (the cow) = to milk (a cow)

long-handles = long underwear

mash = to crush or smash; to push (a button)

mumble-peg = mumblety-peg

roasting ear = sweet corn

run off = to have diarrhea

seed = the stone of a peach, cherry, or plum

shock or **hay shock** = a small pile of hay in a field; haycock

sick at (one's stomach) = queasy, nauseated

singletree = the moveable bar to which the traces of a harness are attached; whiffletree

slough = a swamp or backwater

sowbelly = bacon

sultry = (of the weather) warm and humid

taw = (in marble play) the shooter

taw line = (in marble play) the lag line

The Atlantic South Layer (Map 5.2)

batteau = a small boat

bell a buzzard = to do the simplest task: "He hasn't sense enough to _____."

bellowsed = (of a horse) short of breath

brownie = a penny

Brunswick stew = a stew made with vegetables and usually game meat, especially squirrel

bush hook = a hand tool for cutting underbrush

butt-head(ed) = (of a cow) without horns; a muley

catfish stew = a stew made with catfish

conjure = to cast a spell on someone

cooter = a turtle

co-wench = a call to summon cows from the pasture

cowitch (vine) = a tropical woody vine, cowage

cracker = a poor, countrified person; "poor white"

crocus bag = a coarse loosely woven sack; gunnysack

dog fly = stable fly; a biting fly resembling the common housefly

dope = a carbonated, usually cola, soft drink

dual lane (highway) = a divided highway

duck = a cigar or cigarette butt

elbow = in the phrase "go around one's elbow to get to one's thumb (nose, mouth)": to do something in an indirect or complicated way

find = (of an animal) to give birth to

firedogs = andirons

frog skin = a paper dollar

frogsticker = a large jackknife

fussbox = a finicky, fussy person; one who frets or worries over trifles

ground pea = a peanut

hopping John = a dish made with meat, usually pork, peas, and red peppers

kernel = a fruit seed, usually peach

key = the handle used to remove the lids of a wood-burning stove

lightwood = dried pinewood used for fuel or kindling

liver pudding = a sausage made of ground liver and pork trimmings

lull = (of the wind) to subside

sandspurs = the seeds of certain weeds, especially burr grass, that stick to clothing and skin

shad = an inedible freshwater fish

skeeter hawk = dragonfly

sorry = poor quality, low-grade

stick broom = a house broom with a long handle

stick-frog = mumblety-peg

stock hog = a boar

sweep = a kind of plow

syrup candy = a homemade candy made from cane syrup

tabby (cat) = a cat with fur of mixed colors

tail = buttocks

turn [of wood] = an "armload" or other amount carried in one load

turn plow = a kind of plow

whicker = the sound made by a horse

The Delta South Layer (Map 5.5)

armoire = a large, sometimes ornate, wardrobe or clothespress

bayou = a small slow-moving stream or tributary

coon-ass = a person of Acadian French heritage; a Cajun

cream cheese = cottage cheese

gallery = a porch or veranda, usually roofed

gaspergou = a croaker or freshwater drum

gumbo = a stewlike dish containing okra, with vegetables and meat or seafood

jambalaya = a rice dish made with tomatoes and herbs and with ham, chicken, shrimp, or oysters

lagniappe = a small gift given for good measure with a purchase; a bonus

neutral ground = the median strip of a highway

pirogue = a dugout canoe or other crude open boat

poule d'eau = a coot (*Fulica americana*) or mudhen

praline = a confection made with pecans and brown sugar

salt meat = bacon

tie vine = wild morning-glory

The Delta South Layer (Map 5.6)

(Isoglosses and map numbers from Atwood 1962)

armoire (50) = a piece of furniture like a wardrobe

banquette (44) = a sidewalk

bayou (53) = a stream

cream cheese (52) = cottage cheese

cush-cush (45) = a cornmeal or semolina dish

gallery (57) = a porch

girdle (29) = a saddle girth

gumbo (56) = a kind of soup

lagniappe (18) = something extra, a bonus

pirogue (48) = a kind of canoe

praline (55) = a pecan candy

salt meat (47) = salt pork

shivaree (46) = a mock wedding serenade when remarriage is involved

want to get down (49) = want to leave or get off (a bus)

The Lower South Layer (Map 5.8)

Adam's housecat = "I don't know him/her from _____."

ball = a hair bun worn on the top of the head

beau dollar = a silver dollar

b from bull's foot = anything at all: "He doesn't know _____."

big daddy = grandfather

big mama = grandmother

blate = the noise made by a calf

bray = the sound a horse makes

bream = any of various sunfishes, especially a bluegill

buck naked = totally naked

carry = to escort (someone)

cat squirrel = a reddish coated fox squirrel or the common European squirrel

chinquapin = a chestnut

chitterlings = deep-fried hog intestines

chunk = to throw

clearseed or **clearstone peach** = a freestone peach

collard (greens) = a smooth-leaved kale

cotton (is low) = a coy expression telling a woman her slip is showing

croker sack = a gunnysack

disremember = to forget

drink(s) = a carbonated, soft drink

drop = to plant (a crop)

farm-to-market road = a secondary or country road intended only for local traffic

fat pine = resinous pinewood often used for kindling

fritter = fried cornmeal bread

grind(ing) rock = a circular stone with a flat edge used to grind or sharpen tools

grits = coarsely ground corn or wheat

ground rattler = a massasauga rattlesnake

hamper = a container used to store or transport fruit, especially peaches

hey = hello, hi

high yellow = a mulatto or black person with light skin color

hog('s) head cheese = a meat loaf made of the head, feet, and heart of a pig

hop scot = the children's game of hopscotch

low = the sound made by a cow or calf; to make this sound

middle buster = a double moldboard plow

mosquito hawk = dragonfly

mulligrubs = a fit of bad humor, a melancholy mood

pinder = a peanut

pine straw = pine needles

poor = (of humans) thin, weak, sickly

potato bank or **potato hill** = a mound of root vegetables covered with straw and earth for protection against the weather

press peach = clingstone peach

rain frog = a small green frog

rawboney = gaunt, skinny

red bug = chigger

safe = a container for storing bread, cake, or pastries

shed room = a room added on to a house

sling blade = a hand tool for cutting weeds and grass

snap bean = any of various beans eaten whole with the pod

sore head = a poultry disease

splinters = kindling

squirts = diarrhea

storm pit = an underground storm shelter

suckhole = whirlpool, eddy

Swiss broom = a whisk broom

tip = to walk very quietly

Tom walkers = stilts

tumbled = in disorder, mixed up

tumbleset = a somersault

wiggler or **Georgia wiggler** = mosquito larva, often used as fishing bait

yard broom = a broom usually made of twigs and branches for outdoor use

The Outer Delta Layer (Map 5.12)

butcher calf = veal calf

cannonball = an express train

earscrews = earrings with screw fasteners

goggle-eye = a sunfish, especially warmouth or rock bass

grindle = a fish of little food value inhabiting the Great Lakes and the Mississippi Valley; bowfin or mudfish

low-quartered shoes = a low-cut shoe, an oxford shoe

net wire fence = a fence made from woven wire

nigger navel = black-eyed susan

niggerhead = black-eyed susan; purple coneflower

slide = a flat sledge used to carry stones from a field

storm house = an underground shelter against storms

urp = to vomit

The Upper South Layer (Map 6.2)

backstick = backlog

bad sick = very ill

blink(ed) = slightly sour milk; (of milk) sour

brickle = brittle, fragile

bull tongue plow = a simple plow with a single shovel

cap bundle = cap sheaf

checklines = reins

corn dodger = a small cake of corn bread

co-sheep(ie) = a call to sheep

cuss fight = an argument; a verbal fight

double shovel plow = a plow having two shovels

dram = a small amount of liquor, easily drunk in one swallow

feel of = to feel

fernent (or **fornent, forninst**) = opposite; near to; against

fescue = a kind of perennial grass sometimes used for hay

fireboard = the mantel over a fireplace

flitter = pancake

flux = diarrhea

goober pea = peanut

half-runner bean = a firm white pea bean

hidy = hello

jake-leg = a paralysis caused from drinking bad liquor; delirium tremens

jar fly = cicada

orchard grass = a tall hay and pasture grass

plum peach = clingstone peach

redeye gravy = an unthickened gravy made with water and the grease from fried meat, usually ham

sack = a cow's udder

salt shake = salt shaker

sandrock = sandstone

scuttle hole = hay chute

set = to plant (a crop)

smothering spell = a momentary physical condition characterized by weakness, rapid heart beat, and difficult breathing

sorghum = syrup made from the juice of sorghum plants; sorghum molasses

sugar orchard = a grove of sugar maple trees

The Inland South Layer (Map 6.3)

ambeer = saliva colored by chewing tobacco or snuff

blinky = (of milk) sour

buck ager/ague = nervousness of an inexperienced hunter at the sight of game; "buck fever"

bumfuzzled = confused, mixed up, perplexed

calf-rope = used by children as a cry of surrender: "I give up," "uncle"

careless grass = any of several kinds of weeds

carrion crow = vulture

catalpa worm = the larva or caterpillar of the catalpa sphinx moth frequently used as fish bait

crawfish = to back down (from an argument, position, commitment)

cur dog = a mongrel dog

dog-irons = andirons

French harp = harmonica, mouth organ

hay frame = a wagon for carrying hay

house shoe = a slipper for indoor wear

hydrant = an (outdoor) water faucet

nicker = the sound of a horse; to neigh

piece = a certain distance

saw = a command to make a cow stand still

scoot (over, down) = to move or slide (oneself or something) over

shad = a freshwater fish

town ball = a bat-and-ball game resembling baseball but usually with fewer players

turning plow = moldboard plow

The Midland Layer (Map 6.5)

Midland

belly-buster = a belly-flop (on a sled)

comb = the metal or wood strip covering the ridge of a roof

donsie = unwell, slightly ill, sickly

fat meat (poultice) = bacon or salt pork

fishing worm = earthworm

fourteen-day pickle = a kind of pickle soaked in brine for two weeks

gaps = a disease of chickens

hedge apple = Osage orange

hedge fence = a hedge used as fencing

horse corn = field corn

indian turnip = jack-in-the-pulpit

mango (pepper) = a sweet or bell pepper

meat house = a small building for curing or smoking meat or fish

medium (strip) = the middle area separating the lanes of a highway; median strip

papaw = a tree of the custard apple family

poke = a sack or bag, usually made of paper

rick (of hay) = a hay stack; hay cock

sheep(ie) = a call to sheep

smartweed = any of various knotweeds (*Polygonum*) having a smarting acrid juice

snake feeder = dragonfly

sook (cow, calf) = a call to cows or calves

strand = a necklace, especially one made of beads or pearls

sugar tree = a sugar maple tree

sweat bee = any of numerous small bees that are attracted by perspiration

white mule = moonshine; illegally made whiskey

woolly worm = caterpillar

Midland-and-West

armload = the amount of something (such as wood) that can be carried in one trip

bawl = the noise a calf makes

bedfast = confined to bed because of illness

blinds = a roller window shade

coal bucket = a container for coal

coal oil = kerosene

crawdad = freshwater crayfish

hull = to remove the outer covering of a bean

mud dauber (wasp) = "mud wasp"

muley (cow) = a hornless cow

off (want off) = used in requesting to disembark from a bus: "I want off at the next stop."

rock fence = a fence made from fieldstones, usually without mortar

sled = a sledge or "drag" for removing stones from a field

sop = gravy

The Southeastern Pennsylvania Layer (Map 6.9)

all = completely gone, finished: "The potatoes are all."

baby coach = a baby carriage

barn burner = a wooden friction match

caretaker = highway superintendent

chicken corn soup = soup made of chicken, corn, and dumplings

dressing = gravy

fastnacht = a deep-fried cake

flitch = bacon
got awake = woke up; awakened
gum band = a rubber band
medial (strip) = (of a highway) median strip
viewing = a funeral wake
washboard = baseboard or mopboard

The Lower North Layer (Map 6.15)

Lower North

andy-over = a children's game in which a ball is thrown over a building to another player
belling = shivaree
black man = a children's tag game
cap sheaf = the top bundle of a shock of grain
carry in (dinner, meal) = potluck
cave = storm shelter
cave = a place for storing root vegetables
chicken tracks = illegible handwriting
dip = syrup or sweet liquid poured over pudding or ice cream
doodle = a small pile of hay; haycock
dope = ice cream syrup
dornick = a small stone
dressing = a sweet liquid or syrup used on pudding and ice cream
flip flop = somersault or handspring
fresh fried potatoes = raw potatoes sliced and fried
fuss-button = a person who worries and frets a lot
gathered ear = an infected, suppurating ear
goose drownder = a heavy or steady rainfall
go to it = to fight or brawl
hedge tree = Osage orange
hot potato salad = a hot dish made with potatoes
Johnny-jump-up = any of various pansies or American violets
meat platter = a large meat dish
mud boat = a sledge or drag used to remove stones from a field
pinch bug = a large beetle
pound sand down a rathole = to do the simplest task: "He/she hasn't sense enough to _____."

smarty = a know-it-all; smart aleck
sneak = to walk quietly
snipe = a cigar or cigarette butt
spatzie = a sparrow
spouting = the metal trough at the edge of a roof for carrying off rainwater; downspout
stake-and-rider fence = a fence made with crossed vertical stakes and a bar on top
stool = a toilet
sugar camp = a grove of sugar maple trees
sugar maple grove = a grove of sugar maple trees
tea towel = dish towel
umbrella plant = mayapple
wakened = participle: "have wakened"

Eastern Lower North

bank barn = a two-story barn built into a hillside such that both stories have entrances
bealed = (usually of an ear) infected, suppurating
belly-smacker = belly-flop (in water)
berm = the shoulder of a road
minnie = minnow
pasture bred = (of a horse) bred by accident
peanut heaven = the upper balcony of a theater
redd (up) = to clean or straighten (a room); to clean or clear off (a dinner table)
run = a stream
scrapple = headcheese
smearcase = cottage cheese
soup bean = a small white bean
summer kitchen = a kitchen addition usually built adjacent to a house for warm-weather cooking
trestle = sawhorse

The West Layer (Map 7.2)

bear claw = a kind of pastry
bull snake = any of several North American snakes that feed primarily on rodents

canyon = a steep-sided valley cut into a mountain by a stream

catch colt = a child born out of wedlock

chippie = a woman considered to have loose morals

civet cat = a skunk

corral = a fenced-in area for keeping livestock

frontage road = a side road connecting businesses along a highway

jerky = strips of beef, dried and usually highly seasoned

ketch colt = the offspring of an unintentionally bred mare

lug = a fruit crate, especially for peaches

mountain lion = cougar or panther

mush = cooked cereal

parking strip = the grass strip between sidewalk and curb

raise cain = to behave wildly, to "raise hell"

sourdough bread = bread leavened with sourdough

water witcher = a person who divines water

The South Texas Layer (Map 7.12)

(Isoglosses and map numbers from Atwood 1962)

acequia (4) = an irrigation ditch

arroyo (15) = a gulch, ravine, creek bed

chaparral (5) = brush-covered terrain

frijoles (17) = kidney or pinto beans

hacienda (7) = the main house of a ranch

llano (3) = a plain

olla (14) = an earthenware pot or crock

pelado (3) = a Latin American

pilon (18) = a bonus, lagniappe

reata (7) = a rope or lasso

resaca (2) = a small body of water

toro (4) = a bull

vaquero (2) = a cowboy

The Central Texas Layer (Map 7.13)

(Isoglosses and map numbers from Atwood 1962)

clook, cluck (40) = a setting hen

cook cheese, kochcase (41) = a soft cheese cooked and poured into jars

grass sack (39) = a burlap bag

lunch (42) = a snack

plunder room (38) = a storage room

roping rope (40) = a lariat

settee (43) = a couch or sofa

smearcase (41) = cottage cheese

tarviated road (38) = a paved or blacktopped road

tool house (39) = a toolshed

wood house (39) = a woodshed

Regional Counterparts

Most regionalisms do not have contrasting distributions; that is, if a term is used in, say, the South, there may or may not be a corresponding regional synonym used in the North. The corresponding term might instead be in widespread use. For example, the Southern *free-hearted* does not seem to have a Northern regional counterpart. Instead, *generous* would be the most likely Northern usage, a standard term that is of course in common use throughout the South as well. There are, however, a substantial number of regionalisms that have geographical counterparts, each set offering a miniature essay on the distinctiveness of the American dialect regions.

The following is a selected list of regional counterparts, and although for the most part the terms of each set are synonymous, each word has its own history and connotations. Moreover, the synonymy is often very broad, so that many words have a very specific meaning that is not strictly speaking synonymous with the other words in the set. For example, the terms for sweet pastries usually refer to a specific kind. An extreme example of a set of words that are only in the very broadest sense synonymous, are those in the set "kinds of wind." A *chinook* wind refers to a warm southwest wind, while a *norther* is a cold northern wind. Thus, in using this list caution must be exercised and the index, or better, the *Dictionary of American Regional English* should be consulted.

1. **Of the wind: to decrease or die down**
   - to lay or lay by: *South II*
   - to lull: *Atlantic South*
   - to go down: *Inland Upper North*
2. **Kinds of winds**
   - nor'easter, nor'wester: *Eastern New England*
   - chinook: *Northwest*
   - norther, blue norther: *Texas, southern Oklahoma*
3. **A heavy rain**
   - gullywasher, toad strangler, frog strangler: *South II*
   - goose drownder: *Lower North*
4. **A running stream**
   - crick: *Inland North-and-West*
   - branch: *South I*
   - brook: *Northeast*
   - bayou: *Louisiana*
   - run: *Eastern Lower North*

5. **Exterior wood siding**
    weather boarding: *South I*
    clapboard: *Northeast*
    battens: *Far West*

6. **Troughs to carry off rain**
    eave(s) trough/spout: *Eastern Lower North*
    spouting: *South-and-West, New England*
    gutters: *Upper South*

7. **A padded bed cover**
    comforter: *North-and-West*
    comfort: *South I*
    counterpin: *South II*

8. **The round cover on a wood stove**
    griddle: *Upstate New York*
    eye: *South II*
    cap: *Upper South*

9. **A loosely woven cloth bag**
    croker sack: *Lower South*
    crocus sack: *Atlantic South*
    tow bag: *Eastern North Carolina*
    tow sack: *South II*
    grass sack: *Virginia, Kentucky, Louisiana*
    gunnysack: *Greater West*

10. **A broom usually made of bundled twigs for outdoor use**
    yard broom: *Lower South*
    stick broom: *Atlantic South*
    corn broom: *Northeast*

11. **Indoor toilet**
    stool: *Lower North*
    commode: *South I*

12. **Rubber band**
    elastic (band): *Upper North*
    gum band: *Pennsylvania*

13. **Bread purchased in a store**
    boughten bread: *North*
    baker's bread: *North-and-West*
    loaf bread: *South II*

14. **Wheat flour bread**
    whitebread: *North-and-West*
    lightbread: *South I*
    raised bread: *Eastern New England*

15. **Pancake**
    griddle cake: *North*
    wheatcake: *Inland Upper North*
    flitter: *Upper South*

16. **Doughnut**
    cruller: *Northeast*
    friedcake: *Inland Upper North*

fastnacht: *Pennsylvania*

sinker: *North-and-West*

17. **A sweet pastry**

danish (pastry): *North*

bear claw: *West*

maple bar: *Northwest*

long-john, bismarck: *Upper Midwest*

18. **Bacon**

sowbelly: *South-and-West*

middlins: *South II*

breakfast bacon: *Atlantic South*

salt meat: *Louisiana*

fat meat: *Midland*

flitch: *Pennsylvania*

19. **A loaf meat made from the head and other parts of a hog**

headcheese: *North-and-West*

scrapple: *Lower North*

souse (meat): *South I*

hog('s) head cheese: *Lower South*

haslet: *Atlantic South*

20. **Sliced and fried potatoes**

fresh fried potatoes: *Lower North*

panfried potatoes, home fried potatoes: *Northeast*

raw fries: *Inland North*

American fries, American fried potatoes: *Upper Midwest*

21. **Thick, soured milk**

bonnyclabber: *Northeast*

clabber: *South I*

lobbered milk: *Upstate New York*

22. **Cottage cheese**

sour-milk cheese: *Eastern New England*

pot cheese: *Hudson Valley*

smearcase: *Eastern Lower North*

clabber cheese: *South II*

cream cheese: *Louisiana*

23. **A social gathering to which a person brings a dish to share**

potluck (dinner or supper): *North-and-West*

carry in (dinner or meal): *Lower North*

dinner on the ground: *South II*

24. **Carbonated soft drink**

pop: *Inland North-and-West*

soda: *Northeast*

tonic: *Eastern New England*

cold drink: *South II*

drink: *Lower South*

dope: *Atlantic South*

25. **Of a vegetable: old and dried out**

woody: *North-and-West*

pethy: *South I*

gone by: *Eastern New England*

26. **Sweet young corn**

sweet corn: *North-and-West*

roasting ear: *South-and-West*

27. **Field corn**

horse corn: *Midland*

cow corn: *Inland New England*

28. **Peanut**

pinder: *Lower South*

goober pea: *Upper South*

ground pea: *Atlantic South*

29. **The large seed of a peach, plum, or cherry**

pit: *Inland Upper North-and-West*

seed: *South-and-West*

kernel: *Atlantic South*

30. **A peach whose flesh does not cling to the seed**

clearseed peach: *Lower South*

soft peach: *Virginia Piedmont*

31. **A peach whose flesh clings to the seed**

plum peach: *Upper South*

press peach: *Lower South*

32. **To milk a cow**

pail: *Inland North-and-West*

juice: *South-and-West*

33. **A hornless cow**

muley (cow): *Midland-and-West*

butt-head(ed): *Atlantic South*

buffalo (cow): *Eastern North Carolina*

34. **The noise made by a cow or calf**

blart: *New England*

blare: *Eastern New England*

blat: *Upper North*

blate: *Lower South*

bawl: *Midland-and-West*

loo: *South II*

low: *Lower South*

35. **Hay wagon**

hay frame: *Inland South*

hay rack: *North-and-West*

36. **A bull**

gentleman cow: *North*

sire: *North-and-West*

top cow: *Eastern New England*

toro: *Eastern New England, Southwest*

male cow: *South I*

37. **The sound made by a horse**

whinner: *Upper North*

nicker: *Inland South*

bray: *Lower South*

whicker: *Atlantic South*

38. **The sound made by a sheep**

blat: *Upper North-and-West*

blate: *South I*

39. **Call to cows**

boss, co-boss: *Upper North-and-West*

sook (cow): *Midland*

co-wench: *Atlantic South*

40. **Call to sheep**

ko-day: *Upper North*

sheep(ie): *Midland*

co-sheep(ie): *Upper South*

41. **A pile of hay**

(hay)cock: *Upper North*

tumble: *Northern New England*

rick (of hay), hayrick: *Midland*

doodle: *Lower North*

shock: *South-and-West*

42. **To plant a crop**

set: *Upper South*

drop: *Lower South*

43. **A stone for sharpening tools**

wetstone: *North*

rifle: *Eastern New England*

whetrock: *South I*

grind(ing) rock: *Lower South*

44. **The pivoting bar to which the traces of a harness are fastened**

whippletree: *Upper North*

whiffletree: *Northeast*

singletree: *South-and-West*

45. **The pivoting bar to which whippletrees are fastened**

evener: *Upper North*

doubletree: *South-and-West*

46. **The lines of a harness for attaching the draft animal to a vehicle**

tugs: *North-and-West*

trace chains, hame strings: *South II*

47. **A partial load (of something)**

jag: *North-and-West*

piece of a load: *South II*

48. **A wheelless vehicle for transporting stones from a field; a drag**

stoneboat: *Upper North-and-West*

stone drag: *New England*

mud boat: *Lower North*

sled: *Midland and West*

slide: *Outer Delta*

49. **A support for sawing wood**
    sawbuck: *Inland North-and-West*
    trestle: *Lower North*
    (saw)rack: *South II*

50. **A mortarless fence made of fieldstones**
    stone fence: *Inland North*
    stone wall, dry wall: *Northeast*
    rock fence: *Midland-and-West*

51. **The area in a barn for storing hay**
    (hay) mow: *North-and-West*
    (hay) loft: *South-and-West*

52. **A fenced area, usually next to a barn, for keeping livestock**
    lot (barnlot, cowlot, etc.): *South I*
    cuppen: *Virginia Piedmont*
    corral: *West*

53. **A place for storing root vegetables**
    root cellar: *North-and-West*
    cave: *Lower North*
    potato bank: *Lower South*
    potato hill: *Atlantic South*

54. **A toilet (indoor or outdoor)**
    biffy: *Northern Upper Midwest*
    necessary (house): *Eastern New England*
    garden house: *Eastern North Carolina*
    johnny: *South*

55. **A divided highway**
    parkway: *Inland New England*
    throughway: *Upstate New York*
    dual highway: *Upper Atlantic South, New Jersey, New York, Missouri*
    dual lane (highway): *Atlantic South*

56. **The center strip separating the opposing lanes of a highway**
    mall: *Upstate New York*
    medium (strip): *Midland*
    medial (strip): *Pennsylvania*
    neutral ground: *Louisiana*

57. **A common worm, often used as fishing bait**
    angleworm: *Upper North-and-West*
    nightcrawler: *North-and-West*
    nightwalker: *Northeast*
    eace worm: *Narragansett Bay*
    mud worm: *Eastern New England, Atlantic South*
    fishing worm: *Midland*
    wiggler: *Lower South*
    bloodworm: *Upper Atlantic South, New Jersey, Metropolitan New York*

58. **Toad**
    toad: *North-and-West*
    toad-frog: *South I*
    hop-toad: *Northeast*

59. **Dragonfly**
    (devil's) darning needle: *Upper North*
    snake feeder: *Midland*
    snake doctor: *South I*
    mosquito hawk: *Lower South*
    skeeter hawk: *Atlantic South*
    ear sewer: *Northern California*

60. **A wasp that builds a mud nest**
    mud wasp: *Northeast*
    mud dauber: *Midland-and-West*
    dirt dauber: *South II*

61. **A grove of sugar maple trees**
    sap orchard: *New England*
    sugar bush: *Upper North*
    sugar (maple) grove, sugar camp: *Lower North*
    sugar orchard: *Upper South*

62. **The sticky sap from trees, especially pines**
    pitch: *North-and-West*
    rosin: *South I*

63. **Tired, exhausted**
    all in: *North-and-West*
    wore out, give out: *South I*

64. **To throw (something)**
    heave: *Upper North-and-West*
    chunk: *Lower South*

65. **A child born out of wedlock**
    old-field colt: *Virginia Piedmont*
    woods colt: *South II*
    catch colt, ketch colt: *West*

66. **A noisy mock serenade to newlyweds**
    shivaree: *Greater West*
    horning (bee): *Upstate New York*
    skimmilton: *Hudson Valley*
    serenade: *Northern New England, Pennsylvania, Atlantic South*
    belling: *Lower North*

67. **Sick _____ one's stomach**
    to: *Upper North-and-West*
    at: *South-and-West*
    on: *Atlantic South, Pennsylvania*

68. **Funeral wake**
    calling hours: *Inland New England*
    viewing: *Pennsylvania*
    sitting up: *South II*
    visitation: *Eastern Upper Midwest*

69. **A person who uses snuff**
    snuffer: *North*
    snoose: *Northwest*
    snuff dipper: *South I*

70. **A drunkard**
    souse: *Upper North*
    rummy: *Northeast*
    sot: *South I*

71. **A game in which a jackknife is thrown into the ground**
    mumble-peg: *South-and-West*
    stick-frog: *Atlantic South*

72. **A bat-and-ball game for a few players**
    one-old-cat: *Inland Upper North-and-West*
    town ball: *Inland South*
    work-up(s): *Greater West*

73. **The place where "it" counts in hide-and-seek**
    goal: *Upper North*
    base: *South-and-West*

74. **A running dive onto a sled with the front of the body striking first**
    belly-flop(per): *North-and-West*
    belly-bump: *Eastern New England*
    belly-buster: *Midland*

75. **A dive into water in which the front of the body strikes first**
    belly-flop(per): *North-and-West*
    belly-smacker: *Lower North*
    belly-buster: *South-and-West*

76. **Seesaw**
    teeter-totter: *Inland North-and-West*
    teeter: *Northeast*
    tilting board: *Southeastern New England*
    teedle board: *Northeastern Massachusetts*

77. **A social gathering usually involving a special activity**
    ice-cream social: *Inland North-and-West*
    pie supper: *Upper South*

78. **A finicky, worrisome person**
    fussbudget: *Upper North-and-West*
    fusspot: *Inland New England*
    fuss-button: *Lower North*
    fussbox: *Atlantic South*

79. **"Meaner than _____"**
    dirt: *Upper North*
    the devil: *South I*

80. **To be in accord, agree with, fit in**
    jibe: *North-and-West*
    hitch: *Upper North*
    gee(-haw): *South I*

81. **Askew, crooked**
    skew-gee: *Upper North*
    antigodlin: *South II*

82. **As far as**
    all the farther: *Inland North-and-West*
    all the far: *South II*

Abbreviations

AmSp	*American Speech, a Quarterly of Linguistic Usage*
Annals	*Annals of the Association of American Geographers*
DA	*Dictionary of Americanisms*
DAE	*Dictionary of American English*
DARE	*Dictionary of American Regional English*
EDD	*English Dialect Dictionary*
Handbook	*Handbook of the Linguistic Geography of New England*
LAGS	*Linguistic Atlas of the Gulf States*
LAMSAS	*Linguistic Atlas of the Middle and South Atlantic States*
LANCS	Linguistic Atlas of the North Central States
LANE	*Linguistic Atlas of New England*
LAPC	Linguistic Atlas of the Pacific Coast
LAUM	*Linguistic Atlas of the Upper Midwest*
OED	*Oxford English Dictionary*
OEDS	*Oxford English Dictionary Supplement*
PADS	*Publication of the American Dialect Society*
WG	*A Word Geography of the Eastern United States*, Kurath 1949.

Bibliography

Abernathy, Thomas Perkins. 1965. *The Formative Period in Alabama 1815–1828*. University, Ala.: University of Alabama Press.

Adams, James Truslow, ed. 1943. *Atlas of American History*. New York: Charles Scribner's Sons.

Adams, Ramon F. 1944, rev. ed. 1968. *Western Words: A Dictionary of the Range, Cow Camp and Trail*. Norman: University of Oklahoma Press.

Ahlstrom, Sydney E. 1972. *A Religious History of the American People*. New Haven, Conn.: Yale University Press.

Ainsley, W. Frank, and Florin, John W. 1973. "The North Carolina Piedmont: An Island of Religious Diversity." *West Georgia College Studies in Social Sciences* 12:30–34.

Allen, Harold B. 1958. "Minor Dialect Areas of the Upper Midwest." *PADS* 30:3–16.

———. 1959. "Haycock and Its Synonyms." *AmSp* 34:144–45.

———. 1960. "Semantic Confusion: A Report from the Atlas Files." *PADS* 33:3–13.

———. 1971. "The Primary Dialect Areas of the Upper Midwest." In *Readings in American Dialectology*, edited by Harold B. Allen and Gary N. Underwood, pp. 83–93. New York: Appleton-Century-Crofts.

———. 1973. "Two Dialects in Contact." *AmSp* 48:54–66.

———. 1973–76. *The Linguistic Atlas of the Upper Midwest*. Vol. 1, *The Project and the Lexicon*. Vol. 2, *The Grammar*. Vol. 3, *The Pronunciation*. Minneapolis: University of Minnesota Press.

———. 1977. "Regional Dialects, 1945–1974." *AmSp* 52:163–261.

Allen, Harold B., and Underwood, Gary N., eds. 1971. *Readings in American Dialectology*. New York: Appleton-Century-Crofts.

Anderson, Hattie M. 1937. "Missouri, 1804–1828: Peopling a Frontier State." *Missouri Historical Review* 31:150–80.

Arbingast, Stanley A. 1973. *Atlas of Texas*. Austin: University of Texas Press.

Atwood, E. Bagby. 1951, reprint 1971. "Some Eastern Virginia Pronunciation Features." In *A Various Language: Perspectives on American Dialects*, edited by Juanita V. Williamson and Virginia M. Burke, pp. 255–67. New York: Holt.

———. 1953. *A Survey of Verb Forms in the Eastern United States*. Ann Arbor: University of Michigan Press.

———. 1962. *The Regional Vocabulary of Texas*. Austin: University of Texas Press.

Atwood, E. Bagby. 1963, reprint 1971. "The Methods of American Dialectology." In *Readings in American Dialectology*, edited by Harold B. Allen and Gary N. Underwood, pp. 5–35. New York: Appleton-Century-Crofts.

Avis, Walter S. 1955. "Crocus Bag: A Problem in Areal Linguistics." *AmSp* 30:5–16.

Babington, Mima, and Atwood, E. Bagby. 1961. "Lexical Usage in Southern Louisiana." *PADS* 36:1–24.

Bailey, Charles-James N. 1968. "Is There a 'Midland' Dialect of American English?" Educational Resources Information Center (ERIC) document ED 021 240.

———. 1973a. *Variation and Linguistic Theory.* Arlington, Va.: Center for Applied Linguistics.

———. 1973b. "The Patterning of Language Variation." In *Varieties of Present-Day English,* edited by Richard W. Bailey and Jay L. Robinson, pp. 156–86. New York: Macmillan Co.

Bailey, Charles-James, N., and Shuy, Roger W., eds. 1973. *New Ways of Analyzing Variation in English.* Washington, D.C.: Georgetown University Press.

Bailey, Richard W., and Robinson, Jay L., eds. 1973. *Varieties of Present-Day English.* New York: Macmillan Co.

Barnhart, John D. 1953. *Valley of Democracy: The Frontier versus the Plantation in the Ohio Valley, 1775–1818.* Bloomington: Indiana University Press.

Bergquist, James M. 1981. "Tracing the Origins of a Midwestern Culture: the Case of Central Indiana." *Indiana Magazine of History* 77:1–32.

Billington, Ray Allen. 1956. *The Far Western Frontier: 1830–1860.* New York: Harper and Row.

———. 1960, 2d ed. *Westward Expansion: A History of the American Frontier.* New York: Macmillan Co.

Birdsall, Stephen S., and Florin, John W. 1981. *Regional Landscapes of the United States and Canada.* New York: John Wiley and Sons.

Bloomfield, Leonard. 1933, reprint 1958. *Language.* New York: Henry Holt and Co.

Bogue, Alan G. 1963. *From Prairie to Corn Belt; Farming on the Illinois and Iowa Prairies in the Nineteenth Century.* Chicago: University of Chicago Press.

Bright, Elizabeth S. 1971. *A Word Geography of California and Nevada.* Berkeley: University of California Press.

Brown, Ralph H. 1948. *Historical Geography of the United States.* New York: Harcourt, Brace, Jovanovich.

Callary, Robert E. 1971. "Dialectology and Linguistic Theory." *AmSp* 46:200–209.

Carlson, David R. 1973. "The Common Speech of Boston." Ph.D. dissertation, University of Massachusetts.

Carmony, Marvin. 1965. "The Speech of Terre Haute: A Hoosier Dialect Study." Ph.D. dissertation, Indiana University.

———. 1972. "Aspects of Regional Speech in Indiana." In *Studies in Linguistics in Honor of Raven I. McDavid, Jr.,* edited by Lawrence Davis, pp. 9–24. University, Ala.: University of Alabama Press.

———. 1979. "Indiana Dialects in Their Historical Setting." *Indiana Folklore* 2.3:1–51.

Carr, Donna H. 1966. "Reflections of Atlantic Coast Lexical Variations in Three Mormon Communities." Master's thesis, University of Utah.

Carver, Craig M. 1986. "The Influence of the Mississippi River on Northern Dialect Boundaries." *AmSp* 61:245–61.

Cassidy, Frederic G. 1978. "Another Look at Buckaroo." *AmSp* 53:49–51.

———. 1980. "The Place of Gullah." *AmSp* 55:3–16.

Cassidy, Frederic G., ed. 1985–. *Dictionary of American Regional English.* Cambridge, Mass.: Harvard University Press, Belknap.

Cassidy, Frederic G., and Duckert, Audrey R. 1953. "A Method of Collecting Dialect." *PADS* 20.

Chambers, J. K., and Trudgill, Peter. 1980. *Dialectology.* Cambridge: Cambridge University Press.

Clark, Thomas L. 1972. "Marietta, Ohio: The Continuing Erosion of a Speech Island." *PADS* 57:1–55.

Clough, Wilson. 1954. "Some Wyoming Speech Patterns." *AmSp* 29:28–35.

Combs, Josiah H. 1916. "Old, Early and Elizabethan English in the Southern Mountains." *Dialect Notes* 4:283–97.

Cook, Albert B. 1978. "Perspectives for a Linguistic Atlas of Kansas." *AmSp* 53:199–209.

Cook, Stanley J. 1969. "Language Change and the Emergence of an Urban Dialect in Utah." Ph.D. dissertation, University of Utah.

Couch, William Terry, ed. 1935. *Culture in the South.* Chapel Hill: University of North Carolina Press.

Crisler, Robert M. 1948. "Missouri's 'Little Dixie.' " *Missouri Historical Review* 42:130–39.

Crozier, Alan. 1984. "The Scotch-Irish Influence on American English." *AmSp* 59:310–31.

Cummings, Richard O. 1941. *The American and His Food: A History of Food Habits in the United States.* Chicago: University of Chicago Press.

Cussler, Margaret, and DeGive, Mary L. 1952. *'Twixt the Cup and the Lip; Psychological and Socio-Cultural Factors Affecting Food Habits.* New York: Twayne.

Dakin, Robert F. 1966. "The Dialect Vocabulary of the Ohio River Valley: A Survey of the Distribution of Selected Vocabulary Forms in an Area of Complex Settlement History." 3 vols. Ph.D. dissertation, University of Michigan.

_____. 1971. "South Midland Speech in the Old Northwest." *Journal of English Linguistics* 5:31–48.

Davis, Alva L. 1948. "A Word Atlas of the Great Lakes Region." Ph.D. dissertation, University of Michigan.

_____. 1951. "Dialect Distribution and Settlement Patterns in the Great Lakes Region." *Ohio State Archeological and Historical Quarterly* 60:48–56.

_____. 1971. "Developing and Testing the Checklist." *AmSp* 46:34–37.

Davis, Alva L., and McDavid, Raven I., Jr. 1949. "Shivaree: An Example of Cultural Diffusion." *AmSp* 24:249–55.

_____. 1950. "Northwestern Ohio: A Transition Area." *Language* 26:264–73.

Davis, Alva L.; McDavid, Raven I.; and McDavid, Virginia G. 1969. *A Compilation of the Work Sheets of the Linguistic Atlas of the United States and Canada and Associated Projects.* Chicago: University of Chicago Press.

Davis, Lawrence M. 1971. "Worksheets and Their Variants." *AmSp* 46:27–33.

_____. 1973. "The Diafeature: An Approach to Structural Dialectology." *Journal of English Linguistics* 7:1–20.

_____. 1983. *English Dialectology.* University, Ala.: University of Alabama Press.

Davis, Lawrence M., ed. 1972. *Studies in Linguistics in Honor of Raven I. McDavid, Jr.* University, Ala.: University of Alabama Press.

Dearden, E. J. 1943. "Dialect Areas of the South Atlantic States as Determined by Variation in Vocabulary." Ph.D. dissertation, Brown University.

Dickinson, Donald. 1952. "Speech Characteristics of the Rio Grande Valley, New Mexico." Master's thesis, University of New Mexico.

Dil, Anwar S. 1980. *Varieties of American English: Essays by Raven I. McDavid, Jr.* Stanford: Stanford University Press.

Dillard, Joey L. 1972. *Black English: Its History and Usage in the United States.* New York: Random House.

Drake, James A. 1961. "The Effect of Urbanization upon Regional Vocabulary." *AmSp* 36:17–33.

Duckert, Audrey. 1956. "Gutter: Its Rise and Fall." *Names* 4:146–54.

Dumas, Bethany K. 1971. "A Study of the Dialect of Newton County, Arkansas." Ph.D. dissertation, University of Arkansas.

––––––. 1975. "The Morphology of Newton County, Arkansas: An Exercise in Studying Ozark Dialect." *Mid-South Folklore* 3:115–25.

Eaton, Clement. 1966, 2d ed. *A History of the Old South.* New York: Macmillan Co.

Ernst, Joseph A., and Merrens, Harry Roy. 1973. "The South Carolina Economy of the Middle Eighteenth Century: A View from Philadelphia." *West Georgia College Studies in the Social Sciences* 12:16–29.

Evans, E. Estyn. 1965. "The Scotch-Irish in the New World: An Atlantic Heritage." *Journal of the Royal Society of Antiquaries of Ireland* 95:39–49.

––––––. 1966. "Cultural Relics of the Ulster-Scots in the Old West of North America." *Ulster Folklife* 12:33–38.

––––––. 1969. "The Scotch-Irish: Their Cultural Adaptation and Heritage in the American Old West." In *Essays in Scotch-Irish History,* edited by E. R. R. Green, pp. 69–86. London: Routledge and Kegan Paul.

Faries, Rachel B. 1967. "A Word Geography of Missouri." Ph.D. dissertation, University of Missouri.

Fasold, Ralph W. 1981. "The Relation between Black and White Speech in the South." *AmSp* 56:163–89.

Feagin, Crawford. 1979. *Variation and Change in Alabama English: A Sociolinguistic Study of the White Community.* Washington, D.C.: Georgetown University Press.

Fenneman, Nevin M. 1928. "Physiographic Divisions of the United States." *Annals* 18:261–353.

Fisher, Hilda B. 1950. "A Study of the Speech of East Feliciana Parish, Louisiana." Ph.D. dissertation, Louisiana State University.

Florin, John. 1977. "The Advance of Frontier Settlement in Pennsylvania, 1638–1850: A Geographic Interpretation." *Papers in Geography.* Pennsylvania State University.

Foley, Lawrence M. 1972. "A Phonological and Lexical Study of the Speech of Tuscaloosa County, Alabama." *PADS* 58:1–54.

Folk, Mary L. P. 1961. "A Word Atlas of North Louisiana." Ph.D. dissertation, Louisiana State University.

Foscue, Virginia. 1967. "Background and Preliminary Survey of the Linguistic Geography of Alabama." Ph.D. dissertation, University of Wisconsin.

––––––. 1971. "A Preliminary Survey of the Vocabulary of White Alabamians." *PADS* 56:1–46.

Francis, W. Nelson. 1958. *The Structure of American English.* New York: Ronald Press Co.

––––––. 1983. *Dialectology, an Introduction.* London and New York: Longman.

Frank, Yakira. 1948. "The Speech of New York City." Ph.D. dissertation, University of Michigan.

Frazer, Timothy C. 1971. "Combining Atlas, DARE, and Checklist Materials." *AmSp* 46:58–65.

––––––. 1973. "Midland Dialect Areas in Illinois." Ph.D. dissertation, University of Chicago.

––––––. 1978a. "Cultural Geography in Illinois: Regional Speech and Place Name Sources." *Great Lakes Review* 4.2:19–30.

––––––. 1978b. "South Midland Pronunciation in the North Central States." *AmSp* 53:40–48.

––––––. 1979. "The Speech Island of the American Bottoms: A Problem in Social History." *AmSp* 54:185–93.

––––––. 1982. "Language Variation in the Military Tract." *Western Illinois Regional Studies* 5:54–64.

––––––. 1983a. "Sound Change and Social Structure in a Rural Community." *Language in Society* 12:313–28.

_____. 1983b. "Cultural Assimilation in the Post-Frontier Era: Linguistic Atlas Evidence." *Midwestern Journal of Language and Folklore* 9.1:5–23.

Friis, Herman R. 1940. "A Series of Population Maps of the Colonies and United States, 1625–1790." *Geographical Review* 30:463–70.

Garland, John H., ed. 1955. *The North American Midwest: A Regional Geography*. New York: John Wiley and Sons.

Garreau, Joel. 1981. *The Nine Nations of North America*. Boston: Houghton Mifflin Co.

Gastil, Raymond D. 1975. *Cultural Regions of the United States*. Seattle: University of Washington Press.

Gaustad, Edwin Scott. 1976, rev. ed. *Historical Atlas of Religion in America*. New York: Harper and Row.

Gawthrop, Betty. 1973. "The Speech of the Calumet Region." Ph.D. dissertation, Purdue University.

George, Albert D. 1951. "Some Louisiana Isoglosses, Based on the Workbooks of the Louisiana Dialect Atlas." Master's thesis, Louisiana State University.

Gerlach, Russel L. 1976. *Immigrants in the Ozarks: A Study in Ethnic Geography*. Columbia: University of Missouri Press.

Gibbons, V. E. 1966. "A Progress Report on a Word Geography of Indiana." *Midwest Folklore* 11:151–54.

Gibson, James R., ed. 1978. *European Settlement and Development in North America*. Toronto: University of Toronto Press.

Gillespie, Paul F., ed. 1982. *Foxfire 7*. Garden City, N.Y.: Anchor Press, Doubleday.

Gimlin, Hoyt, ed. 1980. *American Regionalism: Our Economic, Cultural and Political Makeup*. Washington, D.C.: Congressional Quarterly.

Glass, Joseph W. 1971. "The Pennsylvania Culture Region: A Geographical Interpretation of Barns and Farmsteads." Ph.D. dissertation, Pennsylvania State University.

Glassie, Henry. 1968. *Pattern in the Material Folk Culture of the Eastern United States*. Philadelphia: University of Pennsylvania Press.

Gordon, Milton M. 1961. "Assimilation in America: Theory and Reality." *Daedalus* 90:263–85.

Gould, Peter R. 1969. *Spatial Diffusion*. Resource Paper no. 4. Washington, D.C.: Association of American Geographers.

Green, E. R. R. 1969. *Essays in Scotch-Irish History*. London: Routledge and Kegan Paul.

Greenway, John. 1958. "Australian Cattle Lingo." *AmSp* 33:163–69.

Griffin, Paul F.; Chatham, Ronald L.; and Young, Robert N. 1968, 2d ed. *Anglo-America: A Systematic and Regional Geography*. Palo Alto, Calif.: Fearon.

Grigg, David. 1965. "The Logic of Regional Systems." *Annals* 55:465–91.

Hagerstrand, T. 1967. *Innovation Diffusion as a Spatial Process*. Chicago: University of Chicago Press.

Haggett, P. 1965. *Locational Analysis in Human Geography*. London: Arnold.

Hancock, Ian F. 1980. "Gullah and Barbadian—Origins and Relationships." *AmSp* 55:17–35.

Hankey, Clyde T. 1960. "A Colorado Word Geography." *PADS* 34.

_____. 1961. "Semantic Features and Eastern Relics in Colorado Dialect." *AmSp* 36:266–70.

Hansen, Marcus L. 1961. *The Atlantic Migration, 1607–1860*. Cambridge, Mass.: Harvard University Press.

Harris, Jesse W. 1946. "The Dialect of Appalachia in Southern Illinois." *AmSp* 21:96–99.

Hart, John Fraser. 1967. *The Southeastern United States*. New York: Van Nostrand Reinhold.

_____. 1972a. "The Middle West." *Annals* 62:258–82.

———. 1974. "The Spread of the Frontier and the Growth of Population." In *Man and Cultural Heritage: Papers in Honor of Fred B. Kniffen,* edited by Bob F. Perkins, pp. 73–82. Baton Rouge: School of Geoscience, Louisiana State University.

Hart, John Fraser, ed. 1972b. *Regions of the United States.* New York: Harper and Row.

Hartman, James W. 1966. "Pressures for Dialect Change in Hocking County, Ohio." Ph.D. dissertation, University of Michigan.

Hawkins, J. D. 1941. "The Speech of the Hudson River Valley." Ph.D. dissertation, Brown University.

Hill, Archibald A. 1979. "Buckaroo Once More." *AmSp* 54:151–53.

Hilliard, Sam. 1969. "Hog Meat and Cornpone: Food Habits in the Ante-Bellum South." *Proceedings of the American Philosophical Society* 113:1–13.

Hilliard, Sam B., and Irwin, Dan. 1972. "Indian Land Cessions." *Annals* 62:374 and map enclosure.

Hoff, Patricia J. 1968. "A Dialect Study of Faulkner County, Arkansas." Ph.D. dissertation, Louisiana State University.

Holbrook, Stewart H. 1950. *The Yankee Exodus: An Account of Migration from New England.* New York: Macmillan Co.

Houck, Charles L. 1970. "A Statistical and Computerized Methodology for Analyzing Dialect Materials." Ph.D. dissertation, University of Iowa.

Howren, Robert R., Jr. 1958. "The Speech of Louisville, Kentucky." Ph.D. dissertation, Indiana University.

———. 1962. "The Speech of Ocracoke, North Carolina." *AmSp* 37:163–75.

Hsu, Mei-Ling, and Robinson, Arthur H. 1970. *The Fidelity of Isopleth Maps: An Experimental Study.* Minneapolis: University of Minnesota Press.

Ivic, Pavle. 1962. "On the Structure of Dialectal Differentiation." *Word* 18:33–53.

———. 1964. "Structure and Typology of Dialectal Differentiation." In *Proceedings of the Ninth International Congress of Linguists,* pp. 115–19. The Hague: Mouton.

Jackson, Elizabeth H. 1956. "An Analysis of Certain Colorado Atlas Field Records with Regard to Settlement History and Other Factors." Ph.D. dissertation, University of Colorado.

Jaffe, Hilda. 1973. "The Speech of the Central Coast of North Carolina: The Carteret County Version of the Banks 'Brogue'." *PADS* 60.

Jensen, Merrill, ed. 1965. *Regionalism in America.* Madison: University of Wisconsin Press.

Jones, Mabel Jean. 1973. "The Regional English of the Former Inhabitants of Cades Cove in the Great Smoky Mountains." Ph.D. dissertation, University of Tennessee.

Jones, Maldwyn Allen. 1960. *American Immigration.* Chicago: University of Chicago.

Jordan, Terry G. 1967. "The Imprint of the Upper South on Mid-Nineteenth Century Texas." *Annals* 57:667–90.

———. 1969. "Population Origins in Texas, 1850." *Geographical Review* 59:83–103.

———. 1970. "The Texan Appalachia." *Annals of the Association of American Geographers* 60:409–27.

Kimmerle, Marjorie. 1950. "The Influence of Locale and Human Activity on Some Words in Colorado." *AmSp* 25:161–67.

———. 1952. "Bum, Poddy, and Penco." *Colorado Quarterly* 1:87–97.

Kimmerle, Marjorie, and Gibby, Patricia M. 1949. "A Word List from Colorado." *PADS* 11: 16–27.

Kimmerle, Marjorie; McDavid, Raven I., Jr.; and McDavid, Virginia G. 1951. "Problems of Linguistic Geography in the Rocky Mountain Area." *Western Humanities Review* 5:249–64.

Kirk, John; Sanderson, Stewart; and Widdowson, John. 1985. *Studies in Linguistic Geography*. London: Croom Helm.

Kniffen, Fred B. 1953. "The Western Cattle Complex." *Western Folklore* 12:179–85.

_____. 1965. "Folk Housing: Key to Diffusion." *Annals* 55:549–77.

Kniffen, Fred B., and Glassie, Henry. 1966. "Building in Wood in the Eastern United States." *Geographical Review* 56:40–66.

Kurath, Hans. 1939, reprint 1973. *Handbook of the Linguistic Geography of New England*. Providence, R.I.: Brown University.

_____. 1939–43. *Linguistic Atlas of New England*. 3 vols. Providence, R.I.: Brown University.

_____ 1949, reprint 1966. *A Word Geography of the Eastern United States*. Ann Arbor: University of Michigan Press.

_____. 1972. *Studies in Area Linguistics*. Bloomington: Indiana University Press.

Kurath, Hans, and McDavid, Raven I. 1961. *The Pronunciation of English in the Atlantic States*. Ann Arbor: University of Michigan Press.

Labov, William. 1963. Review of *The Regional Vocabulary of Texas*, by E. Bagby Atwood. *Word* 19:266–72.

_____. 1972a. "The Recent History of Some Dialect Markers on the Island of Martha's Vineyard, Massachusetts." In *Studies in Linguistics in Honor of Raven I. McDavid, Jr.*, edited by Lawrence Davis, pp. 81–122. University, Ala.: University of Alabama Press.

_____. 1972b. "Some Principles of Linguistic Methodology." *Language in Society* 1:97–120.

_____. 1973. "The Boundaries of Words and Their Meanings." In *New Ways of Analyzing Variation in English*, edited by Charles-James N. Bailey and Roger W. Shuy, pp. 340–73. Washington, D.C.: Georgetown University Press.

Lance, Donald M. 1977. "Determining Dialect Boundaries in the United States by Means of Automatic Cartography." *Germanistische Linguistik* 3.4:289–303.

Lance, Donald M., and Slemons, Steven V. 1976. "The Use of the Computer in Plotting the Geographical Distribution of Dialect Items." *Computers in the Humanities* 10:221–29.

Lang, Elfrieda. 1954. "Southern Migration to Northern Indiana before 1850." *Indiana Magazine of History* 50:349–56.

Leach, Douglas Edward. 1966. *The Northern Colonial Frontier 1607–1763*. New York: Holt, Rinehart and Winston.

LeCompte, Nolan P., Jr. 1967. "A Word Atlas of LaFourche Parish and Grand Isle." Ph.D. dissertation, Louisiana State University.

Lemert, Ben T. 1935. "The Knit-Goods Industry in the Southern States." *Economic Geography* 11:368–88.

Lewis, Peirce F. 1975. "Common Houses, Cultural Spoor." *Landscape* 19.2:1–22.

Lineback, Neal G. 1973. *Atlas of Alabama*. University, Ala.: University of Alabama Press.

Lord, Clifford L., and Lord, Elizabeth H. 1955, rev. ed. *Historical Atlas of the United States*. New York: Henry Holt.

Lynch, William O. 1943. "The Westward Flow of Southern Colonists Before 1861." *Journal of Southern History* 9:303–27.

McDavid, Raven I. 1948a. "Postvocalic /-r/ in South Carolina: A Social Analysis." *AmSp* 23:194–203.

_____. 1948b. "The Influence of French on Southern American English." *Studies in Linguistics* 6:39–43.

_____. 1951a. "Midland and Canadian Words in Upstate New York." *AmSp* 26:248–56.

_____. 1951b. "The Folk Vocabulary of New York State." *New York Folklore Quarterly* 7:173–92.

————. 1955. "The Position of the Charleston Dialect." *PADS* 23:35–49.

————. 1958. "The Dialects of American English." In W. Nelson Francis, *The Structure of American English*, pp. 480–543. New York: Ronald Press Co.

————. 1966. "Sense and Nonsense about American Dialects." *PMLA* 81:7–17.

————. 1973. "The Folk Vocabulary of Eastern Kentucky." In *Lexicography and Dialect Geography: Festgabe for Hans Kurath*, edited by Harald Scholler and John Reidy, pp. 147–67. Wiesbaden: Franz Steiner.

————. 1983. "Retrospect." *Journal of English Linguistics* 16:47–54.

————. 1984. "Linguistic Geography." *PADS* 71:4–31.

McDavid, Raven I., and McDavid, Virginia G. 1951. "The Relationship of the Speech of American Negroes to the Speech of Whites." *AmSp* 26:3–17.

————. 1960. "Grammatical Differences in the North Central States." *AmSp* 35:5–19.

————. 1969. "The Late Unpleasantness: Folk Names for the Civil War." *Southern Speech Journal* 34:194–204.

McDavid, Virginia. 1963. "To as a Preposition of Location in Linguistic Atlas Materials." *PADS* 40:12–19.

McManis, R. Douglas. 1974. *Colonial New England.* New York: Oxford University Press.

McMillan, James B. 1977. "Naming Regional Dialects in America." In *Papers in Language Variation: SAMLA-ADS Collection*, edited by David L. Shores and Carole P. Hines, pp. 119–24. University, Ala.: University of Alabama Press.

Marckwardt, Albert H. 1940. "Folk Speech in Indiana and Adjacent States." *Indiana History Bulletin* 17:120–40.

————. 1957. "Principal and Subsidiary Dialect Areas in the North-Central States." *PADS* 27: 3–15.

Marshall, Howard W., and Vlach, John M. 1973. "Toward a Folklife Approach to American Dialects." *AmSp* 48:163–91.

Mason, Julian. 1960. "The Etymology of 'Buckaroo'." *AmSp* 35:51–55.

Mathews, Lois Kimball. 1909. *The Expansion of New England: The Spread of New England Settlement and Institutions to the Mississippi River 1620–1865.* Boston: Houghton Mifflin Co.

Mathews, Mitford M. 1948. *Some Sources of Southernisms.* University, Ala.: University of Alabama Press.

Meigs, Peveril. 1941. "An Ethno-Telephonic Survey of French Louisiana." *Annals* 31:243–50.

Meinig, Donald W. 1965. "The Mormon Culture Region: Strategies and Patterns in the Geography of the American West, 1847–1964." *Annals* 55:191–220.

————. 1969. *Imperial Texas: An Interpretive Essay in Cultural Geography.* Austin: University of Texas Press.

————. 1972. "American Wests: Preface to a Geographical Interpretation." *Annals* 62:159–84.

Meredith, Mamie J. 1933. "Charivaria: Belling Bridal Couples in Pioneer Days." *AmSp* 8:22–24.

Meriwether, Robert L. 1940. *The Expansion of South Carolina 1729–1765.* Kingsport, Tenn.: Southern Publishers.

Merk, Frederick. 1978. *History of the Westward Movement.* New York: Knopf.

Merrens, Harry Roy. 1964. *Colonial North Carolina in the Eighteenth Century: A Study in Historical Geography.* Chapel Hill: University of North Carolina Press.

Metcalf, Allan A. 1972. "Directions of Change in Southern California English." *Journal of English Linguistics* 6:28–34.

————. 1971. *Riverside English.* Riverside: University of California.

Miller, Tracey R. 1973. "An Investigation of the Regional English of Unicoi County, Tennessee." Ph.D. dissertation, University of Tennessee.

Minshull, Roger. 1967. *Regional Geography: Theory and Practice*. Chicago: Aldine.

Mitchell, Robert D. 1972. "The Shenandoah Valley Frontier." *Annals* 62:461–86.

Molloy, Robert. 1947. *Charleston, a Gracious Heritage*. New York: Appleton-Century-Crofts.

Montgomery, Michael B., and Bailey, Guy H. 1986. *Language Variety in the South: Perspectives in Black and White*. University, Ala.: University of Alabama Press.

Morris, John W., and Reynolds, Edwin C. 1965. *Historical Atlas of Oklahoma*. Norman: University of Oklahoma Press.

Murphy, Raymond E., and Murphy, Marion. 1937. *Pennsylvania: A Regional Geography*. Harrisburg, Pa.: Pennsylvania Book Service.

Newton, Milton. 1974. "Cultural Preadaptation and the Upland South." In *Man and Cultural Heritage: Papers in Honor of Fred B. Kniffen*, edited by Bob F. Perkins, pp. 143–54. Baton Rouge: School of Geoscience, Louisiana State University.

Norman, Arthur M. Z. 1956. "A Southeast Texas Dialect Study." *Orbis* 5:61–79.

Nostrand, Richard L. 1970. "The Hispanic-American Borderland: Delimitation of an American Culture Region." *Annals* 60:638–61.

O'Cain, Raymond K. 1972. "A Social Dialect Study of Charleston, South Carolina." Ph.D. dissertation, University of Chicago.

––––––. 1979. "Linguistic Atlas of New England." *AmSp* 54:243–78.

Odum, Howard W. 1936. *Southern Regions of the United States*. Chapel Hill: University of North Carolina Press.

Odum, Howard W., and Moore, Harry Estill. 1938. *American Regionalism: A Cultural Historical Approach to National Integration*. New York: Henry Holt and Co.

O'Hare, Thomas J. 1964. "The Linguistic Geography of Eastern Montana." Ph.D. dissertation, University of Texas.

Owsley, Frank L. 1945. "The Pattern of Migration and Settlement on the Southern Frontier." *Journal of Southern History* 11:147–76.

Pace, George B. 1965. "On the Eastern Affiliations of Missouri." *AmSp* 40:47–52.

Parkins, Almon E. 1938. *The South: Its Economic-Geographic Development*. New York: John Wiley and Sons.

Parslow, Robert L. 1967. "The Pronunciation of English in Boston." Ph.D. dissertation, University of Michigan.

Paullin, Charles O., and Wright, John K. 1932. *Atlas of the Historical Geography of the United States*. Washington and New York: Institution of Washington and the American Geographical Society of New York.

Pearce, T. M. 1958. "Three Rocky Mountain Terms: Park, Sugan, and Plaza." *AmSp* 33:99–107.

Pease, Theodore Calvin. 1919. *The Frontier State [= IL], 1818–1848*. Chicago: A. C. McClurg.

Pederson, Lee A. 1968. *An Annotated Bibliography of Southern Speech*. Atlanta: Southern Educational Laboratory.

––––––. 1969. "The Linguistic Atlas of the Gulf States: An Interim Report." *AmSp* 44:279–86.

––––––. 1971a. "Southern Speech and the LAGS Project." *Orbis* 20:79–89.

––––––. 1971b. "An Approach to Urban Word Geography." *AmSp* 46:73–86.

––––––. 1971c. "Chicago Words: The Regional Vocabulary." *AmSp* 46:163–92.

––––––. 1973. "Dialect Patterns in Rural Northern Georgia." In *Lexicography and Dialect Geography: Festgabe for Hans Kurath*, edited by Harald Scholler and John Reidy, pp. 195–207. Wiesbaden: Franz Steiner.

———. 1974. "The Linguistic Atlas of the Gulf States: Interim Report Two." *AmSp* 49:216–23.

———. 1976. "The Linguistic Atlas of the Gulf States: Interim Report Three." *AmSp* 51:201–7.

———. 1980. "Lexical Data from the Gulf States." *AmSp* 55:195–203.

———. 1981. "The Linguistic Atlas of the Gulf States: Interim Report Four." *AmSp* 56:243–59.

———. 1986. "A Graphic Plotter Grid." *Journal of English Linguistics* 19:25–41.

Pederson, Lee A.; McDaniel, Susan Lea; Bailey, Guy; and Bassett, Marvin. 1986. *Lingusitic Atlas of the Gulf States*. Vol. 1, *Handbook for the Lingusitic Atlas of the Gulf States*. Athens, Ga.: University of Georgia Press.

Pederson, Lee A.; McDavid, Raven I., Jr.; Foster, Charles W.; and Billiard, Charles E., eds. 1974, 2d ed. *A Manual for Dialect Research in the Southern States*. Atlanta: Georgia State University Press.

Perkins, Bob F., ed. 1974. *Man and Cultural Heritage: Papers in Honor of Fred B. Kniffen*. Baton Rouge: School of Geoscience, Louisiana State University.

Petyt, K. M. 1980. *The Study of Dialect: An Introduction to Dialectology*. London: Andre Deutsch.

Pickford, Glenna R. 1956. "American Linguistic Geography: A Sociological Appraisal." *Word* 12:211–33.

Pilch, Herbert. 1972. "Structural Dialectology." *AmSp* 47:165–87.

Pillsbury, Richard. 1970. "The Urban Street Pattern as a Culture Indicator: Pennsylvania, 1682–1815." *Annals* 60:428–46.

Pooley, William Vipond. 1908. "The Settlement of Illinois from 1830 to 1850." *Bulletin of the University of Wisconsin* vol. 1, no. 4.

Potter, Edward E. 1955. "The Dialect of Northwestern Ohio: A Study of a Transition Area." Ph.D. dissertation, University of Michigan.

Powell, Sumner Chilton. 1963. *Puritan Village: The Formation of a New England Town*. Middletown, Conn.: Wesleyan University Press.

Power, Richard L. 1953. *Planting Cornbelt Culture: The Impress of the Upland Southerner and Yankee in the Old Northwest*. Indianapolis: Indiana Historical Society.

Raitz, Karl B. 1973. "Ethnic Settlements on Topographic Maps." *Journal of Geography* 72: 29–40.

Randolph, Vance, and Wilson, George P. 1953. *Down in the Holler: A Gallery of Ozark Folk Speech*. Norman: Oklahoma University Press.

Read, William A. 1945. "Notes on 'Gaspergou'." *AmSp* 20:277–80.

Reed, Carroll E. 1949. *The Pennsylvania German Dialect Spoken in the Counties of Lehigh and Berks: Phonology and Morphology*. Seattle: University of Washington Press.

———. 1952. "The Pronunciation of English in the State of Washington." *AmSp* 27:186–89.

———. 1956. "Washington Words." *PADS* 25:3–11.

———. 1957. "Word Geography of the Pacific Northwest." *Orbis* 6:86–93.

———. 1961a. "Double Dialect Geography." *Orbis* 10:308–19.

———. 1961b. "The Pronunciation of English in the Pacific Northwest." *Language* 37:559–64.

———. 1977, rev. ed. *Dialects of American English*. University of Massachusetts Press.

Reed, Carroll E., and Reed, David W. 1972. "Problems of English Speech Mixture in California and Nevada." In *Studies in Linguistics in Honor of Raven I. McDavid, Jr.*, edited by Lawrence Davis, pp. 135–44. University, Ala.: University of Alabama Press.

Reed, Carroll E., and Seifert, Lester W. 1954. *A Linguistic Atlas of Pennsylvania German*. Marburg: Lahn.

Reed, David W. 1954. "Eastern Dialect Words in California." *PADS* 21:3–15.

Reed, David W., and Spicer, John L. 1952. "Correlation Methods of Comparing Idiolects in a Transition Area." *Language* 28:348–59.

Rehder, John B. 1973. "Sugar Plantations in Louisiana: Origin, Dispersal, and Responsible Location Factors." *West Georgia College Studies in Social Sciences* 12:78–93.

Rooney, John F.; Zelinsky, Wilbur; and Louder, Dean R., eds. 1982. *This Remarkable Continent: An Atlas of United States and Canadian Society and Cultures.* College Station: Texas A&M University Press.

Rowe, H. D. 1957. "New England Terms for 'Bull'. " *AmSp* 32:110–16.

Sale, Randall, and Karn, Edwin. 1979. *American Expansion: A Book of Maps.* Lincoln: University of Nebraska Press.

Samuels, M. L. 1972. *Linguistic Evolution.* Cambridge: Cambridge University Press.

Sauer, Carl O. 1916. "Conditions of Pioneer Life in the Upper Illinois Valley." In Carl O. Sauer, *Land and Life: A Selection from the Writings of Carl Ortwin Sauer,* edited by John Leighly, pp. 11–22. Berkeley: University of California Press.

———. 1920. *The Geography of the Ozark Highland of Missouri.* The Geographical Society of Chicago Bulletin No. 7. Chicago: University of Chicago.

———. 1925. "The Morphology of Landscape." In Carl O. Sauer, *Land and Life: A Selection from the Writings of Carl Ortwin Sauer,* edited by John Leighly, pp. 315–50. Berkeley: University of California Press.

———. 1927. "The Barrens of Kentucky." In Carl O. Sauer, *Land and Life: A Selection from the Writings of Carl Ortwin Sauer,* edited by John Leighly, pp. 23–31. Berkeley: University of California Press.

———. 1962. "Homestead and Community on the Middle Border." In Carl O. Sauer, *Life and Land: A Selection from the Writings of Carl Ortwin Sauer,* edited by John Leighly, pp. 32–41. Berkeley: University of California Press.

———. 1963. *Land and Life: A Selection from the Writings of Carl Ortwin Sauer.* Edited by John Leighly. Berkeley: University of California Press.

Sawyer, Janet B. 1957. "A Dialect Study of San Antonio, Texas: A Bilingual Community." Ph.D. dissertation, University of Texas.

———. 1959. "Aloofness from Spanish Influence in Texas English." *Word* 15:270–81.

———. 1964. "Social Aspects of Bilingualism in San Antonio, Texas." *PADS* 41:7–15.

Schele de Vere, Maximilian. 1872. *Americanisms; the English of the New World.* New York: C. Scribner.

Scholler, Harald, and Reidy, John, eds. 1973. *Lexicography and Dialect Geography: Festgabe for Hans Kurath.* Wiesbaden: Franz Steiner.

Shaw, David. 1974. "Statistical Analysis of Dialect Boundaries." *Computers in the Humanities* 8:173–77.

Shores, David L., and Hines, Carole P. 1977. *Papers in Language Variation: SAMLA-ADS Collection.* University, Ala.: University of Alabama Press.

Shuy, Roger W. 1962. "The Northern-Midland Dialect Boundary in Illinois." *PADS* 38.

———. 1967. *Discovering American Dialects.* Champaign, Ill.: National Council of Teachers of English.

Sledd, James H. 1966. "Breaking, Umlaut, and the Southern Drawl." *Language* 42:18–41.

Smith, Max D. 1968. "The Dragonfly: Linguistic Atlas Underdifferentiation." *AmSp* 43:51–57.

Sopher, David E. 1967. *Geography of Religions.* Englewood Cliffs, N.J.: Prentice-Hall.

Southard, Bruce. 1983. "The Linguistic Atlas of Oklahoma and Computer Cartography." *Journal of English Linguistics* 16:65–77.

Starkey, Otis P., and Robinson, J. Lewis. 1969. *The Anglo-American Realm.* New York: McGraw-Hill.

Stewart, William A. 1967. "Sociolinguistic Factors in the History of American Negro Dialects."

In *Black-White Speech Relationships,* edited by Walter A. Wolfram and Nona H. Clarke, pp. 74–89. Washington, D.C.: Center for Applied Linguistics.

————. 1970. "Toward a History of American Negro Dialect." In *Language and Poverty,* edited by Frederick Williams, pp. 351–79. Chicago: Markham.

Stockwell, Robert P. 1959. "Structural Dialectology: A Proposal." *AmSp* 34:258–68.

Stone, K. H. 1965. "The Development of a Focus for the Geography of Settlement." *Economic Geography* 41:346–55.

Strickland, Arney L. 1970. "A Study of Geographical and Social Distribution of Some Folk Words in Indiana." Ph.D. dissertation, Ball State University.

Taeuber, Conrad, and Taeuber, Irene B. 1958. *The Changing Population of the United States.* New York: John Wiley and Sons.

Tarpley, Fred A. 1970. *From Blinky to Blue-John: A Word Atlas of Northeast Texas.* Wolfe City, Tex.: The University Press.

Thomas, Charles K. 1947. "The Place of New York City in American Linguistic Geography." *Quarterly Journal of Speech* 33:314–20.

Thompson, Daniel Garrison. 1956. *Gateway to a Nation: The Middle Atlantic States and Their Influence on the Development of the Nation.* Peterborough, N.H.: William Bauhan.

Thompson, John H. 1966. *Geography of New York State.* Syracuse: Syracuse University Press.

Trudgill, Peter. 1975. "Linguistic Geography and Geographical Linguistics." *Progress in Geography: International Reviews of Current Research* 7:227–52.

————. 1983. *On Dialect: Social and Geographical Perspectives.* New York: New York University Press.

Turner, Lorenzo D. 1949. *Africanisms in the Gullah Dialect.* Chicago: University of Chicago Press.

Underwood, Gary N. 1968a. "Vocabulary Change in the Upper Midwest." *PADS* 49:8–28.

————. 1968b. "Semantic Confusion: Evidence from the Linguistic Atlas of the Upper Midwest." *Journal of English Linguistics* 2:86–95.

————. 1968c. "Slop Pail: An Example of Dialectal Blending." *AmSp* 43:268–76.

————. 1975. "American English Dialectology: Alternatives for the Southwest." *International Journal of the Sociology of Language* 2:19–40.

————. 1981. "The Dialect of the Mesabi Range." *PADS* 67.

U.S. Bureau of the Census. 1909. *A Century of Population Growth in the United States, 1790–1900.* Washington, D.C.: Government Printing Office.

Vance, Rupert B. 1935. *The Human Geography of the South.* Chapel Hill: University of North Carolina Press.

Viereck, Wolfgang. 1973. "The Growth of Dialectology." *Journal of English Linguistics* 7:69–86.

Wacker, Peter O. 1975. *Land and People: A Cultural Geography of Preindustrial New Jersey; Origins and Settlement Patterns.* New Brunswick: Rutgers University Press.

Walsh, Harry, and Mote, Victor L. 1974. "A Texas Dialect Feature: Origins and Distribution." *AmSp* 49:40–53.

Watson, James Wreford. 1963. *North America: Its Countries and Regions.* London: Longmans, Green and Co.

Weinreich, Uriel. 1953, reprint 1974. *Languages in Contact.* The Hague: Mouton.

————. 1954a. "Is a Structural Dialectology Possible?" *Word* 10:388–400.

————. 1954b. "Linguistic Convergence in Immigrant America." *Georgetown Univ. Monograph Series on Language and Literature* 7:40–49.

Weinreich, Uriel; Labov, William; and Herzog, Marvin I. 1968. "Empirical Foundations for a Theory of Language Change." In *Directions for Historical Linguistics,* edited by W. P. Lehmann and Yakov Malkiel, pp. 95–195. Austin: University of Texas Press.

Wertenbaker, Thomas Jefferson. 1938. *The Founding of American Civilization: The Middle Colonies.* New York: Charles Scribner's Sons.

———. 1949. *The Old South: The Founding of American Civilization.* New York: Charles Scribner's Sons.

Wheatley, Katherine E., and Stanley, Oma. 1959. "Three Generations of East Texas Speech." *AmSp* 34:83–94.

Whittlesey, Derwent. 1954. "The Regional Concept and the Regional Method." In *American Geography: Inventory and Prospect,* edited by Preston E. James and Clarence F. Jones, pp. 19–68. Syracuse: Syracuse University Press.

Wigginton, Eliot, ed. 1973. *Foxfire 2.* Garden City, New York: Anchor Press.

Wilhelm, Hubert G. H. 1982. *The Origin and Distribution of Settlement Groups: Ohio 1850.* Athens, Ohio: Department of Geography, Ohio University.

Williams, Frederick, ed. 1970. *Language and Poverty.* Chicago: Markham.

Williamson, Juanita V., and Burke, Virginia M., eds. 1971. *A Various Language: Perspectives on American Dialects.* New York: Holt, Rinehart and Winston.

Wilson, A. H. 1948. "English Spoken by Pennsylvania Germans in Snyder County." *AmSp* 23:236–38.

Wilson, Charles Morrow. 1929. "Elizabethan America." *Atlantic Monthly,* August, pp. 238–44.

Wilson, H. Rex. 1958. "The Dialect of Lunenburg County, Nova Scotia." Ph.D. dissertation, University of Michigan.

Wolfram, Walter A. 1971. "Black-White Speech Differences Revisited." In *Black-White Speech Relationships,* edited by Walter A. Wolfram and Nona H. Clarke, pp. 139–61. Washington, D.C.: Center for Applied Linguistics.

Wolfram, Walter A., and Clarke, Nona H. 1971. *Black-White Speech Relationships.* Washington, D.C.: Center for Applied Linguistics.

Wolfram, Walter A., and Christian, Donna. 1976. *Appalachian Speech.* Arlington, Va.: Center for Applied Linguistics.

Wood, Gordon R. 1961. "Word Distribution in the Interior South." *PADS* 35:1–16.

———. 1963. "Dialect Contours in the Southern States." *AmSp* 38:243–56.

———. 1971. *Vocabulary Change: A Study of Variation in Regional Words in Eight of the Southern States.* Cambridge, Ill.: Southern Illinois University Press.

Wright, Louis B. 1976. *South Carolina, A Bicentennial History.* New York: W.W.Norton and Co.

Zelinsky, Wilbur. 1951a. "Where the South Begins: The Northern Limits of the Cis-Appalachian South in Terms of Settlement Landscape." *Social Forces* 30:172–78.

———. 1951b. "An Isochronic Map of Georgia Settlement, 1750–1850." *Georgia Historical Quarterly* 35:191–95.

———. 1961. "An Approach to the Religious Geography of the United States; Patterns of Church Membership in 1952." *Annals* 51:139–93.

———. 1967. "Classical Town Names in the United States: The Historical Geography of an American Ideal." *Geographical Review* 57:463–95.

———. 1970. "Cultural Variation in Personal Name Patterns in the Eastern United States." *Annals* 60:743–69.

———. 1973. *The Cultural Geography of the United States.* Englewood Cliffs, N.J.: Prentice-Hall.

————. 1977. "The Pennsylvania Town: An Overdue Geographical Account." *Geographical Review* 67:127–47.

————. 1983. "Nationalism in the American Place-Name Cover." *Names* 31.1:1–28.

Glossary Index

acequia (= an irrigation ditch), 228, 266

Adam's apple (= someone one doesn't know: "I don't know him/her from Adam's apple"), 208

Adam's housecat (= someone one doesn't know: "I don't know him/her from Adam's housecat"), 148, 208, 262

Adam's off ox (= someone one doesn't know: "I don't know him/her from Adam's off ox"), 208

adder (= a snake), 34, 132, 215, 216 (map), 253

adder's tongue (= a dogtooth violet), 59

adobe (= sun-dried clay), 240

agers (= ague, chills and fever), 111, 258

agg (= to incite), 106, 259

airish (= cool, chilly; haughty), 112

airy (= haughty), 112

all (= finished), 187, 264

all (in) free (= a call in the game of hide-and-seek), 63

all in (= tired, exhausted), 63, 255, 273

all the far (*or* fast, high, *etc.*) (= as far [fast, high, etc.] as), 114, 115, 259, 274

all the farther (= as far as), 81, 257, 274

all the tea in China (= anything: "I wouldn't do that for all the tea in China"), 72, 256

allee-allee (all) in free (= a call in the game of hide-and-seek), 63

allee-allee oxen (all in) free (= a call in the game of hide-and-seek), 63

allie (= a superior playing marble; a shooter or taw), 37, 253

altar call (= a challenge or call to church members to come to the altar or front seats and pray), 108

ambeer (= saliva colored by tobacco), 169, 171, 263

amber (= saliva colored by tobacco), 171

amen corner (= a front row section of church seats), 108, 259

amen pew (= a front row section of church seats), 108

American fried potatoes (= boiled potatoes sliced and fried), 84, 257, 269

American fries (= boiled potatoes sliced and fried), 84, 269

andy-over (= a game in which a ball is thrown over a house), 200, 265

angledog (= an earthworm), 28, 30

angleworm (= an earthworm), 72, 85, 256, 272

antigodlin (= askew, crooked), 274

anxious seat (= a special row of seats in a church), 108

apple slump (= a deep-dish apple dessert), 28

arbor (= an open-sided structure with a roof made of boughs), 107

armload (= an armful), 178, 180, 264

armoire (= a clothespress or wardrobe), 141, 261

arroyo (= a small stream; a dry wash; a small valley), 219 (map), 221, 222, 228, 240, 266

ash cake (= a kind of corn bread), 93

ass-end-to (= backwards, reversed), 71

at sword's points (= [of two persons] at odds with each other), 72

awendaw (= a kind of bread made from corn or hominy), 93

ax (= a wagon's wheel axle), 74

a-yuh (= yes), 38, 253

B from bull's foot (= anything: "He doesn't know B from bull's foot"), 148, 262

babushka (= a head scarf), 58, 254

baby buggy (= a small four-wheeled carriage for a baby), 207

baby carriage (= a small four-wheeled carriage for a baby), 207

baby coach (= a small four-wheeled carriage for a baby), 207, 187, 264

back (= to address), 106, 259

backstick (= a backlog), 168, 263

bad (= unwell), 111, 259

bad man (= the devil), 107, 258

bad place (= hell), 93, 259

bad sick (= very ill), 167, 263

baga (= a rutabaga), 84, 257

baker('s) bread (= store bought bread), 62, 93, 255, 268

ball (= a hair bun), 148, 262

banjo (= a stringed instrument similar to a guitar), 149

Subject Index